An Introduction to the Stock Market and Investments

What You Need to Know

Before You Invest

Rod Davis

Unique Ink Press
Prescott, AZ 86305

Copyright © 2024 Rodney G. Davis
All Rights Reserved

International Standard Book Number:
978-0-9847100-8-9

Library of Congress Control Number:
2016910376

20 19 18 17 16   15 14 13 12 11   10 9 8 7 6

No part of this book may be reproduced in any form, stored in a retrieval system, or transmitted in any form or by any means—electronic, mechanical, photocopying, recording, scanning, or otherwise—without prior written permission of the publisher.

Unique Ink Press
Prescott, AZ 86305

uniqueinkpress.com

Dedication:

To Nancy,
my inspiration and motivation.
We're a great team.
Write on.

Acknowledgements:

I would like to acknowledge the contributions of many students at Cerritos College who helped during the time I was writing this book. It was an ongoing project for several years—and still is. Many of you acted as a sounding board for my thoughts and proofreaders for the text. Thank-you very much. If any of you have a story about class experiences, investment results, or anything else related to the class, I would love to hear from you. Email me through the contact link on my website, uniqueinkpress.com.

A stock is not just a ticker symbol or an electronic blip; it is an ownership interest in an actual business, with an underlying value that does not depend on its share price.

Benjamin Graham, *The Intelligent Investor*

Today the conservative investor is being replaced by the get-rich-quick gambler who knows little about what he or she is betting on. The strategy of sound investing has not changed, but neither has the greed of most people. We are our own worst enemies. But if we can overcome our desire for immediate gratification, we will be better investors.

Table of Contents

Preface   1

Introduction   3

Chapter 1
What Is the Relationship Between the Economy & the Stock Market?   10
What Are Market Averages and Indexes?   17
How Do You Find and Interpret Stock Quotes?   25
Should You Invest in the Stock Market?   28
How Do You Know When to Buy or Sell?   34

Chapter 2
What Are Shares of Stock?   42
How Do Companies Sell Shares of Stock?   47
What Are Your Shareholder Rights?   50
Is the Stock Market Risky?   53

Chapter 3
How Do You Open a Brokerage Account?   57
What Account Title Should You Use?   62
How Do You Select a Broker?   64
How Do You Make an Investment?   68
What Is a Margin Account?   74
How Do You Invest for a Market Decline?   81
What Is a Dividend and Yield?   83

Chapter 4
What Is a Bond?   88
What Are the Different Types of Bonds?   91
What Is Compound Interest?   102

What Are the Risks of Investing in Bonds 107
How Do You Buy Bonds? 115

Chapter 5
How Do You Read Financial Statements? 121
What Can You Learn from Financial Statements? 129
Why Are Financial Ratios Important? 137

Chapter 6
What Is Fundamental Analysis? 141
What Are Economic Cycles? 144
What Is the Industrial Life Cycle? 151
How Do You Measure Inflation? 153
What Is the Biggest Economic Problem Today? 160

Chapter 7
What Is Technical Analysis? 168
How Do You Read Stock Charts? 171
What Other Indicators Are Used by Chartists? 178
What Are Some Non-Chart Technical Indicators? 186
How Do You Use Market Timing Techniques? 193

Chapter 8
What Is a Mutual Fund? 197
What Does It Cost to Buy Mutual Funds? 200
What Types of Mutual Funds Are Available? 205
How Do You Select a Mutual Fund? 210
What Are Closed-End Funds and Unit Trusts? 213
What Are ETFs and ETNs? 217
What About Cryptocurrencies? 221

Chapter 9
What Are Put and Call Options? 224
What Happens When You Buy Options? 230
What Happens When You Write a Put? 234

How Do You Trade Options on ETFs & ETNs?	238
What Are Commodities Futures Contracts?	242
What Are Stock Rights and Warrants?	245

Chapter 10
How Are Investors' Rights Protected? 249
What Has Been Learned from Past Events?	254
What Does FINRA Do?	265

Chapter 11
What Types of Investments Offer Tax Advantages? 269
Should You Have an IRA?	274
Should You Participate in a 401(k) Plan?	281
What Investments Are for Education Expenses?	285
What Is an Annuity?	287
What Are Limited Partnerships?	290

Chapter 12
What Issues Will Affect the Economy in the Future? 294
What Causes the Wealth of Nations to Rise and Fall?	301

Glossary 314

Recommended Reading 342

Index 343

Preface

After over forty years of working as a stockbroker and college professor, it was time to retire. I still identify my former profession as "Stockbroker" even though that title has become obsolete. Most brokers use more ostentatious and less specific titles: Investment Advisor, Financial Councilor, Money Guru, etc. By the way, if someone claims to be a "Money Guru," recommend they pick another title. *Money* is a measure of material value, and a *guru* has spiritual wisdom. The words are oxymoronic.

I prefer the title Stockbroker because I associate stocks with capitalism, which is being much maligned today and needs defending. Being able to own shares of a company is what free market capitalism is about. It is closely aligned with other freedoms on which America was founded. Both America and capitalism are under attack for the same reason by those who want to limit our freedom. There is, or course, both a good side and a bad side to freedom. We can choose rightly or wrongly; but the point is, we are free to choose. Freedom does not guarantee success. It simply guarantees we have the right to pursue success.

When I retired I thought I would finally have time to finish writing the books that had been stuck in my head. I especially wanted to finish *The Sisyphus Solution: My Search to the Solution to an Unsolvable Problem.* It is about searching for solutions to unsolvable problems. The stock market, however, is not unsolvable.

I did not want to spend my retirement working on this book. I fully expected it to precede me in death. Yet here I am, trying to keep it alive. What changed? Not me; the market did. The stock market has been betrayed by those who should be protecting its tradition values of free market capitalism. I will sacrifice some retirement time to fight that battle.

What many call capitalism today is the antithesis of what it is supposed to be. The Chinese Communist Party (CCP), for example, claims their economic system is capitalism. But using slaves and underpaid employees to reduce labor costs, disregarding and violating patent laws and intellectual property rights, and the CCP's seizure of 50% of Chinese companies is <u>not</u> capitalism. The CCP is trying to redefine "capitalism" to keep communism alive. They are using capitalist profits to finance plans to support a communist vision that has produced nothing but economic disaster. That is not free market capitalism; nor has communism ever produced a system of equality for all. No communist leader once they have assumed power has sacrificed his own greed for the "greater good".

Misrepresenting capitalism is the reason I have taken time out of retirement to keep this book current. It is the reason I am not having a glass of wine on the patio right now. Well actually, I do sit out on the patio and write, but working on this book is not what I planned on doing. Only now, when capitalism is on the eve of destruction, does the importance of understanding it become clear. I consider this book an apologetic for capitalism. It is the foundation of our traditional values and the reason why America has become so successful. The innovators who built this country did not steal technology, they invented it. When government becomes so corrupt that it violates the principles of free market capitalism, it will fall. When the government can spend trillions of dollars over budget and increase the national debt to unheard of proportions, our cost will no longer be measured in money. It will cost us our freedom.

This book will not likely change the course of people who are hell bent on destroying themselves, but I want to keep hope alive. For that reason, this book should not just quietly pass away. I must warn you, however, it is not a real page turner. It is simply a rule book about how the game should be played. Only coaches, officials, and players read rule books for sports games. Rule books are boring... but necessary. If you want to know the rules of investing, this will tell you. Do not play any game without knowing the rules.

I have not changed much content in this new edition. Over 95 per cent of the content is still the same as the previous one. The changes keep it current with rule changes, such as T+1 settlement date for a security transactions. There is also a brief recap on cryptocurrency. If this book helps you to become a better investor, I will consider it a success and my time well spent..

Introduction

Everything old becomes new again. This book began with the title *What You Need to Know Before You Invest* (which is now the subtitle). It was written over twenty years ago. Maybe that doesn't seem old to you, but stock market years are like dog years (especially if the market is a dog). So, the first edition of that book might as well have been written over a century ago. The original book has long ago outlived its usefulness. The world of investing twenty years ago is unrecognizable from that of today. The market before the turn of the century looked more like it would have been over two centuries ago rather than two decades. Tradition had long been the hallmark of the stock market, but recent technological advances have changed all that. High tech culture is only now in the process of forming new traditions.

Individual investors had previously been described as those having long-term goals, but now such people are an endangered species. Long-term investors are being superseded by short term speculators and, more often, gamblers. The securities industry has undergone revolutionary changes, and trying to keep the print edition of a book up to date is nearly impossible. The first edition of that first edition underwent two revisions within ten years, and some of the revisions became obsolete almost as quickly as the book rolled off the press.

For many investors, the massive volume of data and lightning fast access speeds has had the opposite effect than intended. It was as if the more information that was available, the less comprehensible the market became. I wrote this book to address that issue, to help you focus back on the basics of investing by putting the abundance of information you have at your fingertips into pragmatic focus. Technology alone, without context, can take your attention off the basics of investing.

The most notable change in the securities industry has been that most people who participate in the market are no longer investors but speculators and gamblers. The idea of someone being an investor in the traditional sense is almost lost in today's environment. Investors buy and hold securities for years. Speculators measure the holding period for securities in weeks; a gambler, in minutes; and some high-tech market manipulators, in milliseconds.

Someone who owns a stock for milliseconds—or, for that matter, minutes, hours, days, or weeks—never considers the significance of what stock ownership means. Such people are certainly not planning to attend an annual shareholders' meeting, or vote proxy cards on corporate issues. They could care less about the company's business. They are only obsessed with betting on a bouncing price, like the numbers on lottery balls. For high tech traders, there is nothing material attached to ownership of stock.

The idea of being a long-term investor can easily be lost in today's investing environment, but it shouldn't be. When I began this introduction with the adage everything old is new again, I was not referring to this book, but to the way investors approach the market. Traditional investors are becoming a rarity on Wall Street, but it is time for them to come back. I am not advocating a Luddite resurgence. I am saying that to make the best use of technology you need to put it in the proper framework of how the market works.

People need to be reminded of why the stock market was created. Traditionally the market has turned many average Joes into millionaires, but today it is more likely to turn millionaires into average Joes. The most successful investors have always taken a long-term approach. People do not become millionaires by gambling. That is a fun recreation, not a sound financial plan. So, how did it come to this? How did investors transition from financiers participating in a business into gamblers betting on a horse race, trying to turn paper into gold? That's an interesting story. Like any story it begins at the beginning.

On May 17, 1792, 24 stockbrokers first met under the now-legendary buttonwood tree on Wall Street to decide how to organize a central marketplace for "buying and selling of bonds and company shares". They also began formulating the rules and regulations that would govern the trading of these securities. About 25 years later, on March 8, 1817, they officially signed the Buttonwood Agreement that created the institution we now call the New York Stock Exchange. For about two centuries, those rules worked just fine for facilitating stock and bond trading.

However, all that changed on March 7, 2006. When the New York Stock Exchange merged with Archipelago Holdings, a publicly traded company that ran an *electronic communications network* (ECN) for executing buy and sell orders. Now, mergers and acquisitions happen all the time on Wall Street, so what was different about this? Henceforth, the New York Stock Exchange would be a publicly traded company. For about 200 years the NYSE had been a non-profit organization whose purpose was to create and maintain capital by facilitating the transfer of public ownership of corporations. But on that date the NYSE became a corporation itself, and its goals changed from facilitating the creation of wealth for others to the creation of wealth for itself. Anyone could participate in the profits and losses of this great American institution, and investors took full advantage. However, it was no longer the same institution it had been for the last 200 years.

Few people realized the impact of what had happened at the time. But the stock exchange had just transformed itself from a nonprofit organization into a for-profit corporation. It was no longer monitoring and regulating the greed of others; it was participating in it. A year after going public the NYSE would merge with the largest securities exchange in Europe, Euronext, to become an even more massive global securities exchange. That would be followed by several other mergers and acquisitions shortly thereafter, and it now owns twelve other exchanges and marketplaces.

The NYSE was steadily moving further away from its origins. It would introduce trading of foreign securities, derivative products, futures, options, ETFs, and ETNs. These were all securities that had never before been traded on the NYSE. They were generally highly speculative, but they

The façade of the NYSE has not changed in over 100 years, but the interior has changed many times over.

were also highly profitable for the NYSE. Then in 2013 the 221-year-old NYSE was purchased by the then 13-year-old Intercontinental Exchange (ICE), an Atlanta based commodities exchange.

Thousands of new products have been introduced on the NYSE designed to appeal to a new type of participant in the securities market—the gambler, specifically the high-tech gambler. Hundreds of new terms were introduced into the language of investing that made no sense to traditional investors: algorithmic trading, binary options, black box trading, dark pools, flash crashes, high frequency trading (HFT), and 3X bull and bear ETFs. If the entrepreneurs who had founded the NYSE had heard this language, they would have thought they were on a different planet. Perhaps they were.

For about two centuries, the NYSE served as a nonprofit organization providing a service to investors who wanted to participate in the ownership of public companies. Those original financiers could have never imagined that in the future their institution would become a platform for gambling. The effects on securities trading from high frequency traders has undermined investor confidence in the process of old-fashioned investing. Those with the fastest computers are bound to win the race for the best price, and to be able to exit the market before the trend reversal can be verified by everyone else.

Consequently stock market investing has been attracting fewer and fewer individual investors. The percentage of individual investors who own stocks (not including those who only participate in the market through surrogate means, such as retirement accounts or bank savings accounts) has been steadily declining for several years. The decline has come despite that the overall market has been doing quite well. Since the real estate and banking crisis in 2008, the stock market has been rapidly rising.

The growth in the market during those years came despite the U.S. economy undergoing one of the worst periods of economic recession and slowdown in its history. That, probably more than any other factor, was the real cause of investor wariness. Unemployment and, more importantly, _under_employment is a chronic problem plaguing the economy.

I would grant that most people approach the stock market anticipating a higher rate of return than what they would get from their bank savings accounts. There are a myriad of reasons why people want to accumulate wealth: retirement, security, comfort, power and prestige. People look to investing as a means of achieving such goals.

However, there is a prevalent attitude today that corporations are evil for no other reason than they make a profit. If that were true, then the government would be a much greater evil than corporations. Politicians profit immensely from their seats of power, and they can generally outspend corporate CEOs. They do not have to earn the money they spend.

The problem is that government cannot do what the private sector does. The government cannot create self-sustaining jobs. The jobs created by the private sector are necessary to generate tax revenue to fund the government. In a democracy, the government only spends other people's money; it does not create wealth; it diminishes it. The government relies on tax revenues from its citizens. So, government jobs would not exist without private sector jobs supporting them. If the private sector does not generate profits that can be used to produce tax revenue, there would not be any government jobs.

The balance between public and private sector jobs is crucial. It is the responsibility of the government to regulate or referee business and commerce. Government oversight is necessary to prevent monopolies or unethical business practices. The U.S. government was never intended to be a player in the game, for that would create an obvious conflict of interest. The job of a referee is to ensure the game is played fairly, not to compete in it. If referees compete with players, the game is rigged. Who referees the referees? When government abandons its role as a nonpartisan regulator of economic commerce and assumes the role of a player, free market capitalism is no longer free. When government officials begin picking winners and losers to benefit themselves, they are not acting in the best interests of all but to favor political allies. In that case, the economy is doomed; political greed will destroy it.

Free market capitalism will succeed only if the government ensures a fair and level playing field for all participants. A competitive environment will work properly only if all competitors play by the same rules. Only then is government properly providing for the welfare of all.

The job of politicians is to police the irresponsible behavior of corporations. But if politicians are irresponsible, who polices them?. Problems in a free market capitalist system that are created by unethical, greedy individuals are not limited to corporate executives. Everyone is greedy—politicians as well as corporate executives. Unchecked greed is never in the best interests of the economy as a whole.

The introduction to this book is not intended to solve all the political and economic problems today. What I hope to accomplish is to offer a better understanding of the stock market, investments, and the economy. But for anything worthwhile to be accomplished, it has to be based on reality. Greed will play a big part in your success or failure as an investor. So you need to begin with an understanding of what that means. You will learn why greed is not your friend in the first chapter.

The stock market is still one of the best places to invest and to accumulate wealth. However, most people do not understand how it works. Basic information about market mechanics has been replaced with a flood of new get-rich-quick schemes. Many personal finance books emphasize investment strategies and fail to integrate those strategies with fundamental information about the nuts and bolts of the market.

To understand how a particular investment strategy works, you first need to understand how the economy works and how the securities markets relate to it. Making successful investment decisions is not easy. You are going to have to do the work. This book will give you an understanding of the market, but that is only the foundation, not the building. However, for any structure to stand, it must be built on a solid foundation. Without that, whatever you create is destined to collapse.

So, the purpose of this book is simply to teach you how the stock market functions. You will not find any hot stock tips or secret formulas for "proven" success. You will not find shortcuts to making investment decisions without having to learn what you are doing. The stock market was founded as a means of facilitating people's ability to participate in free market capitalism. Through the stock market, everyone could help finance and share in the profits of visionaries. You do not have to be an inventor to be able to profit from the inventions and innovations of others.

But first you need to learn the rules of the game. Only when you know what you are doing will you be able to formulate a successful strategy. The stock market was never intended to be a casino. If you invest like you gamble, you will lose. As with any game of chance, you can play the odds; but they will never be in your favor.

Lesson one is to explain why economics seems so confusing to most people. There is a great debate among economists about how it functions best. But if you do not understand the basic premise of that debate and the fundamental ways that different economic theories portray the markets, then you have lost the game before you begin. You just don't know it yet. This book is designed to fill a need in the gaps of most people's understanding of the stock market and investments. As the subtitle states, Your road to success begins by learning *What You Need to Know Before You Invest*.

Tevye, the protagonist in the long-running musical *Fiddler on the Roof*, sang about tradition. The stock market was founded on a tradition of free market capitalism.

Chapter 1

How Does the Stock Market Relate to the Economy?

The psychological state of the economy can best be described as bipolar, continuously bouncing between euphoria and despair. There is never any stability in the economy; it is in a constant state of flux. It cannot stand still. It is continually in the throes of a dramatic mood swing—up, down, up, down. You might say the economy is like a teen drama queen.

Economists, the caretaker/parents of the economy, are aware the behavior of their charge is unpredictable. There are too many variables. They cannot be sure what will send the economy into a tailspin depression. They can only try to take action and make recommendations designed to address the economy's immediate needs, hoping to change its mood. But they don't know what the economy's mood is going to be from one moment to the next.

Also, the economy goes through stages of aging, and it does not age gracefully. It can alternatively act mature one moment and like a melodramatic child the next. No one seems to be able to accurately psychoanalyze the economy. For something that has no mind, it certainly seems to have a mind of its own.

If the economy were a person, it would certainly be a teenager. Teens are at an age when they are most inclined to describe themselves with the epithet, "No one understands me". The economy can go through dramatic growth spurts that are usually followed by long periods of lethargy. The economy usually has the juvenile tendency never to remain stationary. It seems impossible to get it to stand still and focus on adult instruction.

The economist parents (at least the ones who consider themselves so), never come to a point where they feel their job is over and complete. They can never say, "Stop everything. Stand still. You are just perfect as you are. Don't change a thing". Whether anyone wants it or not, the economy is going to change. There is no way to stop it, and there is no way to predict exactly what it will be up to next.

Also, the nature of the economy is such that there is always a problem looming just around the corner. To a drama queen, everything is a life-or-death situation. It is continually confronted with one earthshaking crisis after another. Regardless of the actual size of the problem, it always looks ominous. "This time it's different. Nobody understands me. I am the most misunderstood and miserable economy ever".

Economists can never be certain whether their child's problems are relatively minor and easily solved, or a potential meltdown that could last years. It is difficult to tell whether that blemish is a simple pimple, problematic acne, or a cancerous growth. Accurate diagnoses of economic problems are always difficult. Does this problem require a bandage, prescription medicine, or radical surgery? Such uncertainty heightens the tension around the search for a solution to every problem. You can never be completely sure the proposed solution will cure the ailment, or even whether it will address the problem.

In addition, the nature of the economy is such that every solution inevitably creates another problem. If the symptom of a problem is lethargy, an economist may recommend a strong dose of caffeine, such as lower interest rates, to stimulate it. However, the caffeine jolt may create a whole new set of problems, such as hyperactivity and inflation, requiring a prescriptive sedative to reverse. There is always the possibility that mother's admonition was right—caffeine really does stunt your growth.

However, the real problem with the teenager economy may not be simple lethargy. It may be manic depression, in which case a stimulant may only worsen the problem and create an even deeper depression. Economists are continually trying to figure out what went wrong with their charge, and they blame each other for their lack of parenting skills. What has happened to this child whom we have loved and nurtured? It has turned on us. How did it go so wrong? What's the matter with kids today?

The stock market acts like a convex mirror to the economy. It magnifies every economic imperfection. When the economy looks good, the stock market looks glamorous. When the economy looks bad, the stock market can look downright hideous. Understanding

12 ◊ The Stock Market and the Economy

the behavior of the economy and the stock market's reaction to it is a subject of great debate.

There are two popular schools of thought regarding economic theory currently being debated: Keynesian Theory and Austrian School Economic Theory. There are many complexities to this debate, but the key component affecting the markets is government's role in the economy. Under the view advocated by John Maynard Keynes, government has a duty and responsibility to intervene in the economic activities of the private sector because of market inefficiencies. The Austrian School view, advocated by Friedrich A. Hayek and others, is that economies run best under a policy of *laissez-faire*, a French phrase connoting let alone or "hands off." *Laissez-faire* implies an economic environment relatively free of government intervention. Hayek's view was that a competitive marketplace should be the determiner of the success or failure of commercial enterprises.

This economic debate is not new. Although Keynes and Hayek were both early 20th century economists, the role the federal government should play in the economic development of the U.S. has been ongoing since the beginning. The founding fathers debated these questions intently throughout their political careers. There was never a universal consensus about what the government's role should be regarding its citizens' business ventures, and that debate continues to this day.

Some prominent presidents who would fall into the Keynesian camp would be Theodore Roosevelt, Woodrow Wilson, Franklin Roosevelt, Jimmy Carter, and Barack Obama. Some prominent Austrian School advocates would be Calvin Coolidge, Richard Nixon, Ronald Reagan, George H.W. Bush, and Donald Trump. George W. Bush's legacy was clouded by his actions in his last few months in office when confronted with the imminent failure of several large corporations and financial institutions. His action in the creation of TARP, the Troubled Asset Relief Program, to support failing companies with federally guaranteed loans was a Keynesian action. But TARP was designed to be a temporary stopgap measure and required collateralization and repayment of the loans. TARP loans were subsequently paid back, and some even returned a profit. However, similar programs enacted by Barack Obama had no collateralization requirements or payback provisions. Most were not loans, but gifts. This lack of oversight and excessive deficit spending resulted in a low growth economy (stagflation) for his entire term in office.

Whatever your political views, you should be aware that the economic theories being debated drive political policies that directly affect your quality of life. The basic question is how much control should government have? So, when one side of a political debate resorts to name calling or exaggerated hyperbole, realize that those are distractions intended to redirect your focus away from the issues. Making policy decisions regarding the economy based on emotions and rhetoric, rather than logic and reason, can be a very costly mistake. Which economic theory will work best to keep the country on a path to economic stability?

According to Bloomberg, a business news agency, the number of publicly traded companies worldwide is about 65,000. You literally have tens of thousands of ways of vicariously experiencing both good and bad economic times through free market capitalism facilitated by the stock market. So, some company somewhere is going to be reflecting every possible juvenile antic of the economy imaginable. "When it is good, it is very, very good; but when it is bad, it is horrid". What exactly is the stock market, and how does it work?

The **stock market** is a system whereby shares of ownership in public companies, or other similarly structured businesses, can be exchanged from one entity to another. The owner may be either a person or an institution. Implied in that definition is the fact that the stock market does not create the shares being bought and sold; it simply acts as a facilitator for the transfer of ownership. Thus, the places or means of executing these buy and sell transactions are referred to as *exchanges*.

The two largest exchanges in the U.S. are the NYSE/Euronext, formed by the merger of the New York Stock Exchange and Euronext, and the Nasdaq Exchange. NASDAQ started out as an acronym for National Association of Securities Dealers Automated Quotation system, but the NASD organization merged with the NYSE Regulatory Committee in 2007 to form the Financial Industry Regulatory Authority, FINRA. So, even though there is no longer a NASD, the Nasdaq name for that exchange has remained.

There has been a continuing trend of mergers among stock exchanges. However, at the time of this writing, major worldwide exchanges would include the Shenzhen, Hong Kong, and Shanghai in China; the Tokyo in Japan, the Bombay in India, the Frankfurt in Germany, the FTSE in the UK, the Toronto in Canada, the Bovespa in Brazil, the Bolsa in Mexico, and many more. Most countries around the globe have stock exchanges, either an ECN or a physical location, where those who want to buy securities are able to be matched with those who want to sell, and vice versa.

The term **securities** is used to describe a wide variety of investment instruments issued by businesses, usually corporations or partnerships. Securities may be bought or sold through broker/dealers, one of the many different types of companies in the *financial services industry*. Securities would include not only shares of stock, but also mutual funds, bonds, options, futures, partnerships, and more. The various types of securities will be explained in an orderly manner throughout this book.

There are many common misconceptions about securities markets. For example, you may have heard someone say, "The market was up because there were more buyers than sellers", or "It was down because there were more sellers than buyers". Such statements are misleading. On any exchange, there are never any more shares bought than sold, or sold than bought. Exchanges only provide a service for facilitating change of ownership. Every time someone purchases a security, someone else sells it. Consequently, you might hear the market described as having "a zero sum gain", meaning the same amount of money lost by someone was gained by someone else.

Stock exchanges are called secondary markets. New shares for companies are not created by the exchange, but through a system called the primary market. This will be described in greater detail in the next chapter. Any newly created security is referred to as an **initial public offering**, **IPO**. Only after the IPO shares have been issued does the security begin trading on the secondary market.

Security exchanges provide an efficient means for arriving at an agreed upon price between two parties and facilitating the legal aspects of transfer of ownership. They are not the cause of price fluctuation. The buyers and sellers themselves usually determine that. Security exchanges are free market capitalism at work.

The Stock Market and the Economy ◊ 15

The reason why the prices of shares of stock rise and fall can be expressed by the classic economic model of supply and demand.

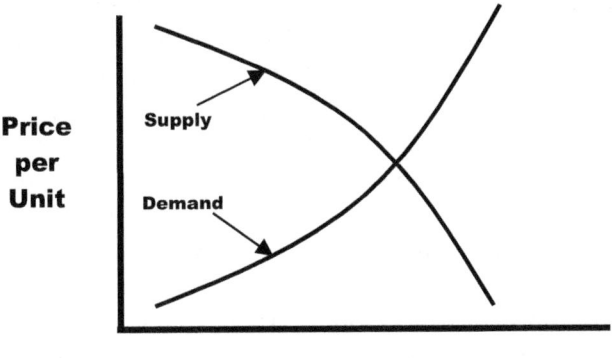

This illustration demonstrates the relationship between supply and demand curves. If supply is high and demand is low, the price per unit will be low. But increasing demand causes supply to decrease, and the price per unit will be driven higher. Only at the point where the supply line crosses the demand line, does the price of an item remain relatively stable. That is the price that a securities exchange facilitates for those who want to buy or sell shares of stock. An economist would say that the worth of something is the price that the market will bear. In other words, the buyers and sellers themselves determine the prices of securities.

The economic principle of supply and demand explains the movement of stock prices because every company has a relatively fixed number of shares available, thus a limited supply. This number is said to be *relatively fixed* because, within certain limits, a company can occasionally issue more shares. Many companies may choose to issue new shares of stock or options to purchase shares at a lower than market price as employee bonuses. These are popular perks used by employers as incentives for meeting productivity goals. The details of that will be explained later, but with those provisos aside, the supply of shares of a publicly traded company is considered to be fixed. Unless a company amends its charter, it cannot issue more shares than has been authorized.

Since there is a limited supply of shares available, the more motivated investors are to buy those shares, the higher the price they may be willing to pay for them. Increased demand will drive the price higher. Conversely, the more motivated owners of a stock are to sell those shares, the lower the price they may be willing to accept, increasing supply. Stock prices tend to follow the same up and down patterns of the supply and demand curves economist use to describe price volatility for any commodity or service.

Shares of stock on U.S. exchanges trade in increments of dollars and cents. Usually the smallest incremental change in price per share is one cent ($0.01). The incremental change for some high-priced shares may be at a higher minimum, such as five or ten cents ($0.05 or $0.10). Also, some low-priced shares, usually below one dollar, can trade in increments of one-tenth of a cent ($0.001) or even one one-hundredth of a cent ($0.0001). Some high-priced stocks can trade in increments of $1.00 per share or more, but those cases are rare.

The term used to describe the incremental change in a stock's price is a **tick**. Thus, if someone says, "The stock is on an up-tick"; it simply means the last trade for that stock was at a price higher than the previous trade. A down-tick would indicate a lower price than the previous trade. The scrolling video of securities and prices of trades that you see featured on televised business news broadcasts is referred to as the ticker tape. The letters represent the computer codes for the names of companies and are referred to as ticker symbols.

You might hear business reporters refer to the **closing tick** at the end of the market session. It is the number computed by subtracting the number of companies whose last trade of the day was on a down-tick (sell) from those companies whose closing trades were on an up-tick (buy). The purpose is to indicate the sentiment of buyers and sellers just before the market closed. That could be an indicator of how the market might open on the next trading session. A high closing tick number would indicate that there was a surge of buying activity at the end of the trading day that might carry over into similar activity when the market opens the next day.

Contrary to what some people assume, the price of a stock does not have to open the next trading day at the same price it had closed at on the previous day. Investors may put in orders to buy and sell securities after the market is closed to be executed at the next open. Major stock exchanges in the U.S. are open every business day from

9:30 a.m. to 4:00 p.m. Eastern Time in New York City, which would be 6:30 a.m. to 1:00 p.m. Pacific Time on the West Coast.

Also, there are companies that provide afterhours trading over **electronic communication networks, ECNs**. Although, investors should note that afterhours ECNs do not trade the same volume of securities as the larger exchanges and this lack of liquidity can affect execution prices. In most cases, investors are likely to get a better price, whether buying or selling, during regular trading hours. The high volume of trading usually benefits investors.

As stated earlier, the stock market is a pure expression of a free market economy in action. Individual investors can decide for themselves whether the price of a stock, for either a buyer or a seller, is acceptable and fair. A free market economy depends on a competitive environment to determine what a fair price is. A free market capitalist environment affords investors the opportunity to choose how they want to participate in the market.

What Are Market Averages and Indexes?

When you hear someone say, "The market was up (or down) today", they are not referring to the total market value for all securities, or the total of the securities on the New York Stock Exchange, NYSE. They are usually referring to the percentage change in price of just the few representative companies. Most commonly, in daily use, they are referring to the Dow Jones Industrial Average, the Dow. You may also see it identified as DJI, DJIA, or some other variation of that acronym. However, some market commentators may be referring to the Standard & Poor's 500 Index, which will be discussed later.

The Dow is made up of just thirty companies. But each of them is a leader in its industry, has a large capitalization, is actively traded, and usually pays a dividend. A dividend is a payment made to shareholders of a company representing a portion of that company's earnings. The Wall Street jargon for the type of companies that are included in the Dow is **blue chip**. Blue is the color of the gaming chip with the highest value in most store bought poker sets.

18 ◊ THE STOCK MARKET AND THE ECONOMY

The fact that the term "the market" seems ambiguous is another example of how slowly traditions change on Wall Street. The Dow Jones Industrial Average started in 1884, when Charles H. Dow and Edward D. Jones began computing it by hand. The average included eleven stocks and grew to thirty by 1928. Originally the closing prices of the stocks were added up, and the total was divided by the number of companies to get a simple arithmetic average. However, because of stock splits, which will be explained shortly, and additions and deletions of the companies that make up the average, the **divisor** has evolved from just the number of items included in the list (30) to a factor of less than one. In recent years is has been in a range of roughly 0.12 - 0.16.

The divisor is useful because it gives you a reference point for figuring out how much the price movement of individual stocks affects the total market average. Consider how much the market would be changed if all thirty companies in the Dow were up exactly one point. Dividing the total number of companies, 30, by a divisor of 0.15, reveals the market would be up about 200 points (30/0.15 = 200).

If you wanted to determine how much one particular company is factoring into the total change of the Dow, you can divide its price by the divisor. For example, assume that the market is up about 60 points, but one of the companies in the DJIA is up 10 points. By dividing that company's price change (10) by the divisor (0.15), the result will reveal how much that one stock contributed to the total market performance. In this case, those ten points alone would account for the whole 60-point rise and then some (5/0.15 = 66.66). Consequently, you could deduce the other 29 companies in the Dow would average out to about a -6.66 of the total.

Many professional investors and analysts are critical of using the Dow as an indicator of the overall market because it is composed of so few companies. But there is also a mathematical reason to criticize it. The DJIA is described as **price-weighted**. Using a simple arithmetic average for computation means that higher-priced stocks contribute more to the total than lower-priced ones. A $100 company adds ten times as much to the total as a $10 company does. This heavier weighting toward higher priced stocks might skew the average to a lower overall percentage change than a more equally weighted one would. For example, a $1 increase in the price of the

$100 stock is only 1% (100/1 = 0.01). However, a $1 increase in a $10 stock is 10% (10/1 = 0.1)—ten times as much. It is more likely that a $100 stock will move up $1 than a $10 stock.

Next, consider how the DJIA divisor has changed due to stock splits. When a company undergoes a **stock split**, the number of shares an investor owns will increase and the price per share will decrease by the same proportion. The total market value of the shares owned will be the same after the split as it was before. In other words, the percentage of the price reduction after the split will be the same as the percentage of the increased shares resulting from the split. When a stock splits 2-for-1, for example, the total number of shares an investor owns will be doubled, but the price per share of the stock will be cut in half. The number of shares that will be added as a result of the split will be 50 percent of the new total. Thus the market value of the investment remains the same.

Consider the effect of a 2-for-1 split for a stockholder who owns 100 shares of a $50 stock. The total investment is worth $5,000. After the split that investor will receive 100 more shares for a total of 200. However, the post-split price per share will be reduced from $50 to $25. So the total market value of the investment will remain the same, $5000 (200 × $25 = $5000). One hundred shares of a $50 stock has the same market value as 200 shares of a $25 stock.

Additionally, stock splits may be done in any proportion, not necessarily just 2-for-1. A 3-for-2 stock split, for example, would result in investors owning 150 shares if they originally owned 100 shares. If the price of the pre-split stock was $50, after the split the price would be $33.33. The 33 percent price decrease in the price of the stock would be equivalent to a 33 percent increase in the number of shares owned after the split (150 × $33.33 = $5000, rounded off). Also, a 4-for-3 split would result in ownership of 125 shares worth $40 per share (125 × $40 = $5000).

The announcement of a stock split is generally viewed very favorably by investors. Stock splits are a sign that the price of the stock has appreciated substantially. The Board of Directors of the company has decided they would like to keep the company in a lower price range, hoping to attract more investors. However, investors should be aware there is no direct material benefit. The total value of their investment is not affected.

So let's go back to the effect of stock splits on the DJIA divisor. To illustrate how it has been reduced from 30 to 0.15 over the last 140 plus years, imagine what would have happened if the original 30 companies had all split 2-for-1 simultaneously. (That, of course, has never happened; and this is only a hypothetical illustration.) To keep the Dow at the same number after a split, you could either multiply the post-split share prices of each company by 2 and continue to divide by 30 or simply reduce the divisor by one-half, from 30 to 15. Since adjusting the prices of each entry involves many more computations than only adjusting the divisor, that seems the most practical method. Stock splits happen irregularly and unpredictably, and simply adjusting the divisor makes computation of the Dow Jones Industrial Average coherent.

Also, there have been many deletions and additions made to the 30 companies that make up the Dow Jones Industrial Average over the last two centuries. Usually companies whose status as blue chip stocks has faded are replaced by other companies that have emerged as new leaders in their industries. This has resulted in some people criticizing the Dow as artificially improving the market average, as underperforming companies are replaced by those more likely to perform better.

If companies that have done poorly had been left in the average, the market would not appear to be doing as well as the historical record would indicate. This is not only a potential problem with the Dow Jones Industrial Average, but with other market measurements as well. Some of those other market indexes will be discussed shortly. However, while the DJIA may make changes once or twice a decade, other market measures may be adjusted once or twice a year. Suffice it to say that formulating a completely accurate method of measuring the market is difficult.

Even though computers have made using the Dow as an overall market indicator obsolete, the primary reason why investors continue to follow it is simply that it is traditional. The culture of Wall Street has deep roots in tradition. The current state of stock market trading has become a melding of tradition and high tech innovation, and traditions die hard.

There are many other market indexes than the Dow Jones Industrial Average, such as the S&P 500 and the Nasdaq, that have rendered the Dow obsolete. Most institutional money managers, such as those who administer mutual fund portfolios, use the S&P 500 Index as their market benchmark. **Mutual funds** are defined as professionally managed portfolios in which each share of the fund represents ownership of many different individual securities. (Mutual funds will be discussed in detail in Chapter 8.)

As opposed to just 30 companies being included in the Dow Jones Industrial Average, the S&P 500 Index is composed of the 500 largest companies selected by Standard & Poor's. S&P estimates that their index includes companies representing about 75 percent of the total market value of all shares traded in the U.S. So, it is a much broader representation of the U.S. market than the Dow.

Note that the Dow is called an average, but the S&P 500 an index. The difference between an average and an index is the method used for their computation. An index is usually weighted by something other than the prices of the stocks. Also, an index begins its measurement with a base being assigned as a starting point. The base number of an index may be selected on an arbitrary basis such as 0, 50, 100, or any other number assigned by the creators of the index. The S&P 500 was first published in 1957, but its oldest computation dates back to 1923. The importance of an index to any investor is that any point on it may be used as a starting point, allowing you to determine the percentage change from that point to any other future date.

The S&P 500 is described as a **value-weighted**, or market cap, index because each entry used to compute the index is not the price of the stock but the total market value of all the shares outstanding for that company. The total market value is called market capitalization, or just market cap. **Market cap** is the price of the stock multiplied by the number of shares outstanding. So, price determines only part of the index total. Each company's weighting in the index is determined by more than price alone; it is the total amount of money that shareholders currently have invested in it. For the S&P 500 index, and all other indexes published by Standard & Poor's, high priced stocks do not necessarily add more to the weighting of the market measure.

For example, a shares of a company priced at $50 that has 100 million shares outstanding would have a total market capitalization of $5 billion. But a company at $25 with 2 billion shares outstanding would have a market cap of $50 billion. In this example, the company whose stock is selling at half the price of the other represents a market capitalization twice that of the one with the higher price, because of the greater number of shares outstanding. In the price-weighted Dow, a $50 stock would factor in twice as much as a $25 one to the total. But in the value-weighted S&P 500 Index the $50 stock in this example would represent a factor of only half as much as the $25 one.

Here is a chart of the DJIA and the S&P 500 over a recent ten-year period. Notice that even though the two indicators use different components and different methods of computation, they still consistently fall within about a four percent variation of change. Despite all their differences, these two indicators still closely correlate. Over longer periods of time, they do diverge to a greater degree than in this illustration, but they tend to move in sync.

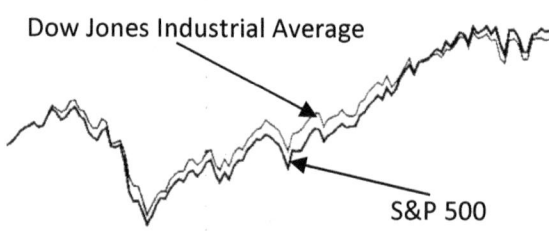

Investors should be aware that regardless of whether they are watching an index or an average, the relevance of the computation is not the number itself, but rather the relative change in that number over time. If the DJIA was at 20,000, for example, and went up 2,000 points in one year, the market would be up 10 percent for that time period. Two thousand is 10 percent of 20,000 (2000/20,000 = .10). Correspondingly, if the S&P 500 Index was at 3,000, it would only need to go up 300 points for the index to be up 10 percent. The number that is reported for the DJIA or the S&P 500 is not important in and of itself. It is only useful as a benchmark for measuring change in the market from one point in time to another.

Dow Jones is a financial publishing company and a subsidiary of News Corp. Standard & Poor's is another financial publishing company and a subsidiary of McGraw-Hill Corp. There are many other financial publishers of note, but those two are the largest and probably most followed. Both companies publish information on several other indexes meant to measure more specialized markets.

In addition to the Industrial Average, Dow Jones publishes the Transportation Average of 20 companies, the Utility Average of 15 companies in the electric, gas, or telecommunications business. It also publishes a Composite Average of the 65 companies comprised of all three market measures. In addition to the S&P 500 Large Cap Index, Standard & Poor's publishes the S&P 400 Mid Cap Index, the S&P 600 Small Cap Index, and the S&P Composite of all 1500 companies. Both companies, and several others, also publish information on many other indexes. The criteria for categorizing companies as large cap, mid cap, or small cap is based on the S&P method of determining total **market value**, price per share times number of shares outstanding. However, the size of companies is a constantly moving target, for the price changes daily, and the number of shares outstanding will also change over time.

At the time of this writing, the approximate sizes of the market capitalization of companies in the S&P indexes was: small cap, $1 - $2 billion; mid cap, $2 - $10 billion; large cap, $10 - $80 billion. Companies under $1 billion are referred to as micro-cap, and over $80 billion as mega-cap. Market cap constantly changes as prices and total shares change. So setting the limits for these categories is also constantly being adjusted, and the categories will often overlap. The S&P website provides updated current information. There are many companies who now have a market cap over $1 trillion.

Additionally, the number of specialized market indexes has been mushrooming. These indexes can be bought and sold in the same way shares of stock can be. The price for trading indexes is usually adjusted by a fixed multiple of the actual number in the index. For example, if the S&P 500 Index is at 2000, the equivalent unit cost of investing in the index would be $200.00, because the multiple of the index is set at 0.1. More information about this process will be included in Chapter 9.

A complete list of tradable market indexes is beyond the scope of this book, but a few of them are worth noting, based on popularity. The S&P 500 Index is the most active and is referred to as the Spider, which is the pronunciation of the acronym for Standard & Poor's Depository Receipt, SPDR. The Nasdaq 100 is composed of one hundred of the largest companies trading on the Nasdaq Exchange. It is usually referred to as the Qs because its trading symbol is QQQ. The NYSE Composite consists of over 2000 of most of the actively traded companies on the NYSE. The Russell Small Cap 2000 is composed of that number of U.S. companies whose market cap ranks below the top 1000. The Value

Line Composite Index is composed of the approximately 1700 companies on which Value Line publishes research data. Lastly, the Wilshire 5000 Index is the broadest market index, designed to include all the publicly traded companies for which price data is readily available. The number of companies in the Wilshire 5000 Index exceeds 5,000.

As the world becomes more economically interdependent, there are many important global market indexes. A couple worth noting would be the S&P Global 1200 Index, which is designed to capture approximately 75 percent of the world's trading in stocks and the Dow Jones Global Equity Commodity Indexes, a series of indexes comprised of companies involved in various commodities industries such as energy, agriculture, precious metals, and so on.

Finally, there are dozens of stock indexes that are specific to one country or one continent. For speculators who want to trade in geographically delineated areas, most foreign indexes trade on U.S. markets. A short list would include: the Shanghai Composite in China, the Hang Seng in Hong Kong, the Nikkei Stock Average in Japan, the S&P/ASX 200 in Australia, the Kospi in South Korea, the Bombay Sensex in India, the Stoxx in Europe, the DAX in Germany, the CAC 40 in France, the FTSE 100 in the UK, the S&P/TSX Composite in Canada, the Bolsa IPC in Mexico, the Sao Paulo Bovespa in Brazil, and many more.

With so many choices, how do you figure out which stocks will be the best investments? No one has figured out the consistently correct answer to that question, and no one ever will. If someone tells you they have a fail-proof secret formula, run away. Investing is more of an art than a science, and as with buying art, go with what you like. Such an approach may not assure you of a good investment, but if you like it, chances are many other people will like it as well. But first you need to know what you are looking at.

How Do You Find and Interpret Stock Quotes?

The biggest problem most people have when they begin looking up stock information is figuring out how to find and interpret price quotes. Financial websites usually have a link on their home page for accessing quotes. Usually there will be a box that says "get

THE STOCK MARKET AND THE ECONOMY ◊ 25

quotes" or something similar. However, in order to get the information you need to know the stock's ticker symbol.

The **ticker symbol** is a computer symbol identifying a security by a series of one to five letters. In some cases, there may also be an extension following a dot (.), which would likely indicate a stock trading on a foreign exchange, or some other class of stock. You will need to put that symbol in the quote box to get the price and other information about the security. To find the symbol start typing the name of the company in the "get quotes" box. You should get a dropdown menu with a list of names of companies that match what you are typing. Click on the name of the company you want, and the correct symbol will automatically be put in the box. Hit enter, and your quote information will pop up.

However, there may be several companies on the dropdown list that match your request. So you need to determine which one to choose. If this is a large company, it will likely trade on several different exchanges worldwide. The specific exchange will be listed to the right of the name of the company. The most likely exchange you will want to select will be the NYSE or Nasdaq.

Companies that trade on foreign exchanges will have a symbol followed by an extension identifying which one. Unless you are looking for a foreign stock quote, do not click on these symbols. The quote will represent that foreign exchange only and usually in the currency of that country. The exchanges will be listed on the right side of the dropdown menu. For example, .TO will be Toronto, .L London, .F Frankfurt, .AX Australia, .HK Hong Kong, .BO Bombay, .MX Mexico, .SA Sao Paulo, etc.

Foreign securities usually trade on U.S. exchanges in the form of an **American Depositary Receipt**, **ADR**. An ADR is not the same as common stock. It is a designation for shares of a foreign company trading on a U.S. exchange. The foreign shares are put on deposit at a U.S. financial institution, which then reissues a new class of shares being in printed in English and quoted in U.S. dollars. On the Nasdaq ADRs are usually identified when the fifth letter of the symbol is a *Y*.

If you are looking for a small company that does not trade on the NYSE or Nasdaq exchange, you will probably want to select a company with a four or five letter symbol followed by the extension *.PK* or *.BB*. Those extensions identify securities that trade on the

OTC Pink Sheets or Bulletin Board. Not all quote services use the same extensions, but the symbol should be recognizably close to that. OTC is an acronym for over-the-counter and is the obsolete term for the Nasdaq market. Pink Sheet and Bulletin Board stocks will have less data available than companies that trade on an exchange. Most brokerages will not assign analysts to research and follow Pink Sheet or Bulletin Board stocks.

Companies trading on the NYSE or Nasdaq must meet several minimum requirements. Some of these requirements would be the number of shares outstanding, size of the market cap, number of shareholders, trading volume, and so on. Stocks that trade on the Pink Sheets or Bulletin Board, usually do not meet all the exchange requirements. Stocks trading there may also be referred to as Additional Over-the-Counter.

When you have selected the stock you want from the dropdown list, click on it and its ticker symbol will automatically be inserted in the quote box. Your quote information will immediately pop up. Different services provide different information. The following illustration is meant to be a generic presentation of a common format. Although the format of different websites will look differently, the data will be the same. It is from the same source.

Unique Inc. (UIQ)

Last Trade:	28.34 ↑0. 28 (0.1 %)		
Prev Close:	28.06	**Bid:**	28.32
Open:	28.10	**Ask:**	28.35
High:	28.35	**Vol:**	7,320
Low:	28.06	**PE:**	18.52
52 Wk Range:	18.82 – 28.63	**EPS:**	1.53
Divd:	$0.80	**Yield:**	2.82%

The name of the company, Unique Inc., and its ticker symbol, UIQ, are listed at the top. The letters of the ticker symbol are recognized by the ECN to identify the company. *Last Trade* is the most recent price at which a trade was executed. During the day this will change as new orders are entered until all markets have closed. The information that follows is the amount of the dollar and percentage change from the *Prev Close*, previous close, or the prior day's last traded price. *Open* is the quote at which the price of the stock first traded when the market opened on that day. The *High* and *Low* prices are the highest and lowest prices at which the stock has traded so far on that day. The difference between the high and the low is the day's range. The *52 Wk Range* is the lowest and highest price the stock has traded at over the last year. It shows the investor whether the stock is trading closer to the low or high end of its recent range.

The **bid** is the highest price at which a buyer is offering to purchase shares. The **ask** is the lowest price at which a seller is currently offering to sell shares. If you want to purchase shares, you could buy them at the current lowest ask price; and if you want to sell, you would receive the highest current bid price. This will be explained in greater detail in Chapter 3. *Vol*, short for volume, is the total number of shares that have been traded so far on this day. Sometimes volume is expressed as the number of 100 share units. One hundred shares is called a *Round Lot* and is the traditional quantity for trading stock.

PE stands for **price earnings ratio**. It is sometimes written like the fraction, P/E, because it is the market price of the stock ($28.34) divided by the **EPS**, **earnings per share** ($1.53). In this example, 28.34/1.53 = 18.52. EPS is the net income the company made for the last year (four quarters), divided by the number of shares it has issued. The significance of this will be explained in Chapter 5.

Finally, *Divd* is the current annual dividend, the dollar amount of payments the company will make to its shareholders. The dividend represents that part of the company's earnings per share it will pay out to its shareholders. In this example the $0.80 annual dividend will be distributed in four $0.20 quarterly payments. *Yield* is the **dividend yield** and is computed as the dollar amount of the annual dividend divided by the current market price. In this example, the yield is 0.80/28.34 = 2.4%. The dividend yield is analogous to the interest rates that banks would pay on saving accounts. If you were to put $28.34 in a bank saving account paying 2.4% interest, you would receive $0.80 by the end of the year.

Investors should keep a close eye on the quarterly earnings reports to make sure they are sufficient enough to cover the dividend payment. Companies sometimes go through down cycles where they don't have enough quarterly earnings to cover the quarterly dividend. However, companies are not likely to change their dividend distribution policy because of one bad quarter. When a company declares a dividend, there is an implied expectation that the company will continue paying at that rate in the future.

There will be a more detailed description of the information available on stock quote systems presented in Chapter 6. The presentation here is only meant to give you an overview. The significance and implications of the data go well beyond this summary. You need to know a little about what a stock is before you can decide if you want to invest in it.

Should You Invest in the Stock Market?

Even if you think you don't own any investments in the stock market, you probably do, through a surrogate. Most Americans participate in stock market investing at some level, even though they don't realize it. If you have an insurance policy, pension or profit-sharing plan, a 401(k), an IRA, or even a bank or credit union account, some of your money is likely to be invested in the stock market.

It is not a coincidence that so many different financial entities invest in the market. Any professional **fiduciary**, someone who is responsible for managing finances on behalf of another, realizes the stock market has given a long-term inflation adjusted average return higher than any other alternative investment class.

In the last few years the percentage of individuals who hold investments in the stock market has held fairly steady at around 60 percent, according to a Gallup poll survey. However, the number of individual investors has been declining. The high percentage of stock ownership is due to accounts managed by institutions. People tend to look at the stock market as a high risk-high reward venture. But treating the stock market only as high-risk probably contributes to more ill-timed, wrong-headed investment decisions than any other factor.

Although it would be difficult to prove statistically, it is possible this is because so many new entrants into the market are speculators or, more likely, gamblers. As with any gambling venture, practically everyone loses money over an extended period of time. That experience and the negative chatter around the water cooler might tend to discourage others from the stock market.

There is always risk in the stock market, but by the same token, there is always risk in any venture. We live in an environment of unpredictability. The end result of almost any undertaking is undeterminable. That is also the nature of life. You cannot eliminate risk; the best you can do is mitigate it. So, do not assume more risk than you are comfortable with. Investors have made millions of dollars investing in stock markets, but you should note that those same millions were lost by someone else. Most of the legendary billionaires who made their fortunes in the stock market have advocated the same consistent strategy: slow and steady. So, follow their example and be a long-term investor, not a short term gambler.

If you grasped the implications of the analogy that the economy is like a hyperactive drama queen at the beginning of this chapter, you should have realized the economy is inherently unpredictable. The biggest risk to any investment is inflation. Most people think of inflation as rising prices. It can be that, but it is more.

Economists usually define **inflation** as the measure of the loss of the purchasing power of money. Superficially, rising prices and loss of purchasing power sound the same. But economists' definition highlights the reason that goods and services cost more is because money is too readily available. The supply of money exceeds the demand for goods and services.

Inflation is an almost constant economic reality. Seldom does the economy go through periods of contractions, or recessions, longer than a few months. When it does, the economy has even more problems with which to deal—high unemployment, falling real estate values, and a general distrust of economic policymakers. Most people prefer the risk of inflation over the alternative.

So, because of inflation, the greatest risk you can take with your capital is to do nothing. Do not keep your money in a mattress, or in any other way sleep on it. If you do nothing to cause your money to grow faster than the rate of inflation, you are shrinking it. Inflation is constantly eroding the purchasing power of your money, guaranteeing you will lose at least part of it. Your **net worth**, the total market value of your assets minus what you owe on those assets, will steadily decline. The economy does not allow anyone to stand still.

Do you remember what it cost you to go to a movie when you were younger? Do you know what your parents paid for their car or their house? How about the cost of a college education? You don't need to have a very long memory to realize that a dollar does not go as far today as it used to. Only if you make investments that at least maintain pace with the rising cost of living will the dollar you have in your pocket today be able to buy an equivalent amount of goods and services next year.

For the last century, the best performing inflation-adjusted investment option, of all investment possibilities, has been common stocks—averaging over 10% growth with dividend compounding factored in. Other investments may have outperformed stocks for short periods of time, but compared to bonds, gold, real estate, oil, diamonds, collectibles of all sorts, or any other investment, the stock market has consistently produced the highest long-term returns.

You should note that recent stock market activity has generally been providing returns below historic averages. But the market has always demonstrated remarkable resiliency. A long-term chart of the market shows consistently rising prices in spite of constantly negative news—wars, global terrorist activities, assassinations, natural disasters. There was never a time when the world was in a worry-free state of peace and harmony. The stock market will react downwardly to each new negative event, but then it will continue climbing upward.

There is a place for equity investments in almost everyone's financial plan. Regardless of your current economic status, you could benefit in some way from securities. But first you need to have a financial plan.

A boilerplate financial plan, although most are very thorough, might not address your specific issues; everyone is unique. Your individual circumstances need to be personally addressed in order to make all the diverse pieces of your financial situation fit into place like a jigsaw puzzle. Everyone's financial plan will be as unique as the individual. However, there are some basic guidelines you should follow.

Your financial plan should begin with an itemization of all your marketable assets. These can be broadly separated into financial assets and real assets. Financial assets would include bank accounts, brokerage accounts, insurance, and retirement plan investments, and so on. Real assets would include your house, car, jewelry, marketable collectibles, household assets, and so on—everything for which you could determine a fair market value.

Next, itemize your debt, or liabilities. You might list your home mortgage balance remaining, outstanding auto loan, credit card debt, annual property tax, income tax, and any other debt you may have incurred.

Finally, subtract the total market value of your assets from your total liabilities. The difference between the two will be your **net worth**, or equity. It is the hypothetical amount of money you would have if you were to sell everything you own and pay off all your debt. You'll see how corporations calculate their net worth in Chapter 5.

Certified Financial Planners, CFPs, have completed a very rigorous course, granting them the right to use that title. Many people may call themselves financial planners, but have not met the requirements to use the CFP title. However, not all CFPs are created equal. If you are considering using a financial planner, find one with whom you can work well, who understands your individual needs. The person who helps you manage your life savings should be someone who listens to your questions and answers them in terms you can understand.

Most financial planners organize your personal spending and investing priorities something like this: (1) insurance or risk management, (2) home ownership, (3) tax and estate planning, and (4) capital accumulation. Quite honestly this list looks like it was organized by (1) insurance salespeople, (2) real estate salespeople, (3) attorneys, and (4) bankers. Some financial planners may imply that stock market investing is for risk capital only, that there is no place for stock market investments until you have met all your other financial goals. That assessment assumes all securities are high-risk, but that is simply not the case.

Certainly risk capital should be on the bottom of any list of financial priorities. But securities markets should not always be approached with the idea of investing risk capital only. There are many investments that are low risk. Securities can be used to help you attain each of your goals, falling into the four priorities listed in that model.

Financial planning is simply a logical approach to evaluating your economic situation. Consider you own basic personal needs. They are the same now as they were in childhood. Most children are taught that the four basic necessities in life are: food, shelter, safety, and love. Sound financial planning should be prioritized on the same basis.

First and foremost, you need to provide for adequate personal income to meet all your current and anticipated future needs. In other words, you need to keep food on the table. If you don't have finances, you don't need a financial plan.

Secondly, your goal should be to achieve home ownership—shelter. The real estate market has evolved into a maze of complex legalities. Some worry that there will be another collapse in the housing market like the one in 2008. But be assured that the real estate market will follow the economic law of supply and demand, the same as any other commodity. As the population increases, the demand for housing will increase. During periods of declining property values, fewer homes are being built. If supply is decreasing and demand is increasing, housing prices will inevitably rise. To enter the housing market, you will need to have a predictable source of income and enough money saved up for a down-payment.

Thirdly, financial safety should be addressed through proper insurance coverage. You need to protect your assets from loss due to natural disasters, what insurance companies call "acts of God". You also need to provide for your dependents in the event of your demise with life insurance. Additionally, you should fund long-term accounts to adequately cover your loss of income when you retire. This is especially important since the federal government's plan, the Social Security System, will not likely be there if your planned retirement is over 30 years in the future.

Last on the list of personal needs is love, and, as every country and western singer knows, "Money cain't bah luv". In fact, some would say that money is a hindrance to true love; but that is a topic for another book. Your fourth financial goal, however, is to anticipate the future financial needs of your loved ones. Set up provisions for your children's college education or other major expenses. I believe it is important for financial plans to also include provisions for charitable giving or tithing.

THE STOCK MARKET AND THE ECONOMY ◊ 33

Anyone who has capital to invest has a good reason to take advantage of opportunities in securities markets, no matter what your financial status is. At all levels of financial planning, there are some security investments that could help you achieve your goals. If you approach investing with a desire to study and be involved in your investment decisions, you will avoid common pitfalls of novice investors. You will also increase your chances of achieving your goals.

This brief discussion about financial planning is only meant to introduce you to the subject. It is only a secondary topic in this book. You would be well advised to seek the counsel of a professional Certified Financial Planner, or access some of the online sources offering guidelines for financial planning. A complete financial plan will help you avoid some otherwise unforeseen problems. Without a financial plan, most people myopically deal only with problems as they arise. Such an approach inevitably leads to more problems. Having an overall financial picture will help you anticipate potential problems and give you tools for solving them. Securities investing can be one of those tools.

Do not approach the stock market with a get-rich-quick mentality. Do not take unnecessary risks with any part of your investments. A little psychological study of how your investments affect your emotions can be invaluable to your success. When it comes to making good investing decisions, too often you are your own worst enemy.

How Do You Know When to Buy or Sell?

Perhaps the most difficult question for anyone regarding investing in the stock market is, "When should I buy, and when should I sell?" There have been innumerable books written on that subject, but none of them has found a definitive answer. Someone once said that the stock market exists to make smart people look stupid. Certainly market timing is more an art than a science.

The best advice on the subject of market timing has come from studies on the psychology of investing. Those studies resulted in a theory known as the **Greed-Hope-Fear Cycle**. This cycle illustrates the fact that an investor's emotions tend to be their worst enemy when it comes to investment timing. So, if investors are able to separate emotions from logic, they will greatly improve the timing of their buy and sell decisions.

The Greed-Hope-Fear Cycle is also called the Individual Investor Cycle, or sometimes the Small Investor Syndrome. That appellation is condescending toward individual investors. It implies that this cycle represents unsophisticated individuals, which if you are reading this now, you are not one. It should be noted that corporations are made up of individuals, and the most dramatic illustrations of the Greed-Hope-Fear in action have come from institutions, not individual investors.

On October 19, 1987, a date referred to as Black Monday, the Dow crashed over 500 points for the first time. That was the largest numerical drop for the market up till that time. The market has subsequently gone through several periods of greater volatility—notably, following 9/11 in 2001 and the real estate collapse in 2008. However, all stock market volatility has paled in comparison to the Great Crash of 1929. From peak to trough the market drop following October 19, 1929 was almost 90 percent. That, of course, was the beginning of the Great Depression in the U.S. and a worldwide global recession.

It is important to note that the market drops following 9/11, and the housing crisis of '08 were bear market reactions perpetuated primarily by institutional—not individual—investors. Insurance companies, pension and retirement funds, brokerage firms, and mutual funds were primarily responsible for the huge increase in trading volume during those times. In fact, several insurance companies announced increases in their premiums as a result of investment losses they incurred from market volatility. However, many astute individual investors, bought stocks at relatively low prices during periods of extreme volatility Consequently most market indexes returned to their previous levels, and on to new highs, within a year or so after each drop.

I believe individual investors actually have an advantage over institutional ones in many ways. They answer only to themselves, not to a manager who has no skin in the game. Also, institutions are generally dealing with hundreds of millions or billions of dollars. So they tend to panic more quickly over volatile markets than individual investors. You are in a better position than most professional to evaluate your situation than most outsiders.

To illustrate the Greed-Hope-Fear Cycle, here is a typical example of how some investors choose what stocks to buy and when to buy them. Usually, curiosity about a particular company is initially aroused when you happen to overhear an intriguing conversation among your co-workers, neighbors, relatives, friends, barber, or hair stylist. Seldom does such a conversation begin with a professional financial advisor.

The conversation will follow along the lines that some company has developed an innovative product that is going to change life as we know it. Though you may listen with a justifiably skeptical ear to this conversation, your curiosity has been sufficiently aroused so that you start to follow how this company is doing. You go online and begin investigating into it.

To your surprise, this company's product really is revolutionary. This company could be the next big deal. So, you start watching the stock price. It started out around $20 per share and over the next few days has run up to $24.50. Doing a little simple arithmetic, you realize an investment of $2000 for 100 shares would now be worth $2450. That would be a $450 profit, or a 22.5 percent return on your original investment—in less than a week, no less! Hey, that beats the CD rate you just put your money into hundreds of times over. So, you figure if that stock backs down a bit, you're going to finally get your feet wet. Why should everybody else get rich and not you? So, you continue to watch the stock more intently. Low and behold it does start to back off a bit. It comes down to $22.75. Just a little bit more, and you'll make the plunge. But now you begin to think, "Hey, maybe this will drop back down to a price below $20".

So you continue to watch the stock with conflicting emotions. If it goes down, you worry it may go down further. If it goes up, you worry it is going to cost too much. It drops a little more to $21.35. "Maybe I should pull the trigger now," you think. "No, it was $20 just a week ago, and it's coming down. I'll wait".

However, over the next few days you watch the stock steadily climb up and up. It goes over $23. "Too expensive now, I'll wait". It comes down a bit. "It hasn't hit the bottom yet, I'll wait." You sit on your hands as you watch it methodically march higher a few days in a row—$24, $25, $26, $27. "Whoa, hold on here. Where's the pullback?" You start beating yourself up. "What a fool I am. If I had just bought that stock when I first heard about it, I'd be rich now. If I had bought a thousand shares at $20, that stock would be worth over $27,000 today! Why don't I ever act when I should?"

The stock continues to work its way up a bit and down a bit as you do nothing but watch, sitting on your hands with your head spinning and a knot in your stomach. "I can't take this. My whole body aches". Down to $26, up to $28, down to $27, up to $30, up to $32. Then something happens. The company puts out a press release explaining how this new product really will change life as we know it. The stock immediately shoots up over $40 per share.

You just can't sit still any longer. It's too depressing to compute how much money you have lost by not investing when you knew you should. You know the product works. There it is on your computer screen. In a fit of desperation you click on a link to one of the online brokers. You set up a trading account in a matter of just a few minutes, and you immediately purchase 100, no make it 200, shares of this company. You put in a market order, and it quickly comes back filled at $43.45. "Yes! I did it. I didn't plan on spending that much on the stock. Let's see—$8690 plus a commission and a fee. That's over $8700! But it's worth it. Look at what the stock has done over the last few months."

Over those last few months you have watched this stock run from around $20 to over $43. Your emotions are running high in anticipation that the next stop for this stock will probably be around $80 or even $100. "Dare I dream bigger?" However, if you were to set aside your emotions for a moment and consider the logic of your investment decision, where would you realistically expect the stock to go from here? Is it rational to think that stock could go up that high? All those people who have been buying the stock over the last few months, what price did they think it was going to hit? Those who bought at 20 have more than doubled their money already.

Examine the motivation for your buying decision. It is purely and simply GREED. You became so obsessed with how much money you could make from that investment you failed to analyze the overall picture. Greed caused you to buy the stock at the top of the market. So, or course, the next day the stock closes at 41.50. The following day 39.85. "Okay, I can live with that. I should have known the stock was going to pull back somewhat. Lesson learned. But I'm still going to make a fortune from this investment. You'll see. I just hope my wife doesn't find out".

You may still be in denial, but you bought at the top of that market cycle. The next few days you watch as it drops and drops—37.43, 35.25, 33.45. Your heart is sinking along with your stock. Over the last week or so, you have lost $10 per share. "Wait a minute. That's $1000. No, it's not; it's $2000. I bought 200 shares, remember? My God, what have I done?"

Your attitude toward this investment has rapidly deteriorated. The greed that motivated you when you first bought it is now a faint memory. As you click on the stock quote each day, it's not with eager anticipation to see how much money you've made. You know that's not going to happen. In a relatively short period of time, your attitude toward your investment has transformed into a firm resolve that if that turkey ever gets back close to what you paid for it, you'll sell it in a heartbeat.

Your emotional attachment to your carefully planned foray into the world of high finance has subtly changed from greed to HOPE. You hope you can just get out of this debacle without it costing you too much. You have learned your lesson—never invest in the stock market again. You'll write off this one as the cost of a valuable learning experience.

But wait. Now as you despondently watch your company, it is begins to come back. (Hope springs eternal.) It moves slowly up from the low 30s to around 35. In a few more days, it hits 36.25. You begin thinking maybe this isn't the catastrophe you thought it would be. It's moved up over 3 points in just 3 days. A little more and you'll be able to get out without being hurt too badly.

However, the following day is a big disappointment. You find yourself staring at the number 34.50 on your computer screen. "Oh, no! That's the wrong way. I should have sold when I had the chance. Should I cut my losses here? Well, it did go up about 5 points in only a few days. It could do that again".

You decide to wait and see. As you carefully watch, the stock goes up one day, and you're hopeful it's coming back. But it's down the next, and you're in the throes of despair. Up, down, up, down. You are starting to think you just can't take this anymore.

Your stock has worked its way back down to the low 30s. The further away it gets from your $43.45 price, the dimmer the glimmer of hope. Gradually your attitude toward this company is turned from hope to despair. So, you decide to stop watching the stock altogether. "What can I do now? I'm not going to get my money back. I'll have to ride this one out. I'm not going to eat that much of a loss. I can't afford it".

A few weeks go by. You periodically check your stock's price, but it's going nowhere. It seems to be staying in the low to mid 30s. Then one day you log on to your computer and there on the home page of your internet service provider is a news article that you notice mentions your company's name. Normally you don't pay much attention to these articles, but this is about your company. The headline is not good.

The new product your company developed that was supposed to change life as you know it has some fatal flaw, and the CEO of the company has absconded with $50 million from the company's coffers. "Oh, my God", you think. "That company may not change life as we know it, but it sure has changed my life!" Quickly you log on to your quote page. Not quite as quickly as you would like, because your heart is racing, you are hyperventilating, and your fingers move clumsily and are slippery from sweat. There it is—the stock quote. You knew it would be red, but not that red. It's at 19.50. "That's down over 12 and a half points. Oh, my God. What am I going to do?"

Quickly you log back on to your brokerage account. The news is worse there. You watch in quiet desperation as the stock keeps flickering back and forth as trades come fast and furious—19.43, 19.44, 19.43, 19.42, 19.41, 19.43. You look at the volume, over 27,000,000 shares and counting. That stock has never traded over 5 million shares before.

Blinded by an adrenaline rush, your mind goes blank. In a panic you hit the wrong button to enter an order. "I can't even remember how to enter a sell order". You close your eyes and take a deep breath. You calm down enough to gather your wits. Finally you click Sell. Your order report doesn't pop up "filled" like it is supposed to. You wait a few desperate seconds, that seem to last an hour. You watch the stock continue to trade—lower. Your execution report suddenly pops up on the screen. Order filled at 18.98. You sigh. "What just happened?"

Now, consider how your attitude toward your investment has changed. You long ago abandoned your original attachment to the stock—GREED. You can hardly remember a time when you expected this investment to be your best chance to get rich quickly and retire early. "Was that really only a few months ago?" Now, your HOPE of ever recouping your money has come to a final conclusion. What caused you to sell? FEAR. Fear of losing everything. You are left with only your thoughts. You ask yourself, "What have I learned from this experience?" The answer quickly pops into your mind. "Never, never, never do this again".

However, consider what will probably happen to this stock next. You've watched it go from 43.45 to 18.98 in only a few months. Logically, without emotional confusion, where do you think this company is likely to go from here? The next day the stock closes at 20.28. In a week the company issues a press release that insurance will cover the money the CEO stole from the firm, and he will spend his retirement in a federal penitentiary.

The stock shoots up over 23, and in a month it is at 25. Less than a year later the company comes out with another press release stating that flaws in their product have been corrected and that the next generation of the product will be in full production by next quarter. The stock jumps to over 30. A few months later the company reports that sales of its next generation product have greatly exceeded everyone's wildest expectations. The stock pops back up over 40.

This narrative is meant to be a somewhat exaggerated and simplistic look at the emotional swings that investors go through in the Greed-Hope-Fear Cycle. Unfortunately for some, it may be too close to real-life to be humorous. The point, however, is this: Your emotions are always going to be working against you when it comes to making good market timing decisions. The best time to buy is when the majority of people are selling, and the best time to sell is when the majority is buying.

You may have heard market commentators advising investors to be contrarians, and this is an illustration of what they mean. If you had been a buyer of securities after one of the stock market "crashes" in the last few decades, in most cases you would have doubled your investment within the next two years. Keep in mind that trading securities is a zero sum gain. For every share of stock that was being sold in that panicky FEAR part of the cycle, someone was buying those shares. It didn't seem like there were many investors scrambling to buy on those down days, but the smart buyers were the contrarians.

Buying at the bottom of a Fear cycle emotionally goes against the grain. To buy when most people are selling or to sell when most people are buying is not easy to do. We are, after all, emotional individuals. That is true whether one is an amateur individual investor or a professional. Everyone is an individual, even those who are employed by financial institutions. So, referring to the Greed-Hope-Fear Cycle as the Small Investor Syndrome or the Individual Investor Cycle is just as applicable, and I believe more so, to institutions as it is to individuals.

Lesson one to becoming a good investor is to avoid falling victim to the Greed-Hope-Fear Cycle. Successful investors need to make decisions based on logic, research, and analysis, not on emotions. When it comes to investing your emotions will be your worst enemy. They will cause you to make bad market timing decisions.

The hypothetical investor's mistake in this illustration was not that he did not act quickly and buy the stock when he first heard about it. His mistake was that he did no research or analysis before making his investment decision. He let his emotions control the decision making process.

Smart investors would have examined the company's financial statements. They may have also analyzed the company's market potential, competitive advantage, and managerial style. Then they could have made a more well-informed decision based on logic, not emotion. The hypothetical person in this example was a gambler, not an investor. The following chapters of this book will present some basic tools for making better investment decisions. But never forget lesson one: Do not succumb to the Greed-Hope-Fear Cycle.

The Stock Market and the Economy ◊ 41

Don't get blown up by venturing where you don't understand the risks. Your road to success begins by learning what you need to know before you invest.

Chapter 2

What Are Shares of Stock?

Businesses in the U.S. are organized as sole proprietorships, partnerships, or corporations. A **sole proprietorship** is a business owned by an individual, who is personally responsible for its success or failure. Proprietorships are often retail businesses serving a local market, a professional or private practice, a home business, etc. Self-employed individuals are often sole proprietors. Businesses will generally remain proprietorships as long as their owners do not need to raise additional money for expansion, beyond that available from their own resources.

If the proprietorship grows to the point that the individual owners need to raise more capital for expansion than is available from their own resources, the next logical step could be to take on a partner. The addition of a partner will require changing the business structure from a proprietorship to a **partnership**. The profits and losses of the partnership will be divided between the partners in whatever arrangements they agree upon. Usually this sharing arrangement is in the same proportion as the amount of capital each partner has invested in the business.

More business than you might think are organized as partnerships. Some large family-owned businesses have remained in the family for generations and have never opted to expand beyond their partnership status. In recent years, there has been a wave of partnership-financed buyouts of public corporations. In these cases, multimillion-dollar financiers have raised enough personal capital or have borrowed enough money to buy out large public corporations. Thus, they have reversed the more common method of business expansion, turning corporations back into partnerships.

The laws applicable to business formation are set by the states, not the federal government. Although most state laws tend to be similar, following guidelines established by the Uniform Partnership Act (UPA), there are many distinct differences. The

UPA established rules and regulations for **Limited Liability Partnerships, LLPs**. These business models are favored by many professionals, such as attorneys and accountants. An LLP business structure generally offers tax benefits and liability protection of personal assets to some degree.

If a business continues to grow beyond the bounds of a partnership structure, its next move may be to incorporate. There are two basic options under which a small business may become a corporation: an S-Corporation and a Limited Liability Corporation, LLC. S-Corps are so named because of the special tax election under which they are covered is Subchapter S of the Internal Revenue Code. They are limited to no more than 75 shareholders. These types of small businesses can shelter the owners' personal assets from corporate liability.

LLCs offer more flexibility of revenue sharing, and generally require less paperwork, document filing, and record keeping. Both business structures, however, act as pass-through vehicles for income tax purposes. That means all corporate profits are passed through to the individual owners, who then pay taxes on those profits. Taxes are not paid both by the corporation and again by the individual owners.

Small business owners who are considering reorganizing their operations under one of these private business models would be well advised to seek legal counsel. This can be an ever evolving and complex area of the law. However, one basic distinction between an S-Corp. and a LLC is worth noting. Income reported under an S-Corp. would not be subject to self-employment tax for Social Security, but LLC income would be. Owners of an S-Corp. only pay self-employment tax on their salary, not their business profit.

These corporate structures are referred to as private companies. In fact, that term may also be applied to almost any company owned by a small number of shareholders, regardless of its corporate structure. Such companies are private because they have few owners and seldom sell shares to outsiders. Consequently, they are not required to disclose financial information to the general public about their business finances. The shareholder/owners of a private company keep all the profits and share all the liabilities from the business. They are solely responsible for making all financial decisions regarding the company.

44 ◇ Shares of Stock

Companies that allow the general public to invest in them are labelled C-Corporations. Other than this brief description of private companies, almost every other company referenced in this book will be a C-Corp. When the word company is used, it will refer to a publicly traded C-Corp.

Corporations have two basic methods of raising capital. They can borrow money, or they can sell a share of their equity ownership to outside investors. To borrow money, they could get a loan from a bank or other financial institution, or they can borrow it from other investors by issuing bonds. A **bond** is simply a loan that can be easily traded on organized exchanges. If a company raises capital by borrowing, either from loans or bonds, it will need to pay interest on the amount borrowed and is required to pay back the principal when the loan comes due or the bond matures.

If a company decides to sell shares of equity, it will not have the same interest payment obligation or refund of principal that it has with bonds. However, the company could lose some control over the operations of its business. At the very least, allowing the general public shares of ownership, obligates the managers of the business to address issues raised by those owners. Companies that want to raise a large amount of capital by becoming a C-Corp. must go through the process of going public.

Going public means the company will make available shares of stock, representing a percentage ownership of that business. By going public, the new company will raise additional capital, but now it must disclose to its new shareholder owners, and usually the general public as well, all its financial information. It is important to note that, even though the company has shareholder owners, it will continue to be managed by corporate personnel.

Following is an example of a paper stock certificate for Scantron. If this were a negotiable security, the name of the owner would be imprinted where the word SPECIMEN is stamped. Scantron is no longer a publicly traded company on its own. Notice the words COMMON STOCK imprinted over the writing on the lower half of the certificate. The name of the Transfer Agent is imprinted vertically in the lower right hand corner. Every stock certificate will have a unique identification number, usually in a box on the upper left-hand corner, and the number of shares in the similar box on the upper right-hand side.

SHARES OF STOCK ◊ 45

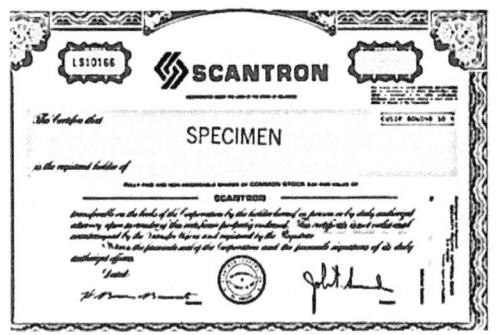

Front ↑   Back →

Paper stock certificates are seldom issued to individual investors any more. They are normally held by the brokerage firm. But the look of them has not changed much in over 100 years. Certificates are usually printed on banknote paper, the same kind of high cotton-fiber paper on which money is printed. The borders of stock certificates are usually embossed. The ink used in the printing process is raised off the paper, giving the feel of texture to the certificate.

The back of a certificate must be properly endorsed by the registered owner, and stamped with a Medallion Signature Guarantee by an authorized representative before shares that are registered in the owner's name can be sold. This endorsement will reassign registration of the shares to the broker. Because of the legal technicalities of transferring ownership of paper certificates, brokers seldom issue paper certificates to individual investors.

When your broker holds stock certificates in your account, they are usually registered in **street name**, also referred to as nominee name. In that case, instead of your name being on the face of the certificate, it will be held in a designation representing the brokerage firm. When you decide to sell shares held by the broker, you will not need to endorse the certificate, for it is being held in negotiable form. You can simply authorize your broker to sell, and the broker can quickly and easily transfer ownership.

A publicly traded company must update shareholders of its financial operations on a quarterly basis. The quarterly cycle for the company begins in the month the company first starts publicly trading, and ends on each sequential three-month period after that.

The beginning and end of the first four quarters defines the company's **fiscal year**.

Some companies continue to use the fiscal year that was established when they were initially formed. However, after companies have been in business a few years, they often opt to adjust their fiscal year to correspond to the calendar year, one beginning January 1 and ending December 31. In that case, their first quarterly statement will cover the months of January through March. Their second, third, and fourth quarters will end in the months of June, September, and December.

Because so many companies have changed their fiscal year to correspond to the calendar year, the eight weeks following those regular quarters are referred to as **earnings seasons**. The large number of companies filing earnings reports during those periods can cause higher than normal market volatility. Speculators cause that volatility as they buy or sell companies based on their expectations of how the earnings report will match up with analysts' forecasts. Often if there is a miss in earnings for a company that is a leader in a particular industry group, not only that company but others in that industry will be sold off as well.

This style of speculation (or gambling) is frequently touted by some online brokers, whose profits depend on high volume trading. However, such speculators play a dangerous game. Press releases from analysts, or from the companies themselves, may contain wording meant to prejudice readers toward positive or negative expectations. It is illegal for companies to post their earnings before the scheduled press release, but most companies offer guidelines meant to aid analysts.

Investors would be well warned not to compete with professionals at this strategy. Those people who have made a career of rapidly trading stocks around earnings reports usually have better intuition, if not better information. Investors have a competitive advantage with their patience. Understanding corporate business formation puts into context what investors' relationships are with the companies they own. This insight is lost on those who imagine the stock market as a casino. To an investor, it is better to own the game than to play it. Businesses usually set long-term goals, and so should their owners, the stockholders.

This discussion of business formation highlights that taxes are probably the most frequently sited consideration for determining the best business structure. However, income tax rates are not a good reason for incorporating. Corporate income tax brackets are generally higher than, or equal to, those for personal income tax. Also, keep in mind that tax law can change quicker than ink can dry on the documents that created it.

Perhaps a more important difference between sole proprietorships, partnerships, and corporations is the financial liability assumed by the owners. With the exception of LLPs, proprietorships and other partnerships can leave the business owners' personal assets vulnerable to lawsuits. If the business fails, those who loaned money to the business, the creditors, have a legal right to seize not only the business assets, but possibly some of the owners' personal assets as well.

If the business is sued over something like a personal injury case, the owners' personal assets could be vulnerable. Thus small businessmen are well-advised to purchase liability insurance to protect their personal assets. The risk of running a proprietorship or partnership is not limited to the amount of capital an individual has invested in the business. When a sole proprietorship or partnership fails, or declares bankruptcy, the owners are often forced to declare personal bankruptcy as well.

Corporations, however, become a separate legal entity. The assets of individual investors in public corporations cannot be subject to liability claims brought against a corporation under normal circumstances.

How Do Companies Sell Shares of Stock?

The process of bringing shares of stock to market is called underwriting, and it is the function of investment bankers. The market for an **initial public offering (IPO)** of stock is called the primary market. When a company completes its IPO, its shares start trading on an exchange. The NYSE, Nasdaq, and regional exchanges in the U.S., such as Boston, Philadelphia, Midwest, Pacific, are properly referred to as the **secondary market**.

There is also a **third market**, which refers to trading stock off the exchange system by member firms of the NYSE or Nasdaq Exchanges. For example, the broker with whom you enter a buy order might maintain an inventory of that stock and therefore might be able to execute your order at a slightly better price than is currently available on the exchange. In that case the broker is said to be acting as **principal**, rather than as agent. Stock that is traded off the exchange is often referred to as 19c3 shares after the SEC rule that allows it.

Additionally, institutions will sometimes negotiate *block trades*, at least 10,000 shares, between themselves without going through an exchange. The execution of that trade is referred to as the *fourth market*. For example, a mutual fund may want to sell millions of shares of a company. Entering that order on the exchange would upset normal market activity by instantaneously changing the supply-demand balance. So, one mutual fund manager might call its counterpart at another fund and negotiate a trade, thus ensuring each party a fair price and avoiding creating volatility on the exchange.

Additionally, major brokerage firms, as well as most large banks, will have investment banking departments. These departments can be very profitable for the financial institution. The investment banker's job is to advise owners of private companies on their various options for going public.

There are options other than issuing common stock available to owners of private companies planning to raise more capital. An investment banker may advise such owners to issue preferred stock or bonds, rather than common stock. Preferred stock is more like a bond than it is like stock. It pays a fixed dividend like the interest on a bond, but it is equity rather than debt. Common stock represents equity ownership, but the payment of the preferred stock's dividend and bond interest are senior obligations to the common dividend.

So, if the investment banker recommends issuing common stock, the company's decision makers will need to determine the number of shares and the price per share. This will represent the company's initial market capitalization. One of the largest IPOs in history was Facebook in 2012. The market value of the IPO shares offered to the public amounted to about $8 billion. But the price per share revealed that the number of outstanding shares still held by the key principals at Facebook would be about $100 billion.

The only information that can be distributed to the public before an IPO is the preliminary prospectus, called a **red herring**. This is booklet containing full disclosure of the company's operations, including a complete analysis of possible risks to the company's business model. The red herring is so called, not because of the connotations of that word (a clue meant to mislead) but simply because of the red disclaimer statement on the cover page.

The red disclaimer simply states the Securities and Exchange Commission (SEC), the federal agency governing the securities industry, cannot guarantee the authenticity of the information contained in the preliminary prospectus. That doesn't mean a company can't be sued if they make false statements in the booklet, only that you cannot sue the SEC for the company's lies.

While the company is going through the primary market IPO process, the red herring is the only document that may be distributed to investors who request an *indication of interest*. Remember there are no shares yet being traded. Potential investors may only request an indication of interest in them. After the company's stock is priced and released for public trading on a secondary exchange, the **final prospectus** will be issued to all investors. Usually, the only difference between he the final and the preliminary prospectuses is that the red ledger will be removed and the final price and number of shares is filled in where there were blanks on the red herring.

The front page of the prospectus will contain a list of the investment bankers who participated in the offering. This is called the Syndicate Group, and the uppermost name on the list is the Lead Underwriter. The Lead Underwriter is the investment banker who negotiated the offering.

Once the price of the company's stock is set, all potential investors who expressed an indication of interest will pay one flat price per share for all the shares they are allotted. Then those shares are released from the primary market and start trading on a secondary exchange. The business has moved from a private structure to a public one. It is now a corporation, or perhaps another legal designation such as an investment trust, in the hands of its shareholders.

50 ◊ Shares of Stock

What Are Your Shareholder Rights?

Under a public corporate structure the liability of shareholders is limited to the amount of their investment. Investors cannot lose any more money than they paid for their stock. As a corporate shareholder, your personal assets are not at risk, as they could be in a proprietorship or partnership.

However, shareholders do not have nearly as much control over the operations of their corporations as proprietors or partners usually do over theirs. The shareholders may own the company, but they do not manage it. Executive decisions are made by the company's Board of Directors, and operating decisions by its managers. Shareholders do not have a say in running the day-to-day operations of the company.

Common stock shareholders are guaranteed the right to vote on a slate of candidates who will represent their interests on the Board of Directors. Most companies are chartered so that one share equals one vote. Shareholders may also vote on any proposals that would materially change the power of that vote. Thus, if a company wants to increase the number of shares it is authorized to issue, it must get approval from a majority of its existing shareholders.

As explained in chapter 1, the number of shares outstanding remains relatively constant. Thus, your percentage ownership of a company and your voting influence over it remains relatively constant. If you own 100 shares of a company with 100 million shares outstanding, the influence of your vote is a rather insignificant 0.0001 percent (0.000001). However, activist investors, who have amassed a significant voting block of stock, are well equipped to put pressure on the Board of Directors to revise corporate policies.

Many large institutional shareholders, especially pension and retirement funds, have been exercising voting clout more aggressively in recent years. Organizations such as CalPERS and CalSTRS, California Public Employees Retirement System and California State Teachers' Retirement System, two of the largest shareholders in the world, often assert the power of their voting block to influence companies to adopt policies they favor. Frequently this has been to raise the dividend payout ratio. In some cases, however, they have also pressured companies to make changes to the Board of Directors, when they lack confidence with the company's governance. The power of the vote can be very persuasive.

Individual investors may not feel much of a sense of power from their right to vote because they own such a small percentage of the company. But there are some organizations of individual shareholders whose goal is combine a large number of small investors into a unified voting bloc. In the U.S. the right to vote is considered sacrosanct. Although there are occasional proposals to issue nonvoting stock, none has gained much support.

Voting rights should not be taken for granted. Shareholders who only own a few shares of a company with billions of shares outstanding may feel quite powerless to influence corporate management with their votes. However, all those small shareholder votes combined can greatly influence corporate decision making. There is always the potential that if shareholders feel their company is being mismanaged, they can mount a proxy fight to replace the current Board of Directors.

The New York Stock Exchange traditionally maintained a policy of granting voting rights for all shares of common stock listed on that exchange. Consequently other organizations have carried on with that policy. However, when the NYSE merged with the American Stock Exchange, AMEX, in 2008, it began listing stocks with restrictions on voting rights.

The right to vote has been generally maintained. However, there are many publicly traded companies where the majority of voting stock is controlled by a few individuals or a group that votes their shares as a bloc, effectively negating the power of outsiders to influence corporate policies with their voting power. Nevertheless, for most companies, voting shares can be a powerful tool for influencing corporate governance.

Voting is usually accomplished by issuing a **proxy card** to all registered shareholders. A proxy is defined as someone who is given the authority to act on behalf of another. If you own shares of a company on the record date for the annual shareholders meeting, a proxy card will be sent to you a month or so before that meeting. When you sign and return your proxy card, your votes will be cast by designated proxy at the meeting. So you do not have to be physically present to cast your vote.

52 ◊ Shares of Stock

Occasionally companies issue shares of stock that have no voting rights or restricted voting rights. Such shares are called **classified**, identified as a different type (class). Instead of common stock, they will be labeled Class A, B, or some other letter. One prominent example is Berkshire Hathaway, a company founded by billionaire investor Warren Buffett. Called the Oracle of Omaha, Warren Buffet consistently ranks near the top on Forbes 400 List of Richest People. Berkshire Hathaway Class A shares grant full voting rights, but each share of Class B has $1/200^{th}$ of a vote (and also sells at approximately $1/200^{th}$ the price of Class A).

The industry group that is the most likely to put restrictions on voting rights media companies—print and broadcast media outlets. CBS, Discovery Communications, New York Times, Washington Post, News Corp, and many others, issue classified shares, which are either non-voting or have restrictions on voting rights. This is intended to maintain the consistency of the political opinions generally held by the management of those companies, many of which were originally family-owned. Restrictions on voting rights are meant to eliminate the ability of those with an opposing political view from gaining a voting interest in the company and changing the political opinions traditionally held by the company's management...

Although controlled companies may operate as patriarchies, most companies operate, to some extent, as a democracy. Although the voting power of stock seems diminished by Board Room politics, it is potentially still a means of checks and balances on corporate governance. Shareholders' rights to vote should not be taken for granted.

Another basic right of shareholders is the right to participate in the profitability of the company. Many companies have a policy of declaring a regular *dividend*, a payment made to shareholders representing a percentage of income from the company's quarterly earnings report. This is entirely at the discretion of the Board of Directors. There are many companies that do not pay dividends. These are often referred to as growth stocks, but it should be noted that not all of them grow.

Once the Board of Directors declares a dividend payment, there is implied expectation among investors that the company will continue to pay that same dividend, or increase it, for all subsequent payments. Thus, companies usually do not declare dividends unless their projected cash flow and current reserves are adequate to maintain that rate even through unpredictable periods of slowdown or contraction. Companies that have good dividend payout policies may be safer than those that do not. Dividends may mitigate some investment risk.

Is the Stock Market Risky?

Risk is defined as the potential for an unpredictable result, in particular, a potential for loss. The rates of return on investments assume that the investor has an aversion to risk. So, the lower the risk associated with an investment, the lower the expected rate of return. Conversely, the higher the risk, the higher the expected return.

The propensity to assume greater risk with capital is what differentiates investing from speculating. Speculators are obviously willing to assume greater risks in hopes of realizing a higher return. Speculators also set goals of achieving their returns in a shorter period of time than investors.

Investing and speculating both involve making decisions based on adequate research and analysis. To make little or no analysis before putting your money into securities is gambling, not investing or speculating. If you have a mindset toward the market that would properly be labeled gambling, and many do, you should call it that. It is good reminder to keep in focus what you are doing, rather than to use a euphemism, such as a trader.

Almost everybody wants to make money, and there is nothing wrong with wanting to live with financial security. However, you should always question whether promises made about your finances are realistically wise or exaggeratedly foolish. If you act foolishly with your investment capital, do yourself a favor and do not call it investing.

There is always inherent risk, no matter how conservative you are with your money. Life is inherently risky. Risk can only be mitigated, not eliminated. The best you can do to lower the risk factor in your investment decisions is to base them on adequate research and realistic expectations.

You may say a gambler does all that, researching the odds before placing a bet. But a gambler's odds-making methodology is far different from an investor's analysis. A gambler cares little about what game he is playing, only what his chances are. In the market, a gambler looks at a chart, or some other technical indicator, and makes a bet on where that chart goes next.

Investors not only consider the chart but the company—what it does, how it is managed, where it will be a year from now. Investors spend time scrutinizing the company because want to own it. The thought of ownership never crosses the gambler's mind. The stock is not much more than a pair of dice and a winner-takes-all roll.

Gambling is an activity that should properly be called entertainment. There is certainly nothing wrong with entertainment, but you should treat gambling losses as the cost of the entertainment. But if you expect to pay off your credit card debts and home mortgage with your gaming purse, you are in serious trouble. Do not approach investing the same way you would approach gambling.

With that said, risk is extremely difficult to measure. There is no scientific way to quantify and qualify it. It is not a physical commodity. The best analysis of rick must still only be an estimate. Most investors equate a higher level of risk with a higher level of volatility, and volatility can be measured.

The greater the spread between the lowest price of a security and the highest, the greater the volatility. The volatility of stocks can be measured by beta. **Beta** is a means of expressing the historical relationship between the volatility of an individual stock to the volatility of the market. For the purpose of computing beta, the measure for the market is usually the S&P 500 Index.

In other words, if the market was up 10 percent for one year, and your stock was also up 10 percent for the same year, the beta would be 1.0. There was a 1-to-1 correlation between the market and the stock for that period of time. Standard sources for reporting beta usually use a calendar year (Jan. 1 to Dec. 31) for comparison.

If the market was up 10 percent, and your stock was up 15 percent, the beta would be 1.5. But if the market was up 10 percent and your stock was only up 5 percent, the beta would be 0.5. If the market was up, but your stock was down, there is usually no beta or a negative beta reported. There was no correlating relationship between the security and the market. However, if both the market and your stock were down, the beta would have the same correlation as that expressed when the market was up.

You should realize that the percentage relationship of beta always assumes the market change to be 1.0. So, if the market was up 8 percent and your stock was up 2 percent, the beta would be 0.25 (2/8 = 0.25). If your stock was up 16 percent in that same market period, your beta would be 2.0 16/8 = 2.00).

Beta can also be used to measure the volatility of portfolios of investments or mutual funds. Conservative investors generally want to overweight their portfolios with low beta investments—lower than 1. This could indicate that if the market drops, your portfolio might go down at a lower percentage change than the market. However, it needs to be pointed out that whatever the beta of a particular stock or fund was for one year, it will virtually never be the same number next year. Beta is only accurate for the past, not the future. Beta is only a guideline for potential volatility, not an accurate predictor of future volatility.

Investment risk can be broadly categorized as either *macroeconomic* or *microeconomic*. The prefix *macro-* means large. Macroeconomic risk would include factors that affect all investments of like kind. Inflation, recession, interest rate changes, government policies, economic cycles, and business trends would all be examples of macroeconomic risk.

On the other hand, the prefix *micro-* means small. Microeconomic risk factors would include those peculiar to one company or even one particular investment vehicle of a company, such as stocks or bonds. Microeconomic risk factors would include quality of management, structure of the company's finances, the company's competitive position in its industry, the quality of the company's product or service, and the company's ability to control its overhead expenses, etc.

A few key macroeconomic risk measures will be presented in Chapter 6. Emphasis will be placed on inflationary and economic cycles. Macroeconomic risk is a far more extensive topic than will be covered here. This presentation is only an introduction and overview of the topic.

Most of the microeconomic risks of a company require a judgment call. How do you really measure "quality of

56 ◊ SHARES OF STOCK

management"? If you are an employee, how do you rate your boss? Probably each of your coworkers will have a different opinion. Some will like and some dislike him or her, based on personal reasons or experience. There is nothing scientific about that.

Institutional Shareholders Services (ISS), a subsidiary of MSCI Inc. is an organization that has developed a method for ranking corporate governance. They operate a proprietary program called GRId, an acronym for governance risk indicators. It rates governance practices in four categories: Audit, Board of Directors, Compensation/ Remuneration, and Shareholder Rights.

You now have an overview of the economy and the market. You understand how shares of companies come to be publicly traded, and you have some principles for assessing the risks associated with investing. The next step is to learn about the nuts and bolt of investing, how to set up and account and begin making trades.

~$ $ $~ *Investing Tip* ~$ $ $~

As a stockholder, you own shares of a company, but you do not manage it. Ownership allows you to vote for the Board of Directors to represent your interests.

Chapter 3

How Do You Open a Brokerage Account?

The process of opening a brokerage account is similar to that of opening a bank account. Most people should have already gone through that process before they consider establishing a brokerage account. Applicants for brokerage accounts will be asked to provide much the same information they did for the bank. On the Account Application you will be asked to fill out: your name, address, date of birth, social security number, employment information, and information about other financial accounts.

Brokers will also request some additional information not applicable to bank accounts. You will be asked to provide your marginal tax bracket, annual income, and net worth. Lastly, brokers will ask you to rank your investment objectives in order of priority. You will be given a list that will include categories such as: safety and preservation of capital, income, growth, and speculation. (Gambling will not be one of them, but it probably should be in some cases.)

Ranking your investment objectives is meant to help you determine your tolerance for risk, from most conservative to most speculative. The results have important ramifications meant for your legal protection, as well as the protection of the brokerage firm. You should give some thought to this part of the application.

Be completely honest when ranking your investment objectives. Do not rank speculation as your highest priority if you are a novice investor. Everyone's objective is to make money, and most honest people would admit they want to make it as quickly as possible. That is human nature. But the high risk associated with speculation, necessarily involves a greater likelihood of loss. Seriously consider whether you can afford to lose some of your investment capital before you identify yourself to a broker as a speculator.

58 ◇ Brokerage Accounts

The securities industry can be divided into two groups: full-service and discount brokers. Full-service brokers, referred to in the industry as wire houses, offer professional research and analysis and make specific investment recommendations designed to meet your stated financial goals. Discount brokers offer significant savings on transaction costs primarily because they do not have the same overhead full-service firms do. If discount brokers offer research and analysis reports, they will usually come from publicly available sources or low cost proprietary programs

Discount brokers rely on high volume trading to make a profit. That necessarily implies they hope most of their accounts are speculators. Beginning investors are at a complete disadvantage in that arena. For that matter, experienced speculators should be warned they often don't know as much as they think they do. Individual investors are always at a competitive disadvantage to professionals.

As the financial service industry continues to evolve, the distinction between full-service and discount brokers has blurred. Many full-service brokers offer discounted online trading through their proprietary system, and many discount brokers now offer personalized financial advice. Both types of firms will offer many nontraditional brokerage services that are usually associated with banks, such as checking accounts and credit cards.

Probably the most significant response of full-service brokers to the threat of losing clients to discount brokers is managed *wrap fee* accounts. A wrap fee allows the client to execute transactions through a broker without paying a commission for each trade. The broker charges a flat annual fee for this service. Usually this wrap fee is 1 to 1.5 percent of the account value. For large accounts, it can cost less. A wrap fee account may pay off for active traders. However, firms usually put a limit on the number of trades a client can make. Also, many wrap fees are packaged with a managed portfolio of investments.

If you are a long-term buy-and-hold investor, a wrap fee account may require you to pay a lot of money for little or no service. A $100,000 account, for example, might be charged a $1500 per year. If the client only makes two or three trades in a year, that would amount to $750 or $500 in commissions per trade, even if the size of the trades are only a few thousand dollars. So, investors should tailor their accounts to fit their particular trading style. Two or three trades at a discount broker may only cost about $30.

The commissions that a full-service broker charges to execute trades will generally fall into a range from 0.2 percent to about 5 percent of the total amount of the trade. This is a broad range, but the actual commission charged depends on the size of the trade. Most brokers' commission fees are computed by a matrix that includes number of shares, price per share, and total dollars invested. The smaller the trade, the higher the commission as a percent of the amount invested. The larger the trade, the lower the rate as a percentage.

Another way of looking at the commission charged by full-service brokers is that an investor can usually get professional research and analysis for around 1 or 2 percent, on average. That could be a good bargain if the information is insightful. Professional analysts should be able to direct investors into securities that would return more than 1 or 2 percent. There is much discretion in the brokerage business, but an analyst's number one buy rating on a stock is usually only awarded to companies expected to outperform the market by at least 10 percent, or higher.

A final consideration if you select an online broker is internet security. Be assured that wherever financial information is being processed online, computer hackers are trying to figure out a way to break in. Hopefully, if you have gotten to the stage in life where you are considering online trading, you know basic internet security skills. Be sure you have internet security software with anti-virus, anti-spam, and spyware features installed on your computer and access account information using a virtual private network, VPN.

Also, observe all the standard precautions regarding internet security. Do not respond to emails requesting personal information and do not click on hyperlinks in emails from sources with which you are unfamiliar. Log off completely from your online account when you are finished. Protect your password, and select one that is not easily guessed. The passwords with the highest level of security have combinations of letters, numbers, and symbols. Also, they include both upper and lower case entries. The general recommendation is to use 12 or more entries. Also, use particular caution in public access internet areas. Such areas often have a lower level of internet security.

Finally, most online brokers offer tokenization security, which uses block chain technology. Security tokens generate random pass codes that usually change every 30 to 60 seconds. This has proven to be one of the most effective ways of thwarting hackers. Even if an identity thief is able to capture your user name and password using a keystroke logging program, that same program cannot be used to crack constantly changing token codes.

There are advantages and disadvantages to both full-service and online brokers. However, the competition between the two, as well as between each other, has created a very favorable environment for consumers of financial services. The quality and quantity of information readily accessible to individuals about the securities industry has never been as thorough as it is today, and additional improvements are constantly being added. This is the way that a free market economy should function.

In a free market capitalism, competition is the key to the system's success. Giving businesses the ability to compete effectively and fairly is what has made the United States the global economic leader it is. The U.S. has become the largest economy in the world by providing an environment where anyone, rich or poor, who has a creative and marketable idea can capitalize on it. Businessmen and women with the brains and determination to build a better product can prosper from their own creativity and their own abilities to market those ideas.

This is not true of other economic systems, particularly socialism and communism. The fundamental philosophical difference between socialism and capitalism is whether financial rewards for hard work go primarily to the state or to the individual. If the benefits of one's labor are taken away from the individual and ceded to the state, the incentive for working hard is removed. Socialist economic policies have bankrupt many of the member nations of the European Union, and there is a growing movement in the United States clamoring to go down the same path. But there has never been an economically successful example of a socialist or communist system.

Some may point out that communist China has been economically successful. However, although China is still governed by a communist country, it functions like a capitalist economic system. What has allowed China to emerge as the main rival to other economic giants around the world is a change of economic policies. It has realized the benefits of allowing individuals to profit from their labor. China had been reduced to third world nation status under a repressive communist regime. But when it opened up to the capitalist ideas of global trade, it rose to be one of the largest economic powerhouses in the world in just a couple decades. Capitalism, not communism, allowed China to prosper. Predictably, if the communist Chinese government reverts to its past policies of human rights violations, the system will implode. Free market capitalism is still the best path to prosperity.

Most of the wealthiest people in America did not start out with silver spoons in their mouths. Most of the people on the Forbes 400 list of wealthiest people are self-made billionaires, and the few who are not have failed to increase their personal wealth very much since they were put on the list.

What drew millions of immigrants to the United States last century was not the promise of state sponsored welfare, but a culture of allowing people to prosper themselves through their own efforts in "the land of opportunity". The economic model of the U.S. was successful when the government's primary role was oversight of business practices to maintain a fair, honest, and ethical economic environment. But if the government becomes a manipulator or a competitor in the free market system, the economic model will fail. The inefficiencies of the socialist model are being played out today all around the world.

The task of government should be to create a level playing field. In a fair marketplace, the companies that can produce the best product or service at the lowest price will emerge as the most successful businesses. A competitive free enterprise economic environment will inevitably allow the best managed company to prosper. There is always a group espousing a different philosophy, questing whether the competitive market has been the foundation of prosperity in the U.S.

Competition works. It works for countries, and it works for industries, including the financial services industry. Competition among brokers has greatly benefited investors. The emergence of discount brokers has forced full-service brokers to deliver premium service for the higher commissions they charge. What is true for other industries is true for brokers as well.

In a competitive free enterprise market, if full-service brokers charge higher fees, they must provide better service to justify them. As a result of competition from discount brokers, the professional analysis offered by most full-service brokers is probably the best it has ever been. In addition, the price differential between discount brokers and full-service brokers is about as low as it has ever been. The lesson you should take away from this discussion is to select the type of broker that best fits with the trading style you expect to use in your account.

What Account Title Should You Use?

After selecting the type of broker with which you would like to open an account, you will need to decide what legal designation should be on your account title. If you are a single individual opening an account, this is not an issue. However, when investors open joint accounts, such as between husband and wife, there are several choices necessary to clarify how the investment assets should be distributed upon the death of one of the joint account holders.

The most commonly used designation is **Joint Tenants with Rights of Survivorship**, abbreviated **JTWROS** or **Jt Ten**. This designation simply means what it says. The account is jointly owned by both individuals named on the account, and if one tenant dies, the account will become the property of the survivor.

If the two tenants are husband and wife, the account title will usually be changed without any estate tax ramifications. However, if the relationship between the tenants is not husband and wife, it could affect the tax status. Consult with a tax attorney about your situation. Tax laws are in a constant state of flux, and professional advisors who keep current with these changes are valuable.

Other account designations involving two individuals are Tenants in Common and Community Property. A **Tenants in Common** designation, abbreviated **TIC** or **Ten Com**, indicates that half of the account is owned by one tenant and half by the other. There may also be other proportional designations, but that is uncommon. Some accounts might recommend a TIC account title to help with estate tax planning for high net worth individuals. You should check with your tax consultant to determine if that is applicable to your situation.

Community Property designations are relatively rare, and not all states have community property laws. If you live in a state that does, you would likely select this option if you signed a prenuptial agreement with your spouse. A Community Property title means that some designated proportion in the prenuptial agreement, will not be automatically ceded to the surviving spouse, but most of the estate must go through other distribution arrangements. In other words, at least part of the account would go through the probate process, be transferred to a trust, or distributed in some other manner. Community Property laws generally allow high net worth individuals to leave a large part of their estate to beneficiaries other than their spouse. This avoids legal entanglements when a rich elderly person marries a young gold digger who essentially steals the estate from the traditional legitimate heirs.

There is not usually an "*and/or*" designation for brokerage accounts (although this has changed in some states) as there is for bank accounts because securities are property, whereas money is not. Because money is not property, ownership must be identified in a more unambiguous manner. Property cannot generally be owned under a legal designation whereby either one party owns it or the other party and additionally it is owned by both. Lawyers don't like ambiguity.

However, all the standard joint account designations usually allow for either one party or the other to make investment decisions. A broker will not require both the individuals who have title on the account to confirm every buy and sell order. Either party can authorize a transaction. So, in that sense, joint account titles function similar to an "and/or" designation.

A notable exception to the flexibility of entering orders in a joint account occurs if a stock certificate has been issued registered in joint name. In that case, both parties must properly endorse the back of the certificate before the security can be sold or deposited into an account with different title. Most brokers do not recommend that accounts take physical delivery of their stock certificates for that reason.

Stock certificates are usually held in the client's account by the broker in a designation known as **street name**. That means the physical certificate representing a client's ownership of a security is registered in the name of the brokerage firm, usually the *nominee name* of the broker. Thus, the security can be sold or transferred without the beneficial owners having to sign the certificate.

When investors sell shares being held by a broker they may simply tell their broker to sell them, or enter the order themselves in an online account. The brokerage firm can sell the shares without having to obtain the seller's signature authorizing the transaction. Orders for securities being held in street name can be quickly and easily executed with little or no paperwork.

The legal proof of ownership of a security investment is confirmed by the investor's account statements, in the same manner as bank account statements. Just as you should review your bank accounts for accuracy, review your brokerage statements frequently. Updated brokerage account information can be accessed online daily. Paper statements are not generally mailed out unless the client requests it. Finally, it is good advice to maintain a close relationship with your stockbroker, even if you are not a frequent trader.

How Do You Select a Broker?

Most people will, or at least should, spend a great deal of time deciding what investments they want to make. However, most people spend little or no time selecting an investment advisor. This can be a big mistake. A good investment advisor can be worth much more to you than a good investment.

The usual way most people select a broker is after they have picked an investment, they go online or call a broker and take whoever they get. If you call a full-service broker, the receptionist will direct your call to whoever happens to the designated floor broker for the day. This is the person who has been assigned to answer call-ins who do not already have a broker or the regular broker is unavailable. Usually this will be a rookie who is trying to build up a clientele, not usually the most experienced broker.

Not to denigrate rookies or even inexperienced brokers. Most are very knowledgeable, ethical, and personable people. However, the point is you don't know them. You don't know anything about their qualifications, experience, background, or personal biases. Every broker is an individual; not all brokers are created equal. You should make an effort to find a broker who will work with you in a manner comfortable for you. Try to find someone with whom you have compatible personality traits.

Contrary to stereotypical caricatures (especially in motion pictures), most stockbrokers are honest, hardworking, and professional. The standards of ethics in the financial services industry are very high and strictly enforced. However, inevitably there will be some dishonest individuals. You will hear about them in the news. Money can make people do strange things. Bernard Madoff raised the bar for dishonest brokers to previously unknown heights when he pled guilty in 2009 to several federal counts of defrauding thousands of investors and stealing billions of dollars while running a brokerage firm that was operated like a Ponzi scheme. He created fictitious account statements, while redirecting money from clients' accounts to be used for his personal benefit.

The primary government regulators of the financial services industry are the Financial Industry Regulatory Authority (FINRA) and the Securities and Exchange Commission (SEC). Both agencies, especially FINRA, have become increasingly diligent in recent years at prosecuting broker fraud, mismanagement, or other client abuse cases. More information about what resources are available if you feel your broker is mismanaging your account will be discussed in Chapter 10.

Most brokers realize maintaining their clients' best interest is in their own best interest as well. Some critics of full-service brokers are quick to point out that brokers, who are paid from the commissions they generate, have an inherent conflict of interest. Brokers may be inclined to recommend frequent buying or selling simply to generate more commissions. The same critics may also say that brokers whose compensation comes primarily from wrap fees have no incentive to diligently service their clients' accounts. The broker gets paid whether trades are made or not.

There are no perfect answers to all problems that may arise from broker/client relationships. However, brokers who have been in the business a few years are well aware that if they do not make money for their clients, they are probably going to lose them. Brokers know that unless they offer their clients sound financial advice, they will lose their business. So the broker's welfare is inherently tied to the welfare of the clients.

Even though most brokers strive to do a professional job for their clients, some investor complaints are bound to occur. Probably the most common complaint clients have is they feel their broker is making inappropriate recommendations, such as speculative investments for clients who are conservative. However, most brokerages have Branch Compliance Officers who frequently monitor all the daily trading activity. So, if the investments do not match the guidelines the client selected on the New Account Form, these problems can be quickly addressed. Another common complaint is the practice of *churning*, a term used to describe the practice of making frequent buy and sell recommendations without benefitting the investor. However, this too is a practice that a diligent Compliance Officer should easily spot.

If you feel you have a complaint about your broker over any matter, you should first talk to the Branch Manager of the broker's office about the problem. The Manager's interest is in keeping the office profitable and will not want to lose your account at the branch. The manger has the power and authority to make restitution to you if deemed necessary and decide what disciplinary action should be taken against the broker.

Investors should keep in mind, however, that the risk inherent in the market is not something that can be mitigated. All the best research and analysis cannot prevent unforeseen events that affect economic stability. The stock market fallout from events like those on 9/11, the detonation of a nuclear bomb, or any of a thousand possible risks that exist in the world in which we now live will have a major impact on all economies. You cannot hold your broker responsible for unpredictable events.

If the Branch Manager is unable to resolve the issue to your satisfaction, the next logical step would be to contact the Financial Industry Regulatory Authority. FINRA is an independent regulator for all U.S. securities firms. Its stated purpose is "to protect investors by maintaining the fairness of the U.S. capital markets". At the bottom of FINRA's Home Page is a link labeled "Arbitration & Mediation". Click on it, and you will be connected to a site covering a vast array of information and resources FINRA offers to investors, including how to file a claim.

FINRA also maintains a popular BrokerCheck link that allows investors to access information on all its members. The Home Page of that FINRA site claims, "BrokerCheck is a free tool to help investors research the professional backgrounds of current and former FINRA-registered brokerage firms and brokers". The site will link you to databases on all pertinent information regarding any firm or individual, including any disciplinary actions that may have been taken against them. Additionally, FINRA offers the services of a Board of Arbitration made up of professionals in the industry who will hear and rule on client/broker disputes. Again, more information about FINRA will be presented in Chapter 10.

Serious legal matters may also be resolved in a court of law with an attorney. However, investors should note that the securities industry is highly specialized and legally complicated. It may be difficult to find a judge or jury who has a good understanding of the legal nuances of this specialized area. Most disputes can be equitably settled by arbitration. It seems unlikely that FINRA's arbitrators will rule leniently on a flagrantly dishonest broker. Keep in mind that FINRA's reputation is at stake, as well as the broker's.

Hopefully, you will be able to avoid any of these problems by first taking the time to go through the process of selecting a good broker. It is a frequent practice in the medical profession to get a second opinion before making a major health decision. The same practice would be advisable to follow regarding your financial health. If you are looking for a broker, make appointments with several of them and interview them as you would for any professional service. Pay particular attention to how well the broker communicates with you.

Brokers will usually have a specific investment that they may recommend at the time of your interview. That is, after all, their job. If they don't have a good investment recommendation, you should probably be a bit worried. However, consider whether the broker is just trying to sell you something, or if he or she is really listening to your needs and recommending a product that fits your objectives.

You might also ask the broker for two or three referrals. This doesn't seem to be done much in the brokerage business, but it is a frequent practice in many others. People often seem more inclined to ask for references regarding a plumber than they are from the broker to whom they are about to hand over a large portion of their personal wealth. Don't flush your money down the drain by not checking out the broker's referrals. Follow up on them. Keep in mind that brokerage account information is confidential and may not be disclosed. But regarding the broker himself, it will only take a few minutes to talk to a few other people who will have something in common with you.

Finally, if you have any questions about your account, do not hesitate to call your broker. Do not be intimidated by anything you do not understand. No question is trivial or unimportant. The brokerage business is a service industry, and your broker's job is to service your account. Develop a good working relationship with your broker from the beginning. You'll sleep better later on.

How Do You Make an Investment?

Once you have selected a broker, opened your account, and have been assigned an account number, you are ready to make a trade. For an initial purchase, your broker will probably require you to deposit cash in your account to cover the cost, or most of the cost, of your initial investment. However, after your account has been activated and a relationship with your broker established, a transaction timeline will automatically come into play.

In most cases when you make a trade, such as purchasing or selling a stock, bond, or mutual fund, there are two important dates involved—trade date and settlement date. The **trade date** is the day on which the purchase or sale takes place, and the **settlement date** is the day by which the purchase must be paid for or the proceeds of the sale will be distributed.

For regular way trades, there is *one business-day* between the trade date and the settlement date. You will usually see this abbreviated T+1 (trade date plus 1 business day). A **business day** is any day that banks are normally open for business, Monday through Friday, excluding bank holidays. Even though some banks are now open on Saturdays, that still does not make it a normal business day in the eyes of the financial services industry.

To illustrate how trade dates and settlement dates work: if a stock is purchased on Wednesday, it would normally settle on Thursday. If the investment is purchased on Friday, the next business day would be Monday. However, if Monday happens to be a bank holiday, the settlement date would be on Tuesday. So, in that scenario, the next business day would be four days after the trade date. That would be the following business day. These dates are important to an investor who is trading a stock about to make a dividend distribution, as will be explained later in this chapter.

Next, investors should understand the two different types of orders that can be entered: a market order and a limit order. A **market order** is one that will be executed at the best available price at the time it is received by the exchange. As explained earlier, that would be the lowest current ask for a buy order or the highest current bid for a sell order.

When you look at a stock quote, there are three prices you should note: the last trade, the bid price, and the ask price. The **last trade** is the price at which the last buy and sell orders were matched. Remember that exchanges simply match buyers with sellers, and vice versa. There are usually many different bid prices from investors who want to purchase a stock at any particular time, but the **bid price** displayed on the stock quote is the highest of all those offers. For the orders to be filled, the bidders must be matched with sellers of shares, who enter orders a specified **ask price**. Just as there are usually several orders at different bids from investors who want to purchase, there are several ask orders entered by people who want to sell. The lowest ask price at that time you request a quote is the one that is displayed in the stock quote information.

The following illustration is the way a typical order book screen might look. During the hours when the market is open, the bid-ask prices and the size of the orders will be constantly updated as new orders are entered. The price under the name of the company is the last trade. It shows Unique Inc. is up five cents from the previous session's close.

Unique Inc (UIQ)
31.77 ↑ $0.05 (0.16%)
Order Book
Top of Book

Bid		Ask	
Price	Size	Price	Size
31.77	3,900	31.78	2,000
31.75	21,300	31.82	4,600
31.74	2,400	31.95	3,500
31.68	1,500	31.96	700
31.65	5,000	31.98	5,500

Notice that the bid prices are presented in descending order and the ask prices in ascending order. The top price on the bid side is the highest price currently entered by someone who wants to buy the stock. The top price on the ask side is the lowest price that anyone is currently offering to sell shares. A market order to buy in this situation would be executed at 31.78 (the lowest ask), and a market order to sell would be executed at 31.77 (the highest bid).

Most orders on the NYSE are executed electronically, without human intervention. However, the computer system is monitored by a **designated market maker, DMM**. Occasionally, when the market becomes too volatile the DMM can become involved in the order matching process. In those cases, orders may be executed by a DDM. The NYSE rule describing the role of a designated market maker states, "DMMs… must engage in a course of dealings for their own account to assist in the maintenance of a fair and orderly market insofar as reasonably practicable". To fulfill this mandate of a fair and orderly market, DMMs will maintain their own bid and ask if the order spread through the electronic system is deemed so large it will create unusual volatility.

The NYSE also employs another class of market makers called supplement liquidity providers or SLPs. They are similar, but there are some significant differences. The DMMs are paid a flat fee per every round lot (100 shares) traded. The SLPs also receive a fee, although smaller, when asked to act as a backup market maker, but they have fewer restrictions on trading their own accounts.

During regular market hours most orders for stocks traded on the NYSE are routed into the DOT System, an acronym for designated order turnaround. Orders in this system match buyers with sellers as often as possible. Approximately 80 percent of all trades are executed this way. But sometimes, especially during periods of high volatility, the opposite side of a trade may be matched with the DMM's or SLP's account.

Order matching with the DMM's account is only for situations in which it is deemed necessary to maintain a fair and orderly market. DMMs are expected to match orders with their own accounts only during periods of high market volatility. This would be when the size of the order flow is heavily weighted on one side—either buy or sell. Remember supply and demand factors are what moves the market. DMMs need to maintain an inventory of shares and cash to fill orders only during unusual circumstances.

The Nasdaq Exchange only operates as an ECN, electronic communication network. It includes hundreds of market makers all around the world. It has no central location for trading like the NYSE. The high profile cylindrical building in New York's Times Square with the wrap around illuminated exterior screen is a media and news center, not a trading center. You will often see this building featured in business news reports. The exterior screen provides current news and market information, entertaining videos, and advertisements. The function of this building and the function of the NYSE building a few blocks away on Wall Street are completely different.

Nasdaq market makers compete among themselves for the best prices to execute trades. Nasdaq market maker firms will only buy shares for their own accounts from sellers who enter orders there. Nasdaq market makers will then turn those shares and sell them to buyers who enter orders there. These market makers buy shares at their bid, and sell them at the ask.

In the Nasdaq market maker system, and in all other ECN trading systems, the difference between the bid and ask prices is called the *spread*. You should remember that earlier it was noted the spread represents the market maker's current profit for trading shares. If a stock is quoted at 25.22 bid and 25.25 ask, the market maker's profit is three cents. In this scenario, a market order to sell would be filled at 25.22, and a market order to buy would be filled at 22.55. The three cents "spread" represents about a 1.2 percent profit margin for the market maker ($.03 \div 25.22 = .0012$).

If you go online to a financial website or tune in to a live broadcast of a televised business report while the market is open during regular hours, you will notice stock prices are constantly changing. Thus, you may be inclined to conclude after this explanation on the function of market makers that they are the ones setting the price, but that would be inaccurate. For actively traded stocks on the Nasdaq there may be fifty or more market makers, each trying to arrive at the highest bid or lowest ask so they can execute trades. For less active stocks, there may be only four market makers. Consequently, market makers for low volume stocks tend to factor in much higher spreads between their bid-ask quotes. This is not unfair, it is simply a function of supply and demand.

If one market maker's inventory of shares is low, it may be inclined to raise the bid, trying to be more aggressive on the buy side. However, if the inventory is higher than normal, the market maker may be more aggressive on the sell side and lower the ask price. The market maker's decision is primarily based on how many shares of that stock others are trying to buy or sell. The size of the orders, greater demand on the buy side or greater supply on the sell side, is the cause of price fluctuation. The greatest risk that market makers assume in their business is time. They hope to turn around shares very quickly from their inventory and make a small profit. However, if they are holding a large inventory of shares and the market for that company tanks, the market maker will absorb the loss. This is the case both on the Nasdaq and the NYSE, or any other exchange.

The second type of order entry is a **limit order**, which can only be filled at a price you set—or better. Limit orders to buy are set at a lower price than the lowest current ask, and limit order to sell would be set at a higher price than the highest current bid. Limit orders will not be filled unless the volatility of the market brings the price down to your buy limit or up to your sell limit. They can be filled at a better price than your limit if the market gaps through that limit. Limit orders are also referred to as *open orders*.

Nasdaq market makers and NYSE DMMs usually manage their inventory of shares based on the limit orders on their books. Market orders will, of course be a factor as well, but those need to be filled immediately whereas limit orders may indicate more pent up demand on the buy side or increased supply on the sell side.

Consider a hypothetical example. Suppose you want to buy one hundred shares of Unique Inc. The last trade is 18.53; the bid is 18.52; and the ask is 18.54. If you enter a market order, it will be filled at 18.54. But if you think the volatility of the market will probably bring the price down to at 18.50, you might decide to enter an order to buy 100 shares at 18.50 limit. This means the ask price will have to drop $.04 before your order will be filled. If the ask drops to 18.50 or better, you will buy the stock. However, if Unique Inc. begins rallying and the ask price for the stock never comes down to 18.50, your limit order will not be filled. It will remain an open order on the market maker's books.

If there is no designation for the length of time an order is to remain active, it is considered to be a day order. That means that if the order is not filled by the close of the market on that day, it will automatically be cancelled. Day orders are only valid during the normal market hours—for that day only.

However, limit orders are frequently entered on a **good-till-canceled** (GTC) basis. A **GTC order** means it will remain active on the market makers' books until it is either executed or canceled by the one who entered it. The size of these GTC orders, whether they are bids from buyers or asks from sellers, helps the market maker set the two sides of the market at a price the firm thinks the market will bear.

Some of the online sites for stock quotes will also reveal the number of shares on each side of the market, referred to as *size*. This way an investor can compare the size of the highest bid prices with the size of the lowest ask prices. A large imbalance on one side of the market could be a good indicator of the price direction over a short term period of time. For example, if the total size on the bid side is 50,000 shares and the size on the ask is only 1,000, you could reasonably expect the price of the stock to rise because of increased demand and limited supply. An imbalance of size on the ask side would indicate a potential imbalance shortage of supply, and the price will likely drop.

The amount of information for stock quotes is available on three levels. Level 1 quotes are free at many online financial sites. Usually Level 1 quotes can be accessed by clicking on an "order book" or "real time" link. The previous illustration of bid and ask quotes for Unique Inc. was an example of Level 1. That level of service shows the top bids listed from highest down along with the size of the bid at each of those prices. It also shows the best ask prices ranked from the lowest up with the size of the shares being offered at each price. Investors can easily determine whether there is an order imbalance on the buy side or the sell side.

Level 2 quotes are available to individual investors through many online services. They would be most useful to day traders, speculators who buy and sell shares quickly to profit from small price swings. Active day traders may hold a position only a few minutes, or a few seconds, and make several trades on the same day. This is a type of trading activity appropriately labeled gambling.

This book is designed to be more useful to investors than gamblers. Level 2 quotes not only provide the price and size of bids and asks, but also which market makers are listing those offers. For day-traders, if the lead market maker in a stock (referred to as the ax), suddenly starts taking small losses in its position, that could signal they might be trying to reduce their inventory before a price drop.

Level 3 quotes are only available to market makers. It includes all the information in Level 2, but also allows for entering orders. Some online brokerage services offer Level 3 access to investors who have accounts with them, but only on stocks for which they are a market maker. Investors should be forewarned that trying to beat the market makers at their own game is a poor "get rich quick" strategy. Market makers will have more sophisticated algorithmic strategies than average individual investors.

What Is a Margin Account?

When you open a brokerage account, you will be asked if you want to establish a cash account or a margin account. A **cash account** is one for which any investment you make must be fully paid for with your own funds by the settlement date. Brokerage firms usually identify a cash account as type 1. A margin account allowing you to make a partial payment for an investment is usually identified as type 2. Identifying different types of accounts by number is similar to how banks add different extensions to the end of an account number denoting savings, checking, loans, and so on.

A **margin account** is more speculative than a cash account because it is leveraged, allowing you to borrow a percentage of the total cost of the investment from the broker. The broker holding your securities uses them as collateral for your loan. Thus, you are not allowed to take delivery of the certificates for your securities because the broker might need to access the equity in them, which is being held as collateral for their loan.

Margin loans may be easier to understand when compared to real estate mortgage loans. Both mortgage loans and margin loans are similar regarding the use of leverage. When you purchase a house, you do not usually pay the full price with your own money. You invest a down payment, perhaps 20 – 30 percent of the total market value, and then borrow the remainder from a mortgage lender. However, you own the 100 percent of the property. You are entitled to all the profits from the appreciated value of the property and are also responsible for the losses due to depreciation. The mortgage lender has no equity stake in your property and is only concerned that you continue to make your payments.

The mortgage lender does not own a percentage of the house, only a lien on it. If you should default on the terms of your loan by not making payments, the lender can sell the house and use the proceeds to make up for the amount you are in arrears. You own 100 percent of the house, but have paid for part of it with borrowed money. So just as you benefit from rising property values, you also experience the full effect of real estate market declines. Whether the market is up or down, when you sell your house, you will realize a capital gain or loss on the full value of the property. To the lender, the house is simply collateral.

Likewise, a broker's margin loan is collateralized by your stock. One primary difference between a real estate mortgage loan and a stock margin loan is that the mortgage loan has a termination date, but the margin loan does not. You will be charged interest on a regular basis, usually monthly, on a margin loan. However, unlike a real estate loan, none of the interest payments are used to reduce the principal amount of a margin loan.

The maximum amount you can borrow when you invest in equity securities on margin is 50 percent of the total value. The amount of equity you must put up for stock margin accounts is called the **initial margin requirement**. It is set by the Federal Reserve Board (FRB) and by the Financial Industry Regulatory Authority (FINRA) and is called **Regulation T** (Reg. T) for individual investors. If you were to purchase $10,000 worth of a marginable security, you could invest $5000 of your own money and borrow $5000 from the brokerage firm.

The initial margin requirement for debt securities, such as bonds, is much less than for equities. Reg. T for most investment grade corporate bonds is 30 percent. Government bonds can usually be bought on margin for 10 percent or less—the shorter the term, the lower the initial margin requirement. Bonds will be addressed in the next chapter.

Setting Reg. T is the only way that the FRB is involved in the securities industry. It is primarily the regulating agency responsible for overseeing the banking industry, not the securities (investment banking) industry. Federal policies regarding the securities industry are usually set by the Securities and Exchange Commission, SEC, not the FRB. Since the Fed's mandate is to regulate bank activities meant to adjust the rate of growth of the economy, setting the initial margin requirement falls under their jurisdiction. So, the only involvement of the Fed in the securities industry is that it is one of the government agencies that can affect the initial margin requirement in regard to expanding or contracting the amount of capital in the economy through broker/dealers.

The Fed's primary mandate is to keep the economy growing at a healthy, sustainable pace. It attempts to work in coordination with the U.S. Treasury Department and other government agencies by implementing their goals for either stimulating or deflating economic activity. Although, some critics of the Fed have noted there is less coordination and communication regarding policies and goals than there should be.

As noted earlier, when you establish a margin account, the brokerage firm will charge you a margin interest rate on your debit balance. The interest rate on this loan will usually be set at a *marginal* premium above another interest rate known as the broker loan rate. That was probably the etymology of the word margin in this context. The **broker loan rate** is the rate that commercial banks charge brokerage firms to borrow money for the purpose of issuing margin loans to their clients.

So, if the broker loan rate is 5 percent, the margin interest rate may be set at something like 5.25 percent or higher, a 0.25 percent premium or more. The broker determines what premiums they will charge, and it is usually higher for small loans and lower for large. For large margin loans, most brokers may not charge any premium over the broker loan rate, as a courtesy to their most profitable accounts.

The Fed indirectly manipulates the broker loan rate in a process that will be described in Chapter 6. Consequently there is little need for the Fed to manipulate the initial margin requirement, Reg T. Nevertheless, it is a possible tool in the Fed's arsenal for stimulating or slowing the economy. During the first half of the 20th century the initial margin requirement was frequently adjusted, but that is no longer the case.

When you establish a margin account, there is another benchmark to be aware of other than the initial margin requirement. It is the minimum margin maintenance requirement. Brokerage firms that make margin loans also set the minimum maintenance requirement to make sure the amount of their loan is always covered by the amount of equity in the account.

The broker considers margin loans riskless because their money is 100 percent collateralized by your securities. This is the same as mortgage lenders requiring their loans to be always covered 100 percent by the equity in the house for which the loan was made. If the prices of your margined securities drop, the broker sets the minimum maintenance requirement at 30 percent as a safety measure to protect their interests. So, if you put up the 50 percent initial requirement, your securities cannot fall any more than 40 percent, that is 2/5ths of their value, or the broker will require you add more equity to your account.

If market volatility causes the equity in your margin account to drop below 30 percent of the market value, you will be required either to deposit additional funds in the account or to sell some of your securities. This drop in the value of the account will generate a **margin call**, which means that you will need to meet the **minimum maintenance requirement**. If you do not meet the margin call within the time allotted, usually three business days, the broker can sell your shares—even without your authorization. The provisions for a mandatory sale will be stated in the Margin Agreement you must sign before opening a margin account. Most brokers will try to work with clients to resolve margin liquidations amicably, but they are not legally required to do so.

Brokers set the minimum maintenance requirement at 30 percent or higher because the FRB and FINRA set the minimum maintenance level at 25 percent (equity/market value). The brokers must ensure that margin accounts comply with the minimum equity rules. Under some circumstances, brokers may set the minimum above 30 percent. This is usually because of over concentration in a single security or because of low priced securities. Low priced securities are not eligible to be held in margin or require a higher maintenance level. Very low priced securities, penny stocks, must usually be fully paid for with the investor's own funds. They are considered too volatile to be used as collateral for a margin account.

	Buy 200 UIQ at $30/share on margin:	If price drops to $20/share or (33.3%):	If price rises to $40/share or (33.3%):
Market Value:	$6000	$4000	$8000
Debit Balance:	$3000	$3000	$3000
Equity:	$3000	$1000	$5000
	(50% of MV) Per Reg T	Equity drops 66.7%, to 25% of MV Mgn call for $200	Equity up 66.7%, to 62.5% of MV

This illustration shows what would happen when you purchase 200 shares of Unique Inc. at $30 per share on margin. (It has done quite well in the last few pages). The total market value of stock you bought is $6000. You would be required to deposit $3000 (equity) and would borrow the $3000 (debit) from your broker.

There are three components to your margin account: the **market value** ($6000), the total amount of the stock you bought; the **debit balance** ($3000), the amount of money you borrowed from your broker for this purchase; and the **equity** ($3000), the difference between the two. Although you put up the original $3000 equity, that amount will change as the market value of your investment changes. Also, remember that your debit balance is a loan, and you will be charged interest on it.

If the price of Unique Inc. drops to $20 per share, the total market value of your 200 shares will drop to $4000. Your debit balance, the amount you borrowed, remains the same $3000. So your equity, the difference between the market value and the debit balance, dropped to $1000 ($4000 - $3000 = $1000).

That $1000 equity is now only 25 percent of the new market value $4000. So, the brokerage firm will issue you a maintenance call. This will require you to deposit enough money into your account to bring it back up to the 30 percent minimum margin maintenance requirement. The minimum dollar amount of that call will be $200. It would be computed as 30 percent of $4000 (0.30 × $4000 = $1200). Since your equity is currently only $1000, you will need to deposit at least $200 to bring the equity in the account back up to 30 percent.

In the real world, however, the broker will probably require you to deposit a little more than the minimum since the market is in a constant state of volatility. That minimum $1200 equity will only meet the maintenance requirement so long as the market value does not drop below $4000. This computation is for illustration purposes only and would probably not play out exactly as presented here in a real world situation.

In addition to market volatility, this example has not taken into account any interest that you will be charged on your margin loan. So, in a real world situation your margin call would likely be higher, at the discretion of the broker. This example only illustrates the corresponding relationships between the three margin components.

You should also note that if you decide to meet the margin call by selling securities rather than by depositing funds, you will need to sell substantially more than $200 worth of stock. The sale of shares will not only reduce your debit balance, it will also reduce your market value. In the illustration, you would have to sell about $800 worth of stock to get the equity back over 30 percent of the market value. If you do that, your MV will be reduced to $3200 ($4000 - $800 = $3200) and your debit balance reduced to $2200 ($3000 - $800 = $2200). Thus, your equity will still be $1000 ($3200 - $2200 = $1000). However, that $1000 equity now represents 31.25 percent of your new MV ($1000 \div 3200 = 31.25\%$).

The use of margin will magnify your profit or loss by the same percentage as the equity is of the market value. In the example, Unique Inc. dropped $10 per share, from $30 to $20. The total market value of the investment dropped $2000, from $6000 to $4000. That is a 33 percent drop, because $2000 is 33 percent of $6000 ($6000 \times .33 = $2000). However, the equity in the account also dropped $2000, from $3000 to $1000. That percentage drop is twice as much as the market value drop, 67 percent, because $1000 is 67 percent of $3000 ($3000 \times .67 = $1000).

You should also realize if the price of Unique Inc. had risen $10 per share instead of declining, you would have made twice as much money as you would have in a Cash Account. If the share price goes from $30 to $40, the market value of 200 shares will go from $6000 to $8000. The $2000 profit is a 33 percent gain on the $6000 market value (.33×$6000 = $2000). But your equity will have also gone up $2000, and a $2000 gain on your original $3000 equity is a 67 percent gain ($3000×.67=$2000)—twice that of a cash position.

If you invest in a margin account at 50 percent, you will double the gain or the loss you would have from the same investment in a cash account. Your profit or loss will be magnified proportionally by the same percentage as the margin. If you restrict your margin to just 25 percent, the corresponding returns will be half as much as they were at 50 percent. This is called leverage.

Leverage is a general term for describing the process of using a smaller amount of money to control a larger amount of an investment. The use of leverage involves borrowed money. In the previous example, the investor made the same amount of money on his investment as he would have in a cash account ($2000), but he had invested fewer of his own dollars. The margin investor originally only risked $3000 of his own money, instead of the $6000 he would have had to invest for the same position in a cash account.

Leverage adds risk to any investment. For a potentially greater gain there is a corresponding potentially greater loss. Leverage itself is not necessarily bad, but it changes the nature of the investment to a more speculative one.

The most common use of leverage has always been in the housing market. Prior to 2008 real estate was considered by lenders to be an appreciating asset. So, most mortgage brokers had no problem granting highly leveraged loans to home buyers. Very small down payments, or even no-down loans, were common. This practice greatly magnified the losses when the housing market began to decline.

Even if conservative mortgage lenders required a 10 percent down, that still left 90 percent of the market value at risk. So if you bought a home for $250,000, the lender merely required you to put up $25,000 of your own money. The mortgage company loaned you the remaining $225,000. If the house appreciated just 10 percent in market value, from $250,000 to $275,000, your equity appreciated from $25,000 to $50,000. That was a 100 percent return on your money from just a 10 percent rise in market value.

Of course, that wasn't what happened in 2008. The market depreciated 10 percent. That meant your original $25,000 investment depreciated 100 percent. You lost all your money. The lenders had to put so many houses on the market for sale at the same time that it compounded the problem and the market dropped 20 percent, then 30 percent, then 40 percent and much higher in some geographic areas.

This brief discussion of leverage is a simplistic view of a complex problem, but it should heighten your awareness of the risks inherent in using leverage. It does not pay off to leverage an investment unless it appreciates. Excessive leverage for any investment can move from speculation to gambling very quickly.

However, you may have heard of people who make money when the market drops.

How Do You Invest for a Market Decline?

Another example of a leveraged investment is short selling. **Short selling** is the process of selling shares of stock you borrow from your brokerage firm with the commitment to buy back the same number of shares in the future and return them to the lender. Your hope is that the price of the shares you sell short will fall, and you will be able to buy them back at a lower price than your original short sale.

So, short selling is a strategy only appropriate when the price of a stock is going to drop. The proceeds of a short sale may not be withdrawn at the time of the transaction. Those funds are kept in a separate short account, usually identified as type 4. That money will be applied to the cost of repurchasing the stock, referred to as covering the short.

You cannot enter a short sale for a specific stock without first receiving the broker's confirmation that the firm has the shares available to lend you. Before the transaction can be made, you will need to contact the broker for permission. Brokers will usually be able to loan the shares only if they are holding them on margin in other client accounts.

When you set up a margin account, you will need to sign a **Margin Agreement**, also called a Client's Agreement or Loan Agreement. The broker not only has the right to sell securities in your account if you are in violation of the minimum margin requirement, it also grants the broker the right to use some of those shares for their own purposes, such as lending shares to short sellers. The broker, after all, has paid for half of them.

The fact that the broker can loan those shares does not negate their clients' legal ownership of the stock in their margin accounts. If margin holders want to sell their shares, they have the right to do so at any time.

If you sell short, the broker will also require you to deposit funds of 30 percent of the market value of the short sale or have sufficient margin equity to meet that requirement. So to short $20,000 worth of stock you will need to make a $6000 deposit (30% of $20,000) or already have that much equity in a margin account.

Say you think Unique Inc. has rallied up to $40 per share, a point where its next move will likely be downward. (This is a good possibility since its range has gone from around $20 to $40 in this chapter alone.) You could sell 500 shares short, generating proceeds of $20,000 in a type 4 account. Remember that when you sell short you do not own those shares; you are borrowing them from the broker.

Now, if UIQ drops back down to $30, the market value of 500 shares will drop from $20,000 to $15,000. As a short seller at $40, you will make $5000 on your position ($20,000 - $15,000 = $5000). Keep in mind that your original equity commitment for this short sale was only $6000, 30 percent of $20,000. So that $5000 profit represents an 83 percent return on $6000 investment you put at risk when you made the trade.

As long as you maintain a short position, the credit balance in your short account will be monitored daily to maintain an equal amount of cash in the short account to the market value of the short position. The process of keeping the short account completely funded is called **mark to the market**.

After each day's close, the broker will journal, or move, funds back and forth between the short account (type 4) and the equity in the margin account (type 2). If the price of the stock goes higher, marking to the market will require the broker to move funds from the margin account to the short account. This is the reason for the 30 percent equity deposit. Vice versa, if the price drops, the excess equity in the short account will be journaled from type 4 (short) to type 2 (margin).

The risk to a short seller is that the stock's price will rise. If it does, the short seller is in a position where covering the short sale, buying back the shares to return to the broker/lender, will create a loss. If you short the stock at $40 and it goes to $50, you just lost $10 per share, or $5000 on a 500 shares. Note that a $5000 loss on your $6000 equity deposit is an 83 percent loss.

Although there is no specified time limit for how long short sellers can maintain their positions, this is usually as short term strategy. Historically, the stock market goes up more than it goes down. So the odds usually favor the purchaser of stock, not the short seller. Also, the broker has the legal right to cover any short position as any time. The broker may need to deliver the shares to another investor.

Another factor to consider before shorting a stock is that if the company you short pays a dividend, you will have to pay that dividend out of pocket. The broker will issue a dividend claim and debit your account for the dollar amount of the dividend paid on that number of shares. Remember since the broker loaned you the shares from someone else's margin account, that owner is still entitled to receive the dividend. If the shares are not there to physically receive the credit, this must be rectified by the broker.

Dividends are usually paid quarterly, every three months. So, dividend payments could be another reason why short selling is a short term strategy. Having to pay dividends would certainly reduce your profit, especially if you were to hold the position through several dividend cycles.

What Is a Dividend and Yield?

As stated in the section describing stock quotes in Chapter 1, a stock dividend is a payment made to shareholders representing a share of quarterly earnings. The **dividend yield** is rate of interest on an annual basis the dividend payments represent based on the price paid for each share of stock. It is equivalent to the annual percentage rate, APR, paid on bank accounts. So it is the sum of four quarterly dividends payments divided by the current market price of the stock. Although corporations are not under any legal obligation to pay a fixed rate dividend, most companies do have a policy that once they have declared a dividend they will continue to pay that same rate in the future. Investors base their expectations of future dividend payments to be at that rate or higher.

There are four dates that a shareholder should be aware of regarding a dividend payment. They are the declaration date, ex-dividend date, record date, and payable date. A dividend is usually declared when the Board of Directors has their meeting following their quarterly earnings cycle. The **declaration date** will usually be on the day of that meeting,. Remember that a company's dividends are paid from their earnings. So, when a dividend is declared it represents the part of the company's profits it is going to pay out to its shareholder/owners.

The **payable date** is when the dividend will actually be distributed. It will be a date in the near future, usually within the next month or so. However, between the declaration date and payable date, there are two other dates, the record date and ex-dividend date. Those two dates are relevant to the dates involved when you purchase the stock—the *trade date* and the next business day *settlement date*. For dividend payment purposes if you buy the stock the day before the **record date** you will not get that dividend, so that is called the **ex-dividend date**; the prefix ex- means without. The seller of the shares you purchased will be the shareholder of record for that next payment. So, if you want that dividend, you must buy the shares before the ex-dividend date.

In case you think this seems unfair, it isn't. On the ex-dividend date, under normal conditions the share price would be reduced by the amount of the dividend. If Unique Inc. had declared a $0.25 dividend and the stock closed at $35.75 the day before ex-dividend, it will probably open the next day around $35.50. The price of $35.50 would register as *unchanged* from the previous day's close of $35.75, not down $0.25. The seller of the stock on the ex-dividend date will receive the dividend on the payable date. But the purchaser of the stock might save about $0.25 off the price of the stock. So, both investors essentially net out an equivalent price.

Of course, market volatility doesn't stop on the ex-dividend date. So, there is no way to make the situation always equitable. Unique Inc. could just as easily go up 0.25 on the ex-dividend day as down due to market forces and sentiment for that day. There are many other reasons why a stock's price may go up or down that have nothing to do with the dividend payment.

However, the price for any good-till-cancelled (GTC) buy limit order for Unique Inc. will be reduced by the amount of the dividend on the ex-dividend date. An open order to buy the stock at $35 GTC would be reduced to $34.75 GTC on that date. This would also be the case for a sell stop order that was entered at $35 GTC.

An investor can avoid having open buy orders reduced on ex-dividend dates by coding the orders DNR, which stands for do not reduce. The effects of dividend payments can be difficult to analyze and predict. But all of these small dividend adjustments have very little significance to long-term investors.

If you are not planning on selling the stock for several years, whether the 25 cents price difference is a result of a dividend or cost basis has little significance. That dividend represents about 0.7 percent of the price of the stock. So, if you are expecting to make a 50 percent gain on the stock in that length of time, that small percent becomes much less significant.

As mentioned earlier, the source of dividend payments is a share of a company's quarterly earnings. The amount of the dividend payment is usually analyzed by the dividend payout ratio. That is the percentage of earnings that is typically paid out. Usually, the Board of Directors, who vote to approve dividend payments, keep to a policy of specific guidelines for the amount of the payout ratio. If Unique Inc. reported quarterly earnings of $0.75 per share, their $0.25 dividend would represent a 33 percent payout ratio (.25/.75 = .33).

Dividend payout ratios vary widely by industry group, but most companies in the same industry tend to follow similar guidelines. Companies that do not pay a dividend (and there are many of them) are able to retain more of their earnings for corporate needs. These are generally categorized as growth stocks.

Investors usually focus on utility companies—electric and gas—for high dividend payout ratios. Utilities generally have low cash flow needs because their profit margins are regulated by government agencies. The utility industry's historical average dividend payout ratio is around 65 percent of their earnings.

Other industries that are known for generous dividend payout policies are the Pharmaceuticals, Consumer Staples, Banks, and

Mortgage Real Estate Trusts. Companies in industry groups like these are referred to as defensive stocks. They don't necessarily have above average growth potential, but they hold their value better than most other industry groups in down markets.

Finally, many companies offer a **dividend reinvestment program**, or **DRIP**. It allows investors to purchase additional shares of their company's stock with the dividend payments from shares they already own. If you participate in a company's DRIP instead of receiving a payment in cash, you will receive a statement showing the number of shares purchased with fractional shares usually carried out to three decimal places. Many companies have a policy of not charging for this service.

Also, most DRIP programs offer investors the right to purchase additional shares without having to pay a fee or commission. This is a well-kept secret among most brokerage firms, but it is an opportunity worth investigating for long-term investors. DRIPs must be set up directly with the Transfer Agent for the company. Many brokers have a program that will allow you to participate in DRIPs without having to take delivery of your stock certificate, but you will need to ask about it.

There are thousands of companies that offer DRIPs. To participate, you must first be an owner of that company. Some companies allow you to participate in a reinvestment program when they are holding your shares, but some transfer agents may require you to have the security registered in your name, not the street name of your broker. DRIPs allow you to make additional purchases of more shares without going through your broker. So brokers do not have an incentive to tell you about them.

Another important feature is that DRIPs are not limited to just reinvestment of dividends. Some allow you to make purchases directly through the program and may even offer a discount on the share price for additional purchases. Buying shares of stock at a discount and commission free is a broker's worst nightmare, but smart investors would do well to check out the specifics about the DRIPs that might be available for any stock they own or are contemplating purchasing. There are several websites where you can check out current lists of stocks that have DRIPs.

By having dividends reinvested, you will receive future dividend payments on all your previously paid dividends. This is called compounding and will be discussed in the next chapter. It is similar to the compound interest on savings accounts at banks. When interest is credited, you begin earning more interest on that higher credit balance. Compounding dividends means you will earn increasingly higher dividends with each payment. That would not happen with dividends paid in cash.

Selecting a broker is important, but no one watches out for your interests better than you. You are the one who has the most at stake.

Chapter 4

What Is a Bond?

The two primary means for companies to raise capital in the securities markets are by issuing shares of stock or selling corporate bonds. Each share of stock represents a percentage (share) of ownership in the company. But a bond represents debt, money that will have to be paid back to the lender/bond holder. When a company, or any other entity—a sovereign government, a state or local municipality, a government agency, etc.—issues a bond, it is borrowing money from the investor.

When you lend money by buying corporate bonds, you do not have an equity ownership in the company. The company (or other entity issuing bonds) is obligated to pay you back the amount of principle you are loaning. A **bond** by definition is an agreement made by the issuer to pay a fixed rate of interest to the lender for a predetermined period of time and to repay the principal at the end of that period. To the bond issuer this is a liability.

Worldwide the total market value of all bonds issued is over $82 trillion at the time of this writing. The size of all equity investments in the stock markets worldwide is under $50 trillion. Bonds are a much larger market value than stocks, but they are primarily the domain of institutional investors. Individual investors will never come close to the volume of trades made by institutions, but bonds can, and probably should, be a part of most individual investors' portfolios.

Even though you do not have an equity stake in a company when you invest in bonds, you do have a senior claim to corporate assets over stockholders. In the event the company becomes insolvent, that is, does not have sufficient cash to meet its financial obligations, bond holders have a senior claim to assets over stockholders. In bankruptcy, stockholders are at the bottom of the list. Generally speaking, the priority by which creditors get paid in the event of bankruptcy follows the order of the company's payments on its income statement, which will be explained in the next chapter.

In most cases when you hear people talk about **equity** they mean stock, and **debt** means bonds. There are other equity securities than stocks, and other debt securities than bonds, but those are most common. Some of the other examples of equity and debt obligations will be discussed later on in this chapter.

Since learning the language of investing is key to understanding how the market works, you should know one more set of terms you may hear when contrasting stocks and bonds. Stocks may be referred to as **variable return investments**, and the analogous term for bonds as **fixed return investments**. Those terms capture the essential difference between the two types of securities. Variable return obviously draws your attention to the unpredictability of the stock market. There is no way an investor can accurately predict the exact market value of a stock at any given point in the future. However, that is not the case with bonds.

Bonds are called fixed return investments because they will pay a fixed rate of interest over the life of the investment. Then when the bond comes due, or matures, the principal amount you originally invested will be returned to you. Like any other loan, both lender and borrower are aware of the exact term for the bond and when the principle must be fully repaid.

I will make one note about the language of bonds regarding that explanation about debt. You will also hear the bond market referred to as the credit market. Even though the word credit implies the opposite of debt, the debt market is also the credit market. Think credit cards. Also, the label bond market is a catchall phrase for all debt securities, not bonds only, but also notes, bills, and other fixed return securities.

Bonds are classified as collateralized or uncollateralized based on whether or not they are backed by specific assets. A **collateralized bond** will have an asset of the issuer pledged to replace the bond's principal in the event it is otherwise unable to do so, such as from bankruptcy. For corporations, collateralized bonds are usually mortgage bonds. A company will typically pledge its office building, manufacturing site, or other real asset as the specific asset backing the bonds it issues.

Most collateralized corporate bonds are backed by real estate, but that does not necessarily need to be the case. Airline and railroad companies typically back their debt obligations with equipment trust certificates. Airline companies may pledge their planes as collateral, and railroads their *rolling stock*. Corporations may also issue trust bonds that have security investments pledged as collateral, such as shares of stock they hold in other companies.

The word collateralize has gotten bandied about quite a bit and can be used in several other different contexts. So, a note of explanation is necessary for at least a couple of them. Collateralized corporate bonds should not be confused with collateralized mortgage obligations, CMOs, or collateralized bond obligations, CBOs.

A CMO is a security derived from a government agency's reissuance of mortgage debt. These agencies are Ginnie Mae, Fannie Mae, and Freddie Mac and will be explained later on in the section on government agency debt securities. CMO's are backed by the title to the property for which the mortgage was issued.

A CBO is a bond derivative fund containing low grade *junk bonds*. But it qualifies for a higher rating than junk because of its broad diversification, being composed of a large number of bonds. In most cases, very few of the bonds in the CBO may have as high a rating as the fund itself, but the default of any one bond in the fund would have a relatively small effect on the whole fund. The assumption is that it is unlikely all the junk bonds in the fund will default. These topics will make more sense to you as you go through the rest of this chapter. For now, you need only be concerned with collateralized and uncollateralized corporate debt.

An uncollateralized corporate bond is called a **debenture**, and most corporate bonds are debentures. Companies may also issue **subordinated debentures**, which would indicate those bonds rank below other bonds regarding rights to assets of the company. Non-subordinated debentures of the company would be senior debt obligations. This only becomes a factor in the event the company goes bankrupt and needs to liquidate assets to reorganize its debt.

Stockholders are on the bottom of the prioritized list of creditors who have claim to a company's assets in the event of bankruptcy. They are below collateralized bonds, debentures, subordinated debentures, preferred stockholders. So investing in the common stock of a company that is likely to go bankrupt is not a good idea.

Another bond term you need to know is **indenture**, the formal agreement specifying the terms of the bond and the rights and obligations between the bond issuer and the bond investor. The indenture appears on the face of the bond certificate. It will spell out how much interest the bond holder will receive each year, when the bond's principal will be repaid, and any other details regarding that specific issue. With only a few exceptions, bonds pay interest semiannually, every six months. But the rate, as is standard with most interest rates, is quoted at the annual percentage rate, APR.

A complete bond description contains three parts. To identify a specific bond, you need: (1) the title of the issuer, (2) the coupon rate, which may also be called the stated rate, and (3) the due date, or maturity date when the bond's principal will be repaid. So, a complete bond description might be something like Unique Inc. 5% 07/01/2035—name, rate, and date.

Almost all bonds are sold in denominations of $1000 principal amount, or face value. A bond of less than $1000 is called a baby bond, but they are very rare. Some bonds may be sold only in minimum denominations of some other dollar amount, such as $5000, but that would still usually be referred to as five bonds.

What Are the Different Types of Bonds?

Bonds are broadly classified by their types of issuers. The major bond issuers in the U.S. are the federal government (U.S. Treasury Dept.), state and local municipalities, U.S. government agencies (GNMA, FNMA, and FHLMC), corporations, foreign sovereign governments, and foreign corporations or agencies.

Far and away the largest issuers of bonds in the world are governments. The largest single issuer of bonds in the world is the U.S. Treasury Department. The national debt, which, at the time of this writing, is nearing $50,000,000,000,00. That is what the U.S. government owes bond investors, and U.S. taxpayers are obligated to pay. Those bonds will need to be repaid by future tax revenues. That amount of debt represents about $1.6M of debt for every person in the U.S. No country has ever tried to manage that amount of debt, but that is a different topic.

Before going into U.S. government bonds, let's consider another form of government debt. Bonds issued by state, county, and local governments or agencies are called **municipal bonds**, or more commonly just **muni bonds** or just **munis**. The total municipal bond market is a fraction of that for U.S. Treasuries, but they still represent many trillions of dollars and are extremely popular among individual investors.

Muni bonds are a popular choice for high income investors because the interest on these bonds is exempt from federal income tax and from state and local income taxes for residents of their state of issue. Also, bonds issued by federal territories such as Puerto Rico or Guam are tax exempt for all U.S. taxpayers. For most people, the higher the income the higher the tax bracket.

For whatever state in which you are a resident, muni bonds from any issuer within that state will be exempt from both federal and state income tax. However, for a resident outside that state, no federal tax would be charged on the bond's interest, but any applicable state and local income taxes would be. A California resident, for example, would generally not owe federal or state income taxes on any bond issued within the state of California. But if you invested in a muni bond issued from another state, you would probably owe California state income tax on that bond's interest.

The origins of the tax-advantaged nature of muni bonds came with the ratification of Sixteenth Amendment to the Constitution in 1913. This was first legislative authorization allowing the federal government to collect income tax. One of the provision of this amendment was that the federal government could issue bonds with interest payments exempt from state income tax, and under a reciprocity arrangement, the states could issue state and local government bonds exempt from federal income tax. The states took that one step further and mandated that bonds issued by the state would also be exempt from state income taxes for their residents. Thus interest payments on muni bonds were exempt from both federal and state taxes, and interest payments on U.S. Treasury bonds were exempt from federal income tax.

Municipal bonds are usually offered in $5000 denominations; however, that is still referred to as five bonds. Historically muni bonds pay the lowest rate of interest, compared to other bond issuers, such as corporations or the federal government. This is because of the tax-free nature of their interest. When you add the tax savings to the interest you receive from tax-free bonds, the net after-tax return is usually comparable to equivalent taxable bonds.

It should be noted, however, during periods of unusual interest rate fluctuations, the historical relationship between taxable and tax-free bonds can be significantly altered from that normal correlation. You may find some tax-free bonds yielding higher rates than their taxable equivalents. That would make the differential between the two even higher.

For example, imagine you are in a 35 percent tax bracket, and are trying to decide between two equivalent bonds, one taxable and one tax-free, both paying the same rate of interest. So, the tax-free muni bond will give you a 35 percent better after tax rate of return than the taxable corporate bond. If the taxable corporate bond is paying 5 percent and the tax-free muni is paying 5 percent, the after tax rate of return for the corporate bond will be 3¼ percent. Put another way, if the tax-free bond pays more than 3.25 percent, it will yield more than 5 percent to that taxpayer.

If you invest in tax-free munis, you can compute the taxable equivalent rate by using a simple formula: the tax-free rate divided by the result of one minus your tax bracket. For example, if you invest in a muni bond paying 5 percent and your tax bracket is 35 percent (combined federal and state), the taxable equivalent yield would be about 7.7 percent, $5/(1-0.35) = 7.69$. In this example, you would have to invest in a taxable bond paying higher than 7.69 percent in order to receive the equivalent of a 5 percent tax-free bond.

Obviously, if you are in a lower income tax bracket, your taxable equivalent rate on a muni bond will be lower. However, keep in mind the 35 percent bracket being used in this example would include both federal and state income tax. So you could be in a 28 percent federal and 7 percent state income tax bracket and your combined tax liability would be 35 percent ($28 + 7 = 35$). You don't have to be in the top tax bracket to benefit from tax free bonds. It is a relatively simple matter for you to calculate whether you would be better off investing in taxable bonds or tax-free bonds, if you know what your tax bracket is.

Municipal bonds may be broadly categorized either as general obligation, GO, bonds or as revenue bonds. A **GO bond** can only be issued by a taxing authority, such as a state, and it is backed by the full taxing authority of that issuer. A **revenue bond** is backed by the cash flow generated by whatever project the bonds are being used for. Sanitation, landfill, toll roads, and sports arenas are some common examples of revenue bonds.

GO bonds used to be considered the highest standard by which all other revenue bonds were rated. However, during periods of economic downturns, GO bonds of many states have been downgraded significantly. At those times, there are many revenue bonds considered safer and have a higher rating than those backed by tax collections.

Next, consider U.S. government bonds. For federal government debt, there are three different classifications, based primarily on the length of the term for each: U.S. Treasury bills, notes, and bonds. U.S. Treasury bills, commonly referred to as T-bills, have the shortest maturities, ranging from 1 month to 2 years. T-notes range from over 2 years to 10 years at the time of their issue. And T-bonds range from over 10 years to 30 years.

Treasury notes and bonds pay interest on a semiannual basis, like most other notes and bonds. However, T-bills are structured differently. They are sold at a discount to **par value**, the principal amount of the bill received at maturity, and rather than make semiannual payments, the interest rate they pay is factored into the difference between the discounted price at the time of investment and the par value at maturity. The types of credit securities can also be referred to as zero coupon bonds, or original issue discount, OID, securities.

T-bills can be bought in as little as $100 denominations, but most are usually sold in $1000 increments. That is what the bill will be worth on the due date. The price of investing in a T-bill will be at a discounted price from the face value at maturity. The interest rate is the difference between the purchase price and the maturity value. So, if you invest in a $10,000 one-year T-bill, the cost of the bond might be $9,700. The additional $300 you receive at maturity, will be about a 3 percent APR ($9,700 + $300 = $10,000).

Remember that interest rates are always quoted at an annual percentage rate, APR. So, if you were to invest in that same T-bill for a three month period, the cost of it would be about $9925. The $75 you would receive at maturity would represent about a ¾ percent rate of return for that period of time, or about 3 percent APR. You would only own the bill for one-fourth of a year. These numbers were rounded off to simplify the math, but the actual yield would be calculated out to the nearest one-hundredth of a percent.

U.S. Treasury notes and bonds function like all other types of bonds. They will pay interest semiannually. You will receive one-half of the annual interest payments every six months, beginning six months after the date of issue. T-notes and T-bonds are sold in $1000 minimum denominations.

Another type of U.S. government debt issue is Treasury Inflation-Protected Securities, or TIPS. These are bonds that are sold in $100 denominations and make semiannual interest payments based on the rate set when the bond was issued. However, the principal of the bond is adjusted to correspond to the rate of inflation as measured by the Consumer Price Index, CPI. They are sold for terms of 5, 10, and 30 years.

Thus, TIPS investors receive a rate of return meant to maintain the buying power of the dollar. These bonds are considered the most conservative because rising interest rates will not cause the principal to depreciate. So generally speaking, the best time to invest in TIPS would be when you expect interest rates to rise as a result of inflation.

All U.S. Treasury securities are available for purchase directly from Federal Reserve Banks during weekly auctions, free of all fees or commissions. This is the primary market. It can be accessed online at www.TreasuryDirect.gov. Brokerage firms can also submit your auction orders. Most do not charge a fee, but you should ask before buying.

U.S. Treasuries are also available on secondary markets. You would purchase securities from an inventory of bonds. For those bonds, there would be a commission. However, it is usually small; typically $10 per bond.

The next category of fixed-return investing is government agency securities. Most agency debt securities are tied to the real estate mortgage market. However, there are a few other federal agencies whose function is meant to bolster markets other than real estate. Two of the most popular of these would be for student loans and farm subsidies.

The largest of the real estate agencies is the **Government National Mortgage Association**, GNMA, referred to colloquially as **Ginnie Mae**. Ginnie Mae's two siblings are Fannie Mae and Freddie Mac. **Fannie Mae** is a colloquialism for FNMA, the **Federal National Mortgage Association**; and **Freddie Mac** is FHLMC, the **Federal Home Loan Mortgage Corporation**. All three agencies functioned in a similar manner. They purchase several home mortgages, referred to as mortgage pools, from financial institutions, then repackage them as a new security backed by these mortgages.

Ginnie Mae is the only agency with a stated U.S. government guarantee in its charter. It is required to issue only Federal Housing Authority, FHA, or Veterans Administration, VA, approved loans. Fannie Mae and Freddie Mac are bankrupt corporations that have been taken over by the federal government. They were originally created to add liquidity and safety to investing in the mortgage market. Instead, they added illiquidity and risk. Following the real estate market collapse in 2008, the no-longer-collateralized debt of Fannie and Freddie kept the economy in a state of stagnation and uncertainty for many years.

Fannie Mae and Freddie Mac were never truly U.S. government agencies to begin with. They were publicly traded corporations owned by their shareholders. They were created, however, by an act of Congress and were thus usually labeled as quasi-governmental agencies. Most investors assumed there was an implied government backing of the debt securities they issued, even though there was no stated one.

Most of the FNMA and FHLMC individual pools of home mortgages were restructured as several derivative securities. Financial institutions would break up one or more of these individual mortgage pools and create new tradable securities. These were broadly called collateralized mortgage obligations, CMOs, as referenced earlier.

One popular derivative was to split an individual pool into two parts, one representing just principal repayments only, POs, and the other interest only, IOs. Another was to create CMOs with various **tranches**, representing laddered maturity dates. The first tranche would get the first one-third of the interest and principal payments, the second tranche the next third, and the third the last mortgages to be repaid. There were literally hundreds of derivative securities. Many so complex that many investors did not understand what they were buying. Even parts of various pools that remained after other derivatives were created, would often be bundled into one more derivative referred to as a **kitchen sink**.

Fannie Mae and Freddie Mac derivative securities live on in investment company real estate fund portfolios. Because of their very high yield in an economic environment of very low interest rates, these have become popular investments. However, investors should be warned to check out these high yield portfolios. Remember, the higher the yield, the more risky the investment.

The Government National Mortgage Association, Ginnie Mae, has remained above the fray. So, most Ginnie Mae investments are easier to understand and returns are more predictable. However, Ginnie Mae certificates are still different from other debt securities.

Each pool of Ginnie Mae mortgages will be divided into individual securities with a $25,000 minimum initial investment and additional $5000 denominations. Investors in these certificates will receive monthly payments of interest and repayment of principal. If you are a homeowner, you know that the monthly check you send to your lender is applied partly to interest and partly to principal. Your position as a GNMA investor is like that of the lender. Each month you will receive what the lender would receive—part interest and part principal.

At the beginning of the loan, most homeowners' monthly payments are applied to interest only and very little to principal. However, toward the end of the mortgage, most of your payments are applied to principal and very little to interest. This makes owning GNMA securities a bit unpredictable. As an investor in a GNMA, anytime one of the mortgages in a pool is refinanced or sold, the proportional share of that pool will be repaid to you in a lump sum. Also, subsequent interest payments will be reduced by the amount that would have come from that mortgage.

The term of each mortgage pool will depend on the term of the mortgages in that pool. Previously those terms were only 15 or 30 years, but 10, 20, and 40 year terms are also now available. The shorter the term, the more accelerated will be the pay down of principal.

From an investor's point of view, Ginnie Maes are considered as safe as Treasury debt obligations, backed by the full faith and credit of the U.S. government. However, they generally pay a much higher rate of interest than T-bonds. The bond rate will be set by the supply and demand factors in the bond market, but Ginnie Maes pay an interest rate primarily determined by supply and demand factors for home mortgages.

The problem with this method of principal pay back is that, whereas government bonds will pay interest for a defined length of time, the terms of Ginnie Maes are less predictable. Very few homeowners keep the same 30-year mortgage they start with. Most homes are sold or refinanced before the mortgage matures.

So, 30-year Ginnie Mae rates are usually compared to U.S. government bonds maturing in about 12 years. That is approximately the average life of a mortgage. Keep in mind, however, that is only an estimate; it is not fixed. During some economic cycles the population is more mobile than others, and the average terms are shorter. Ginnie Mae investors may use that as a general guideline, but would do well to check with analysts as to the forecasts for average maturities at the time they make a purchase.

If you invest in a Ginnie Mae with a much higher yield than what is currently available for home mortgages, it is not likely that the security will last 12 years. It is more likely that most, if not all, the homeowners whose mortgage is part of that pool will refinance at the lower rate. So, don't count on high yielding Ginnie Maes to last as long as the historical average.

Corporate bonds are the fourth category of bond classifications. Some corporate bonds are listed on the NYSE, but most trade in the third market, from inventories held by financial institutions. They are usually sold in $1000 denominations, but some brokers may require investors to buy a minimum lot from their inventory, in order to avoid having a large number of small bond lots to deal with.

The interest rate on most corporate bonds is subject to both federal and state income tax. Thus, they usually pay a slightly higher rate than do treasuries or munis. However, recent history has not followed historical patterns.

One unique quality of corporate bonds is that some of them may be convertible into the common stock of the issuer. The terms of the conversion factor for a **convertible bond** will be described in the bond's indenture. The price of the shares of stock into which the bond could be converted is represented by the number of shares you would receive from each bond. Since a bond has a par value of $1000, the number of shares would be how many shares you could buy at that price for $1000.

For example, if the bond converts into 50 shares of stock, the price per share would be $20 ($1000/50 = $20). The important factor here is that if the bond is purchased for a price other than $1000, the conversion price for the stock will also be different. Say you buy a bond for $900 and that bond is convertible into 50 shares. The price per share you would pay for the stock would not be $20, but $18 ($900/50 = $18).

How and why bonds trade at prices different from $1000 will be explained shortly. However, it follows that if an investor pays more than $1000 for a convertible bond, the conversion price for the shares of stock would be higher. Also, most convertible bonds will include in their indenture, the terms of the bond printed on the face of the certificate, a clause giving the issuer the right to make conversion mandatory if the stock trades above the conversion price for a given period of time.

Convertible bonds are hybrid securities whose price will be a function of two different markets. Its trading price will primarily be influenced by the bond market when the price of the underlying stock is significantly below conversion parity. But its price will primarily be influenced by the stock market as the price of the underlying security being trading moves close to or above parity.

The last categories of bonds are foreign sovereign debt and foreign corporate debt. Most individual investors do not participate directly in these markets, so not much time will be spent on them. It is a market dominated by institutional investors.

However, you should know a few facts about this market because there are many popular mutual funds or exchange traded funds, ETFs, that offer individual investors the opportunity to participate in those markets. First and foremost, investors should be aware that the accounting principles applicable to the U.S. are not universally accepted around the world. Not only are the accounting principles often different, but auditing standards are sometime difficult to verify.

You would be well advised to avoid investing not only in bonds, but especially in stocks, of foreign bond issuers unless the issuer has a policy of releasing all financial records. Openness is the most important factor, but you must also have independent auditors with high standards of ethics and professionalism who do not have a conflict of interest with the debt issuer. Finally, there must be a system of checks and balances in place, with harsh penalties for illegal or fraudulent behavior.

No system is perfect. Even though the U.S. generally has the highest standards of financial accountability, there have been many high profile violations of those standards in the past. The bankruptcy of Enron Corp. and the Bernard Madoff Ponzi Scheme were two examples in the past of how the system failed to protect innocent investors. The regulatory failures that led to these examples will be addressed in greater detail in Chapter 11.

If you are considering investing in foreign fixed return securities, pick a well-managed fund that specializes in them. Funds that are only concentrated on the sovereign debt of one nation or one agency are usually the riskiest. An investment portfolio that is diversified into several non-correlated areas will mitigate some of that risk. Also, professional management is a necessity in these markets. Well-managed funds have knowledgeable analysts who are in a far better position to make judgment calls than the average individual investor.

Foreign bond funds are becoming increasingly more popular as the higher yields on some of them look very attractive compared to the U.S. bond market. But always remember higher returns usually mean higher risk. Do your homework.

Finally, there are other fixed return securities than bonds. A particularly popular one is a stock-bond hybrid security called *preferred* or *preference stock*. Preferred shares trade like common stock on a stock exchange. However, its price will trade more like a bond than a stock, because it pays a fixed dividend similar to, and in competition with, bond interest payments.

One of the main differences between preferred stock and bonds is that stock has no maturity date. Some preferred shares, however, might have a callable date at which time the underlying principal amount of the shares would be repaid. Preferred shares will be sold initially at a fixed price, representing the principal. Frequently share prices for preferred stock will be $25, $50, or $100 par value. This would be analogous to the $1000 principal amount for bonds.

In most cases, preferred shares will be identified by the dividend rate they pay. So, you might see a preferred listing for Unique Inc as: Unique Inc 6% Pfd Series C. For the issuing company the dividends paid on preferred shares are not a tax deductible expense for their corporate income taxes, but bond interest payments are tax deductible. So, most companies, especially those for which taxes are an issue, would be more likely to issue bonds than preferred stock.

However, corporate investors are more likely to choose another company's preferred stock rather than their bonds. This is because, to a corporation, dividends received from a preferred stock investment can be 70 percent exempt from federal income tax. That tax exemption is not applicable to individual investors. But to a company the tax exemption greatly increases the after tax rate of return.

Nevertheless, individual investors may be attracted to preferred shares for reasons other than tax advantages. Preferred dividends are senior to common dividends, which means that if the issuing company goes into bankruptcy, preferred shareholders get paid before common shareholders.

Almost all dividends on preferred stock are *cumulative*, which means that if a company skips preferred dividend payments because of financial difficulties, they continue to accumulate. All preferred dividends in arrears need to be paid before a common stock dividend will be paid.

Throughout this section, there were frequent references to the changing prices of fixed return securities. The primary cause for the prices of bonds, preferred stock, and other fixed return investments to move up and down is changes in interest rates. There is an inverse relationship price and interest rates. As rates move up, fixed return investment prices move down, and as interest rates move down, fixed return investment prices move up. To understand how this works, you must first understand compound interest.

What Is Compound Interest?

As mentioned earlier, bond interest rates, and most other interest rates for that matter, are quoted at an annual percentage rate, APR. This is especially important, and sometimes confusing, when the pay period for the interest is less than one year.

A three month T-bill, for example, may be quoted at 2 percent interest, but the amount of interest the investor will receive for holding the bill one-quarter of a year, that is three months, would be 0.5 percent—one-quarter of the 2 percent annual rate. If you rolled over the bill to a new one each time the three month bill matured and each new bill was also 2 percent, at the end of the fourth bill, the total interest you received would add up to approximately 2 percent (0.5 x 4 = 2).

This total annualize interest rate was modified with the word "approximately", because you would end up with a slightly higher rate than 2 percent. This is because each time the three month bill matured, you would have that amount of interest to reinvest in a new bill. This is a theoretical example because T-bills are not sold in small enough denominations to add in the extra interest. However, if you could reinvest your interest you would realize a compound interest rate.

Compound interest is a term used to describe the effect of having interest reinvested in another interest earning investment as it is credited from your old one. A compound rate means you are earning interest on your interest. The amount of money you originally invest is called the present value, and the amount you will have when the investment terminates is the future value. For a more complete explanation of the mathematics of compound interest see the Glossary.

Albert Einstein has been credited with saying that compound interest was the greatest invention of man. Compound interest adds to your credit if you are an investor. That would be true whether you are talking about interest rates on bank certificates of deposits (CDs), savings accounts, or money market funds.

However, compound interest works against you if you are borrowing money. So, credit cards, mortgages, auto loans, and the like end up costing you more money than would be calculated without the effect of compounding. The interest rate charged on your outstanding debt continues to accumulate on the balance owed.

A simple formula to help you understand the effects of compounding is the **Rule of 72**. The number of years it will take your fixed return investment to double in value at a compounded interest rate can be approximated by dividing 72 by the interest rate you are receiving. Of course, the same would also be true of interest you are paying.

So, if you are investing in a fixed return investment paying 7.2 percent compound interest, your original investment would double in value in about 10 years (72/7.2 = 10). If your investment is only paying 2 percent compounded, it would double in about 36 years (72/2 = 36). But an investment paying 12 percent compounded would double in 6 years (72/12 = 6). Compounding can either be a blessing for a lender, or a curse for a borrower. That is something to keep in mind before you charge that unnecessary luxury item on your credit card. Some credit cards charge 18 percent interest, which means the cost of your purchase will double every 4 years.

If interest is not compounded, it is called "simple interest". Consider the difference between those examples of compound interest and simple interest. For an investment to double in ten years, it would need to be in a 10 percent investment, not 7.2 percent. A 2 percent investment would double in 50 years, and a 12 percent investment in 8.33 years.

You may think this is all for naught, as bonds don't pay compound interest. However, that is not quite the case. There are some bonds called **zero coupon bonds** that, like Treasury bills, are bought at a discount and mature at par value. They do not pay interest in cash, but the interest is calculated in the rising value of the bond, and this rate is calculated at a compounded rate of return.

The discount price of a zero coupon bond is calculated at a rate that if the bond paid interest every six months, like regular bonds, that interest would be reinvested at that bond's stated rate. This compounding effect on bonds can be illustrated by the following graph.

The following illustration shows two graphs comparing the rate of return on an investment that pays simple interest and one that pays compound interest at the same rate. Simple interest is a straight line, because each year's interest would simply be added to the total.

The compound interest rate graph follows a parabolic curve, because each year's interest earns more interest. For each subsequent interest payment at a compound rate, you will earn interest on the interest that has been previously credited.

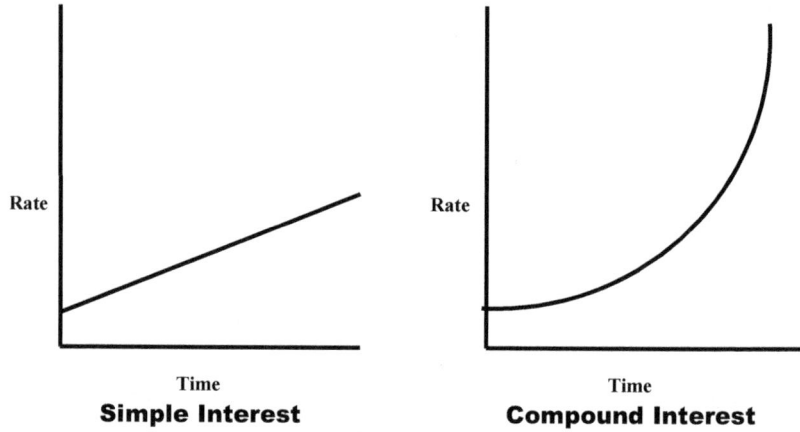

Simple Interest   **Compound Interest**

The stated rate for a particular bond has been referred to as the coupon interest rate. The coupon rate is one of three different rates you need to understand when investing in bonds. The reason it is called a coupon rate has to do with how bonds have changed through the years.

Practically all bonds issued today are registered. The paper certificate for a bond, like that for a stock, will be issued with the name of the bondholder imprinted on it, or the street name for the brokerage firm of the bondholder. Remember that street name, also referred to as nominee name, is the registration brokers use when holding securities for their clients. It allows the bondholder to sell the bond through the broker without having to process any further paperwork. This is the same as for stock certificates.

However, many bonds, especially municipal bonds, were formerly issued in **bearer** form. There was no registered name on the bond certificate. The one who physically possessed the bond could negotiate its sale. This necessitated very high security measures for bondholders. If someone stole the certificates, they might be able sell them or use them as collateral for loans. They were almost as easy to negotiate as paper money.

Bearer bonds had literal coupons attached to the certificate, similar to retail store coupons. They had a dollar amount of interest to be paid and a date on which they could be redeemed. The dates were laddered six months apart, according to the semiannual interest payment schedule. On, or after, the due date the coupons could be cut from the corpus of the bond and cashed or deposited in a bank account. The coupons had to be physically cut from the bond certificate.

This is an illustration of a typical bearer bond from the early 20th century. Notice there is no registered owner on the face of the certificate, and there are coupons attached to the bottom, which would have been cut off and redeemed at semi-annual intervals. So, if the bond paid six percent interest, there would be coupons attached worth $30 each, and incrementally dated every six months for the term of the bond. A six percent bond would pay the bondholder exactly $60 per year in interest, $30 semiannually. Bearer bonds have not been issued in decades, but the stated rate of interest that all bonds pay is still referred to as coupon interest.

The coupon interest rate is not the only interest rate you need to understand when investing in bonds. You will only receive the interest rate stated on the coupon (in this example 6%) if you bought the bond for $1000. If you paid a different dollar amount than that, you would need to know two other rates that will be explained subsequently: the current yield and the yield-to-maturity.

First, if a bond is selling at a price below $1000, it is said to be selling at a **discount**. If its price is over $1000, it is at a **premium**. A bond selling at a discount will have a higher yield-to-maturity than its coupon rate because the bond holder will receive a capital gain on the principal at maturity. A bond selling at a premium will consequently have a lower yield-to-maturity than its coupon rate.

Say a six percent bond is selling at $900, instead of $1000. That bond will pay exactly $60 per year in interest to the registered bondholder. The dollar amount of interest is what is fixed to the bond buyer, and the price of the bond will determine what that yield will be. Sixty dollars per year is not a six percent yield to someone who purchased the bond for $900. So, the **current yield** would be calculated by dividing the dollar amount of the bond's coupon by the price paid for the bond. The current yield for that bond buyer would be about 6.67 percent ($60/$900 = 0.0667). Note the inverse relationship between the current yield and the bond price. If the price of the bond goes down, the current yield on the bond goes up. In that example, the bond buyer paid less than a $1000 to receive the annual $60 in interest. But if the bond buyer paid more than a $1000 for the bond, the current yield of the bond would be lower.

Say a bond buyer pays $1100 for a 6% bond. That bond buyer will still only receive the same $60 in interest. But the current yield at that price is going to be less than six percent. It will be about 5.45% ($60/$1100 = 0.0545). If the bond price goes *down* about 10%, the current yield will go *up* about 10%. Vice versa, if the bond price goes *up* about 10%, the current yield will go *down* about 10%. There is an inverse relationship between bond prices and current yields.

However, the current yield is not the only rate that is affected by the changing bond price. Whether the bond buyer paid $900, $1000, or $1100 for the bond, each will receive the same amount of principal back at maturity—$1000. So someone who bought the bond at a discount will receive an extra $100 over what was paid when the bond matures, but someone who bought the bond at a premium will lose $100 of the original amount paid.

Factoring in this capital gain, or loss, from the cost basis of a bond determines the investor's **yield-to-maturity, YTM**, also referred to as the *basis price*. If the bond had ten years to maturity and you bought the bond for $900, it would be logical to say you would earn an extra $10 per year in capital gains ($1000 - $900 =$100 and $100/10 = $10). However, yield-to-maturity is not calculated on a straight line simple interest basis. It is calculated on a compounded basis, which follows a parabolic curve. The mathematical formula for computing compound interest involves calculus. But if you haven't taken calculus, you can compute it on a financial calculator.

The yield-to-maturity would not actually be 7.78%, the rate you might presume it would be if you received $70 per year ($60 from interest and $10 per year from capital appreciation) on a $900 investment ($70/$900 = 0.0778). But on a financial calculator, it computes out to about 7.44%. This is because you don't get that extra $10 each year while you are holding the bond. You have to wait for 10 years to get the full $100. The future value of $100 is not the same as it would be if you received the $10 each year over a 10 year period.

Next, if instead of investing in this bond at a discount, consider what would happen to the yield-to-maturity if you paid a premium. If you purchased the bond for $1100, you are going to lose that $100 premium you paid over par value when you bought it. At maturity, you are only going to get back $1000. So, the YTM for a 6% bond will factor in that loss of principal and will be something less than the six percent coupon rate. It will be a 5.45% current yield.

Using a financial calculator, the yield-to-maturity will be 4.73% on a six% 10-year bond selling at $1100. That is 1.27% lower than the 6% coupon rate, and 0.72% less than the 5.45% current yield. The loss of $100 in principal has a dramatic effect on the bond's rate of return.

So, now that you know bonds may be bought at prices higher or lower than par value ($1000), let's look at what causes bond prices to fluctuate.

What Are the Risks of Investing in Bonds?

You may have deduced from the previous section that the primary risk of investing in bonds is rising interest rates. When you purchase a bond, you are locked into a fixed rate of return for the term of that bond. If you held it to maturity, there would be no risk to your principal, for you know you will get back your original thousand dollars per bond. However, if you locked in a six percent return and interest rates for comparable bonds rose to seven percent, then you would not be able to sell that bond before the maturity date without losing part of your principal. That is **interest rate risk**.

Consider that you invest in a Unique Inc. 6% 06/01/2030 bond at par value. It would be one paying $60 per year maturing in 10 years if you bought it in 2020. After two years, however, something unexpected happens; and you need to raise money. If you decide to sell your bond at that time, it will be priced to yield what other comparable bonds are yielding then. So, if interest on similar bonds is then about 7%, no one is going to buy your bond at par value if they would only be receiving 6%.

A 6% coupon rate means you will receive exactly $60 per year in interest payments. So, the principal amount of your bond will be reduced in price such that $60 per year in interest will amount to a 7% yield to the bond investor. A 1% rise in interest rates, from 6% to 7%, is equivalent to 17% (1/6 = 0.17).

So, the value of your bond will drop about 17%. It will be priced at about $857.14 ($60/0.07 = $857.14). You would lose about $142.86 from your original $1000 investment. This price is only meant to show you an approximate value. The actual price would be higher because the bond investor would also get the extra capital gain from the cost. So the yield-to-maturity would be adjusted by that amount. This illustration is only meant to show you the cause and effect relationship without getting into exact mathematical accuracy.

Interest rate risk is inherent for all fixed return investments. Some people are inclined to think that safer bonds, such as U.S Treasury bonds, are somehow less vulnerable to interest rate risk. They are not. Every fixed return investment is subject to the same risk to principal if comparable interest rates rise.

The interest rate risk is the same, whether your fixed return investment is in U.S. Treasuries, municipal bonds, corporate bonds, foreign bonds, second trust deed loans, preferred stock, or even bank CDs. Each investment of like kind will be vulnerable to principal loss if interest rates rise. It should also be noted that in the case of bank CDs, the bank may also impose other penalties for early withdrawals. With that in mind, you should note that the shorter the term of the bond the safer the principal. A T-bill maturing in three months is going to be worth par value in about 90 days. So, changes in interest rates will have very little effect on that fixed return investment.

However, a 30-year T-bond would be greatly affected by a rise in interest rates. If interest rates on long-term bonds rise from six percent to seven percent in one year, who knows what they will be in 30 years? Usually when you hear business news commentators on the bond markets, they will reference 30 year bonds because they are the ones that will show the greatest volatility.

The illustration on the next page shows how the relative relationships among bonds of various maturities can change with varying economic circumstances. The left hand side of the graph represents short term bonds, and the right hand side, long term. The shortest term bonds could mature in a few days or months. Long term bonds can run out to as much as thirty years. The yield on short term bonds is almost always lower than long term ones. A normal yield curve is the one represented by the line on the graph that begins and ends between the other two lines. Usually a normal yield curve favors investors who buy bonds with about a ten-year maturity, near the middle of the curve. At that point, investors would capture the highest yield without assuming the higher risk associated with bonds going out to 30 years.

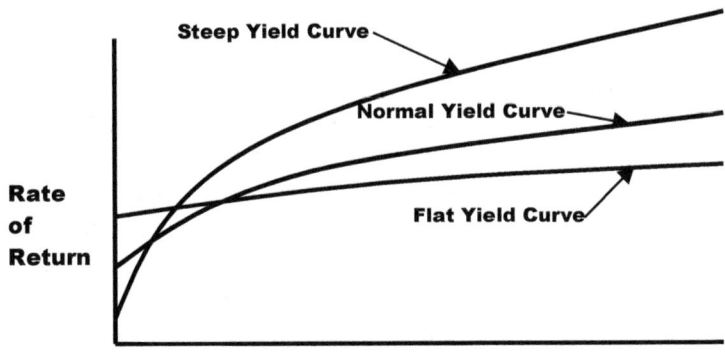

A flat yield curve means that either short term rates have moved higher, and/or long-term rates have moved lower. This type of curve would favor investing at the short end of the curve. A steep yield curve means either short term rates have moved lower and/or long-term ones higher. A steep yield curve is more advantageous for long-term bond investors. Flat and steep curves usually represent periods of transition of interest rates. They are not likely to last very long, and the yield curve will generally move back to a normal relationship.

The most common types of short term bonds, at the low end of the yield curve, are **money market securities.** They are considered the safest debt investments because they come due so quickly. Thus, they are popular choices for low risk investors. **Money market funds** are mutual funds that usually invest in a portfolio of **commercial paper**, corporate debt securities that mature in as little as one day and as long as 270 days. The average portfolio probably runs close to about one month. They may also invest in short term Treasury bills. Money market funds are set at a share price of one dollar. That way they look similar to a bank savings account.

Also, like a bank savings account, you should be aware the interest rate that money market funds pay changes constantly and unpredictably. As some of the short term paper in the fund matures, it will be replaced with new short term paper, probably with a different yield. Remember some of the securities in the money market fund's portfolio will likely mature every day. Thus, even though each security may pay a fixed return, it is only fixed for a few weeks at best or so. New fixed return securities replacing the maturing ones may not pay the same rate.

There have been a few cases where money market funds invested in risky commercial paper and the company issuing it defaulted. That did cause some money market shares to temporarily trade below one dollar per share. However, in those cases, the money market funds net asset value (NAV) only dropped to 98 or 99 cents per share. Because of the large size of money market fund portfolios, there was little damage done to investors.

So, fluctuating interest rates is the largest risk factor to investing in fixed return securities. The second risk factor to be considered is the risk of default. This is called **credit risk**, the measure of the likelihood that the debt issuer will be able to make the required interest payments and return of capital at maturity.

The following illustration shows the three major bond rating agencies that continuously monitor and evaluate the credit risk of debt securities: Standard & Poor's, Fitch's, and Moody's. There are several other rating agencies, but these three dominate the market. It should be noted that in almost all cases, the debt issuers pay these rating agencies to rate their bonds. Thus, some commentators have criticized the rating agencies for the accuracy of their analysis. However, such rating discrepancies have seldom been verified.

Standard & Poor's	Fitch's	Moody's
AAA	AAA	Aaa
AA	AA	Aa
A	A	A
BBB	BBB	Baa
BB	BB	Ba
B	B	B
CCC	CCC	Caa
CC	CC	Ca
C	C	C
D	D	

Bonds are rated from highest (safest) to lowest (least safe or in default) on a scale from AAA to D. The different rating agencies use their own proprietary criteria for evaluating creditworthiness. But equivalent ratings on debt securities represent approximately the same quality. Bonds in the top four categories are considered conservative investments and are referred to as investment grade.

To get a triple-A rating from any of the agencies, the bond issuer must usually generate enough revenue to have a strong likelihood of covering all interest payments and repayment of principal. For a corporate bond, this may mean the company must have enough cash flow to cover the interest by factor of ten or more. However, the rating agencies do not use a mathematical formula for determining their ratings; rather they apply their own proprietary analysis for evaluating the likelihood of the issuer having sufficient future cash flow to cover the debt obligations.

Standard & Poor's and Fitch's have a three-tiered sublevel rating for each category below AAA, a plus, neutral, and minus. The AA rating can be AA+, AA, AA-, and each of the other ratings can have the same sublevel rating from highest to lowest down to a D. Moody's grades each of its lower levels with a 1, 2, or 3 rating system. So the Moody's Aa rating can be narrowed down to Aa1, Aa2, or Aa3 from highest to lowest. A single C rating from Moody's is equivalent to a D rating from S&P or a DDD (or lower) from Fitch. It means the bond is in default.

Different agencies use different standards, and there are factors other than cash flow involved. But the guidelines for a bond issuer to receive the highest rating requires a very high probability of debt coverage. U.S. government bonds obviously don't have to meet that 10 times guideline. The government issues Treasury bonds based on its ability to cover its debt by printing more money. Of course, that means it will need to increase future tax revenue for that purpose. But the government has an indeterminable capacity to increase tax revenues, so it is generally considered to have the lowest risk factor. Historically U.S. government debt has carried an implied triple-A rating.

However, the commonly accepted precept that the government can never go into default because of its unlimited taxing authority is being tested by current deficit spending. The total U.S. debt crossed $20 trillion in 2017. With total U.S. federal tax revenue at around $4 trillion per year, it would take over 5 years to pay off that debt if everyone was taxed at their current rates and all government spending shut down. That, of course, cannot, will not, and should not happen. But how can any reasonable person who understands the magnitude of the situation not be concerned about uncontrolled government deficit spending?

The economies of most of the countries in the European Union (EU), the largest economic entity in the world, have an even greater potential for default than the United States. Bad economic policies, catastrophic spending by a few of the member nations, fomented a crisis for the entire EU. Unsustainable and irresponsible government spending over many years will inevitably lead to this same outcome. If the U.S. continues to follow the European economic model of unfunded deficit spending, can anyone truly be surprised that the outcome will be the same?

This is not meant to be a doom and gloom forecast. The U.S. definitely has the ability to turn the situation around and pursue a more sustainable economic path, but not if it continues to compound the problems without addressing the issues that created them. Every time there is a proposal for additional unfunded spending, even for the most well-meaning of reasons, it is adding to a problem that can only end in fiscal crisis.

Standard and Poor's downgraded their rating on U.S. government debt to AA in 2011. That drew the public's attention to the fact that S&P no longer considered U.S. debt to be "riskless". The irresponsible spending policies and practices no longer met the criteria for their highest rating. A double-A rating is still relatively high, and S&P was not sounding an alarm that default is imminent. But continued unchecked deficit spending will certainly lead to further downgrades and greater risk.

The top four bond ratings, from BBB to AAA, are considered to be **investment grade**. An investment grade bond is important for corporate and institutional bond investors. Financial service agencies, such as pension funds, insurance companies, and banks, usually have to meet fiduciary requirements. A **fiduciary** is someone who is entrusted with investing and managing other people's money. Many fiduciaries are required to purchase only investment grade bonds. So if bonds drop below the top four bond rating categories, interest rates generally rise more dramatically.

Bonds rated below the top four categories, that is, BB and below, are generally referred to as **junk bonds**. The underlying cause of the higher yield on junk bonds is supply and demand. If bond investors are acting in a fiduciary capacity, they will have to sell bonds if they drop from a BBB to a BB. Lower demand for bonds and greater supply, will cause bond prices to follow the same supply/demand curve as other securities.

There are many mutual funds or exchange traded funds, ETFs, that invest in junk bonds, but you will not often find that term being used to describe those funds by the companies that manage them. They are usually called high yield funds. So, knowledgeable investors realize investing in a high yield bond fund means most of the bonds in that portfolio will be rated below BBB. Higher returns generally correlate to higher risks.

The fact that junk bond funds are risky is not necessarily meant to be a warning against them. In fact, high yield funds offer some degree of safety because of diversification and professional management. Also, the yields can be significantly higher than comparable investment grade funds. Investors need to evaluate their own risk tolerance level and income needs. However, you should never assume more risk than that with which you are comfortable.

Like the stock market, the bond market demonstrates a high degree of market efficiency. The term **market efficiency** refers to the fact that prices of securities continuously reflect a fair market valuation. That is the highest price at which one investor is willing to purchase a bond, and another is willing to sell it. Market efficiency also implies rapid adjustments to market valuations, reflecting changes in supply/demand factors. Usually the market will properly price the rate of return on an investment based on the measure of risk assumed.

Bonds rated at the lowest level by each rating agency, a D by S&P or Fitch or a C by Moody's, are in default and unlikely to be able to repay all of the principal and past due interest. That means the issuer of the bond is insolvent and unable to pay the full amount of interest and principal it is contractually obligated to. If the issuer of a bond with a default rating is a corporation, it is probably in bankruptcy proceedings.

The type of corporate bankruptcy filing usually filed is Chapter 11. That is the chapter of the bankruptcy code that allows the company to continue its normal business operations and allows the company temporarily to suspend its payment obligations to creditors. During this time it is required to reorganize its assets and liabilities and work out repayment options with its creditors. Chapter 11 certainly does not mean the end of the company, as some people assume bankruptcy implies. In fact, it is the opposite—allowing the company to stay in business while it negotiates a restructuring plan with creditors. The company's goal is to emerge with a more viable business model. There are other chapters of the bankruptcy code that cover the complete liquidation and dissolution of companies.

A third consideration regarding risks associated with bonds is **call risk**, or early refunding. This type of risk was alluded to earlier during the discussion of high yielding GNMA securities being vulnerable to quicker repayment of principal due to increased refinancing activity of homeowners. Many bond issuers include a call feature in the bond's indenture. A call feature will specify when the bond issuer may opt to pay back principal before the maturity date. Call features have been extremely popular with municipal bonds. The purpose of this feature is to give the issuer the ability to refinance the debt obligations if interest rates decline. There would be no reason for an issuer to call in their debt if interest rates rise higher than the rate they are currently paying.

So, callable risk is assumed by the bond owner, not the bond issuer. If interest rates decline, investors are not likely to have their higher yield locked in for as long as they are expecting. Also, if interest rates rise, the investor remains locked into a lower yield. Some bond issuers may add a small premium to par value for an early call feature. But a one or two-point premium over par value does little to make up for the total amount of future interest income that would have otherwise been realized.

There are other macroeconomic risk factors for bonds than these, but this discussion is only meant to present an overview of some of the more common. Additionally, individual bond issues may have their own microeconomic risk factors. For corporations, a notable microeconomic risk is commonly referred to as financial risk. If a company has too much of its capitalization in debt and not enough in equity, it should be analyzed with greater scrutiny. If a company's business model could be subjected to the vagaries of economic cycles, will it still have sufficient cash flow to meet its fixed income obligations?

All of these risk factors subject bonds to fluctuating prices. So the next topic to be covered is how bond prices are reported.

How Do You Buy Bonds?

Bond quotes look similar to stock quotes, but they are completely different. Remember that bonds are sold in $1000 denominations of principal, and the prices of bonds are expressed as a percentage of that value. A bond priced at 100 means it is priced at par value, that is, 100% of $1000.

Therefore, a bond priced at 95.25 will have a dollar price of $952.50 (95.25% of $1000 = $952.50). Usually bond prices change in increments of one-eighth of a point. This is a throwback to the way that stock prices used to be quoted before they went to the decimal system. One-eighth of a percent for a bond would be equivalent to $1.25 per $1000 (0.00125 × $1000 = $1.25). So, you will usually see bond prices quoted in increments of one-eighth of one percent. Expressed as decimal fractions, the incremental percentage change would be 0.125, 0.25, 0.375, 0.50, 0.625, 0.75, and 0.875. A bond quoted at 88.875 is said to be trading at *eighty-*

eight and seven-eighths. The price of that bond would be $888.75. This fractional pricing system may also get as small as one sixteenth, one thirty-second, or even one sixty-fourth. The smaller increments are especially true of U.S. government securities.

The previous examples were for bonds selling at a **discount**, below par value. But the same pricing also applies to bonds selling at a **premium**, a price above par value. A bond quoted at 105.5 for example would be selling at $1055. Some investors might question why anyone would buy a bond at a premium, since you know you are going to lose the premium amount, in this case $55, when the bond matures. If you pay a premium, you will not get the amount of principal over par value back at maturity. Bond holders can only expect to receive par value ($1000) back at maturity, regardless of what they paid for the bond.

Bonds selling at premiums will be priced at approximately the same yield-to-maturity as equivalent bonds selling at a discount. However, the bonds selling at a premium will have a higher current yield than the ones at a discount. Part of the total return for investors of discount bonds is the appreciation of principal, but that will not be realized until the bond matures. Consequently, discount bonds pay a lower current yield than premium bonds.

Investors in premium bonds, however, know that their yield-to-maturity has factored in the loss of principal they paid over par value. So, they will receive a higher current yield from their premium bonds over those who invested in equivalent discount bonds. You could consider the higher current yield from a premium bond as an early prepayment of the principal you will not get back at maturity.

Discount bond investors, on the other hand, are more likely to be traders. If interest rates go lower, their bonds will rise at a slightly larger percentage rate than equivalent premium bonds. Plus, as the bond moves closer to the maturity date, it will automatically move closer to par value. Remember, the shorter the term, the closer bond prices move toward par value ($1000).

So, whether you choose to invest in a bond at a premium, par, or a discount depends on what your expectations are from that investment. An investor in a premium bond expects higher current income. An investor in a bond at par usually wants predictability, expecting to lock in a yield and probably to hold the bond to maturity. An investor in a discount bond may be hoping to make a capital gain, either from a downward move in interest rates or just from the passage of time. A discount bond will move closer to par value as it moves closer to its maturity date.

During business reports, bonds are sometimes not quoted at the price of the principal, but by the interest rate they are paying. That is what investors are most interested in. The incremental units of change for yield quotes are **basis points**, **bps** (pronounced *bips*). One basis point (one *bp*) is one one-hundredth of a percent (1/100 or 0.01%). So, one hundred basis points is equal to one percent.

If it is reported that the long government bond was up 10 basis points today at 5.73, it means that the yield on the 30-year U.S. Treasury bond was up 10% that day. So the previous day's closing yield on that bond would have been 5.63%. The 10 basis point run up brought the yield up to 5.73%.

If you are interested in investing in bonds, you need to pay attention to how the news about them is reported. If you hear or read a report that says the bond *market* was up today, it probably means interest rates were down, and thus prices were up. However, if the report says bond *rates* were up today, that means the opposite of the previous statement. Bond prices go down when rates go up.

Short term fixed return investments are usually quoted in basis points, rather than price. T-bills are sold at a discount to par value and do not make interest payments. So, quoting the price of the T-bill isn't very useful. You don't know what the yield will be if you only know the price. For example, if a one-year T-bill is quoted at 968.62, you have no idea what the yield will be; but if it is quoted at a 3.24 basis, you do. Also, it is popular to quote all bonds, not just short term ones, at basis points. But investors need to be aware that a higher basis point means a lower price. The market price moves in the opposite direction as interest rates.

Say you are interested in investing in a T-bill on the secondary market, not the primary or auction market. You have a quote that says something like 2.57 bid, 2.55 ask. Like stock quotes, a buyer will purchase the security at the ask price and a seller will receive the bid price. The difference between the two quotes is the spread. However, unlike stock quotes, the ask is expressed in basis points, it will be lower than the bid. This is because basis point quotes reflect yield, not price. A higher yield represents a lower price, and a lower yield represents a higher price. So, you could buy the T-bill at the 2.55 bp ask price, but the one selling the bill will receive the 2.57 bp bid price. The net outcome is the same as with stocks; the buyer pays the higher price and the seller receives the lower. The difference between the two represents the market maker's spread.

A final consideration when buying bonds is **accrued interest**. Regular bonds pay the same amount of interest every six months, semiannually. So, what happens when you buy a bond on the secondary market in the middle of one of these six month periods? Bonds pay the same semiannual payment to all bondholders on the same date. But the bondholder who bought that bond, did not own it for six months and is not entitled to the whole semiannual interest payment. So, when buyers make purchases of bonds trading on secondary markets, they are required to prepay that part of the interest to which they are not entitled. That is called accrued interest, and it represents the part of the bond's interest to which the seller of the bond would be entitled since the last payment date. Buyers of bonds prepay that part of the interest for the period of time they do not own the bond. So, when they get the next semiannual payment, they will net out the correct amount of interest for the period of time they owned the bond.

Accrued interest is calculated using a simple formula. It begins with the assumption that every month is exactly 30 days, even if the actual number is different. So, each month represents one-sixth of the semiannual payment. Each day of the month then represents one-thirtieth of the month. To illustrate, consider that you buy a bond on March 18 whose interest payments are made on January 1 and July 1. It is a 6 percent bond, so its semiannual interest payments are $30 per bond. The amount of accrued interest you would owe would be for 2 months and 18 days.

To calculate the monthly amount of the accrued interest, you would divide $30 by 6, or $5. So you would owe $10 for the months of January and February. Then for the additional 18 days in March, each day would be computed by dividing one month's accrued interest rate by 30 days, $5/30 = $0.167. The amount of accrued interest in March would be calculated as 18 times $0.167, approximately $3. Thus the total amount of accrued interest in this case would be $13 ($5 + $5 + $3 = $13). On July 1, you will receive the regular semiannual interest payment of $30. But since you prepaid $13 in accrued interest, you netted out the $17 interest you were entitled to for the period of time you owned the bond ($30 - $13 = $17).

This may seem like a long explanation for a simple concept and a few dollars. However, bond buyers need to be aware that when they make a purchase on the secondary market, there will usually be this additional initial cost of accrued interest. Even though that will be refunded to you on the next payment date, you will need to allow for this additional expense at the time of purchase.

You can avoid accrued interest by purchasing bonds on the primary market. But if you are buying bonds on the secondary market, from the inventory offered through the broker, there are only two days each year when you will not have to pay accrued interest. There will only be zero days of accrued interest if your bond trade settles on one of the semiannual interest payment dates. Normally the settlement dates for bonds is the same as for stocks. Settlement date is the day following the trade date.

Now you have an overview of the two main types of securities that companies can issue—stocks and bonds, equity and debt. These are the primary ways companies are capitalized, as recorded in their financial statements. You can learn a great deal about companies if you understand some of the basic information on their financial statements. That will be covered in the next chapter.

120 ◇ Bonds

~$ $ ~Investing Tip~$ $ $~

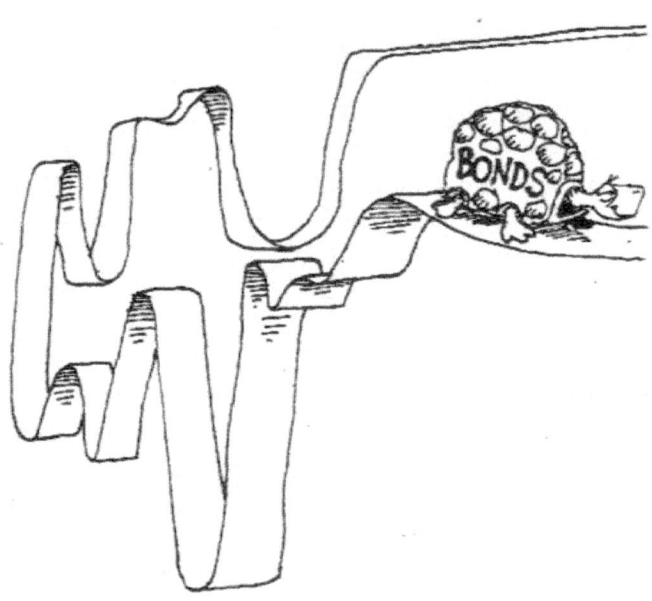

Bond prices move inversely to interest rates, usually at a slower pace than stocks. But they end up at the same level where they started—par value.

Chapter 5

How Do You Read Financial Statements?

There are four basic financial statements you will learn about in this chapter: the balance sheet, the income (or earnings) statement, the statement of cash flows, and the statement of shareholders equity. The balance sheet reveals how the company is capitalized, how it has structured its finances with debt and equity. The income statement presents the company's business operations in the order of priority for paying its financial obligations. The cash flow statement reveals how much of the company's revenues were derived from business operations compared to financing and investing activities. The statement of shareholders' equity explains changes in entries on the equity part of the balance sheet.

The fact that two different words may be used to describe one statement—income or earnings—is indicative of the problem most people have when they begin learning about financial statements. Different accounting agencies use different words to describe the same thing. Many entries on financial statements do not have universal terms to describe them. So, it is important to understand financial statements not by the words, but by the order in which the entries are made. If you understand the order, then no matter what term an accountant may use for that entry, you will know what it is.

The balance sheet is often referred to as a picture, or snapshot, of the company's financial position at a point in time. If the company's financial position were frozen on that day, this is what its finances would look like. The income statement, by similar analogy, is referred to as a motion picture of the company's financial position over a period of time. You can gain a great deal of insight about a company if you understand the meaning and interrelationship of the entries on these two statements.

Financial statements are filed with the SEC as of the end of each quarter of the company's fiscal year, and the quarterly reports will be combined into an annual report. The quarterly reports, 10Qs, and annual reports, 10Ks, must be filed electronically with the SEC through a system called EDGAR, Electronic Data Gathering, Analysis, and Retrieval. Generally 10Qs must be filed within six weeks of the end of quarter, and 10Ks within eight weeks.

The **balance sheet** summarizes the current totals of the company's assets, liabilities, and equity. The balance sheet formula is assets equals liabilities plus equity (assets = liabilities + equity). This is simply another way of stating assets minus liabilities equal equity (assets − liabilities = equity), which probably looks more familiar and is a more logical way of expressing the same mathematical relationship. It is analogous to the way equity is calculated in margin accounts.

UNIQUE INC.

CONSOLIDATED BALANCE SHEET
(In thousands, except per share amount)

Assets:			Liabilities:		
Current Assets:			Current Liabilities		$ 1,585
Cash on hand		$ 9,782			
Marketable securities		64			
Accounts receivable		2,320	Long-term liabilities		4,877
		12,166			6,462
Fixed Assets:					
Property,			Shareholders' Equity:		
Plant & Equipment		21,863	Preferred Equity		21
Other Assets:			Common Equity		
Intangible		97	(11,740,000 shares)		5,870
Goodwill		71	Retained Earnings		21,844
		168			27,735
Total:		$ 34,197	Total:		$34,197

A balance sheet is called such because the total assets ($34,197) will be equal to, or balance with, the total liabilities and equity ($34,197). The traditional way of organizing a balance sheet is to put the assets on the left-hand side of the page and the liabilities and equity on the right-hand side. However, today you are more likely to see balance sheets organized with the assets, liabilities, and equity presented vertically on one page.

Regardless of how it is organized, entries on a balance sheet are still described as either left-hand entries for assets or right-hand entries for liabilities and equity. For example, if a company sells some capital assets and pays off debt with the proceeds, that might be described as moving a left-hand entry to a right-hand one.

The sum of the liabilities and equity of a company make up its **total capitalization**. Companies can either borrow capital, by issuing bonds or taking out loans (liabilities), or they can sell more shares of stock in the company (equity). You can quickly see by looking at the right-hand side of the balance sheet how the company has chosen to finance its operations. Generally speaking, the less debt the company has, the more conservative the financial structure. The following illustration is an example of how a typical balance sheet might be structured. It represents a snapshot of Unique Inc.'s current financial position.

Current assets are those assets that can be quickly and easily turned into cash, such as bank accounts, marketable securities, and accounts receivable. **Fixed assets** would include property, plant, and equipment, or other similar assets that are not readily liquid. In fact, most companies use the phrase Property, Plant, and Equipment instead of Fixed Assets.

Other Assets would usually include illiquid investments, intangible assets, such as the value of patents or trademarks, and goodwill. **Goodwill** is the accounting term for the amount of money a company paid for assets it acquired through a merger or acquisition that exceeded the appraised value of those assets. In other words, when one company acquires another and the value of the company being acquired is smaller than what the acquiring company paid for it, that excess is considered goodwill. This is contrary to the popular belief that goodwill represents that magic number that allows accountants to balance the balance sheet, the number that can make the total of the assets add up to the total of the liabilities and equity.

Current liabilities are those debt obligations that are due within the upcoming fiscal year, which begins the day after the annual balance sheet ends. **Long-term liabilities** are those debt obligations that will come due in more than one year. Also included in the liabilities section of the balance sheet will be any other debt that the company must fund, such as deferred income taxes.

Preferred stock (sometimes called preference stock) is carried on the balance sheet as equity. But as explained in the previous chapter, it is more like a bond than a stock. From the investor's point of view, it is a fixed-income investment. Companies issue preferred stock with a fixed dividend payment. It differs from a bond, however, in that it does not have a maturity date, and it is not a loan from the investor.

Preferred stock is considered equity, because the company is not contractually obligated to pay the dividend as they are bond interest. The Board of Directors must vote on and declare the preferred dividend as they do the dividend for common stock. However, the dividend rate is fixed by the terms of the preferred issue, and the company cannot pay common stock dividends in most cases until they have paid all preferred stock dividends, including those that have been omitted in the past. This would be called a **cumulative preferred** feature. If the preferred is identified as noncumulative, it does not have this feature.

Preferred stock does not usually have voting rights as common stock does. It is rated by the rating agencies like bonds. However, it usually carries a lower rating than a bond with equivalent debt coverage because preferred stock has no maturity date. It may, however, have a callable date. It may also have a convertible feature, where it can be exchanged under certain circumstances for common stock. Thus, because it has similar features to both equities and debt, it is often referred to as a hybrid security.

Common stock is carried on the balance sheet at **par value**, PV. This is simply an assigned amount given to a share of stock for the purpose of determining the equity value for the stock on the balance sheet. For example, if the common stock has a par value of $1 and the company has 10 million shares outstanding, then the common stock will show a value on the balance sheet of $10 million.

But consider that the par value of the stock is $0.50, as it is in the example for Unique Inc. The shareholders' equity on the balance sheet will show the 11,740,000 shares of common stock outstanding at a value of $5,870,000. It is important to note that par value has no relationship to market value and in no way represents the market value of the shares. Most accountants now record the equity value of shares as *no par*, which allows the company to change whatever par value it is using on the balance sheet relatively easily.

Retained Earnings is the running total of previous quarters when the company had net income after paying its fixed-income obligations and dividend requirements. Additions to the retained earnings will come from the bottom line of the company's Income Statement.

The **Income Statement** represents the total revenues and expenses of a company's business over a period of time. If it is a quarterly statement, it would be the total revenues for that quarter, and if it is an annual statement, for the year. The following illustration is an example of the organization of an income statement.

UNIQUE INC.

CONSOLIDATED INCOME STATEMENT
(In thousands, except per share amount)

Net Revenues (Sales)	$ 19,985
Cost of Sales	9,436
Gross Profit	10,549
Administration & Operating Expense	1,722
Operating Income (Earnings Before Interest, Taxes, Depreciation & Amortization, EBITDA)	8,827
Interest Expense	23
Earnings Before Taxes (EBT)	8,804
Taxes	478
Net Income (Earnings)	$ 8,326
Earnings per Share (EPS)	$ 1.41

The income statement is organized from top to bottom according to the order of priority by which the company's financial obligations are paid. So, the top item on the income statement is Total Revenues, or Sales, over that period. You will usually see that listed as Net Revenues, but "Net" does not mean after expenses in this instance. The word Net here means the total of all subsidiary businesses of that company.

The first item deducted from the total revenues is the **Cost of Sales**, sometimes referred to as the cost of goods sold. This would primarily include the cost of the raw materials used to produce the finished product and the cost of labor to produce the product. The **Gross Profit** is equal to the total revenues minus the cost of sales.

The items deducted from the gross profit would primarily be the selling and administrative expenses, research and development expenses, and so on. The gross profit minus those expenses equals the **Operating Income**, sometimes called **EBITDA**, an acronym for *earnings before interest, taxes, depreciation, and amortization.*

As EBITDA implies, the next items to be deducted from the operating income will be interest and taxes. The interest will be the total amount of interest owed on bonds or other debt obligations over that period of time. Taxes are owed on whatever the company has left after that. Depreciation and amortization are accounting terms for writing down the cost of an expensive item over a period of time. For example, the cost of a computer may be depreciated over five years.

The last line is **earnings per share**, **EPS**. This is the net earnings divided by the number of shares outstanding. The number of shares will usually be found in the common stock entry of shareholders' equity on the balance sheet. For example, Unique Inc. had 11,740,000 shares outstanding, and it earned $4,764,000 for that quarter. So, EPS was $0.41 ($4,764/11,740 = $0.41, rounded).

Some investors obsess on this bottom line number, EPS, and their analysis usually stops there. But there is much more in financial statements than the bottom line. Certainly a company's earnings per share is important to analysts trying to forecast the stock price. Also, stock prices can become very volatile as its earnings release date approaches. This is because traders tend to buy or sell shares in anticipation of how the company's earnings report will compare with analysts' published expectations.

The future stock price targets for companies are usually calculated as a function of the earnings forecasts. Corporate earnings form the basis for all **fundamental analysis**, which will be discussed in the next chapter.

An understanding of the **cash flow statement**, or statement of cash flows, can reveal much about the sources of the company's earnings. It begins with the net income from operating activities. This could be different from the income on the Income Statement because it might include income from sources other than the company's operations. The next entries will show the inflow and outflow of money that was included in the determination of that net income. The following illustration is the cash flow statement for Unique Inc.

UNIQUE INC.
CONSOLIDATED STATEMENT OF CASH FLOWS
(In thousands, except per share amount)

Operating Activities:	
Income	$4,764
Accounting Adjustments	(395)
Depreciation and amortization	1,204
Deferred income taxes	1,370
Net cash from operating activities	6,943
Investing Activities:	
Purchase of Property	($ 757)
Sale of securities	548
Net cash from investing activities	($209)
Financing Activities:	
Payment on debt	($435)
Proceeds from common stock	215
Net cash from financing activities	($220)
Cash and equivalents at beginning of year	$1,794
Cash and cash equivalents at end of year	$6,514

Typical accounting adjustments might include depreciation, amortization, or changes in accounting principles. If you are an individual investor with no accounting background, you don't have to be too concerned about how these numbers are determined.

However, the cash flow statement can help you determine the **quality of earnings**. If you observe that a company is losing money from its operating activities, its core businesses, but making up for those losses from its investing activities, you should have a legitimate concern over company's future earnings predictability. The most important information to an individual investor on the cash flow statement is that the company's earnings come primarily from is operating activities.

The statement of cash flows is organized to show the positive and negative movement of funds from (1) operating activities, (2) investing activities, and (3) financing activities. It reveals the net amount of cash *provided by* or *used by* these different segments of the company. The operating activities section of this statement reveals the net difference between the income from sale for the company's products or services plus investment income, and the cost of those sales, such as employees' wages, payments to suppliers, taxes, and so on.

The investing activities section will reveal information on the capital gains or losses on investments or on purchases and sales of assets related to the company's business. The financing activities section will include information on cash flows from the company's debt or equity. These items will not necessarily be as predictable from quarter to quarter as the company's operating activities are.

A quick review of this statement can reveal a wealth of information about how a company uses and creates cash flow. You may be surprised to discover that even though a company may have little or no net income, it may still have hundreds of millions of dollars of cash flow. If some of the negative items are one-time expenses, or short-term in nature, this could indicate the possibility of dramatic earning growth in the future. Also, analysts use the cash flow statement to measure the length of time that outgoing cash flow used for future business development can be turned into incoming cash flow.

The resulting total of all cash flow activities is the net increase or decrease in cash and cash equivalents from the beginning of the fiscal year to the end. So, you can easily see whether the net cash flow is increasing or decreasing from previous years. You are likely to observe that companies in industries showing generally declining cash flows from one year to the next will sell at much lower market prices relative to their earnings (PE ratios will be discussed next) than companies showing increasing cash flows.

The entries made on the statement of cash flows will depend on the various activities in which the company engaged. There may be many entries or only a few. The entries are itemized as to the specific activity. They are not standardized like the entries on a balance sheet or an income statement. The entries on the statement of cash flows for Unique Inc. are typical examples of what you might see on statements for other companies in the same industry.

In addition to the three financial statements already mentioned, annual reports will also include a statement of shareholders' equity. This is simply an itemization of the entries included in the equity portion of the balance sheet. It is designed to give readers a clear presentation of the changes in shareholders' equity from year to year. The statement, like that for cash flow, reveals trends. Hopefully, the equity will be trending upward, since this represents the real net worth of the company.

Once you have an understanding of the types of financial statements that companies issue, you can glean a wealth of information if you know what to look for. By simply picking out a few numbers from the balance sheet and income statement, you can quickly compute a few ratios that will help you decide whether or not this might be a good investment.

What Can You Learn from Financial Statements?

If you are intimidated by the language of the stock market, you will probably be horrified by financial statements. Most individual investors, even when they receive quarterly and annual reports from a company they own, do not bother to look at the balance sheet and income statement. Many people have math anxiety. If you are one of them, it's okay. You don't have to make any mathematical computations from the financial statements if you don't want.

All of the important information on financial statements has already been computed for you by other sources and is readily available from many online services. Research reports from major financial publishers such as Dow Jones, Standard & Poor's, Morningstar, Moody's, or Value Line are available online or in print. The amount of research information available for the stock market has mushroomed in recent years, and continues to do so.

The old-fashioned way was to check out your local library for these sources, and there may be a good reason to continue to renew your library card. Most libraries carry stock market research reports with proprietary information you would have to pay for online. The same reports you can read for free at the library could cost hundreds, or thousands, of dollars from the source. In an age of high tech instant access to everything, people often overlook low tech solutions.

You should realize that, whether you are mathematically challenged or not, you can make a few simple computations from the financial statements. It is not nearly as complicated as most people think, and your results, assuming they correct, are going to be the same as if a professional analyst had made them. In other words, there is nothing mystical about financial statements, and it is not true that only accountants can understand them. Even if you do not make the calculations yourself, you need to understand what they mean.

There are hundreds of financial ratios that could be calculated, but you are going to learn how to compute only six of them here. These are the ones that will be the most helpful in understanding how the company is capitalized and how profitable it is. The three ratios that will help you understand how a company has structured its finances are the debt-to asset ratio, book value, and current ratio. The three ratios that will help you understand how well the company's business is doing are the operating profit margin, net profit margin, and the return-on-equity ratio. Additionally, the price earnings ratio (PE) will be explained.

The **debt-to-asset ratio** is simply the company's total liabilities, both current and long-term, divided by the total assets. The debt-to-asset ratio will let you know at a glance what percentage of the company's total capitalization is funded by debt. The more debt the company has, the greater the financial risk associated with it. The company must pay interest on that debt, whether or not it has any income. So, generally speaking, the lower the debt-to-asset ratio the more conservative the financial structure of the company.

However, there are some notable exceptions to this rule. Most electric or natural gas utility companies finance their operations with much more debt than equity. Although this would be viewed as risky for most other industries, it is not considered so for utilities. Utilities businesses are regulated by state commissions. They set the rates that utility companies can charge customers based on a preset profit margin. However, keep in mind utility companies can also own non-utilities businesses. Profits and losses from those businesses are not regulated and can sharply affect earnings.

In other words, a high debt-to-asset ratio for utility companies is not usually a cause for concern. But if the utility company has transformed itself into a diversified holding company with many non-regulated businesses, a high debt-to-asset ratio might be problematic. A utility company's earnings could be less predictable than the interest it owes on its debt. Investing in unregulated businesses can represent high financial risk in an industry group that has historically been considered low risk.

Look at the balance sheet for Unique Inc. In order to compute the debt-to-asset ratio for this company, you will have to divide the total of the current liabilities and long-term liabilities by the total assets. So, that would be $6,462, total debt, divided by the total shareholders' assets, $34,197. The debt-to-asset ratio is about 18.9% (6,462/34,197 = 0.189). It may be written as a ratio, 6.5:34.2; as a fraction, 6.5/34.2; as a decimal 0.189; or as 18.9 percent.

Another way of looking at the debt-to-asset ratio is to say the debt represents approximately 19% of the assets. So you can assume the company's equity represents about 81% of the assets. Remember that total assets equal total liabilities plus equity.

If a company has no debt, its shareholders' equity will equal its total assets. That might sound like a very conservative investment to some, since the company would have no debt obligations that were senior to the shareholders' equity. However, most companies that have no debt are relatively new startup companies that have recently issued an IPO or are funded with venture capital from risk-oriented investors. They have not been in business long enough to have a need to borrow money through bond offerings or bank loans. Such companies are not usually considered low risk.

There is no magic number for a conservative debt-to-asset ratio. Stock analysts make a judgment call on whether they feel a company with high debt is risking their shareholders' equity. If the figure is greater than 50 percent, then the company has financed its operations with more debt than equity. That is not usually something that shareholders like to see. But you can compare one company's debt-to-asset ratio with other companies in the same industry group and decide which one is the most conservatively financed or least leveraged with debt.

Book value is the shareholders' equity minus intangible assets divided by the number of shares outstanding. Taking out the value of intangible assets is done because those assets are not marketable. The theoretical conclusion drawn from the calculation of book value is that if the company went bankrupt and all of its assets had to be liquidated and all of its liabilities paid off, this is what would be left to the shareholders on a per share basis. Obviously, intangible assets could not be sold.

Book value represents the downside risk to an investor, but it has only theoretical relevance. It is certainly not the value that would likely be realized in the event of the liquidation of a company's assets due to bankruptcy. If a company did go bankrupt, its assets would probably not be sold at the amounts they are being carried on its books. In most cases, however, if the company has a book value close to its current market value, there is little downside risk to the investor.

To compute the book value for Unique Inc. you would divide the total shareholders' equity ($27,735,000) minus the intangible assets ($168,000) and divide that result ($27,567,000) by the number of shares outstanding (11,740,000). This equals about $2.35 (27,735 − 168/11,740 = 2.35). The last three zeros, representing hundreds, were insignificant to the mathematical result.

Assuming Unique Inc. is a growth company, book value wouldn't be too important. The primary reason for investing in a growth stock is future earnings. However, this low book value compared to the current market price does emphasize the high risk of growth companies. If the company went bankrupt and its assets were liquidated, there wouldn't be much left for the shareholders.

The **current ratio** is simply the total current assets divided by the total current liabilities. For Unique Inc. this would be $12,166,000 divided by $1,585,000, which equals 7.67. The only significance of the current ratio is that it tells you whether or not the company has enough liquid assets to pay its liabilities for the upcoming year. Unique Inc. shouldn't have any trouble paying its current liabilities; their current liabilities are covered by their current assets by a factor of nearly eight. With the cash and investments they can easily sell they can cover their liabilities coming due within the next fiscal year almost eight times over.

You'll seldom find a company report on its balance sheet that it will not have enough current assets to cover current debts. However, if you do, that could be a glaring sign of impending trouble. Usually that kind of company makes news.

So far Unique Inc. looks financially healthy. It has conservative capitalization—low debt and plenty of current assets to cover immediate debt obligations. Even though the book value may be low when compared with larger companies, it probably isn't a major concern if the company's earnings are growing. Companies usually build up more book value over years of operation, and Unique Inc. appears to be a relatively young company.

Next, take a look at how the company is doing. Is this a profitable company? To answer this question you will mainly need to look at ratios from the income statement.

The **net profit margin**, **NPM**, is computed by dividing the net profit by the net (or total) sales, that is, the bottom of the income statement divided by the top of it. For this period, Unique Inc. kept $8,326,000 after paying all of its obligations out of the $19,985,000 in total sales. So, to calculate the NPM for Unique Inc. divide $8,326 by $19,985 (zeros were dropped). The result equals about 0.417, or 41.7%. In other words, for every $1.00 in sales that Unique Inc. reported, it kept nearly $0.42. This is a very high net profit margin for any company in any industry. Large cap stocks often have a net profit margin below 10%, and 12% is considered great.

You could also compute the **operating profit margin**, **OPM**, by dividing the EBITDA amount by the net sales. The result would reveal what percentage of the company's revenues it retained after paying its major expenses—cost of sales and administrative and operating expenses. This would represent the company's profit margin before it paid interest on its debt and taxes. For Unique Inc. the operating profit was $8,827. So, that number divided by its total revenue of $19,985 yields 44.2 percent ($19,985/$8,827 = 0.442). It cost the company about $0.56 in overhead for every $1 in sales ($1 - $0.44 = $0.56).

Analysts like to compare NPM to OPM to determine whether the company would be characterized as labor intensive or capital intensive. A labor-intensive business is one whose largest expense is employee wages. A capital-intensive business usually finances its business primarily with more debt—bonds or bank loans. Generally speaking, as sales increase, the net profit margin of a capital-intensive company will increase faster than a labor-intensive one. This is the case because, once the fixed expenses are met, that is, the interest on the debt is covered, almost everything after that is profit. For example, the automobile industry is labor intensive, but the telecommunications industry, with its large commitment to infrastructure expenses to expand its business, is capital intensive.

A labor-intensive business will usually have to hire more employees or work current employees longer hours to produce more goods to sell. Thus, their expenses go up in a corresponding relationship to their sales. A company in this type of business will be able to increase its profit margin, but at a less predictable rate.

High-tech companies are often treated as if they were in a category of their own, neither labor-intensive nor capital-intensive. Because they may produce a new and innovative product that has little or no competition in the marketplace, their profit margins can run very high. However, you never know when new and cutting edge will become old and obsolete. There is high risk in high-tech.

The next ratio to consider is probably the most important one, the **return-on-equity ratio, ROE**. It is first ratio presented that is computed with numbers taken from two different financial statements. To compute ROE divide the net income from the income statement by the total shareholders' equity from the balance sheet.

For Unique Inc. this would be $8,326 divided by $27,735, for a whopping 0.30, or 30%. The significance of the return on equity is that it allows you to compare the percentage return that the company is earning with shareholders' equity. It can be compared to rates on other alternative investments. The equity represents the actual total cash value of the amount of money the shareholders have in the company. They could theoretically take that money out and invest it in something else. However, they would be hard pressed to find an alternative investment that could do that well.

The return on equity ratio is often compared to the **return-on-assets ratio, ROA**. This ratio is computed by dividing the net income by the total assets. Note that ROA will always be a smaller number than ROE, unless the company has no liabilities. In that case, the return on assets will be the same as the return on equity, for assets will equal equity. For Unique Inc. the ROA will be $8,326, total net income (earnings), divided by $34,197, total assets. The result is 0.243, or 24.3%. As you might expect, since Unique Inc.'s ROE is above average, its ROA will be also.

Remember that U.S. Treasury bonds were described as the riskless money rate, being the benchmark for other interest rates. So, if T-bonds are yielding 5 percent, an investment that is higher up on the risk-reward scale should be yielding more. Another way of looking at this would be if a company's return on equity is below 5 percent, then the shareholders could hypothetically make more money if this company were dead than alive.

If a company was only making a four percent return on equity, theoretically the shareholders would be better off if their company liquidated all its assets. It could then pay off all its liabilities and invest the shareholders' equity in T-bonds paying five percent, earning one percent more than they currently did in their own business. Shareholders would be getting a higher return on their investment and would be assuming less risk.

The last ratio was first mentioned in Chapter 1—the **price earnings ratio**, or **PE**. It is computed by dividing the current market price of the stock by the annual earnings per share. As reported by most stock quote websites, it is usually updated to the most recent quarterly earnings report, using the earnings per share (EPS) for the last four reported quarters. However, sometimes the PE is reported based on the earnings for the last fiscal year. So, pay attention to how the computation is made.

The market price of the stock doesn't appear on the financial statements. It changes constantly, so the PE ratio is also changing constantly. However, most websites do not update that number on an intraday basis. The usual method is to use the previous day's closing price.

Assuming the closing price of Unique Inc. is $22, then the computation of the PE ratio would be $22 divided by $1.41, which equals 15.6 (22/1.41 = 15.6). That PE ratio could be compared to those of other companies in the same industry group to determine if Unique Inc. is selling at a relatively high or low relative to the earnings of similar companies in the same business. It could also be compared to the PE ratio of the S&P 500 Index to see how it is trading compared to the overall market.

The PE ratio is also referred to as the **market multiple**, for it is the number that, if multiplied by the earnings per share (EPS), would yield the current market price of the stock. In other words, Unique Inc. is selling at about 15.6 times EPS. The $22 share price is approximately 15.6 times its current earnings of $1.41 (15.6× $1.41=$22). The significance of the PE ratio may be overemphasized because of its high profile with daily stock quotes.

Generally speaking, a low PE, when compared to other comparable companies in the same industry, would mean that the stock is selling at a relatively low price relative to its earnings. The PE ratio will fall into different ranges for different industry groups. For instance, high-tech companies with rapid earnings growth potential usually sell at much higher PEs than low-tech or mature companies with limited growth potential.

From an investor's point of view, the PE ratio computed for past earnings is not as important as what it will be in a year or so. Investors are more concerned about what the PE will be in the future, when an investor may want to sell the stock. If a company's earnings are forecast to grow at a rate of about 25% per year, then the current PE ratio would be about 25% lower next year if the stock's price remained the same. So, it may be a bargain at this price. But if the company's earnings decline 25% next year, the stock may be currently overpriced. A low current PE does not guarantee the stock is a bargain.

Some companies that maintain a high popularity with the investing public consistently sell at higher than average multiples. If you waited for them to come down before you invested, you may end up never buying the stock. Suffice it to say, in order for the PE to be useful to an investor, much more information is required than the number itself.

Many financial websites report an estimated **future PE**, sometimes called a forward PE. Instead of using the earnings for the previous year, they use the consensus forecast for next year's earnings from the analysts who follow the stock. This consensus is usually an arithmetic mean of all the published forecasts. Of course, the company's actual earnings may or may not match the estimates, but the future PE can give investors a better way of evaluating the stock's potential.

With that being said, many times investors are quite surprised when a company reports higher earnings, and instead of causing the stock to rally, they see the share price drop. Normally one would expect that when a company reports higher earnings, it indicates it is becoming more profitable, or expanding its business, or both. Such good news usually causes the stock to appreciate in price. However, sometimes positive earnings don't translate into a positive reaction from investors. This could be because some analysts were expecting even higher earnings, or it could be because the quality of the earning was poor. There is often more art than science behind financial analysis.

Quality of earnings is a term analysts used to describe the breakdown of the sources of that income. If most of the growth of the income came from an industry sector that is viewed as being in decline, this would not be a good sign. Analysts are always looking at future growth, not at the current situation.

So, if a growth stock came in with a good earnings report, but the source of those earnings was primarily due to sales of a product with outdated technology, most investors would not be very impressed. A good investor is always looking around the corner. The current situation for a company is not as important as its outlook for the future.

Why Are Financial Ratios Important?

None of the ratios you just learned about is very important in and of itself. The ratios become significant only when they are compared with the ratios of other similar companies in the same industry. If Unique Inc. is a media publishing company, then you could compare its ratios with other publishers to see which ones operated the most efficiently, had the highest profit margins, and gave shareholders the best return on equity. It would be meaningless to compare financial statements of Unique Inc. with those of companies in other unrelated industries.

Most financial statements will include last year's result side by side with the current year. This way you can easily see how the company has improved, or weakened, year over year (yoy). Many financial information services even include the last three years, or more. Thus you can interpolate a pattern of growth or shrinkage. Of course, the same pattern may not continue for the next few years. However, past financial statements give you a basis for making future projections.

This process of comparing side-by-side numbers from financial statements is called horizontal analysis, also referred to as trend analysis. An investor can compute the percentage change in each of a company's entries on its financial statements by subtracting the previous year's entry from the current year, and then dividing by the previous year. That will reveal the percentage gain or loss from one year to the next for that entry. Since this process can be done for every item on the financial statements, you can detect not only trends in sales and earnings, but also trends in such items as operating expenses or taxes.

Vertical analysis, on the other hand, involves computing the percentage difference of each entry on the financial statements for the same year. On the income statement, for example, you would consider the total sales and revenues for one year as 100 percent. Then, by subtracting the cost of sales and dividing by the total revenues, you can compute of the percent of total revenue the cost of sales represents. None of these computations for either horizontal or vertical analysis involves very complex mathematical calculations. However, the insight an investor will gain by taking a little time to do them can be very revealing.

You will find the financial statements online or in the back of the company's annual report. The first part of the annual report will be the message to the shareholders from the chairman of the board or the CEO (Chief Executive Officer) of the company. This will usually be followed by a description of the company's products or business. The last part will be the financial statements and footnotes. The **footnotes** are an integral part of the statements themselves. They can clarify the reasons for changes in the financial data. You should pay particularly close attention to footnotes regarding any unusual or irregular entries on the statements, such as an expense that did not occur in the previous year's report.

Professional analysts will use the financial ratios they compute as the primary basis for their recommendation. Usually, analysts will follow most, or all, of the companies in the same industry. This is why they can compare the ratios of several companies in the same report and explain why they prefer one company over another.

You can also compare the financial ratios of various companies within the same industry. If you were considering investing in Unique Inc., you could also compute similar financial ratios for other media publishing companies: News Corp., McGraw-Hill, Moody's, Dun & Bradstreet, and others. The most significant ratios are the profit margins, identifying which company is the most efficiently managed. Also compare the return-on-equity (ROE) ratio to see which company is the most profitable.

There has never been a time when so much information has been available to individual investors. In fact, whether through computer databases or other publicly available reports, individual investors today have more information at their fingertips than did the wealthiest institutional investors a couple decades ago; and the amount of information continues to grow.

You don't need to compute the financial ratios yourself. But if you understand how the computations are determined, then you will know what they mean. Being able to comprehend financial information will make you feel more comfortable with your investment decisions. You don't need to feel intimidated by financial statements.

The information presented here is not meant to be all-inclusive. There are many more ratios and information you can get from financial statements not included here. However, you should realize you do not have to be an accountant to compute a few ratios and draw some logical conclusions from your own analysis. With a few clicks of a calculator you can evaluate the degree of risk a company has assumed by the way it has structured its capitalization. You can draw conclusions about its financial stability, analyze its profitability, and so on. You are able to make a better informed decision and feel more at ease about your decisions. The intent of this brief description on financial statements is not intended to turn you into an accountant, but simply to help you sleep at night.

This chapter is meant to demythologize financial statements and give you some insight into what can be gained from a few simple calculations. You will be a better investor if you understand how companies report their finances. If you are inspired to go further, take some accounting classes or read some other books on the subject. There is much more information and many more ratios you can use. Next we'll go beyond the ratios and look at some of the macro factors of fundamental analysis.

140 ◇ Financial Statements

The bottom line to being a good investor is you must understand how to read financial statements.

Chapter 6

What Is Fundamental Analysis?

There are two schools of thought regarding securities analysis: fundamental and technical. The basis of fundamental analysis is that the most important consideration for selecting an investment is future earnings. However, to forecast a particular company's earnings, you must also take into account the outlook for the economy as a whole and the outlook for the industry group in which that company competes.

Most fundamental analysts would say that to select a good investment you should first start with macroeconomic analysis. Begin by studying the indicators for overall economic trends and then narrow down your study to the outlook for a particular industry group. Finally, you should narrow down that study to selecting the best company or companies within that group. That would involve analyzing the microeconomic factors of those companies, the microeconomic factors of those companies, as presented in the last chapter. This is referred to as a **top-down** approach—from macro analysis to micro analysis.

There are also fundamental analysts who use a **bottom-up** approach. This simply means they forego the macro analysis and begin by looking for individual companies, regardless of economic indicators or industry selection. Bottom-up analysts are looking for unique factors that might distinguish a company, either positively or negatively. You might hear these companies referred to as story stocks, implying there is something going on with the company that causes the stock to move regardless of how the economy does.

Technical analysis is a completely different approach from fundamental analysis. Technical techniques employ methods for selecting investments primarily on supply and demand factors. It relies heavily on interpreting chart patterns showing the past performance of the stock's price. These methods of analysis will be discussed in greater detail in the next chapter.

142 ◊ Fundamental Analysis

Most of the information presented so far regarding analyzing financial statements and studying economic cycles and industry trends are disciplines of fundamental analysis. By far the single most important factor in fundamental analysis is the direction of interest rates. If you want to be a good student of the stock market, you must first be a good student of interest rates. As is the case with bonds, there is a cause-and-effect inverse relationship between interest rates and stock prices. As interest rates rise, stock prices tend to fall. This is the case because rising interest rates will generally result in lowering corporate earnings forecasts.

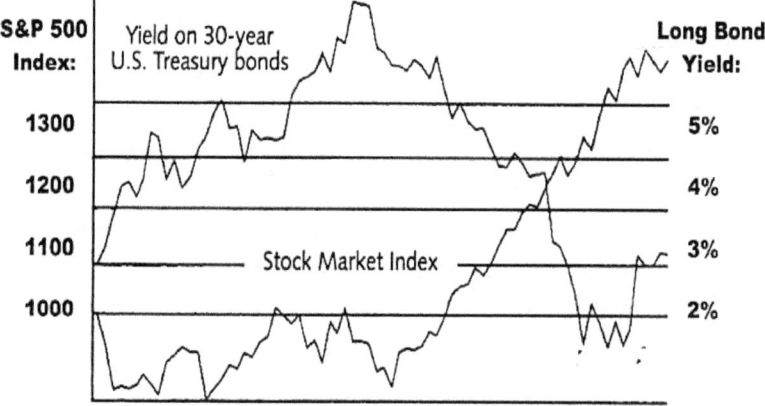

This illustration shows the S&P 500 index versus the yield on the 30-year Treasury bond over the same period of time. It represents a five-year period when interest rates were particularly volatile. Note that as interest rates moved higher, the market generally moved lower; and when interest rates dropped, the stock market rallied. The two lines are not mirror images, but they generally correspond in an inverse relationship.

Remember from Chapter 4 that bond prices move in the opposite direction as interest rates. So, as interest rates rose, bond prices would have been falling, somewhat in correlation to stock prices. There are several fundamental reasons for the inverse relationship between stock prices and bond yields. A company's stock price generally moves in a proportional relationship to expected earnings. If the cost of doing business goes up because of higher interest rates, a company's earnings are negatively affected.

Most companies rely on funding their capitalization partly with bonds, and some of that debt could be tied to adjustable-rate bank loans. If that is the case, it is easy to see that when rates go up, the company's interest expense will go up. The more money the company has to pay on its debt, the less it will be able to retain on its bottom line. A company will have to increase its earnings at a rate equal to its increased interest expense just to maintain the same net income.

Even if a company does not have adjustable-rate loans, investors, always looking ahead, anticipate that when the company's bonds come due, they will have to be refinanced at a higher rate. So, you will likely see a reaction from investors even if there isn't a direct cause-and-effect relationship, as there would be with adjustable rate loans. Investors should be constantly anticipating where the market will likely go in the future.

Also, many investors, particularly institutions that follow a **balanced approach**, continuously rebalance their portfolio by transferring assets between debt and equity, based on projected returns. So, as interest rates are expected to move downward, these investors would likely sell bonds and buy equities. The opposite is also true. If interest rates have risen to a place where the next move will likely be lower, investors using this approach might sell stocks and buy bonds.

Most mutual fund portfolio managers offer a balanced fund that follows this type of strategy, but the influence of this investment approach goes well beyond institutions. They influence many other individual investors to follow suit. In other words, some investors who do not normally move their positions between stocks and bonds might be influenced to make changes in their portfolios based on what they believe institutional investors might do. In that regard, you might say this becomes a self-fulfilling prophecy.

It is much easier to anticipate interest rate changes or economic cycles than it is to accurately predict how one particular company will do. Although you have some valuable tools for drawing basic conclusions about the future earnings of a company, being able to do in-depth analysis to forecast earnings trends for a company is beyond the scope of this book. The more you know about a company's business, the better able you will be to anticipate events that will affect its earnings potential.

There are many sources of information available through local brokerage firms or local libraries for getting professional analysts' opinions and earnings forecasts. Standard & Poor's, Moody's, Morningstar, Argus Research, and Value Line, to name a few popular ones, might be available in most libraries. Also, those research companies, and many more, maintain websites offering some free information. However, proprietary research is usually only available on a subscription basis.

What Are Economic Cycles?

Fundamental analysis deals primarily with forecasting economic trends and cycles. An economic cycle is a period of either sustained inflation or recession. Inflation implies that the price of most goods and services is rising and the size of the total economic base expanding. So, you could say that if your total net worth is not expanding at the same rate, your percentage participation in the economy is shrinking.

This is a simplistic way of looking at inflation, but consider the total size of the economy as a pie, and your net worth is your slice of the pie. If the pie grows bigger, but your slice remains the same size, your piece of the pie has become a smaller percent of the whole. Unless your net worth grows as fast as the economy, you are losing buying power.

Economists say some inflation is an indication of a healthy economy. An economy grows because it is producing an increasing quantity of goods and services. This means more people are employed producing those goods and services. Exactly what represents a healthy rate of growth is a matter of debate among economists. It should grow at a faster rate than the population is growing. Usually, economists like to see wages and salaries growing at about the same rate as inflation.

The negative side of inflation is that because people are generally making more money, the cost of goods goes up correspondingly. When people have more money to spend, the prices of the items they want to buy go higher. This is due to supply and demand factors. So, the ideal economic environment is one of low unemployment and low inflation, a state that is usually difficult to maintain.

If a state of full employment is achieved, then prices of most consumer items are likely to rise sharply. Most economists define full employment as the level when nearly all qualified laborers are employed. However, when the unemployment level reaches about two percent, the anticipated scarcity of laborers tends to put pressure on increasing wages. Companies may then be forced to raise salaries, or labor costs, to attract enough qualified workers.

As wages rise, more of wage earners' salaries become *disposable income*, and this causes greater inflation. So, for practical purposed most investment analysts refer to **full employment** as the state achieved when any further increase in the employment level would be inflationary. Usually this is achieved at about the five percent unemployment level. When the economy reaches full employment, it is likely that the rate of growth of consumer prices will outpace the individual's ability to increase earnings. When the economy reaches a point where too many individuals no longer earn enough to be consumers of products at those price levels, then those prices will decline. This will begin a recessionary cycle.

Recession means that the size of the economic base is shrinking. Yes, this does mean that the economic pie is getting smaller. So, if you are one of the lucky ones whose earning power is going up during a recession, the relative size of your slice would be growing relatively larger. However, for most people, as the pie gets smaller, their slice gets smaller as well. During a recessionary cycle many people are unemployed due to the fact that fewer goods and services are being produced. Thus, for many individuals the fact that the pie is shrinking does not benefit them. They do not have a job and do not have disposable income to capitalize on lower prices.

Most economists define a recession as two consecutive quarters of declining gross domestic product. **Gross domestic product**, **GDP**, is the measure of the total output of all goods and services within a country. It will be explained in more detail in the next section. However, recent economic activity has caused many economists to question that traditional measure of a recession. The economy can feel recessionary if consumers are cautious about spending or worried about the future even though GDP is expanding.

The main weapon used to combat inflationary and recessionary cycles is interest rates. The Federal Reserve Board, the agency that regulates the banking industry, is responsible for initiating U.S. government domestic economic policy, and its primary tool for managing economic activity is the manipulation of interest rates.

Although the Fed only directly controls the policies of banks that are members (shareholders) of the Federal Reserve System, the influence of this board extends far beyond that. Nonmember banks, state chartered ones, are not directly under the authority of the Fed; but they still must comply with Fed bank guidelines. They can still be penalized for noncompliance.

The Federal Reserve Board's ability to control interest rates affects virtually all aspects of the U.S. economy. But its influence does not stop there, for it can also affect many of the economic policies of other countries around the world. It frequently mandates the central banks of other sovereign banks to set monetary policies meant to influence currency exchange rates. The world is becoming much smaller by being economically interdependent.

One of the most followed interest rates by market analysts is the **Fed funds rate**. It is the interest rate that banks, not just federally chartered ones, lend money to other banks. These loans are usually for the purpose of meeting deposit reserve requirements. Most banks are required to keep at least 10% of their customers' deposits on hand. So, if a bank makes loans one day that brings its cash on hand below the reserve requirement, it will need to borrow funds to be in compliance. Fed funds are called overnight loans and are usually due within 24 hours. It is important to note that the Fed funds rate is set by the lending bank, not directly by the Fed. The Federal Reserve Board only sets a target, or range, that they expect all other banks to follow.

Business reporters frequently inform their audience about the movements of the Fed funds rate because it affects all other interest rates. However, the Fed funds rate is itself a function of another rate set by the Fed, the **discount rate**. It is the interest rate the Federal Reserve Bank charges federally chartered member banks for loans.

The fact that the source of many Fed fund loans is money borrowed from the Federal Reserve Bank at the discount rate illustrates one of the means by which the Fed influences all bank lending policies, even nonmembers. The Federal Reserve Board can raise or lower the discount rate to indicate where they want them to set the target for the Fed funds rate and all other bank lending rates. This is their main tool for influencing economic activity. The Fed can attempt to slow inflation by raising the discount rate or stimulate economic growth by lowering it.

When the Fed raises the discount rate, it triggers a rise in most other bank rates. The prime rate, the broker loan rate, and personal consumer loans are all based on a certain premium to the discount rate. The **prime rate** is the rate at which banks lend to their best corporate customers. However, even though individuals may not be able to borrow at the prime rate, it is an important gauge for other business and consumer loans. The **broker loan rate** is what securities brokers can borrow from banks to secure funds that they relend for margin loans.

One of the important rates that the Fed does not directly control is mortgage interest. Those rates are usually competitively set by mortgage brokers based on supply and demand factors for real estate. However, since the collapse of the real estate market in 2008, many of the independent mortgage brokers were bought by commercial banks. So, the Fed now wields more influence over mortgages than they had previously.

Also, adjustable-rate mortgages (ARMs) may be benchmarked to a rate influenced by the Fed's monetary policies. ARMs may be indexed to T-bills, the discount rate, the 11th District (St. Louis Fed) Cost of Funds (COF), or one of several other options. But the most common index benchmark is LIBOR, the London Interbank Offered Rate.

Rising interest rates have the effect of slowing down the rate of growth of the economy. Higher rates mean that consumers will probably be less willing to purchase items that would normally be bought on credit. Big ticket items, such as houses and automobiles, are the most obvious consumer products that are usually purchased on credit. The volume of sales of such high priced items is obviously affected by higher financing costs.

However, inflation has the same effect on less costly items as well. During periods of high interest rates, people generally consume less—even items that are not bought on credit. The high rates of returns consumers can receive on their savings accounts make it more advantageous to invest rather than to consume. Conversely, low interest rates usually make spending more advantageous than investing.

During periods when interest rates are significantly higher than inflation, investors are more inclined to put their disposable income, the part not needed for necessities, into investments. This takes some money out of the consumption cycle, at least for a while.

The abbreviations used by the Federal Reserve Board for measuring money supply are M1, M2, and M3. **Money supply** is the total amount of cash and liquid investments in circulation. The three tiered level of reporting is organized from the most liquid to the least.

M1 is the total amount of coins and paper currency in circulation plus the amount of money in checking (demand deposit or DDA) accounts, liquid saving accounts, and travelers' checks. **M2** includes the total of M1 plus other saving deposits such as money market funds and certificates of deposit (CDs). It is the most watched measure. M3, the broadest measure of money supply, includes the total of M2 plus slightly less liquid accounts, such as jumbo CDs ($100,000 or more) and institutional money market funds.

If the Fed is more concerned about the looming possibility of recession, rather than inflation, the board of governors will likely lower the discount rate and the target for the Fed funds rate. When the other related interest rates are lowered following that reduction, it should have the effect of stimulating consumption. Savings accounts become less desirable because of the low rates available on bank deposits, and the interest expense on credit purchases should be lower.

If the Fed needs to slow the rate of inflation, they could raise the discount rate and Fed funds target. That then would hopefully cause investors to put more money into savings accounts, rather than spend it. Savers and investors could take advantage of the higher cash flow they could receive from bank savings accounts or higher yielding securities. Thus, raising rates should reduce consumption, as the cost of financing would increase.

The Federal Reserve Board is a very interesting organization. It was created by passage of the Federal Reserve Act in 1913. Prior to that, banks operated independently. Originally, the intent of Congress was to create a central bank that would be large enough to bail out banks in financial crises. Having a run on banks, where a large number of depositors attempt to withdrawal their money at the same time, was not uncommon during those tense economic times.

Although the Federal Reserve was created by an act of Congress, it is not a government agency. It is a private corporation owned by its member banks. Every federally chartered bank is required to purchase shares of stock in the Fed. State chartered banks may become members by meeting certain requirements. But even if they are not members, they must nevertheless conform to the monetary policies of the Fed.

The Federal Reserve Board is one of the most powerful and least public organizations in the world. No outside auditors have the authority to examine its financial statements, which gives rise to frequent criticism about full disclosure.

The Fed publishes a balance sheet, but it bears no resemblance to the ones you learned about in the previous chapter. It is a statement simply revealing how many government bonds it holds and how many it has issued to banks. There is more talk about the size of the Fed's balance sheet than about the balance between the central bank and its members. The size indicates how much fiat money the Fed currently has at its disposal.

The Chairman of the Federal Reserve Board is required to give testimony before the House Ways and Means Committee and the Senate Finance Committee twice a year to answer questions about the Fed's policies and actions. The Chairman's appearance before these committees is referred to as Humphrey-Hawkins Hearings. It was one of the mandates of the Full Employment and Balanced Growth Act.

The requirement of the Fed Chairman's testimony before Congress was meant to be a check and balance on its power. However, the hearings often turn into a dramatic demonstration of the economic illiteracy of many congressmen and reveal the Fed's unchecked authority to control monetary policy. The Fed has often asserted itself as an independent agency by taking such actions as coordinating bilateral monetary regulation with other countries. That authority was never granted to the Fed in its charter. Thus Fed critics frequently point out that the agency is hardly accountable to Congress.

The twelve members of Federal Reserve Board of governors is composed of seven permanent members, appointed to 14-year terms like the chairman. The terms of these appointees begins on two-year alternating cycles, so that the composition may change more frequently. The other five seats are filled by Presidents drawn from the 12 District Federal Reserve Banks, with New York being a permanent member. These seats are for five year terms. All of this minutia about the terms of FRB Board of Governors may seem of little interest to investors, but it does highlight the fact that the general public knows very little about who is running the economy.

Aside from influencing the levels of interest rates, the other main tool used by the Fed for controlling economic cycles is **open market operations**. The Board of Governors is referred to as the **Federal Open Market Committee (FOMC)**. It meets about every month and a half (approximately six weeks) to decide whether it wants to buy or sell securities to member banks on the open market.

If the Fed purchases securities, such as T-bills or government agency obligations, it will expand the money supply by pumping more funds into the banking system, increasing banks' excess reserves. This also reduces banks' need to borrow money at the Fed funds rate, so that rate will usually be lowered. If the Fed wants to tighten the money supply, it will sell securities to member banks in its open market operations. That will create a reduction of money in the banking system.

If a change of monetary policy is anticipated, the days prior to an upcoming FOMC meeting can be volatile ones for securities markets, especially bonds. Commodity traders in bond derivative contracts, or other speculators, attempt to position their holdings by second-guessing what the FOMC will do. Commodity futures are highly leveraged contracts, where a small movement in interest rates can produce a large gain or loss in derivative contracts. They will be discussed in greater detail in Chapter 9.

You should realize that these methods of manipulating the economy through cycles of inflation and recession are unending. The economy never comes to a point where everything stands still. It never reaches a state of stasis. The economy is a dynamic system that never stops evolving.

Every solution to one economic problem will inevitably create another problem. Low interest rates can fuel inflation, causing your slice of the economic pie to shrink. High interest rates can send the economy into a recessionary cycle, creating high unemployment. It is the job of the Federal Reserve Board to regulate those cycles and try to bring order to chaos.

There has never been a time in the history of the stock market where you could not find someone forecasting economic disaster. Because of the very nature of the economy, disaster is perpetually just around the corner. Every prophet yelling, "The end is near", can usually give a plausible rationale for that statement. There is never going to be an ultimate solution to all the problems of the economy. However, if you understand how the economy functions, you will be less likely to buy into the extremist doom and gloom philosophy.

What Is the Industrial Life Cycle?

In addition to inflation and recession cycles, another predictive tool for the sales of a new product that investors should understand is the **industrial life cycle**. It is a conceptual model for forecasting expected growth of a new product or industry. Although it is not related to inflation/ recession cycles, this seems like an appropriate time to interject it. The following illustration shows the three stages of a typical industrial life cycle. It represents the expected growth potential for a specific product, or the company that developed that product. That growth is not necessarily related to the economy or other macroeconomic factors. It is particularly important companies in industries where new products are constantly being patented, such as the biotechnology, energy alternatives, etc.

The industrial life cycle is separated into three stages. Each stage is meant to represent the growth potential of any new product. During the development stage, at the beginning of a new industry, a company; is likely to move up only moderately. During this phase, the company will be testing and verifying the marketability of its new product. There is always the possibility that the product may not be readily embraced by consumers. At this stage companies are likely to be funded by venture capital. Next, the company will enter into the marketing stage. As the new technology or product

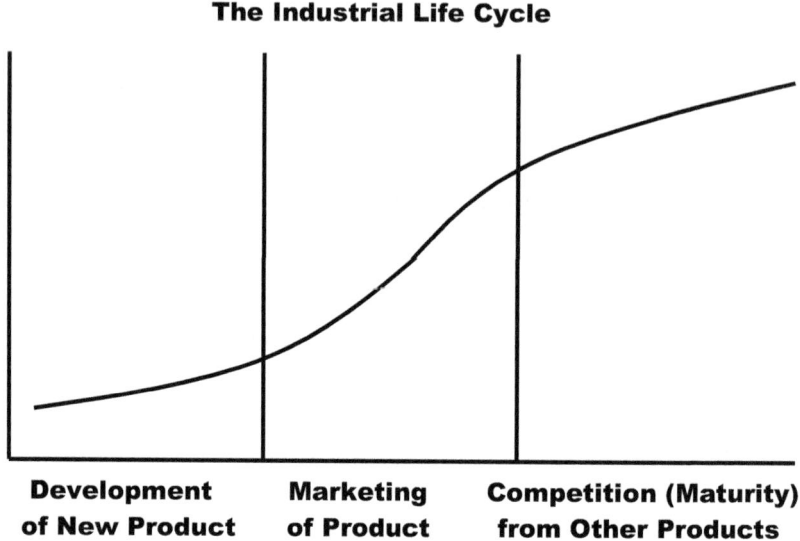

becomes more generally accepted, the company's business will expand very rapidly. A company will usually broaden its marketing approach to a wider range of consumers.

Investors who are looking for growth choose might choose to buy a company near the end of the development stage, before it enters the marketing stage. The industrial life cycle illustrates that the greatest potential for capital appreciation will be after that time. However, it is also the time of the greatest risk. No one knows at that point what the market for the product will become.

After the product has been in commercial production for a while, the company will enter the competition, or maturity, phase of the industrial life cycle. Competition in the marketplace will narrow the profit margins, and the company will enter a period of a slower rate of growth for profit. This does not necessarily mean that the company should be sold, only that it will now be more attractive to more conservative investors who want greater earnings predictability. Also, companies that have reached this stage are more likely to have a higher dividend payout ratio.

So, the cycle illustrates the movement from the most speculative stage to the most conservative stage. Note that the chart has no time frame. It does not predict the length of time it will take for a company to go through these various stages. Depending on the industry, it could represent decades, or for some fad products perhaps only a few months. The graph is meant to represent a guideline regarding general expectations for a company's growth, giving investors a frame of reference for how much risk they are assuming.

Predict what new and innovative products may be developed in the future is difficult. However, there are some industries where you can see at all three stages of the life cycle simultaneously. Consider the pharmaceutical industry. Biotechnology companies would represent the development stage—companies that do not yet have a product on the market, but are testing new discoveries. Examples of pharmaceuticals in the marketing stage might be those that have obtained FDA approval for their patented products. But that may only last for a few years from the time the product comes to market. Although a new pharmaceutical product is granted a 20-year patent, that begins from the time it is discovered and the patent application filed. Then it may take 8 to 12 years or so to complete the FDA required tests for approval to market the product. Finally, companies in the competition stage would include those that manufacture generic versions of products whose exclusive patent has expired.

Also, keep in mind that the industrial life cycle does not represent a chart of the company's stock price. It is only a generic model for the expected growth of the size of the company and its revenue. Sometimes the stock price may appreciate most significantly while the company is still in the development phase, as speculators attempt to capitalize on the anticipated earnings growth resulting from increasing revenues. It is simply meant to give investors a frame of reference on what to expect during each of these stages.

How Do You Measure Inflation?

It would appear that in order to qualify as a noteworthy measure of inflation, the indicator must be easily reducible to a three-letter acronym, such as GDP, CPI, PCE, PPI, LEI, or CRB. However, probably the most important inflation indicator doesn't follow that rule—M2, which was already discussed.

The broadest measure of inflation is GDP, which as you have already learned, stands for gross domestic product. The **gross domestic product** is the total output of goods and services produced within the geographic borders of a country. There are three different methods of determining GDP, all of which should theoretically total up to the same number. These three are output (production), income, or expenditure. As implied in the definition, the most straightforward method is output. The income and expenditure numbers should obviously be equal, as all the money you make must go somewhere.

GDP is the total of consumer spending, investing, government spending, and net exports (exports minus imports) over a period of time. It is often written $C + I + G + (Ex - Im) = GDP$. The GDP for the United Sates is reported quarterly and compiled by the Commerce Department. However, the report is revised twice after its first release, as more data is revised from earlier estimates. It is such a large number and the calculations of some of its components are so complex that it takes three months to compile and verify the accuracy of all the data.

For each quarterly report there will be a preliminary report, a revised report, and a final report. Each one will follow the other by about one month. Only the final report, which will not be released until three months after the end of the reporting quarter, will present complete GDP data. Even then its accuracy is sometimes questioned by scrutinizing analysts. Investors should be aware of the way the GDP numbers are released because even though the data represents a quarterly cycle, the release dates can affect the stock market monthly. The data is released at the end of the month, and the preliminary release is not going to be the same as the final.

Statistically more important than nominal GDP is **Real GDP**. It is computed by adjusting the GDP numbers to exclude price increases, and thus more accurately represent volume increases only. This adjustment is expressed in percentage form as the GDP Deflator. Real GDP is intended to measure the actual increased (or decreased) amount of output in the economy without the value being distorted by cost inflation. Whenever you read or hear reports on GDP, they are usually referring to Real GDP.

The amount of the adjustment to determine Real GDP is based on the previous year's prices and is called a "chain price index deflator". Such an adjustment shows the net percentage increase in spending and investing, without including increased prices due to the declining purchasing power of the dollar. The reason why more emphasis is placed on Real GDP is that it represents the actual expansion of the economy without the distortion of price increases.

There are as many different economic points of view as there are people with opinions. But most economists would say that for a developed economy, like that of the U.S., a healthy GDP growth rate would be in a range from about 2 to 4 percent. This would indicate moderate inflation levels. It indicates that the economy is expanding, but most wage earners still have the ability to increase their income at the same or a higher rate. By most standards, the ideal state is to have the GDP growing slightly slower than the rate of the more volatile consumer price index.

The **consumer price index, CPI**, is the measure of price changes in a market basket of goods and services purchased by most consumers. It measures inflation at the retail level, the level at which most people are concerned. The CPI tells you, in an ongoing basis, how much the cost of frequently purchased items is increasing.

The components of the CPI include all the products most consumers buy—food, gasoline, clothing, medical care, automobiles, housing, public transportation, reading materials, and so on. There are literally thousands of components that make up the index, which are weighted by price and frequency of purchase as determined by the Bureau of Labor Statistics, BLS.

The Bureau of Labor Statistics is a division of the U.S. Labor Department. It releases the details of changes in the CPI on a monthly basis, about two weeks after the end of the month for which it is reporting. The monthly figures will also be adjusted to show what the rate would be if it were compounded annually. Information on the consumer price index and many other important statistics can be found at www.bls.gov.

CPI statistics are divided into two reports: CPI-U and CPI-W. Usually when you read or hear references to the CPI in media reports, they are referring to the CPI-U. It measures the changes in spending patterns of urban consumers, covering about 87 percent of the population. The CPI-W is a subset of the broad urban consumer index, primarily representing clerical workers—about 32 percent of the population. More than 30,000 individuals and families provide information on their spending habits to compute the CPI.

Price comparisons from the previous month are made on items in more than 200 categories of goods and services. These categories are divided into eight major groups: food and beverages, housing (rent and other costs), apparel, transportation (including gasoline), medical care, recreation, education and communication, and other goods and services.

There is a common misconception that the CPI is the same as the cost-of-living index. They are close, but not exact. Although both indicators measure price fluctuations of a market basket of goods and services, the BLS makes several adjustments to the CPI to establish the cost-of-living index. It more heavily weighs certain components to represent a more accurate method of measuring the actual changing cost of maintaining the same standard-of-living for most consumers. It also includes adjustments for many intangible expenses, such as public safety, education, and health.

Many government programs, such as employee pensions, 457 plans, and social security benefits, use this index, referred to as the **cost-of-living adjustment, COLA**, as a basis for pegging payments to the rate of inflation. The index is much more influential than that, however, because many private organizations and corporations also follow the same percentage adjustments as COLA.

The two most volatile sectors of the consumer price index are energy and food. These are also the most heavily weighted components of the CPI. A separate computation called Core CPI, with food and energy prices excluded, will also be released simultaneously with the CPI. Core CPI is usually lower than actual CPI. The lower number is meant to make you feel better by showing you how low inflation would be if you did not eat or drive a car. In other words, it has very little relevance to the real world of consumers.

Personal consumption expenditures, PCE, is an index similar to the CPI computed by the Commerce Department, which you will recognize as the government agency responsible for computing GDP. The PCE is a chain weighted index, like the CPI. However, it is intended to more accurately reflect what average consumers are actually spending money on. For example, whereas the CPI includes housing prices, the PCE does not. Houses are not one of the items frequently purchased. The PCE generally runs a bit lower than CPI because of the weighting. Whereas the CPI measures the price changes in a fixed market basket of goods and services, the PCE adjusts the weighting from quarter to quarter based on consumer behavior.

The Federal Reserve Board frequently cites the PCE as the inflation indicator they follow, as opposed to the CPI. Thus, it should probably become an increasingly important indicator for investors. However, it does have its critics. The PCE does not have as long a history as the CPI does. It uses 2005 as the base year with a value of 100. Also it does not have a sufficiently large enough database of consumers for the survey to comply with the normal statistical probability of error.

Closely related to the CPI is the **producer price index**, **PPI**, which like the CPI, is reported by the Bureau of Labor Statistics. The PPI is the measure of the rate of inflation at the wholesale level, as opposed to the consumer price index which measures retail prices. The PPI reports on the changes in prices of raw materials and wholesale goods. It will be reported one or two days prior to the CPI. It is generally viewed as a forecaster of what the CPI is likely to be. Wholesale prices usually go up before retail prices do.

The **index of leading economic indicators**, **LEI**, is a private-sector compilation of economic statistics, designed to predict future economic activity. It is supposed to forecast what the economy will be doing in about a year or so. Like the CPI and PPI, it is reported monthly, but the data are released about two weeks after the end of the month for which the figures apply.

The LEI was first reported in 1938 when Henry Morgenthau asked the National Bureau of Economic Research, a private organization, to compile a statistical indicator to predict when the Great Depression would end. There are also indexes of lagging indicators and coincident indicators. Their function and significance is primarily useful to verify the accuracy of the leading indicators.

The list of leading economic indicators includes: (1) weekly hours worked in manufacturing, (2) new unemployment claims, (3) new orders for consumer good reported by the Institute for Supply Management (ISM), (4) manufacturers' backlogs of durable goods orders, (5) the consumer confidence index, (6) growth of M2, the measure of money supply, (7) the Standard & Poor's 500 Index, (8) building permits for new homes, (9) the performance of vendors' deliveries to factories, and (10) new plant and equipment orders. Individual components of the LEI have often been emphasized by the press or by financial strategists during certain economic periods.

Most of these indicators have an obvious reason for being there. There is a direct relationship between low unemployment, and increasing rate of new orders, a rising number of building permits, and so on, and an increase in the future level of the economy. The one component that gets the most attention, however, is the one that surprises most people as a leading economic indicator: the S&P 500 Index. Why would higher stock prices be an indicator of economic expansion in the future?

As you already know, stock prices go up when demand for them increases. However, the LEI model assumes most people do not invest in stocks with the intent of selling them next day, next week, or next month. Investors are not traders and speculators. They invest in stocks to sell them at some future date-perhaps in a year or so. Investors expect the stocks they are buying today to be worth more in the future. Thus, stock prices are an indication of investors' expectations for the future of the economy. Thus they are included.

The monthly indicators become statistically more important when they show a consecutive trend for at least three months. Because of the volatile nature of the indicators, a one-month report that departs dramatically from other recent reports is likely to be considered an aberration. However, if the trend is verified for one quarter, then analysts consider it a trend. If the leading economic indicators decline three months in a row, this indicates that the economy could be heading into a recession. A single month's statistical data is not as significant as a trend verified by several successive months.

Perhaps one of the most popular inflation indicators followed by institutional investors is the Commodity Research Bureau Index, or **Thomson Reuters/CRB index** of commodity prices. The Commodity Research Bureau is best known for its research an analysis on commodities market, but many professionals consider the CRB index one of the most important inflation forecasters. The Federal Reserve Board has often cited increasing commodity prices as a key indicator of future inflation, even when other economic indicators were not rising as fast. The index includes the price changes on the futures markets for oil, natural gas, live cattle, pork bellies (bacon), soybeans, cocoa, coffee, sugar, cotton, gold, platinum, silver, and many more.

Since inflation is so important in predicting future economic developments (particularly interest rates), many economists or financial analysts look for indicators that will predict inflation before the inflation indicators. Essentially, analysts are looking for indicators that will predict a rising CPI before it actually rises.

The media is constantly trying to second-guess which indicators are most important to the Federal Reserve Board. Trying to decipher the mind of its Chairman has become a national pastime. At one time or another, the media has focused on money supply, the employment cost index, the unemployment rate, the consumer confidence index, changes in consumer saving and spending, and so on.

Sooner or later every economic indicator, obscure or not, will have its 15 minutes of fame in the media spotlight. In recent years, more emphasis has been placed on the effects of geopolitical influences on the economy than on economic indicators. Whatever the economic indicator du jour, bear in mind that it may be more media hype than substance. Economics is more art than science.

Two other important economic reports that affect investors' perceptions of inflation or interest-rate movements are the U.S. trade deficit and foreign exchange trading, or forex. The fluctuating value of the U.S. dollar versus the currencies of those countries with whom the U.S. has a large trade deficit has a direct effect on retail prices. The U.S. dollar index is a good indicator of how much foreign currency exchange rates could add to rising consumer prices in the near future. This index should be given greater emphasis by business reporters.

What Is the Biggest Economic Problem Today?

The biggest economic problem today will probably also be the biggest economic problem long after this book is out of print. In 2024 it was approaching a $50 trillion problem. It is, of course, the U.S. national debt. Check out the website usdebtclock.org to see what you, Mr. and Mrs. Taxpayer, owe on the national debt at the time you read this. Based on the current growth assumptions, it will soon be about $1 million per taxpayer. If this is the first time you have heard about this, ask you elected representatives why that is.

About three quarters of the national debt is in the form of U.S. Treasury bills, notes, and bonds. The remainder is in other government obligations, such as Series Saving Bonds. Also, the debt can be separated by the classification of the bond owners--public and intra-governmental agencies. Public debt is that part represented by investors outside the government, including the Federal Reserve System, which, although it was created by an act of Congress, is not considered to be a government organization because it is owned by its member banks. Intragovernmental debt is owed to federal agencies such as Social Security and Medicare.

A standard formula for selling books is to write a doom and gloom scenario, that the U.S. federal debt will ultimately cause a global economic collapse. On the other hand, some economists point out that, despite the size of the debt, it has gone through many periods of shrinking as a percentage of the gross domestic product. If the amount of debt slows to a pace below that of the growth of the GDP, the problem would appear to be manageable.

Although the total debt and the GDP are unrelated economic statistics, it is popular to compare the two numbers. When the size of the U.S. debt surpassed the size of the GDP in 2012, the United States became another country in a long list that were in serious jeopardy of being unable to fund the massive amount of accumulated excess spending. The government literally had borrowed more money than the total output of all goods and services in the nation.

Most people realized that if their elected public servants controlled spending costs, they could reduce the debt and ultimately solve the problem. However, an inherent conflict of interest puts most elected officials in a position where their political futures depend on pleasing the short-sighted needs of their constituents rather than the long-term welfare of the populace as a whole. Not until both the elected and the electorate realize that their futures depend on solving macroeconomic problems, not just micro ones, will real progress be made at reducing the debt.

The government does not have many options for dealing with the debt problem—raise taxes and/or reduce spending. The government's revenue source is almost completely limited to taxes. However, raising taxes can be counterproductive as it leads to a reduction in the labor force. Higher corporate tax rates result in fewer new hires, and thus fewer taxpayers. Also, as government expenditures have increased, they have become increasingly entangled in bureaucratic waste, fraud, and inefficiency.

Compounding the problem, every time tax revenues have increased, government spending has increased at an even faster rate. Politicians are not much different from everyone else. There is always something for which government officials need to spend more money. At least when individual consumers run up credit card debt, the issuers put a limit on the amount. But the government has a credit card with no limit, and they are spending other people's money. So, there is no inherent incentive to be thrifty.

Elected representatives who are knowledgeable about economic issues and are fiscally responsible are desperately needed to confront the debt problem. No real progress is likely to be made toward reducing the debt until our elected public servants fight as vehemently for the long-term common good as they do for the short term good of their own constituents.

The national debt creates other economic problems because all other bond issuers—corporations, municipalities, or even foreign governments—must compete with the U.S. government for investors' dollars. So, if the government raises interest rates to attract investors to U.S. Treasuries, then other bond issuers are forced to raise their rates to remain competitive.

The deficit could grow larger than the pool of investors needed to fund it. There will come a point where there are simply not enough people who want to put their money in U.S. Treasury securities, if government spending habits continue on the same course. Also, economic analysts are concerned that the U.S. government will have to raise interest rates to such high levels in order to attract enough investors to fund the debt that other competitors for these investors' dollars, such as state or local government agencies or corporations, could be forced into bankruptcy by having to pay such high interest rates on their debt.

All investors should be very concerned that those responsible for managing the debt do their job. But many of those responsible for government spending do not take the situation seriously. This has turned a relatively small problem into a potentially devastating one. The debt problem will extend for many future generations. Let us hope that rational minds will be able to diffuse the national debt bomb before it explodes. One way or another, this problem is going to be resolved—either through fiscal responsibility or by an economic meltdown. But how did it come to this?

People have a tendency to think that the way it is now is how it has always been. That is untrue. There have been extended periods of time in the past when the U.S. incurred a large amount of debt, usually as a result of war. However, there has never been a peacetime economy that has run up so much debt, not only in total dollars, but as a percent of the total economy.

All the government spending intended to boost the economy during the Great Depression of the 1930s never exceeded 60% of GDP. When the U.S. entered World War II in 1941 the debt quickly ran up to over 100%, but when the war ended the debt to GDP ratio dropped back down to under 60%. It continued a steady decline to below 40% by 1980.

The current debt crisis began in 2008 with the collapse of the real estate market. This was due, at least in part, to more lenient government policies in the mortgage loan business. Government regulators either encouraged, or did not discourage, Fannie Mae (FNMA) and Freddie Mac (FHLMC) to purchase mortgage loans from lenders that did not meet previous conforming loan standards.

Consequently, demand for homes exceeded supply, and many referred to the real estate market as a bubble—it was inflating so quickly it appeared insubstantial and likely to pop. Over the next few years housing prices doubled, tripled, and quadrupled. The housing market came to a head in 2008 when the economy started to go through a recessionary cycle. As many of those new home purchasers became unemployed or were simply unable to make the payments, they began putting their homes up for sale.

A supply-side imbalance of homes quickly followed. The natural consequence of oversupply is a decline in price. So, as housing prices dropped, more homeowners saw the quick equity they had gained in a short period of time start to decline. More homeowners decided to exit the market. In a matter of months, all the homeowners equity was gone, and almost all new homeowners found themselves underwater. Their mortgages were higher than the market value of their homes.

Now, the homeowners were not the only ones losing money, the banks and mortgage lenders were as well. This quickly turned into a financial crisis. It is estimated that in September 2008, just prior to the end of President George W. Bush's term in office, a "run" on the banks drained over $2 trillion from accounts.

In a panic, Congress passed TARP, the Troubled Asset Relief Program. This created about $1 trillion in government loans to rescue failing banks and other corporations. Major TARP loans were made to AIG, Citigroup, Bank of America, General Motors, and many other corporations teetering on the brink of bankruptcy.

The TARP loans contained provisos for repayment, and, for the first time granted the federal government rights to ownership of shares of stock in these companies as collateral for the loans. This was a complete departure from the *laissez-faire* policies that had formed the foundation of the U.S. economy since its inception. The reality of the situation is that U.S. taxpayers had bought about $1 trillion worth of distressed stock.

Stock ownership turned the federal government into not only a regulator for the securities industry, but a participant in it. This was a complete conflict of interest. To use a competitive sports analogy, it was like the referees in the game had become the opposing team. They were not only enforcing the rules, they were making them up as they went along—while they were playing the game.

However, in spite of this inherent conflict of interest, most of the TARP loans were eventually paid back in full. Either through direct repayment or through profits from the sale of the government owed shares of stock. In some cases, the government not only received back the original loan, but made a profit on the sale of stock.

Although this turned out well for the government, it opened the door for the potential of horrendous abuse in the wrong hands of future politicians. There were no checks and balances in place for the government to wield that kind of power. An economic recession might have been averted at that time, except there was a change of leadership in the White House.

At least partially due to economic weakness, the Republicans lost the majority of the elections in 2008, not just the executive branch, but the legislative as well. The seat of power was transferred from President Bush to President Obama in the midst of this fiscal crisis. Since much of the banking industry was still in financial distress, President Obama immediately set out to enact his own version of TARP with a program usually referred to as the Economic Stimulus bill.

Less than a month after taking the oath of office, President Obama, with a Democrat majority in both houses of Congress, passed the American Recovery and Reinvestment Act of 2009. The bill provided for an additional approximately $787 billion in direct federal spending, none of which was backed by offsetting revenue. More importantly, there were no provisions to pay back the principal, as there had been with TARP. Even before this additional debt, the federal budget had already been running at over a $1 trillion annual deficit.

Actually, Congress was never able to pass an actual budget (as they were required to by law). Expenditures were simply paid with fiat currency and little or no budgetary analysis. There was never an overall strategy for managing taxpayers' money. In two years when the Republican Party gained a majority in House of Representatives, they would pass a budget, but the Democrat controlled Senate would never consider it. Then the two parties would accuse each other that it was their fault. This was partisan politics at its worst.

Obviously, the economic stimulus package did nothing to stimulate the economy, and high unemployment continued to weigh heavily on any hope of a quick recovery. So, a second effort was initiated by the Federal Reserve the following month, March 2009. It was called TALF, the Term Asset-Backed Loan Facility. It provided over $1 trillion of asset backed loans. Since this was action being taken by the Fed, it did not require outside auditing. Some economists estimate the amount of money spent on TALF was actually close to $2 trillion.

One of the main strategies for the use of TALF money was to follow the economic policies popularized during FDR's New Deal, to create government jobs. However, more bureaucracy was not the answer either. Although some government jobs are vital to the general welfare, many are not.

It is important not to lose sight of the reality that jobs funded by the taxpayers are revenue consuming. Only jobs funded by the private sector are truly revenue producing. It takes private sector jobs to create the tax revenue to fund government created jobs. When the fragile economic balance leans too far to the consumption side of employment, debt is bound to expand. For an economy to thrive, the private sector needs to produce the lion's share of employment.

Much of the TALF money has never been accounted for, and may never be. The Fed did provide banks with hundreds of billions of dollars of short term Treasury bills. Those funds could be easily audited; but according to several researchers, billions of dollars were transferred to offshore accounts to unidentified parties with no provision for accountability. It should come as no surprise to anyone that this also did not stimulate the economy. So, the Obama Administration continued to allude to the necessity for more rounds of quantitative easing.

Quantitative easing, QE, is the term used to describe the Fed's policy of increasing the quantity of money in circulation. Some people awkwardly refer to quantitative easing as printing money. That is not how it works, but referring to it that way helps some people understand the implications of what the Fed is doing.

The logic behind the necessity of more QE was that even though two trillion dollar QEs had done nothing, maybe more would. Proponents argued that what was needed was simply more spending. What all the excess capital created by past QE programs had been unable to accomplish, more trillion dollar spending programs would. This time would be different. The double talk of proponents for more QEs was meant to mask reality. The economic stagnation dogging the economy was obviously caused by government deficit spending. So, more spending was certainly not going to solve it.

So, quantitative easing added to the problem, not the solution. Money supply was being increased though the issuance of more

Treasury debt. It created more wasteful deficit spending, as taxpayer funds were funneled into corporations or organizations the administration deemed their political allies. This is typical of big government, regardless of party affiliation. The quantitative easing programs were using taxpayer money to finance the downfall of the free market. The net effect of the QE policies was to use tax revenues from the many to fund the political causes of a few.

The African nation of Zimbabwe is a notable example of modern quantitative easing run amok. As the government printed more and more money to stimulate the economy, the buying power of the currency kept falling. A cycle of printing larger and larger bills in order to stimulate economic growth came to a head with the issuance of the world's first $100 trillion bill in 2008. With it, you could buy about $5 worth of goods. Here is what the bill looked like. The rocks on the bill represent the  Chiremba Balancing Rocks. Perhaps if the country had been able to balance its budget as well as nature balanced the rocks, it would have been worth more. Zimbabwe's bills are now collectibles.

The situation in Zimbabwe is unprecedented. Usually economists label runaway inflation hyperinflation. However, they needed a new word to describe what happened in Zimbabwe. Perhaps ultra-hyperinflation or hyper-hyperinflation. Just calling it hyperinflation does not capture the unbelievably dramatic loss of purchasing power for that currency. This crisis came to an end when the currency was replaced first with the Chinese yuan and then a year later with the U.S. dollar.

To summarize, the debt problem cannot be solved by issuing more government debt. It began with government subsidizing the real estate market, continued with government subsidizing the banking industry and others, and has been exasperated by government spending trillions upon trillions of dollars without any plan to fund it whatsoever. During the Obama administration no budget bill was ever passed. The government simply resorted to printing more money in the hopes that no one would realize what was going on. In the Biden era the problem was exasperated.

How will this problem be resolved? No one knows. I hope explaining the problem will motivate people to evaluate political candidates' economic policies with greater scrutiny. I hope that voters realize political promises of free stuff without economic accountability is a sure recipe for disaster. The U.S. is a democratic republic, and you still hold the power to determine your fate in your own hands—in the voting booth. Do not let that right be lost.

The dual mandate of the Federal Reserve Board is to keep inflation low and employment high, but there is a monster lurking behind the stats.

Chapter 7

What Is Technical Analysis?

As previously stated, **technical analysis** involves methods of studying indicators based on supply and demand factors. Most indicators are intended to predict whether or not the supply of securities is sufficient to meet current demand. A pure technician is one who cares little about future earnings, as that would be in the area of fundamental analysis. Earnings would simply be considered another technical indicator, the potential for increased demand due to earnings growth. However, people who rely solely on technical indicators to make decisions are speculators, not investors.

A technician is usually first and foremost concerned with interpreting chart patterns. Therefore, technical traders often refer to themselves as chartists. They attempt to interpret chart patterns to predict the direction of the security's next move. However, you must know what the chart is saying before you make a decision. Chart patterns alone should not be the final determiner of an investor's decision. In addition to charts, there are several other supply and demand indicators that technical analysts follow.

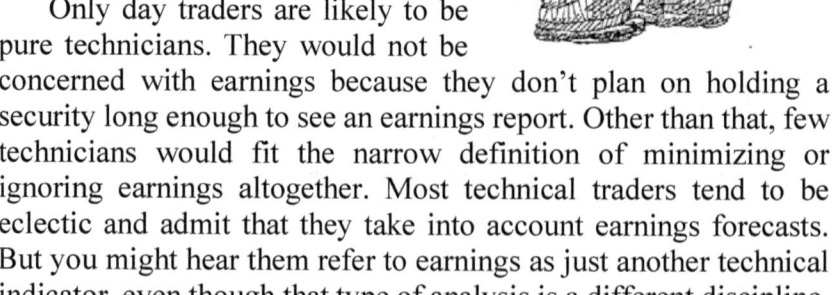

Only day traders are likely to be pure technicians. They would not be concerned with earnings because they don't plan on holding a security long enough to see an earnings report. Other than that, few technicians would fit the narrow definition of minimizing or ignoring earnings altogether. Most technical traders tend to be eclectic and admit that they take into account earnings forecasts. But you might hear them refer to earnings as just another technical indicator, even though that type of analysis is a different discipline.

The fundamental and technical approach to security analysis serve different purposes. Investors use fundamental analysis to select *what* to invest in (something with good earnings growth) and use technical analysis to help them decide *when* to invest in it (when there is a supply side imbalance). Technical analysis is most valuable for offering guidelines on investment timing. In addition to the typical use of technical indicators for timing investment decisions, some other mechanical market timing techniques will be discussed at the end of this chapter.

Market efficiency is the term used to describe the concept that the market, and the price of any security at any time, is constantly fully valued. In other words, the market is continuously selling at the fair market price at that moment. Efficiency implies that the market rapidly adjusts prices to reflect all the factors that would go into evaluating the price of that security.

Some market commentators, particularly pure fundamentalists, have stated market efficiency demonstrates that the technical approach to investing is flawed. Efficiency implies that there is never a time when a stock is undervalued or overvalued, since the price of all securities is constantly and continuously fully valued. However, technicians would point out that although a security may be fully valued all the time, the value will obviously change as circumstances change in the future.

Some critics of technical analysis take market efficiency to an extreme and have proposed what is called the **Random Walk Hypothesis**. It is a theory that the direction of a particular stock is no more predictable than the path of a drunken man walking down the street. As there is no logical way to predict where the drunk's next step will fall—to the right, left, or straight ahead—there is no basis for predicting where the price of any given security going next—up, down, or sideways.

Whether the market follows a random walk or a predictable path is probably a question that will not be answered to the satisfaction of both sides of the debate. However, you can draw your own conclusions from the following descriptions of some of the methods of technical analysis. It should be noted up front that there are very few universally accepted and followed technical indicators. Almost everyone picks and chooses the technical indicators they prefer.

Technicians inevitably put their own spin or personal preferences on how they use the information.

Technical analysis has gained popularity recently because there are so many new tools being provided for online investors. These tools are meant to appeal to a certain personality type—those who think they can come up with their own secret formula for success. Perhaps a quick reminder of the lesson in Chapter 1 is in order.

Remember the Greed-Hope-Fear Cycle, also called the **Small Investor Syndrome**. That title implies that the cycle only refers to the psychological mindset of *small* investors. But that is completely inaccurate. Small investors are certainly not the only ones who are subject to the temptation to buy at market tops and sell at market bottoms. However, the intent of that discussion was to point out that human nature is most likely to tempt you to buy and to sell at the wrong times in market cycles. When it comes to making investment decisions, you are probably going to be your own worst enemy.

Online technical tools are often designed to appeal to greed. But technical indicators are not a philosopher's stone. They cannot turn lead into gold. Investors should be cautioned that they are more likely to turn gold into lead. There is no secret recipe for success, other than hard work and a disciplined approach to investing. Online trading tools are designed by brokers with an agenda to motivate high volume trading. That may be profitable for them, but it is a trap for you. Do not get caught up in a gambler's mentality of trying to beat the system. All successful investors have pursued a disciplined path using fundamental analysis. That is the approach of this book. The gambler may win a few bets and hit a lucky streak, but can you think of anyone who became a millionaire by gambling? Or if they have, have they been able to keep their millions?

The proper function of technical analysis is to help investors with market timing techniques, not to be used to wager on the next ten cent move. So, with that word of caution, let's take a look at how you can use technical indicators.

Technical indicators can be separated into three areas: charts, corresponding indicators, and contrarian indicators. These are not three different approaches. They are simply three methods of trying to predict the same thing: whether or not there is likely to be a supply-side or a demand-side imbalance.

How Do You Read Stock Charts?

Charting has gone through three evolutionary stages. Charts have grown from basic line charts, to bar charts, to candlestick charts. You will find all three options on most online chart services. These three styles of charts all represent the same closing price data, but each will add one more layer of useful information.

Originally charts were laid out with a horizontal axis representing time and a vertical axis representing price. The closing prices of stocks were plotted by dots on the chart and zigzag lines were drawn to connect the dots. For traders there are intraday charts available representing prices on an hourly basis, or some fraction of an hour.

Bar charts were introduced to add the trading range for the period. Typically charts were for daily prices, so the range would be represented by a vertical bar between the high and low prices for the day. Then the opening and closing prices were added to the range bar. A hash mark was placed on the left side of the bar showed the opening price. A hash mark on the right side of the bar showed the closing price, which had been the only price information on the line chart.

With a quick glance at a bar chart you could estimate the normal trading range for a stock and look for trading patterns on those days where the volume was higher or lower than normal. A longer range bar revealed a more volatile day of trading, and a shorter one a less volatile day. This was useful data, because you could look at the chart and immediately determine if the stock had closed higher or lower on those highly volatile days.

Candlestick charts were the next evolutionary step. The **candlestick chart** added an open or closed cell between the opening hash mark and the closing one. An open cell meant that the stock had closed at a higher price than it had opened. A filled in, or closed, cell meant that the closing price was lower than the opening one. Some chart services filled in the cells green for higher, and red for lower. This is essentially the same information as the bar charts, but it is visually easier to follow because the hash marks on each side of the range bar were more difficult to see.

The following illustration shows that when ranges were added to chart information, it made channel patterns easier to spot. With a glance at any chart you can immediately notice a certain direction that the price of the stock is heading—higher, lower, or sideways. The opening and closing hash marks referred to in the description of bar charts were left off this illustration because its purpose is simply to represent a channel.

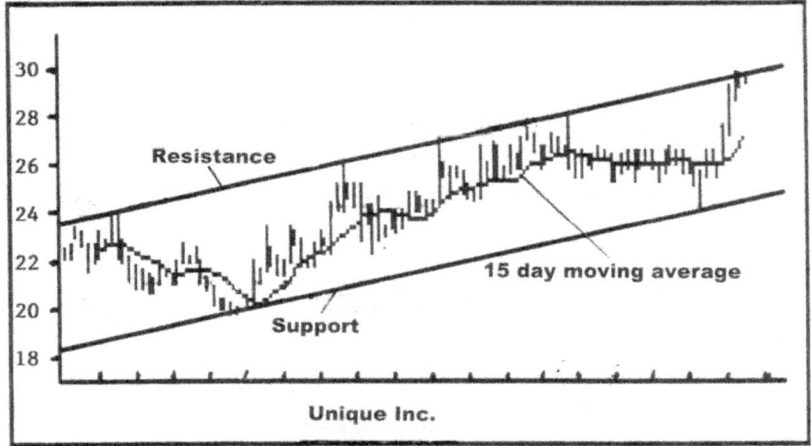

If you were to draw a straight line connecting all the low points where the stock reversed a short downward move and began moving higher and then another line connecting all the points where a stock hit a high and reversed to move lower, those lines would define the boundaries of a channel. For the period of time covered, the stock always traded within the lower and upper lines defining that channel.

The lower line is referred to as the support line and the upper as resistance. The expectation would be that if the stock were to drop to a price that would hit the support line, the stock would reverse its direction and begin moving upward. Also, if the stock were to rise to a price that hit the resistance line, you would expect the stock to drop. There is no guarantee that this channel will always represent the trading range. It is only a presumptive expectation. Sooner or later the stock will break out of that channel, and when it does, it will begin forming a new one.

Relating a stock chart's channel pattern back to supply and demand terms, the support line of a channel would be where a stock is likely to find increased **demand** as more investors attempt to buy it at a low price. The resistance line would represent a high price where the stock would likely come under pressure from an influx of sellers taking a profit, creating an increased **supply** of shares. So, a channel pattern in a chart represents a price where a downward move would likely be reversed by more buying activity, and an upward one by increased selling.

In the language of Wall Street, an upward channel would be **bullish**, a downward one **bearish**, and a sideways one neutral. To a technical analyst, the best bullish investment would be a stock in a steep upward channel trading near the support line. A technician with a bearish bias would look for a stock in a steep downward channel trading near the resistance line. However, short term speculators might look for a stock with a long sideways channel where they could trade the tops and bottoms.

If the sideways channel only covers a short time, most technicians would probably consider it a **consolidation period**, not indicative of a trend that is likely to continue. An example of this would be for a stock whose price had been running in an upward channel, but then it had broken below the support line and began trading sideways. In that scenario, the stock needs to go through a cooling off period—sideways—because there were not enough buyers to keep the stock running upward. Then, once the oversupply of stock in that price range is reduced, the stock will continue its previous upward pattern.

The type of chart pattern that most technical traders would ignore is one for which there is no clearly defined channel, except perhaps a very broad one. Of course, a stock that is trading all over the place should scare anyone away, not just chartists. Both long-term investors as well as short term speculators should be looking for predictability—at least a history of predictable behavior.

The parameters of support and resistance levels, although open to some interpretation among chartists, will generally follow agreed upon channels. However, there are many other chart patterns that rely as much on intuition as logic. Most chartists pride themselves on having a unique perspective on interpreting patterns. A few common patterns recognized by chartists are included in the following illustration: double tops, double bottoms, head and shoulders, and inverted head and shoulders. There are many more chart patterns, but the following illustration is a simple graphic representation of some patterns that might predict a change in future trend for a stock. Do not consider this a complete discussion of chart analysis. It is only meant to keep your focus on helping you to identify likely patterns that fit the Greed-Hope-Fear Cycle. When you identify these types of chart patterns, sell at the top and buy at the bottom.

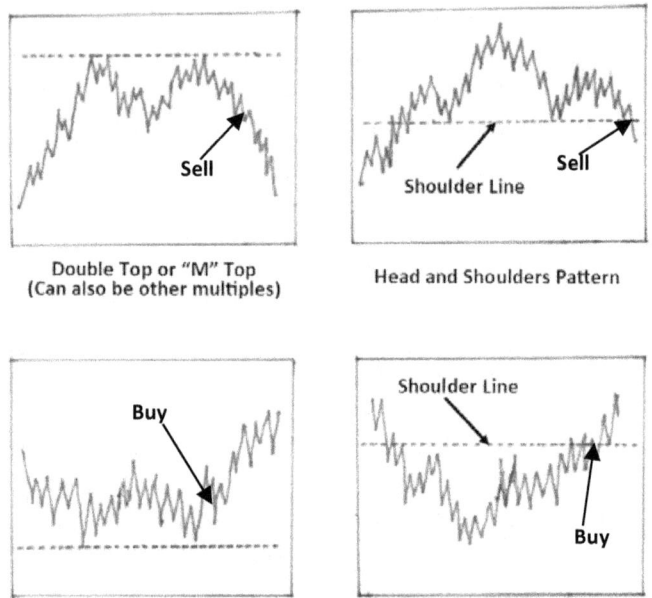

Double Top or "M" Top (Can also be other multiples)

Head and Shoulders Pattern

Double Bottom or "W" Bottom

Inverted Head and Shoulders

A **double top**, also referred to as an **M top**, is a chart pattern where a stock has risen to a new high, pulled back, rallied up to a similar high, then pulled back again. The double top would imply there was too much resistance for the stock to continue above that level. Thus, it could be a forecaster of a trend reversal if it breaks below the previous pull back. The stock would be expected to begin trading in a new downward channel if does not hold at the support line. Sometimes a double top pattern may become a triple top. To a chartist the more tops formed the more bearish the indicator. The tops should be verified by lower volume on the days when the security is up and higher volume on the days when it is lower.

A **double bottom**, also called a **W bottom**, is the reverse of the double top. It is a pattern where a stock has dropped to a new low, rallied up a bit, dropped back down to approximately the same low, then reversed again. The chart would identify an increased demand for the security at that support level. This would also represent a trend reversal, and a chartist would expect it to begin forming an upward channel. Again, the pattern would be verified by higher volume on the up days.

A variation of double tops and bottoms is the **head and shoulders** pattern and **inverted head and shoulders**, also referred to as a *head and shoulders top* or a *head and shoulders bottom*. With a head and shoulders pattern a security rallies to a new high and then pulls back (first shoulder), next it rallies up to an even higher high (head), pulls back to about the same level as the first one, then rallies back up again to about the level of the first high point (second shoulder). Breaking the support line after forming this pattern would indicate a trend reversal. A chartist might short the stock on the second shoulder. But keep in mind that if the security does not break the support level formed on the two sides of the head, it would be viewed as a continuation of the bullish trend. The head and shoulders would be nothing more than a brief consolidation.

An inverted head and shoulders pattern would be a reversal of the one just described. It would indicate a breakout from a bearish trend to a bullish one. For most chartists, head and shoulders patterns are some of the most accurate indicators. In principle, they are variations of triple tops or triple bottoms.

For these chart patterns, technical analysts would buy after the stock has moved up from its lows or down from its highs. This is why you often see stocks that sell at a new high continue to set more new highs. Also, stocks that hit new lows often continue to set more new lows.

Critics of those who make decisions on the basis of chart patterns, often claim that stocks follow these patterns simply because there are so many chartists who follow these guidelines that it becomes a self-fulfilling prophecy. It is difficult to scientifically prove that theory one way or another. However, investors should be aware of how technical chartists are looking at these patterns and make their own investment decisions accordingly.

Finally, it is important to chartists that any gaps in a stock's chart be filled. A **gap** is created when a stock opens at a price well away from the previous closing price, either higher or lower, and never goes back to trade in the previous range. In other words, the gap was never filled. To a chartist this is a dangerous pattern. If a gap on the upside isn't filled, a chartist would consider that the stock would always be in danger of dropping back down to the last price before the gap was created. The same would be true of a gap on the downside. The stock would need to rally up to the last close before a chartist might feel bearish enough to short the stock.

Gaps in a stock's chart can usually happen either overnight or from a halt in trading. Overnight gaps can result when market moving news is released after normal trading hours. Then when the market opens on the next day, the supply/demand imbalance creates a situation where the stock opens at a sharply different price from the previous day's close.

A halt in trading might happen if some event creates a market imbalance on either the bid or the ask side during normal market trading hours. Typically such an event could be a buyout rumor or some news that will significantly affect a company's earnings. Whatever the event, it is important enough so that the market makers do not have enough supply of shares to meet immediate demand (upside or breakaway gap) or enough demand to meet immediate supply (downside or panic gap). Trading will be halted long enough for the market makers to find a point of equilibrium where they will be able to match the bid and ask sides of the order books.

Now that you understand some of the basics of charts, you are ready for a few technical indicators you can apply from that data. However, consider a brief word of caution before you dive in. Most technical indicators are only designed to predict short term market moves. In Wall Street terminology, these are *momentum indicators*. They are trying to predict which direction the market momentum will take the stock next.

Becoming too involved in momentum indicators is a trap. It is meant to appeal to greed. Short term technical indicators should not become the main focus of investment decisions. You should first research the company's fundamentals. If the company has poor earnings projections, it is not worth examining its technical indicators. Proceed with caution.

What Other Indicators Are Used by Chartists?

Most website providers that offer charting information will also offer other basic technical tools. These will present supplemental information that can be helpful for interpreting chart patterns. Some of the basic tools might include moving averages, Bollinger bands, volume, rate of change, relative strength index, money flow index, MACD, fast and slow stochastic; and there are many more. In this section you will learn about some common technical indicators. However, this is not meant to be exhaustive. The area of technical indicators is constantly evolving.

The first and most important topic related to charting is moving averages. Many financial websites automatically default to include a curving line snaking through the chart. A **moving average**, **MA**, is a linear graph computed by adding up the closing prices for a certain period of time and averaging those prices to create one point on the graph. The following day, the oldest closing price is dropped from the average and the new day's close is added into the total to be averaged. The moving average is meant to help the chartist visualize trends. It will level out the peaks and troughs to present a more discernable short or long-term direction in price.

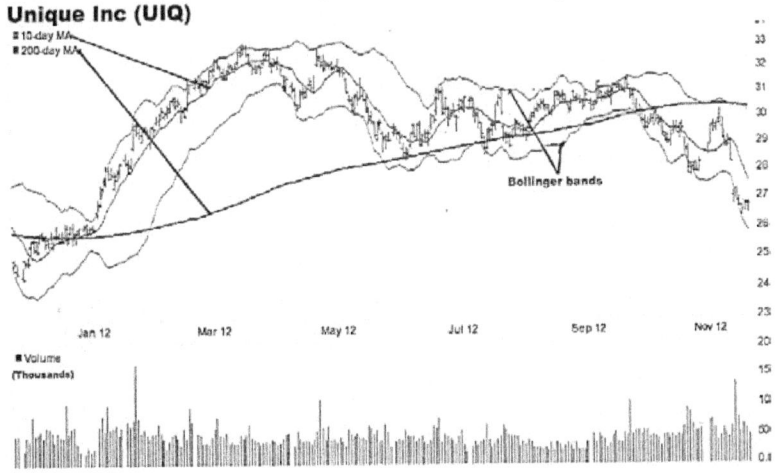

A moving average (MA) and Bollinger bands will be presented first. They are technical tools represented as chart layovers. They are indicators appearing on the chart itself. Other technical indicators will appear on a separate graph below the price chart. The term moving average usually implies a **simple moving average** and is sometimes abbreviated **SMA**. Most technical indicators use a simple moving average, but a few, especially high price securities, use an **exponential moving average**, **EMA**, which denotes that the lengths of the marks on the y-axis are denominated as a percentage change rather than an equal incremental numerical change.

If the technical indicator identifies an EMA, the length on a graph between 2 and 4 would be the same as the length between 1 and 2, not twice as long as it would be if the graph were numeric. The lengths on an exponential graph from 1 to 2 and from 2 to 4 are equal because they both represent a 100 percent change from the lower point. The length on the graph between 4 and 8 and 8 and 16 would also be the same distance as between 1 and 2. Some technical indicators use an EMA to flatten out the volatility.

Moving averages are computed by taking the current day's closing price and then adding it to a number of previous days' closing prices. That total is then divided by the number of days making up the total to compute an arithmetic average. (If the chart represents units other than days, the moving average will be for whatever unit that is, such as hours, weeks, or months.) A 20-day moving average, for example, would be computed by taking the current day's closing price, adding it to the previous 19 closes, and dividing the total by 20. On the next day, that closing price would be added to the previous 19 and averaged. Thus, the oldest number is always being dropped from the average as the new one is added.

Short term moving averages can typically be for 5, 10, 15, or 20 days. Longer term moving averages are usually for 50, 100, 150, or 200 days. Some sites allow you to input any number of days you want to personalize the information. The shorter the term of the moving average the wavier the line will appear. The longer the term, the more it will flatten out, reducing out the short term spikes.

A 5-day moving average will represent the average closing price for one week. There are usually only 5 business days when the market is open per week. So, a 10-day moving average would represent the average price for 2 weeks; 20-days would be about one month; and 100-days about 5 months.

The longest moving average is typically 200 days. That would represent about 40 weeks, representing nearly 80 percent of one year. The 200-day moving average will be a relatively flat line compared to those with shorter periods. Whether it is sloping upward or downward would indicate the long-term trend for the price of that stock. It is also important to a chartist to note whether that line is accelerating or decelerating. An upwardly moving bullish line that shows a recent decrease in the upward slope would be said to be decelerating. That would be interpreted by chartists as a possible forecast that the long-term trend may be about to move in a more bearish direction. Observe the deceleration of the 200-day MA in the previous chart. The last trading activity for Unique Inc. might imply a trend reversal from the previous upward bias.

To a chartist, the importance of moving averages is their use for forecasting trends. Usually a chartist will select a short term moving average and overlay it with a long-term one. The point at which the short-term MA crosses the long-term one could indicate a trend reversal.

So, consider that you select the chart of a stock and input a 15-day moving average for the short term and 200-day for the long term. This is a common selection because the short term represents about three-quarters of a month, and the long term about three-quarters of a year. The 15-day average had been trading below the 200-day, but you notice that it has risen to a point where it has crossed over the long-term trend line and has begun a trading pattern above it. This would be a bullish indicator to the chartist, as you know the long-term line will begin a steeper upward slope. The new numbers being added to the moving average are going to be higher than the older ones being taken off.

The numbers cited in that example would be useful to a long-term investor. However, traders are more likely to use a 5-day moving average as their short term indicator and a 20-day moving average as their long term. The directional indicator for those moving averages is going to be much more frequent and for a much shorter term. However, the methods used for either short term trading or long-term investing are the same.

Bollinger bands are one of the most popular chart overlays used by technicians. Like moving averages, they are meant to predict a change of direction of the trending price of a security. The computation of Bollinger bands begins with the calculation of a 20-day simple moving average, SMA. Next the standard deviation for that 20-day period is calculated. Standard deviation is an approximation of the difference between the average price change for the period as compared to what the price change was for the last day. Standard deviation is already calculated for you, so you don't need to learn the formula. However, here is a brief explanation. The difference between the daily change and the average change is squared, and the numbers for the period are totaled, giving only a positive number, even for a negative change. Then the square root is taken of the average of those numbers. This is just a mathematical method of ensuring the standard deviation number will always be positive. The final calculation for the bands is made by multiplying the standard deviation number by 2. That result is added to the SMA to plot the point on the upper band and subtracted from the SMA to plot the point on the lower. As the volatility of the investment increases, the width of the Bollinger bands widens; and as volatility decreases, the width narrows.

Many technicians consider that if the price of the investment hits the lower band it is a buy signal, and hitting the middle SMA line is a sell. However, some traders do not consider the indicator a sell, or short, until the price hits the upper band. Other momentum speculators might interpret the bands similar to the way they do moving averages. If the price touches or crosses below the lower band, it is a sell. If it touches or crosses above the upper band, it is a short term buy signal.

If you are interested in creating your own Bollinger bands, or your own [Insert Your Name Here] bands using criteria you select, there are several websites that offer detailed information about how to do that. Bands of various ranges can be a useful technical indicator for fundamental investors. John Bollinger, the inventor of the bands, maintains sites offering more detailed information and additional indicators beyond those bands.

Probably the first technical indicator that most traders consider, after those that are chart overlays, is the **volume** graph. Many websites will automatically include a graph showing the volume of trading below the price chart. The volume will be a bar with an index scale on one side showing the total number of shares traded on that day. Observe the volume indicator below the bar chart for Unique Inc. in the previous illustration. Simply by looking at high volume days and comparing them to the price movement corresponding to that day, a chartist can determine how significant the price movement was. High volume indicates a correspondingly high investor sentiment for the future direction of price of the investment. Volume is used to authenticate trends.

If the investment has been trending lower on low volume days, it would not be as much of a concern to a technical trader as it would be on high volume days. The volume graph is also a factor in some of the other indicators. Consider these three technical indicators, ROC, RSI, and MFI. When you select technical indicators, they will appear below the chart for the price of the security.

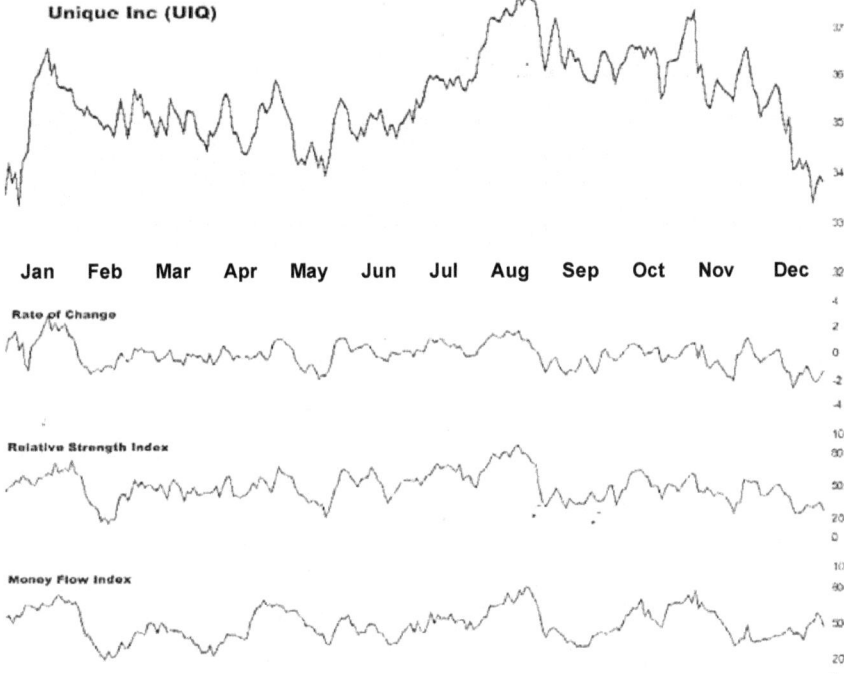

Whereas volume indicators are meant to predict the direction of price movement, the **rate of change**, ROC, indicator is meant to predict the speed at which the security is likely to move. Usually ROC simply measures the percentage difference between the current closing price of the stock and what the closing price was ten days ago. However, many sites have tools allowing you to set the period for computing the rate of change at other increments.

ROC represents percentage change of the price of a security relative to a zero line. Above the line means the stock is higher than ten days ago, and below the line means lower. So, observe from the graph that Unique Inc. was about $36 ten days ago, and today it closed about $34. The point on the ROC graph for that day would be about 5.6 percent below the zero line. The stock was down $2 from its $36 base (2/36 = 0.056 or 5.6 percent). A 5.6 percent move would be a very volatile one considering the short time period for which the indicator is being calculated. A downward move of 5.6 percent over a ten day period would be equivalent to about 140 percent APR. There are about 250 business days in a year, so there are about 25 10-day periods (25×5.6% = 140%).

You might assume that the steeper the line is moving upward the more bullish the technical indicator, and the steeper the slope downward, the more bearish. However, many technical analysts use ROC as a predictor of a change of direction, especially if it is used in conjunction with other technical indicators. Once the upward rate of change starts slowing, a trader might anticipate a change in the direction of the indicator. So the flattening of an upward slope would be a bearish indicator, and a flattening of a downward one could be bullish.

Somewhat related to the ROC indicator would be the **relative strength index**, RSI. It is a technical indicator that measures the ratio of higher closing prices to lower ones over a period of time, usually 14 days. The RSI entry would be a positive number if the current day's closing price was higher than the previous day's closing. It would be a negative number if the close was lower from one day to the next. The index is not concerned about the size of the change, simply with whether it was higher or lower.

The RSI is represented as an oscillating indicator on a scale from 0 to 100. If the stock has 14 straight days of closing higher prices, it would be at 100. If it has 14 straight days of closing lower, it would have an RSI of zero. Obviously, 7 up days and 7 down days would put the index at 50, a neutral rating. If the RSI rises above 80, it is interpreted as an indication of an overbought condition. A trader might use that as a contrarian sell (bearish) signal for a short term momentum trade. If the RSI drops below 20, a trader might consider that a buy (bullish) signal. Also, financial websites that allow you to personalize technical indicators might enable you to compute the relative strength of a company compared to the range of the index for its industry group or to the market in general.

Similar to the relative strength index is the **money flow index**, MFI. Whereas the RSI uses the price of the investment to generate the technical indicator, the MFI adds further clarification by adjusting the index from a simple price weighting to a dollar value weighting of money flow. Like the RSI, the MFI uses an index scale from zero to one hundred and also puts overbought or oversold indicator lines at 80 and 20.

Money flow calculation is based on the measure of the *typical price*, computed as the average of the high, low, and closing prices for the day. Then that typical price is multiplied by the volume of shares traded. That result would represent the approximate dollar value of the shares traded for that day. If that day's typical price is higher than the previous day's, it would indicate positive money flow; a lower one would indicate negative money flow. The money flow ratio is then determined as positive money flow for the trailing 14-day SMA divided by total money flow for the period, the sum of both positive and negative money flow.

The oscillator for MFI will usually approximate the RSI. Divergences between the two indexes would be of significance to the technical analyst. Consider that the price-weighted RSI is at 20 but the value-weighted MFI is at 30. An astute technician might interpret that buy rating of the RSI as invalid, for it is not verified by the MFI. In other words, the selling of the stock that created the low RSI is on lighter volume than average for the stock. Unless the volume of selling picks up and the MFI drops to at least 20, it might be like a false bullish indicator.

The final two indicators to be considered here are MACD and stochastics. They are probably the most useful ones. **MACD** is an acronym for **moving average convergence/divergence**. Convergence means moving closer together, and divergence, moving farther apart. Fast money traders who do not want to wait for two moving averages to cross might use MACD to anticipate when such a crossover is coming. Moving averages will have to start converging before they meet. The MACD indicator uses an EMA, as opposed to a simple moving average.

The MACD results provided by a chart service may not align with your own moving average numbers because there are proprietary factors used in their calculation. The MACD chart looks something like the short term and long-term moving averages you just learned about—one more volatile (shorter term) and one smoothed out (longer term). However, the smoother line is equivalent to the short term moving average would be the 9-day represented by a 26-day EMA minus a 12-day one. Then the line EMA of that number.

184 ◇ Technical Analysis

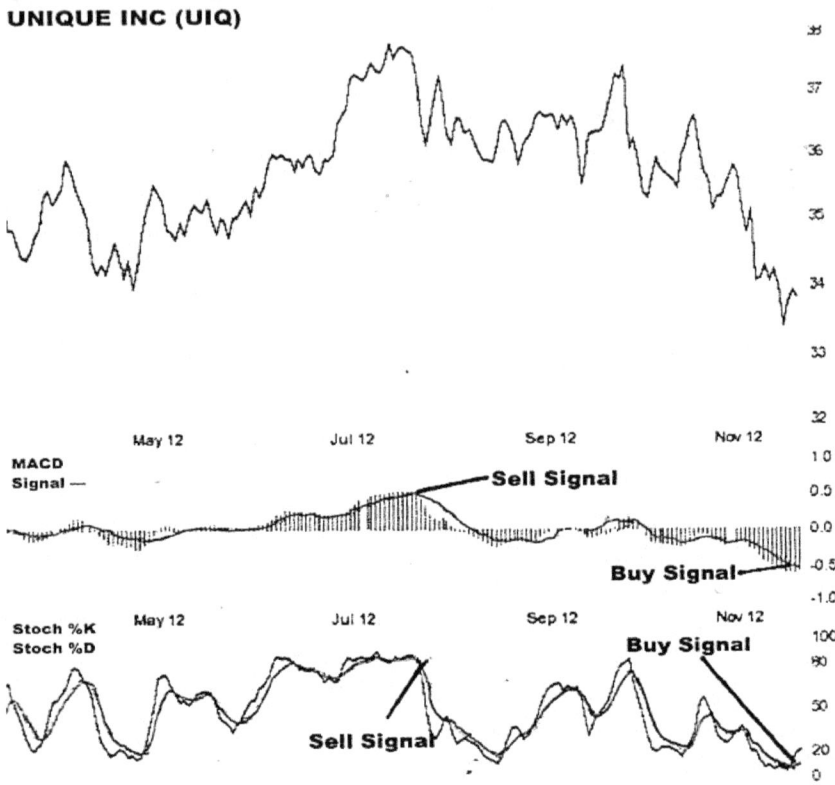

MACD is illustrated by a bar chart called a histogram. When the more volatile (9-day) EMA is smaller the less volatile (26-day – 12-day) EMA, the bar on the histogram will be below the zero line. When the more volatile EMA is greater than the less volatile, the histogram will be above the zero line. You can see when the shorter term moving average would be diverging from the longer term as the bars on the histogram grow longer. A lengthening of the lines represents divergence and a shortening of the lines represents convergence. This is the case whether the bar is below the zero line or above it—below is diverging lower, and above diverging higher.

Usually chartists use an upward crossover, from below the zero line to above it, as a buy signal. Conversely, a downward crossover would be a sell signal. However, most traders don't bother waiting until the indicator crosses the zero line. If it looks like a stock's price has reversed its short term trading pattern from diverging to converging, many traders make buy or sell decisions based on where they think MACD is going next.

A **stochastic** is a moving average of a different sort. It measures the closing price of a stock relative to its recent range. Stochastic indicators are separated into two components abbreviated **%K** and **%D**. The %K numbers are computed by measuring the closing price of a stock relative to the high/low trading range of that stock over a 14-day period (for daily charts). It then plots the closing daily price of the stock as a percent between zero and one hundred. Zero would be the low of the range and 100 the high. The %D number is simply the 3-day moving average of the %K 14-day MA. It is meant to smooth out the high volatility of the graph.

To illustrate this, say that the range for Unique Inc. over the last 14 days has been 30 to 40. The difference between the high and the low is 10 points, so that represents 100 percent. If the stock closes at 32, it would be represented by a point on the %K chart at 20 percent, 2 points above the low end of the range (10). If the stock closes at 35, the %K point will be at 50 percent; at 38, 80 percent; at 40, 100 percent. Keep in mind that with each new computation the range will change if the oldest number, which is being dropped off the SMA, happened to be the high or the low for the period.

The %K and %D numbers are used to compute two main stochastic indicators—fast and slow. Both fast and slow use a volatile number compared to a smoothing average of that number. A **fast stochastic** technical indicator uses the %K (14-day MA of the stock price) as the more volatile line and the %D (3-day MA of %K) as the less volatile number.

The **slow stochastic** indicator is more important to investors, but it is the most confusing to explain. The more volatile line for the fast stochastic becomes the less volatile line for the slow stochastic. So, what was referred to as the less volatile %D line for the fast indicator becomes the more volatile %K line for the slow. If you followed that, your next question should probably be if %K becomes %K, then what is %D? Good question, nice to see you've got it. The %D for a slow stochastic is the 3-day moving average of the %D 3-day moving average. That average just flattens out the peaks and troughs a little more—the same way as the two %K stochastic indicators did. You might have to read this paragraph a few times before it makes sense.

A stochastic is another short term momentum indicator, attempting to identify overbought or oversold situations. To relate this back to the original discussion of channel patterns, an overbought indicator would be where the stock is trading near the resistance (upper) level of the channel. An oversold one would be near the support (lower) level. Usually overbought situations are identified when %D is above 80 percent of the slow stochastic. Oversold situations are when %D is below 20 percent of the slow stochastic.

There are many more technical indicators than those presented here. However, this section is only meant to explain a few common ones. If you understand them, you are probably ten times more knowledgeable than many of the traders who use (or abuse) them through online trading services. Remember, the value of anything is derived from the amount of time and effort you put into it.

A few topics not covered here, but popular among technicians, are Williams %R, Parabolic SAR, Ichimoku Clouds, Pivot Points, Triple Exponential Average (TRIX), McClellan Oscillators, the Elliot Wave Theory, Fibonacci Retracement, Dow Theory, and many more. If you want to continue to expand your knowledge of technical indicators, there are literally thousands of websites on various related topics. Don't be intimidated by them. If you understood the basics of those presented here, you will have a good foundation for understanding the logic behind other indicators.

In addition to chart patterns, there are a few other technical indicators you should know about that are not related to charting.

What Are Some Non-Chart Technical Indicators?

Perhaps the most popular technical indicator not based on chart patterns is the **put/call ratio**. A more complete explanation of puts and calls will be presented in Chapter 9. However, to understand the usefulness of this technical indicator, you simply need to know their definition. They are called options, highly leveraged contracts that allow the owner to participate in the ups and downs of a security without having the purchase that security.

TECHNICAL ANALYSIS ◊ 187

Puts and calls are contracts giving the purchaser the right, or **option**, to sell (put) or buy (call) a specified quantity of an investment (100 shares) within a specified period of time (up to about 2½ years) at a specified price per share. For speculators, puts and calls have become popular because they are not only available on stock, but also on derivative securities meant to mirror the performance of market indexes, commodity prices, industrial sectors, and many more.

In a broad sense, the term **derivative security** implies an investment whose value is determined by (derived from) the price of another investment. Options are derivative securities because their value will be based on the price of the underlying shares. That means an index option is a derivative of a derivative. The value of the derivative option is based on the value of a derivative index, a function of the securities that make up the index. The most popularly traded index options are those on the Nasdaq 100 with the ticker symbol QQQ (referred to as the Qs) and the S&P 500 Index, SPY, (referred to as the Spider).

The word derivative was introduced in Chapter 4 on bonds. It was used to describe the securities created by financial institutions that were formed from splitting up the pools of Fannie Mae and Freddie Mac mortgage securities for the purpose of creating new tradable securities, such as *collateralized mortgage obligations* (CMOs). The market price of CMOs is derived from the market value of the original securities from which they were created.

The important factor to a technical analyst is that call options, since they represent the right to buy the underlying security, go up when the security goes up. The price of the option corresponds to the direction of the value of the underlying security.

Consider that you buy a call option giving you the right to buy 100 shares of UIQ at $30 per share over the next six months. The stock is currently trading at 30, and you pay $200 for the call option. Now, if the stock goes up to $40 within the next six months, the value of your call would go up to about $1000. The value of the call goes up if the price of the stock goes up. The value of a contract giving you the right to buy 100 shares of a stock for $30 per share whose market price is currently $10 higher than that will be worth about $1000 (100 × $10 = $1000).

Next consider what happens if you buy a put option. The corresponding put gives you the right to sell 100 shares of UIQ at $30 per share expiring in six months, and you pay $200 to own that put. If the stock drops to $20, then the value of your put goes up to about $1000. You own the right to sell 100 shares of stock at $30, so a contract like that is worth about $10 per share. A thousand dollars is the market value of 100 shares worth $10 per share. So, the value of the put goes up if the value of the underlying security goes down. Rather than correspond to the direction of the stock, the put moves in the opposite direction.

So, the value of calls goes higher when the market goes higher, but the value of puts goes higher when the market goes lower. The higher the market goes, the higher the call; the lower the market goes, the higher the put. Calls represent bullish sentiment, and puts a bearish one. You should also note that if you invest in a put or a call and the market does not go the way you wanted before it expires, you are likely to lose your entire investment in that option.

The Put/Call Ratio is a technical indicator expressing the relationship of bearish sentiment to bullish sentiment based on the decisions of those who buy options. Speculators who think the market is going to drop would want to buy a put, and speculators who think the market is going to rally, a call. Buying an option is highly speculative because the contract is only in force for a limited time period. You will have several choices, from a few days or weeks to over two years.

Daily norms are difficult to categorize because the options markets can be extremely volatile. However, people are generally more positive about the market than negative. So, a normal range for the Put/Call Ratio generally runs between about 60 percent and 100 percent. The lower the index, the more bullish the indicator. So, below 60 percent, would be a bullish buy signal to a technician. Above 100 would be a bearish sell signal.

Looking at this another way, if you were to consider 75 percent a normalized ratio, which many technicians do, then for every 4 bullish speculators, there would be about 3 bearish ones. There are approximately 3 puts bought for every 4 calls (3/4). At 60 percent there would be about 3 puts for every 5 calls (3/5), and at 100 percent, about 3 puts for every 3 calls (3/3).

As the number of calls increases, the ratio declines and thus represents a more bullish sentiment. As the number of calls decreases, the ratio increases and represents a more bearish sentiment. So, the Put/Call Ratio moves in the opposite direction of the market forecast.

However, this indicator is not as easy to interpret as you might think. Some technicians use it as a contrarian indicator. Even though a high number would appear bearish, a number much higher than 100 may be interpreted by a contrarian as bullish.

Going back to the Greed-Hope-Fear Cycle in the first chapter, when fear is the dominant emotional reaction to the market and almost everyone is yelling, "Sell! Sell! Sell!", that is the time a contrarian should buy. A Put/Call Ratio that is unusually high is the option traders' equivalent of being at the bottom of the Fear Cycle of the market. Of course, too low of a Put/Call Ratio could be interpreted as being at the top of the Greed phase of a market cycle and would thus be a sell signal to a contrarian.

This seems like a good place to remind you that technical indicators are as much art as science. Being more complicated does not make an indicator more reliable. Do not substitute technical indicators for the hard work of fundamental analysis. Do not be a lazy investor. No technical tool is 100 percent inerrant. The tool itself creates nothing. The one who uses the tool does the creating.

Poor carpenters cannot build good houses even if they have the best tools in the business. But a good carpenter can build a good house even with inferior tools. It's the skill of the one using the tools that's important. You are the one who will create something with these tools. For it to be of value, you must apply as much art to the process as science. Rigidly following formulas will not work.

Another popular technical indicator is the **breadth of market**, which is graphed as the **Advance/Decline Line**, ADL. The breadth of market is the measure of the total number of companies that closed at a higher price than the previous day's close versus the number that closed lower. This is usually presented both as a total number and also as a percent of the total number of companies traded. For example, if there were 3200 companies traded on the NYSE, the report might indicate there were 2000 (62.5 percent) issues advancing, 1000 (31.75 percent) declining, and 200 (5.75

percent) unchanged. That would be reported as 2-to-1 on the upside. There were twice as many companies advancing as declining.

When the breadth of the market is 2-to-1, it would be a bullish indicator for the day. However, investors who follow this indicator are much more interested in the trend than in the daily number.

The numbers in this illustration are slightly bullish, but not enough to be meaningful to a technical investor. Note the up volume is slightly greater than down volume. But not significantly enough to be a meaningful bullish indicator. Also, note there are a large number of new highs on the NYSE, but that is offset by the new lows.

	NYSE	Nasdaq
Advances	1,831 (59%)	1,404 (57%)
Declines	1,176 (38%)	960 (39%)
Unchanged	113 (4%)	102 (4%)
Up Vol*	1,194 (64%)	722 (73%)
Down Vol*	629 (34%)	249 (25%)
Unch. Vol*	38 (2%)	14 (1%)
New Hi's	100	33
New Lo's	43	36

The **Advance/Decline Line** plots the number of advancing issues minus the declining ones over a period of time. Thus, the line presents a general market direction, trending upward or downward.

The **High-Low Index** is an indicator used to predict market trends based on the number of companies closing at new 52-week highs versus the number closing at new 52-week lows. The index is calculated by dividing the new highs by the sum of new highs and new lows. So, the indicator is the percentage of stocks closing at a new high out of all the those closing at new highs and new lows. Based on the information from this illustration with 100 new highs and 43 new lows, the High-Low Index would be at 70 percent, that is $100 \div (100 + 43) = .699$.

Most technicians would not consider this indicator significant unless the number of new highs is over 100. For example, approximately the same percentage would be reached if the number of new highs was 12 and new lows was 5 ($12 \div 12 + 5 = 0.706$). Such small numbers of new highs and lows are not indicative of a market trend.

A bearish indicator would be one where the number of new lows exceeds the number of new highs. If there were 100 new lows and 10 new highs, the indicator would be at 9.1 percent, that is 10

÷ (100 + 10) = 0.091. A neutral rating of this index would be at 50 percent. That would indicate the same number of new lows as there were for new highs. Usually technicians consider the High-Low Index to be trending bullish if it is over 70 and trending bearish under 30. But there are many differing opinions about the point where the indicator becomes significant.

A popular variation of the ADL is the **McClellan Oscillator Index, MOI**. It is a moving average of the ADL, calculated with a proprietary method of using two EMAs of advances minus declines. The most efficient use of the oscillator and summation indexes is to predict trend reversals. Say the market has been rising in a bullish trend, but the oscillator reveals that the number of advancing issues has been declining. That would indicate to a technician an overbought situation. Even though the market is still showing more advances than declines, the momentum of the rally is slowing and may soon reverse direction. The opposite would also be true, if the market is in a bearish decline, a flattening of the oscillator would mean there were fewer declining stocks. That could indicate a trend reversal—a bullish indicator. You can check out the McClellan Oscillator website if you are interested in more information.

The **Short Interest Ratio** is a measure of the percentage of shares of a company that have been sold short. You should remember that short selling is a strategy of making a profit when the price of the security declines. Short Interest is not only expressed as a total number of shares but also as a ratio of the average daily volume. If the volume has been running at about 100,000 shares and the number of shares sold short is about 500,000, the short interest would be reported as 5. It would take about 5 days volume to cover the entire short position.

To a fundamental investor, a short interest of 5 would be a bearish indicator. It would simply mean that a large number of speculators are trading to make a profit on the decline in the stock's price. However, to a technical trader a high short interest could be a contrarian indicator. A short interest ratio over 5 (some say over 6) would indicate the opposite of what it does to a fundamentalist. Pure technicians would probably consider it a bullish sign.

The rationale for this contrarian interpretation is that the speculators who have shorted a stock will need to become buyers to cover those short positions. Short selling is a short term trading strategy. So, based on supply and demand factors, the basis of technical analysis, that would indicate pent up demand.

If the market is rallying unexpectedly on a particular day, it is common to hear business reporters describing it as a "short squeeze". Remember that short sellers lose money when the security goes up. So reporters are implying that buying activity is being fueled by short covering. The short trader could either be trying to protect a profit or cut a loss.

Of course, a conservative investor will need to do much more analysis on a company than just considering its short interest ratio. If the fundamentals of the company are poor, it is not a good investment regardless of the short interest. A company that is about to go bankrupt would not be an attractive buy regardless of how many shares have been sold short. It is not going higher if it has no positive fundamentals.

The last indicator to be covered in this section is the **Odd Lot Trading Theory**. Remember that an odd lot is a quantity of shares less than 100. One hundred shares is a round lot, the traditional increment for trading stock. The Odd Lot Trading Theory is based on the Small Investor Syndrome, presented in Chapter 1.

This indicator is hardly worth mentioning as it has been disproven by several studies over the years. Nevertheless, it remains a staple in most books on technical analysis. The basis of the Odd Lot Trading Theory is that the small investor is always wrong. So, if an increased number of investors who can't afford to buy a round lot start buying, the technician considers this bearish; an increased number of odd lot sellers would be bullish.

It is worth noting that some studies on the Odd Lot Trading Theory have demonstrated that small investors are right at least as often as institutional investors, and sometimes even more often. Large investors are much more vulnerable to the psychological profile of the Greed-Hope-Fear cycle. When the market goes into a precipitous decline, institutional money managers may be losing billions and consequently panic more easily. The small investor who understands the cyclical nature of the market is less likely to sell into the Fear Cycle.

Institutions are only motivated to look good in comparison to other institutions. So they tend to follow a herd mentality more than individuals. You should be aware that as an individual investor you actually have an advantage over large institutions. You do not have to be accountable to anyone else, such as shareholders or CEOs. You are accountable only to yourself. Thus, you may be in a better position to take advantage of Fear Cycles than institutions.

How Do You Use Market Timing Techniques?

Technical analysis is useful to an investor or speculator for timing investment decisions. The indicators are designed to predict where there is likely to be increased supply or demand. However, there are a few other non-technical market timing techniques. Even though they are not technical indicators as such, they are being added to this chapter because they relate to this discussion of market timing.

The two most common mechanical market timing techniques used by investors are dollar cost averaging and fixed amount investing. However, for small investors these timing techniques are probably more appropriate for investing in mutual funds or other related types of securities. Mutual funds will be explained in the next chapter. If you are investing in individual stocks, this may not be a workable strategy.

Dollar cost averaging is a strategy of investing the same dollar amount in the same investment at fixed time intervals. Investors usually have the option of investing in mutual funds in relatively small dollar amounts, often as little as $25. They can sign a *letter of intent* to invest the same amount of money in the fund every month and may benefit by paying a lower commission rate if the total amount invested over a year exceeds a breakpoint. Dollar cost averaging might help some investors be more disciplined with their money, motivating them to save rather than spend. It may also lower the cost basis for the investment.

The following illustration assumes an investor puts in $1,000 initially and adds $100 per month over the next year, making a $2,100 total investment for that period of time. If the investor had put in the full $2,100 initially, rather than using dollar cost averaging for future investments, the price per share would have been $10, and the investor would own 210 shares. However, by dollar cost averaging, the price per share was brought down to an average of $9.31, and the investor ended up with a total of 225.62

shares. That is 15.62 more shares for the same amount of money, due to the fact that the price of the investment dropped below $10 for several months during that period.

Dollar Cost Averaging

Date	Price/share	# of shares	$ Amount
1/30	$10.00	100.00	$ 1000
2/28	9.50	10.53	100
3/31	8.75	11.43	100
4/30	7.25	13.79	100
5/31	7.50	13.33	100
6/30	8.00	12.50	100
7/31	8.10	12.35	100
8/31	8.50	11.76	100
9/30	9.40	10.65	100
10/31	10.00	10.00	100
11/30	10.50	9.52	100
12/31	10.25	9.76	100
Total	$ 9.31	225.62	$ 2100

The logic behind this strategy is that when you purchase a fixed dollar amount in the same security every month, you will buy fewer shares when the price goes higher and more shares when the price goes lower. The result of dollar cost averaging will change the cost basis of your investment. It will lower your overall price per share if the investment averages a lower price than your original cost. But, you should also note that, if the average price is higher than your original cost, it will raise the cost basis of the investment. If the investor in this example had purchased $2100 worth of shares at their lowest point, on 4/30 at $7.25, he or she would have been able to buy 289.66 shares. That would amount to 64.04 more shares than was realized from the dollar cost averaging strategy. As is the case with all investment strategies, timing is everything.

If you are unsure about the future when you make an investment, dollar cost averaging could be an appropriate strategy. But when you have done a thorough analysis of an investment and are convinced it is much more likely to rise in the future than to decline, you might be better off putting your investment capital into it at that point.

Dollar cost averaging only benefits you if the price of the investment declines during the time period you will be putting your money into it. If the price only rises after your initial purchase, you will end up averaging a higher price per share and purchase fewer shares. Of course, the investment could still be profitable; but it would have been more profitable if the dollar cost averaging strategy had not been used.

Fixed amount investing is the strategy of keeping a constant dollar amount in the same investment. This is a long-term strategy, and the portfolio is rebalanced over regular intervals, such as quarterly, semiannually, or annually. Using this strategy, you would sell shares if the total value of the investment went above the value of that investment from the last evaluation to bring the invested value back down to the previous total. You would buy enough shares to bring the investment back up to the previous amount if the current value was below it.

For example, consider that you invested $25,000 in a mutual fund. When you review the fund at the end of the year, you find its value has risen to $28,000. So, you sell $3000 worth of the fund, leaving in only the original amount of your investment. If the next year the market value of the fund dropped to $22,000, you would add $3000 to the fund. Buying new shares at a lower price will reduce your original cost basis.

A variation of this type of mechanical timing technique is **fixed ratio investing**. A popular strategy for mutual fund managers is a balanced fund, often referred to as *income and growth funds*. With these types of funds, the strategy is to keep a constant ratio of growth securities to income securities. Usually the growth side will be stocks, and the income side bonds.

For a balanced fund this ratio is usually 50 percent growth and 50 percent income, but it could some other ratio depending on the investor's preference. If the growth side of this portfolio rises so that the ratio goes to 60 percent, leaving only 40 percent in income investments, the manager will sell enough securities from the growth side to bring the ratio back to the 50-50 relationship. Vice versa, if the growth side drops, the manager will sell some of the income shares and buy more growth shares.

So many references were made to investment companies, such as mutual funds and ETFs, in this chapter, that the next logical topic would be about those kinds of investments. Chapter 8 will deal with all types of funds, professionally managed portfolios of investment companies. Some of these funds will invest in derivative securities, and some will be derivative securities themselves.

Technical analysis relies on interpreting chart patterns, but if you do not integrate it with fundamental analysis, you will miss the mark.

Chapter 8

What is an Investment Company?

Mutual funds, Exchange Traded Funds (ETF), and a variety of other new types of professionally managed investments are popular with today's investors. There are many more publicly traded funds in the U.S. than there are individual stocks. The net effect of this trend toward managed investments has been to turn the majority of individual investors into institutional investors. The growth of investment companies is a major reason why the number of investors in corporate stocks has not been growing at the same rate as the volume of shares being traded. To understand what a mutual fund or ETF is, you must first understand the meaning of the broader term investment company.

The term **investment company** is the corporate identification for a business that manages capital for outside investors. The main difference between investment companies and other types of corporations is the tax status of the company's earnings. An investment company is required to "pass through" at least 90 percent of the net income and capital gains it receives from investments to its outside investors. By so doing, it qualifies under Subchapter M of the Internal Revenue Code to be exempt from paying income tax as a corporation. The taxes on the income and capital gains the investment company receives are thus paid by the recipients of those distributions and capital gains.

The main difference between investment companies and other types of companies is how their profits are taxed. You should note that dividends paid to investors by most corporations, which are not investment companies, are usually subject to double taxation. The corporation pays taxes on its net income, and then shareholders pay taxes on the portion of the company's earnings that are taxable. Although exemptions have been granted on qualified dividends for shareholders, a permanent solution to this taxation inequity remains a legal quandary. It may never be rectified because of the government's insatiable appetite for tax revenue to fund its uncontrolled spending.

Investment company funds fall into three categories: open-end, closed-end, and hybrid. A **mutual fund** is a regular open-end investment company. It is called open-end because the number of shares it can issue is unlimited. So its total capitalization and number of shares outstanding can change daily. A **closed-end fund**, **CEF**, on the other hand, has a fixed number of shares it is authorized to issue, and thus has a relatively fixed capitalization. Shares of closed-end funds are usually classified as **shares of beneficial interest**, **SBI**, as opposed to the common stock classification issued by corporations. Closed-end funds trade on an exchange and their price is subject to supply and demand fluctuations like common stock. They are usually organized by the same investment companies that issue open-end mutual funds. Hybrid funds, exchange traded funds (ETFs) and exchange traded notes (ETNs) have the characteristics of open-ended funds because they have an unlimited number of shares they can issue, but they trade on an exchange like closed end funds.

An open-end mutual fund may be redeemed anytime at the fund's closing net asset value. The **net asset value**, **NAV**, is the total market value of the investments held by the fund divided by the total number of shares outstanding. In other words, it is the value of the fund expressed on a per share basis, net of fees. It is important to note that shares of mutual funds do not trade on an exchange. Purchases and sales are made by the fund itself after the market closes, when the closing net asset value of the shares has been calculated.

Because mutual funds are open-ended, people are sometimes confused because occasionally a mutual fund can amend its charter to limit new investments only to investors who currently own shares. That may not sound very open-ended, but it still legally qualifies, even though the fund still has a variable capitalization. New shares can still be added to the fund, but only current shareholders can make that happen.

Often the motivation for managers to close a mutual fund to new investors is that its size has grown too big for the management team to efficiently continue investing large amounts of additional capital. The size of the fund already taxes the team. Sometimes managers may feel their success could cause an influx of new investors, which might make it difficult to repeat their prior performance.

Such a move could accomplish that objective without jeopardizing their status as an open-end investment company. Mutual funds that limit new investments to existing shareholders will probably be able to maintain a more stable capitalization than funds that do not. Current investors can add as much money as they want, but new investors will have to look for another fund.

Because the share price of mutual funds is expressed as the closing net asset value, you should be aware that you never know what the exact share price will be on the day you enter an order, either to buy or to sell. The only price quote you have available is the previous day's closing NAV. The price you pay per share will be the net asset value based on that day's trades.

Since you never know beforehand what the actual cost per share will be, mutual fund orders may be entered either as an exact dollar amount or as an exact share amount. For example, if you have $10,000 you want to invest in a mutual fund, you can enter that amount. The fund will purchase enough full and a fractional share to match it. The fractional share will be calculated out to four decimal places (one one-hundredth of a cent).

The NAV will usually change as the prices of the securities in the fund change from normal daily activity. However, for most mutual funds, the daily change is usually in small increments. Most mutual funds are composed of many securities. Smaller funds may have a few hundred different securities, and larger funds several thousand. With that much diversification, the NAV of the fund will change in much smaller increments than most of its individual components. Some securities may be up and some down.

Next, you should consider what it will cost you to invest in a mutual fund. In addition to the NAV, you will have to pay any fees associated with the purchase. The fees, or **load**, charged will need some clarification.

What Does It Cost to Buy a Mutual Fund?

Although there have been several attempts made in the past to regulate the costs of investing in mutual funds, none of them has resulted in empowering the Securities and Exchange Commission with such control. However, greater volume and keener competition has brought the fees down considerably from what they had been in the past. The mutual fund industry is another example of how a competitive free-market economy, rather than government intervention, results in price benefits to the consumer. Every fund manager is fully aware that in order to attract new investors it must offer a competitive return at a competitive price.

Past mutual fund performance records are reported on a quarterly basis by Lipper Analytical Services, Morningstar, and other financial services. Then that data is reprinted by most financial media outlets. So, you have many sources for gathering information about ranking mutual fund performance. This information will be broken down into short term performance, such as for the quarter or year, and long-term records, such as five- and ten-years.

Since higher fees will lower the total returns reported by the funds, this exposure of their performance generally has the effect of keeping the fees low. The Morningstar Mutual Fund Rating Service is an excellent source of information on the relative cost of fees for a very broad list of mutual funds. It is available online at the Morningstar website, and a print copy of the complete report will probably be available in libraries and many brokerage offices. This service provides a thorough disclosure of fees charged by the funds.

In addition to these rating services, mutual funds must provide prospectuses to all investors. The prospectus, like the one for all new IPOs in the primary market (Chapter 2), must represent full disclosure of the fund's business. Full disclosure means a thorough and complete discussion of the fund's operations, including risks, fees, and expenses.

Funds must provide a prospectus to all investors as a result of the Investment Company Act of 1940. Since mutual funds have an unlimited number of shares they are authorized to issue, every new sold is a primary market (new issue) share. This legal definition was a result of the Investment Company Act. As with all other primary shares, all advertisements for mutual funds must contain the disclaimer that solicitation for shares is by prospectus only and must advise potential investors to read the prospectus before investing.

The fee charged for investing in mutual funds is called a **load**. On the basis of the fee structure, funds will be generally classified as front-end load (Class A), back-end load Class B), or no-load (Class C). There are other variations of these fee structures, but most of those are only applicable to institutional investors. These are the main types of fee structures with which most individual investors will need to be familiar.

With a **front-end load** fund you will be charged a fee when you purchase the shares. This fee is expressed as a percentage of the net asset value. A typical front-end load fund for an actively managed stock fund may be around 5 percent. It is a onetime fee added to the share price of your investment. Not all front-end load funds charge the same rate. They typically range anywhere from 1 to over 5 percent. Read the prospectus before investing. Because there is a front-end load fee, there is no fee to sell the shares.

The front-end load structure will typically have **breakpoints** that could reduce the percentage of the fee, if you plan to make future investment in the fund over certain specified dollar amounts. Breakpoints follow a schedule like the one shown below. Different investment companies have different breakpoints. So, if you plan to invest over a period of time in a mutual fund, check out the breakpoint structure in the prospectus.

Investment Amount:	Sales Load:
Less than $25,000	5.00 %
$25,000 but less than $50,000	4.25 %
$50,000 but less than $100,000	3.75 %
$100,000 but less than $250,000	3.25 %
$250,000 but less than $500,000	2.75 %
$250,000 but less than $1 million	2.00 %
$1 million or more	0.00 %

This illustration is an example of a representative Breakpoint Schedule for a Class A (front-end load) mutual fund. Remember that investment companies set the breakpoint schedules applicable to their funds. Fees and schedules can vary widely among different investment companies. However, even though you may not have enough investment capital to hit a commission breakpoint, you may still be able to qualify for a lower rate by adding additional funds in the future.

If you anticipate making future additions to a fund, such as by dollar cost averaging as discussed in the last chapter, you can sign a **Letter of Intent**, **LOI**, when you initially invest. An LOI will typically be included as part of the application for a mutual fund. You will usually find it at the back of the prospectus. If your letter of intent, sometimes called a *statement of intent*, specifies that you will be investing a total amount in the upcoming year that would go over a breakpoint, you will be charged the lower fees on each purchase, even though no single investment exceeded a breakpoint.

For example, if you invest $15,000 in a fund and plan to send in an additional $1,000 each month, you could specify by LOI that you intend to invest over $25,000 within the next 12 months. You would then be charged 4.25 percent on each purchase, rather than the 5 percent that would normally be charged for investments under $25,000. In most cases a letter of intent can be backdated up to 30 days after your initial purchase. But if you fail to meet the breakpoint you specified by the end of one year, the mutual fund will deduct shares from your fund in order to make up the difference between what you paid in fees and what you should have paid.

Another cost saving plan that most investment companies offer for front-end load funds is **Rights of Accumulation**, **ROA**. This means that if you plan on purchasing more shares of a fund in which you have previously made an investment and this additional amount will make the total go over a breakpoint, you will receive the lower commission rate. For example, if you had previously invested $35,000 in a fund and plan to add another $15,000, you would receive the lower rate on that additional amount for the breakpoint over $50,000.

As mentioned earlier, mutual funds are quoted at the net asset value based on the previous day's total market value of the securities in its portfolio. The quote for a front-end load fund will also show a different offering price. The **offering price** will be the previous closing NAV plus the maximum load the fund would charge. This is similar to the bid-ask quotes for stocks. You could buy at the offer price, which includes the load; or you could sell at the NAV. So if the NAV is 10.00 for a front-end load fund and it charges a 5 percent load, you would pay $10.50 per share.

However, you should note that if you purchase enough shares to exceed a breakpoint for the fund, your price per share will be lower than the quoted offer price. It will be the NAV plus the reduced load resulting from the breakpoint savings. The quoted price would be based on the maximum load.

If the fund is a back-end load or no-load fund, the offer price column will show NL, no load. Daily mutual fund quotes may also include other information, such as year to date net asset value change or historical rates of return. A fund with a **back-end load fund** is one that charges no commission at the time of purchase, but it charges a fee to redeem the shares within a specified period of time. The technical term for this type of fee structure is *contingent deferred sales charge*, or CDSC. The rate reduction schedule for these fees are set by the investment company.

A back-end load fund might charge 5 percent if you redeem shares within the first year of your initial purchase. The next year the fee might decline to 4 percent, 3 percent in the third, 2 percent in the fourth, 1 percent in the fifth and sixth years, and no charge for redemptions after that. Different back-end load funds will have different fee structures. So, again, read the prospectus to find out the specific fees for the fund you are considering.

Mutual funds typically identify the type of fee structure as different classes of shares. Class A shares are front-end load, Class B shares are back-end load, and Class C shares are no-load. Also, investors will usually have the option of switching between other mutual funds within the same family of funds at net asset value without a fee charge, or for a small transfer fee. However, investors should realize that if they switch funds, they will need to stay within the same class of shares.

Investors could not, for example, invest in Class B shares that charge no front-end load but would charge for early redemption, and then switch to Class A shares that have no redemption fees in order to avoid paying the regular front-end fees for the Class A shares. If you invest in Class B shares of one fund and then you will need to switch to Class B shares of another fund within the same family, the holding period for redemption fees will be carried over from the original investment. Investors do not have to begin a new holding period at the time of the switch.

A Class C **no-load fund** will not charge any commission fees for investing in it, and usually it will not charge any fees for redemption. Some no-load funds, however, charge a fee if you redeem the shares within a short period of time from your initial purchase, such as one month or half a year. Some fund managers initiated this fee to curb the high turnover from short-term traders using no-load funds as surrogates for playing small market swings. This practice by no-load fund speculators can play havoc with the fund managers' strategies and goals, potentially causing them to liquidate part of their portfolio to meet these withdrawals.

After reading these fund descriptions, you may start wondering why anyone would select a load fund over a no-load fund. Why would anyone choose to pay fees if they had an option not to? The answer will become clearer when you realize the selection process has one more step involving fees and expenses.

Mutual funds are businesses, not nonprofit charities. Investment companies intend to make money by providing managerial services for their portfolios. If they do not make money on the load, they must make it somewhere else. So, no-load funds that do not charge a front-end load usually charge higher fees for annual operating and administrative expenses than do other classes of shares.

These operating and administrative fees vary widely among funds, but typically no-load funds charge one percent in annual fees. That one percent is split between a marketing and distribution fee and a service fee. A front-end load fund, on the other hand, will usually charge lower annual fees. It is difficult to broadly categorize the expenses of all funds, but you will typically see front-end funds charging 0.25 percent to 0.5 percent annually.

To put this in perspective, if you bought a no-load fund that charges 1 percent in annual operating expenses, you would pay 20 percent in fees to own that fund for twenty years. Whereas, if you bought a 4.5 percent front-end load fund that charges 0.5 percent in annual expenses, the total cost of owning that fund over a twenty-year period would be 14.5 percent (4.5 percent + 10 percent).

The 5.5 percent savings of owning the front-end load fund over the no-load one in that example is significant. A no-load fund does not mean it will not charge fees and expenses. In this example, an additional 5.5 percent of your investment capital went to the investment company managing the fund and was not invested in securities. For a $10,000 investment that would mean the return on your investment would be approximately $500 lower if you owned the no-load fund ($10,000 x 0.05) instead of the front-end load fund.

Many investment companies now offer no-load mutual funds exclusively. This is the fastest growing area of mutual funds. For a fund to be classified as no-load, FINRA requires that it charge no more than 0.25 percent in annual service fees. However, that does not mean it cannot charge other types of fees, such as operating and administrative fees. Again, read the prospectus to get a realistic understanding of what it will cost you to own that fund.

No-load funds, like all other types of funds, will charge fees to cover overhead expenses. No investment company can stay in business if it does not charge enough to meet it expenses. Such fees vary widely from fund to fund. However, many charge annual fees well below the 1.5 percent used in the previous illustration.

In conclusion, the prospectus or some other analytical report will give you a true picture of what owning that fund will cost. More important than the expenses, however, is to select a fund with a consistently above-average total return. Although "past performance is no guarantee of future results", past performance does represent the management's track record. So, it is a basis for evaluating their style and capabilities. If the management team of the fund has done well in a variety of market environments in the past, they are likely to continue to do well in the future.

What Types of Mutual Funds Are Available?

The mutual funds managed by the same investment company are called a **family of funds**. Some large investment companies, such as Fidelity, may have more than one family of funds under their corporate umbrella. When investment companies present a list of all the funds in one family, they generally organize it from the most conservative to the most speculative.

Typically, a family of finds might contain: a money market fund, a U.S. government bond fund, a tax-free bond fund, an investment grade corporate bond fund, a global bond fund, a high yield (junk) bond fund, a balanced fund, a large cap stock fund, a mid-cap fund, various sector funds, a leveraged fund, a foreign stock fund, a small-cap and/or growth fund, an emerging market fund, and perhaps many others. This list is organized from top to bottom by how most investors would rank the most conservative to the most speculative.

Money market funds are brokerage account surrogates for bank savings accounts. The primary investment in these funds is commercial paper, composed of short-term unsecured corporate bonds, and U.S. Treasury bills. Money market funds price each share at $1.00, and since there is little or no credit risk to these instruments and they are very short term, the share price seldom deviates from $1.00. Most investment companies offer money market funds with no load and low annual expenses. There is little management needed for these funds, and no reason to charge much in fees. Money market funds were originally designed by brokerage firms to be a competitive alternative to bank saving accounts. But because money market funds encroached on bank accounts, and because banks started offering mutual funds to their customers around the same time as money market funds were becoming popular, the boundaries between brokerage and banking industries was dissolved.

The Glass-Steagall Act of 1933 defined the differences between commercial banks and investment banks (brokers). It was eliminated by legislation in 1999. But prior to that, the lines of distinction between the two industries had been crossed. Some commercial banks had already bought brokerage firms and were offering full investment banking services through a subsidiary.

Today there is not much of a distinction between the services provided by banks or brokers. They are all financial services institutions offering everything from traditional bank accounts to brokerage services to insurance products. They all compete in the same market for the same customers. Any bank that is not large enough to offer a smorgasbord of financial products is generally categorized in the Regional Bank Industry, as opposed to large commercial banks in the Financial Services Industry.

Mutual fund investors should also be aware that not all fund portfolios may be exactly what they appear to be. In order for a mutual fund to be called a particular type of fund, it need only invest at least 65 percent of its portfolio in that type of investment. For example, a U.S. government bond fund could invest 65 percent of its total assets in U.S. government bonds and the other 35 percent in high yield (junk) bonds or in foreign bonds. In spite of this portfolio mix, it could still call itself a U.S. government bond fund and might claim to be the highest yielding U.S. government bond.

Now, admittedly most government bond fund managers realize that investors who choose government bonds are conservative, and they would probably not try such deception. Investors, however, should realize that portfolios are not always what they seem to be and should read the prospectus and current annual report to have a clear understanding of the fund's philosophy. All U.S. government bonds are going to pay approximately the same rate of interest to an investor, regardless of whether that investor is a large corporation or a small individual.

Stock funds are subject to the same principle—only 65 percent of the fund's assets need be invested in the area specified by the fund. So a utility stock fund may have only 65 percent of its assets in utilities, a foreign stock fund may have only 65 percent of its portfolio in foreign stocks, and so on. Most funds, however, do keep much more than that minimum required percentage invested in their specified sector.

Another type of stock fund is a leveraged fund. It is so called because it can leverage fund assets to enhance performance. This may be done on margin, as was discussed in Chapter 3, but most of these funds use options as a means of leveraging their equity. Put and call options were discussed in the last chapter, and they will finally be covered in detail in the next chapter.

Equity mutual fund portfolios can be distinguished by industry sectors, total capitalization, leverage policy, or any number of other objectives. The peculiarities of the management strategy for each fund and the cost of owning that mutual fund will be clarified in the prospectus. That is why investors are always cautioned to "read the prospectus carefully before investing or sending money".

Also, the management style of mutual fund equity portfolios can be identified as: value, growth, or blend. These are terms used to identify the methodology managers use to make their selections. Value funds would be more attractive to conservative long-term investors; growth funds to speculators; and blend funds to those who want to be conservatively speculative.

A **Value Fund** is one for which the portfolio managers prefer companies they consider undervalued based on the company's projected earnings. Popular choices for this type of fund would be companies whose share price has dropped because of some negative event that will probably not have much effect on the long-term growth of the company. Value funds are often characterized as being composed of stocks with low PE ratios. Although that may be a characteristic of some undervalued companies, a company that has had a disappointing earnings report due to a one-time event would likely have a high PE ratio but would still be considered undervalued.

Value funds have a much lower turnover ratio than growth funds. The turnover ratio is an approximation of the percentage of the fund's portfolio that has been traded over the last year. For a value fund the turnover ratio is likely to be somewhere in the range of 20 to 30 percent. For an aggressive growth fund, however, a typical turnover ratio could be several 100 percent.

A **Growth Fund** is one for which the portfolio managers usually prefer to select momentum stocks, companies that are moving up in price due to positive events. Often these stocks continue to move higher because of their popularity with investors. This type of fund can be more volatile because a negative event, or even a potentially negative event, can cause a quick sell off in those shares. Growth funds can be very volatile.

If you select a growth fund, it is advisable to maintain a long-term time frame for holding it. Actually, all mutual funds are long-term investments by their nature. However, speculators are often tempted to trade in and out of growth funds, and they often end up on the wrong side of the Greed-Hope-Fear cycle.

When your growth fund is down 20 percent and it costs you nothing to get out of it, there is a great temptation to make that call. But almost inevitably a growth fund that is down 20 percent one year will be up 20 percent the next. Check out the long-term chart for your fund before you sell. It could help put your current situation in a new perspective. You might be more tempted to buy than sell.

A **Blended Fund** is one that combines the investing styles of both value and growth. Blend fund managers will maintain a conservative approach with part of the fund's assets, but will also speculate with part. These funds vary as to the percentage of the investments being blended, so it is difficult to broadly characterize them. This is one way that investors may participate in the growth potential of some momentum companies while also receiving dividend income from the value side, especially if the value stocks are large cap.

Mutual funds are also categorized as large cap, mid cap, or small cap. Market capitalization was presented in Chapter 1. Generally speaking, large cap stocks, with capitalization over approximately $40 billion, are less volatile than small cap ones, with capitalization under $2 billion. Keep in mind, however, that the vagaries of the market are such that any one of these groups may outperform the other two over any particular period of time.

Many investors are introduced to mutual funds when they are asked to select one from a list of their employer's pension fund or 401(k) plan. So, the information in this section should help you select mutual fund investments that are consistent with your goals and risk tolerance levels. You should feel comfortable with the style of the management of the fund you select. However, there is more information that will help you with this process.

How Do You Select a Mutual Fund?

Most investors go about selecting a mutual fund by first deciding on their goals. They may decide on some broad objectives, such as preservation of capital, income, growth, speculation, or foreign securities, and then narrow that down to some industry group they like, or some other narrower objective. Then they compare the past performance of the funds that match those objectives.

Even though, once again, "past performance is no guarantee of future results", a fund's past performance does represent the success or failure of that manager. So, it is a logical assumption that if a fund manager has done well in the past, the performance could be somewhat similar in the future.

That expectation for the performance, of course, assumes that the same fund managers are still at the fund. That is frequently not a valid assumption. Fund managers often transfer, retire, or get fired. So, an investor should check to see how long a particular fund's management team has been there. You may be getting a different manager than the one whose results are being reported.

Usually investors will choose funds on the basis of their investment goals and risk tolerance. If you want safety of principal and reasonably predictable income, you may select a government bond fund or a high grade corporate bond fund, for example. If your goals are for overall growth and you are willing to endure some market volatility, you might select a large cap or mid cap equity fund or perhaps a balanced fund of stocks and bonds. If you want to speculate and are willing to assume higher risks for potentially high returns, you may choose a small-cap fund, a leveraged fund, or perhaps a foreign fund.

Since past performance is the primary basis upon which investors make their selections, you should note that most mutual fund performances have been abysmal. In fact, most funds underperform the average rate of return of the overall market that would theoretically be achieved by random selection. Most mutual funds, and other institutional investors for that matter, compare their performance to the Standard & Poor's 500 Index. This is the case from the discussion of stock indexes present in Chapter 1.

The S&P 500 Index theoretically represents what the market average of randomly selected stocks would be expected to return. However, for almost any reporting period—one quarter, one year, five years, ten years—fewer than 10 percent of all equity mutual funds will outperform the index to which they are being compared. In other words, less than one in ten professionally managed mutual funds has actually shown a better rate of return than what would have been hypothetically attained by random selection.

Why can't professional managers select a portfolio of stocks that would give investors a better rate of return than a portfolio selected by random? This is the unenviable question plaguing all mutual funds. There has never been a year in which anything close to 50 percent of mutual funds has achieved returns equal to or exceeding the market average.

Statistically any randomly selected portfolio should be able to beat the overall average at least half of the time. This is overly simplified, but if you picked ten stocks randomly from the list of S&P 500 companies, those ten should beat the index about 50 percent of the time. In addition, most people would assume that if professional managers are making the portfolio selection, they should be able to beat the average market more than that.

However, there are several logical reasons for poor performance. First, the S&P 500 is always considered to be fully invested; in other words, this index represents a value that assumes all the securities in it are fully paid for and that there is no uninvested cash. A mutual fund, on the other hand, must always keep a certain amount of prudent reserve in cash (usually a money market fund) to meet withdrawal demands without having to liquidate securities in its portfolio. So, a fund manager has to do more with less. The manager will have to beat the market average with only perhaps 95 percent of the equity invested in the market.

Secondly, mutual fund managers are vulnerable to the whims of their investors. They are not in control of the amount of capital they have to invest at any given time. New investors may flock to a mutual fund that has had above-average returns. But to the fund manager this means that many of the securities in that fund might be selling at a higher price than the manager would want to buy them. The managers may get an influx of deposits into their fund at a time when they would rather be sellers of their holdings.

This poor timing by mutual fund investors can happen both when the market is up and when the market is down. In other words, when a fund has had a very bad year, the managers many be faced with a large amount of liquidations, at a time when they may prefer to be buyers of securities rather than sellers. Mutual fund managers are frequently punished both for their successes and failures.

Thirdly, the S&P Index is a moving target. If companies in the index are doing poorly, they will be removed from the list and replaced with companies that are doing better. The index is not static, and changes may be made to the portfolio quite frequently. Now, it is true that mutual funds would make changes in their portfolio much more frequently than the index. Fund managers may change their portfolio whenever they like—sell the losers and buy some winners.

However, you should note the S&P index itself would not show nearly as much growth if the losers had been left in. In other words, the statistics of how well the market has done in the past are improved considerably by changes in the stocks used to represent the historical rate of return.

This discussion of mutual funds has obviously assumed an equity stock portfolio. It is not meaningful to compare the results of bond portfolios to those of stock portfolios. You should compare the results of funds with similar objectives. In the final analysis, a potential mutual fund investor would be well advised to select funds that have good long-term track records, but that might be coming off a bad year or selling at their lows at the current time. This is a good strategy for selecting individual stocks as well.

A list of the popular mutual fund family websites seemed like a good idea. However, so many mutual funds exist that listing a few would be an inadequate way of presenting them. Such a list might be construed as a recommendation for those few funds included on it, while many better funds went unmentioned. If you are interested in a particular type of mutual fund, use a web crawler and narrow down your search by using the words that identify the type of mutual fund in which you are interested.

As a word of caution, when you search online be aware of potential biases of the site you are visiting. The web has many sites offering personal opinions that are not objective or professional. Any frequent user of search engines is well aware that anyone can post anything on some sites. You need to be constantly on guard for potential biases of any source which may attempt to manipulate your opinion. Obviously, this is not just true of internet sources.

What Are Closed-End Funds and Unit Trusts?

As previously explained, mutual funds are open-ended by definition. A **closed-end fund**, **CEF**, is a professionally managed portfolio of investments with a fixed number of shares and they trade on an exchange. Some popular types of CEFs are stock funds, sector (or industry) funds, government bond funds, corporate bond funds, municipal bond funds, foreign funds, country funds, royalty trusts, and real estate investment trusts (REITs).

Usually closed-end funds are created by the same investment companies that create open-end mutual funds. However, most portfolio managers would probably say they prefer managing closed-end funds over open-end ones simply because mutual funds have a volatile capitalization by their very nature, as discussed in the previous section. Portfolio managers of CEFs are less likely to worry that they may be forced to sell securities in their fund at a time when they may not want to.

Unlike their open-end counterparts, CEF managers do not have to worry about what happens to their investment portfolio if a large number of shareholders redeem their shares. The amount of capital they are managing will not change. Like shares of stock, all CEF shares sold will be bought by another investor. So, portfolio managers do not have to worry about being in a position where they may have to purchase additional securities in their fund at an inopportune time because a large number of investors have deposited money into the fund. Closed-end fund managers get to deal with a relatively fixed amount of investment capital.

Most fund managers probably prefer to manage closed-end funds over open-end ones because they do not have to worry about constantly changing their portfolio to accommodate the countercyclical behavior of investors. Open-end fund managers might not like being in the position of having to buy new securities at the top of a market cycle, when a large influx of investors are putting money into their fund. Also, they probably would rather not be forced to sell some of their holdings when an influx of sellers are withdrawing from the fund at the bottom of a cycle.

With a closed-end structure portfolio managers know exactly how much capital they have to work with. They don't have to worry about having to keep a percentage in a liquid money market fund. Generally, this type of structure should improve market timing and keep more money invested in whatever the fund is supposed to be in. The risk to the investor in a closed-end fund, however, is that the share price is now subject to increased volatility.

A mutual fund may be redeemed at any time at NAV, but the price of a closed-end fund is subject to supply and demand fluctuations. The net asset value of a closed-end fund will be computed in the same manner as an open-end fund. However, the market price of the CEF may be higher or lower than the NAV.

As a rule, the market value of shares of CEFs will trade relatively close to their net asset value. But during periods of high volatility, there may be a large percentage difference between the market price and NAV—perhaps 30 percent or more. If investors feel that the NAV of a closed-end growth fund may be going up dramatically in the future, they may scramble into that fund, driving the price up well above the current NAV. Likewise, if investor sentiment changes negatively, they may sell shares of a CEF in anticipation of a NAV drop.

However, there are always investors who are looking to take advantage of price inequities. If you are able to buy a portfolio of securities at a 30 percent discount to its current market value, why would you not do so? That would be like buying a portfolio at 70 cents on the dollar. Thus, efficient market forces generally tend to address any perceived inefficiencies and keep the prices of CEFs relatively close to their net asset values. Supply and demand factors, which are immaterial to open-end funds, can play a significant role in the pricing of closed-end funds.

The makeup of the investment portfolios of closed-end funds will be stated in the name of the fund. Stock Funds, for example, might be classified as Large Cap Value, Small Cap Growth, Technology, Balanced, and so on. Bond funds might be identified as U.S. Government, Municipal (Tax Free), Corporate, or High Yield Bond Funds. Be aware that the term *high yield* is a euphemism for *junk*—bonds rated lower than the lowest investment grade rating BBB. Geographically specific funds are also popular—such as Australia, Brazil, China, India, Japan, South Korea, Taiwan, etc.

Perhaps the oldest type of closed-end funds is the **REIT, real estate investment trust**. It is an investment company that invests only in equity real estate and/or mortgages. REITs are usually identified by the types of real estate in which the fund specializes. Popular types of REITs are commercial property, apartments, hospitals, storage, and many more. These investments offer the small investor a means of being about to participate in a market that is usually available only to wealthy investors.

REITs can be structured three ways: all equity, all mortgage, or a combination of equity and mortgage. You would want to choose an all equity REIT if you were primarily interested in the capital appreciation potential of owning real estate. You may receive some income from an equity REIT due to rental receipts, but the primary objective of this type of investment is capital gains.

For a high income REIT investment you would want to choose an all mortgage one. With this type of structure, all the investments in the REIT would be mortgage backed debt. Your position would be like that of the mortgage lender. This would be an appropriate investment for those whose objective is high income only. You would not likely end up owning the real estate property unless one of the mortgagees reneged on the loan.

For a combination of both growth and income a combination REIT would be your best choice. It is composed of equity ownership and mortgages. The exact structure of the REIT would be explained in the description of the investment company's business. If the REIT is a mutual fund, that description would be in the prospectus. If it is not, you could look up the description of the company from its website, or from another financial website.

A **Royalty Trust** is a partnership investment in a particular industry, quite commonly the natural resource industries. They are usually designated as **Master Limited Partnerships**, **MLP**s. Common MLP royalty trusts include investments in businesses such as oil exploration and production, natural gas exploration, production, or distribution, coal mines, timber harvesting, aircraft leasing, and so on. They are structured somewhat like REITs. Royalty trusts are investments in a partnership, and thus, the investor has a direct ownership in the business.

Most MLPs trade shares of beneficial interest (SBI) on an exchange, which allows for easy transfer of ownership. However, because your position of ownership is that of a partner, you will probably be required to file additional tax forms accounting for your income or the tax-advantaged nature of that income if applicable. The partnership type of business structure avoids the double taxation of the corporate structure. You, as a partner, are liable for filing tax information because you, as a partner, own the business.

This type of investment structure is called a "limited" partnership because your liability is limited to the amount of your investment. Remember from Chapter 2 that regular partnerships (as well as proprietorships) offered no legal protection of most personal assets from the liabilities of your partnership business structure. However, a limited partnership means that your liability is limited. None of your personal assets may be attached to legal losses other than the amount of your investment in the partnership.

Royalty trusts may or may not be leveraged. Many times the income from royalty trusts will be tax advantaged. In other words, some of their distributions may be tax sheltered, or tax advantaged, because of favorable tax laws on domestic energy production.

Some natural gas royalty trusts even qualify to pass through Section 29 income tax credits that amount to a direct reduction of federal income tax owed. Keep in mind that all of these closed-end funds qualify as investment companies because they pass through at least 90 percent of their income to their shareholders.

A related type of closed-end fund is a "unit investment trust". This is a type of fund created by investment bankers that invests in a fixed and usually unmanaged portfolio. Once the portfolio of securities has been put into the trust, whether stocks or bonds, that portfolio usually cannot change. Whereas most other investment companies are actively managed and the portfolio of securities may change frequently, most unit trust investments do not allow changes in the portfolio once the trust has been closed.

Unit trust bond portfolios will pay back principal as the bonds in the fund mature or are called. Unit trust stock portfolios will usually have a stated term and after that time all securities are required to be sold and all proceeds distributed. The trust will then simply be dissolved. It does not have an infinite life as do most other investment company funds.

Unit trusts do not usually trade on secondary markets. Most investment bankers who create and market these trusts, however, stand ready to redeem shares at NAV with no sales charge. Some investment bankers also hold previously redeemed units in their own inventory and maintain a market for those units. So, in some cases it is still possible for an investor to purchase units of a trust after it has already been closed.

Popular investments for unit trusts are portfolios of laddered maturity bonds or other fixed income securities. However, one equity portfolio deserves some mention. It can go by several names, but the most popular is Dogs of the Dow. This is a unit trust that invests in the worst performing companies of Dow Jones Industrial stocks for one year. These unit trusts are usually designed to be liquidated in a specified period of time, such as ten years. There are statistics demonstrating that this is a consistently successful strategy. Additionally, other non-listed securities such as commodities, real estate, or natural resources are common investments in unit trusts.

The fastest growing area of investment company funds over the last few years has been exchange traded funds, ETFs. The way ETFs are capitalized and may be redeemed is like open-end funds, but the way they are traded is like closed-end funds. Although they defy the traditional constraints of open-end and closed-end funds, they are an important investment format for individuals.

What Are ETFs and ETNs?

Exchange Traded Funds, ETFs, and exchange traded notes, ETNs, are the third generation of investment company funds. They are a hybrid of open-end mutual funds and closed-end funds (CEF), combining some features of both. They are often created by the same investment companies as those that manage mutual funds. They are created by investment bankers who act as market makers. Many ETFs and ETNs have put and call options available. For individual investors, the options are often more popular investments than the funds themselves.

Like mutual funds, exchange traded funds may be redeemed, usually by the issuing institutions, at net asset value (NAV). But they also trade on exchanges throughout the day like stocks. However, unlike closed-end funds, the most active index ETFs do not usually trade very far away from the NAV, perhaps one or two percent. This is because there are many arbitrageurs who are constantly looking for small discrepancies between the price of the ETF and the equivalent value of the index. With computer trading that can take place in nanoseconds, program traders are able to profit from arbitrage transactions due to tiny market inefficiencies.

An **arbitrageur** is a speculator who buys and sells the same security, or an equivalent one, at different prices on different exchanges. Arbitrageurs not only trade equity indexes, but commodity indexes, foreign currencies (forex), bonds, gold, and oil. Any investment that trades simultaneously at different prices on other exchanges, or in other forms on the same exchange, may be the subject of arbitrage trading.

The first ETFs were designed to offer portfolios that traded at a share price matching the values of popular equity indexes, or a constant percentage of that index. The S&P 500 Index, (SPY), the Nasdaq 100 Index (QQQ), the Dow Jones Industrial Average (DIA), and the Russell 2000 (RUT), are popular index ETFs. The

SPY trades at a price equal to one-tenth of the index it represents. So, if the S&P 500 were at 5500, the SPY ETF would trade at an equivalent price of about $550. The QQQ trades at one-fortieth of the underlying index, and the DIA at one one-hundredth.

By far the largest index ETF in total capitalization is the SPDR S&P 500. SPDR (referred to as Spider) is an acronym for Standard & Poor's Depositary Receipt. Another mega cap fund is SPDR Gold Index (GLD). It is designed to match the price of an ounce of gold at a ratio of one-to-ten. So, if the commodity contract for gold is at $2,500 per ounce, the price of the SPDR Gold ETF will be at approximately $250. Although the size of this ETF fluctuates dramatically, the gold bars held in its vaults would rank GLD as ninth in the world at about 1,170 tons. But the U.S. holds the most gold at about 8,140 tons (about $625B).

The portfolio of an ETF is designed to mimic the portfolio that makes up the index it represents. On almost every trading day, SPY and the QQQ (the Qs) will likely be on the most active list of NYSE securities. Also, some version of the VIX, volatility index, is another regular entry. The VIX, however, has some peculiarities that will be explained later.

The capitalization of ETFs is like open-end mutual funds, and thus is much more flexible than that of closed-end funds, CEFs. However, new quantities of shares are usually created by institutional investors, and the size of additions to the fund is not a few shares at a time, but usually in large quantities, such as 200,000 shares. Institutions may purchase or redeem these "creation units" at NAV directly from the sponsor. Because the portfolios making up ETFs are readily available, institutional investors may purchase the exact portfolio of securities and exchange them for creation units of the ETF at the NAV. The institution can then act as a market maker for those new shares.

A few of the sponsors of popular ETFs are: Blackrock iShares, Direxionshares, Invesco Powershares, Proshares, Sector Select SPDRs, State Street Global Advisors, Vanguard, and WisdomTree. Additionally brokers such as Bear Stearns, Goldman Sachs, Merrill Lynch, and UBS have launched several ETFs. This is not a comprehensive list, and each investment banker tends to specialize in a particular areas of investing. The number of new companies issuing exchange traded funds is constantly growing. Whatever popular trend that happens to grab the attention of investors will undoubtedly soon be represented by a new ETF, capitalizing on that interest.

Because the number of companies issuing ETFs is growing so rapidly, the number of new ETFs being traded is growing even more rapidly. It is approximately the number of individual companies traded on the NYSE. One factor contributing to this growth is that the SEC has allowed the issuance of actively managed ETFs. These are funds that are not meant to track a particular index or commodity, but are meant to compete for the same investors that would traditionally be interested in open-end equity or bond funds. Of course, although the portfolios of these funds change frequently, the ETF must have the same level of transparency as an index ETF in order that institutions may be able to purchase shares and add creation units.

The benefits to the individual investor of ETFs are many. They offer a low cost way of participating in a large portfolio of securities, much lower than what the cost would be to purchase all the individual securities in the fund. ETFs do not charge sales and marketing fees (12b-1 fees) as mutual funds do. Because the shares trade like stocks, you can purchase shares on margin, sell them short, and enter limit or stop orders. None of those trading strategies are available with mutual funds.

Some investment bankers, ProShares and Direxion to name a couple, specialize in offering highly leveraged index ETFs. Some of their funds are designed to track indexes, but their most popular ones are structured to go up (bull) or down (bear) 2 or 3 times the equivalent move of the underlying index. They appeal to speculators, or more accurately gamblers. Put and call options are also available on most of their ETFs, so if 3 times leverage is not speculative enough for you, you can leverage your market call further with options.

Perhaps the most misunderstood ETFs are the VIXs, volatility index funds. These are pegged to the volatility of a specified index, commodity, or other security. Various VIX contracts are structured differently, but generally they are designed to benefit the speculator if there is excess volatility of the underlying security over the benchmark as represented by the value of contract.

That VIXen, she's a devil in disguise

Thus, if the S&P 500 VIX is at 20, the expectation, based on the price, is that the S&P 500 Index will drop 20 points. But if you buy this index and the market drops 20 points, you will probably get nothing because that is the breakeven point. The index must drop over 20 before that VIX contract is profitable. Confused? So are many of the speculators who have bought them. Do not speculate on something you do not understand. Heed the subtitle of this book; learn what you need to know before you invest.

A variation of exchange traded funds are **exchange traded notes**, **ETNs**. They look and act like ETFs, but there is no asset backing them other than the promise of the issuer. They are similar to an unsecured debt obligation (note) of the issuer for a given period of time. However, instead of paying a fixed rate of interest at maturity, ETNs pay the investor the capital gains or losses on the index to which it was pegged. ETNs are promissory notes of the issuing investment company. Most of them are designed to replicate various indexes or specific commodities, such as gold, bond interest rates, currency exchange, etc. A complete list is impractical because it is so large and ever changing.

ETNs can be traded during normal market hours, and there are put and call options available on most of them. They are often promoted as having no tax consequences to the investor until they mature. However, equivalent ETFs are required to distribute all capital gains realized from the buying and selling of securities to rebalance the portfolio in the year the gain is realized. Those distributions will be subject to taxation in the same manner as any other investment company fund. But there are no assets backing an ETN. So, there will be no realized capital gain until maturity.

Speculators can buy or sell options on most ETFs and ETNs, if they want to bet on the overall market or a market segment for the time limited by the expiration date of the contract. The leverage of these options can be used to hedge a large portfolio of securities. Some investment advisors recommend using index options to limit, or mitigate, volatility. There is increased risk in speculating with options, but there can also be reduced risk to your portfolio if puts and calls are properly used to hedge market risk. However, if you are interested in pursuing these derivatives further, you'll have to go to other sources. The emphasis here is on conservative investing.

What About Cryptocurrencies?

Bitcoin opened the door to the first ever independent and non-regulated alternative to making financial transactions without going through federally monitored financial institutions and avoiding the scrutiny of government agencies. Using innovative blockchain technology to make monetary exchange secure and theoretically untraceable, bitcoin became the first private sector entity to introduce an alternative to government-backed *fiat* currency. The word fiat literally means to create something by decree, to speak something into existence—a god-like power.

The creation of bitcoin publicly exposed the fact that governments create monetary units that are not backed by any asset. Sovereign governments cannot be held accountable for their actions and have unlimited spending power—at taxpayers' expense. Sovereigns have the power to turn hot air into money, but bitcoin was not created by a sovereign. Its inventor simply used the same strategy assumed by sovereigns. The main difference being that bitcoin capped the quantity of currency that could be created. That factor should make the exchange rate of it more stable, but free market forces have turned it into an extremely volatile commodity.

The person or persons who invented bitcoin are unknown, and as far as anyone knows, they prefer to remain anonymous. Whoever they are, their plan and the execution of it was pure genius. No one has ever challenged government bureaucracy so successfully. Because this is a book about extolling the merits of free market capitalism, bitcoin could rightfully be cited as the best example of that ever. Bitcoin and its progenies should be applauded, but there is a downside to investing in cryptocurrencies. The approach to investing recommended here is not gambling. Investors need to understand the potential risks and rewards—especially if taking on sovereign governments as competitors.

The advantage of monetary exchange through cryptocurrencies is that transactions pass through the most sophisticated blockchain algorithms ever conceived. They are created by miners who program extremely complex mathematical algorithms to facilitate cryptocurrency transactions. There is no intermediary financial institution or government agency involved in the exchange. It's called peer-to-peer (P2P). Removing monetary transactions from government oversight is tempting, but it also opens the door to the dark side of human nature.

Cryptocurrencies have become the most popular way to fund criminal activities—particularly sales of military weapons that could be used to overthrow governments and create chaos. They can also be used as a means to hide illicit, although not necessarily illegal, activities such as prostitution or illegal drugs. People in positions of holding power are not usually known for their high standards of morality and ethical practice. Morality and ethics may not be that important to many, but if it is not possible to maintain any decorum by those in power, the world could easily be thrown into a high tech version of the Dark Ages. Moral currency is more difficult to create and maintain than monetary currency.

With that said, this book will not delve any deeper into the topic of cryptocurrency. There are hundreds of derivative investments and thousands of ways to gamble with them. The most popular are CEFs and ETFs, but there are many others. The companies that have created blockchain technology are more interesting investments.

Probably, the best outcome from crypto technology will be to make all financial transactions more secure. It certainly heightens one's awareness of uncontrolled government spending and could be the impetus to put an enforceable cap the government's debt ceiling. No economic system can save people from greed, but Americans still have the power to elect fiscally responsible politicians. Investing in crypto is fraught with many problems. Crypto needs to have some system of accountability put on its use, and the price volatility needs to be subjected to better analysis. That said, the advent of crypto has masterfully taken on sovereign governments at their own game, and I for one wish them well.

Investment Companies ◊ 223

Investment companies that outperform the market are difficult to find. Most underperform the market.

Chapter 9

What Are Put and Call Options?

As stated earlier, an **option** is a contract that gives its owner, called the *holder*, the right to buy or the right to sell a fixed amount of the underlying security, usually 100 shares, at a predetermined price and within a predetermined period of time. The contract giving the holder the option to buy the underlying security is a **call**. The contract giving the holder the right to sell is a **put**.

Defining options is easy; understanding all the implications of that definition, not so much. Trading options is complicated significantly by the use of terminology that is unique to these types of securities. Also, understanding how the options market works probably requires participation.

Understanding options is like understanding computer programs. You have to use them to understand them. It isn't something you can learn about simply as an academic exercise. Reading this chapter, or any other material on options trading, will not result in the same level of useful comprehension that comes from experience. So, be forewarned. Do not invest in options until you have thoroughly grasped of how they work. There are significant inherent risks in options speculation. However, there are also conservative hedging strategies for mitigating risk.

The Options Industry Council (OIC) publishes an Options Education Program (OEP) in which prospective options traders should enroll. It is designed to present a complete understanding of how the options market works. It is updated frequently to keep traders current on this ever changing market. Most brokers recommend options trading applicants complete this program before beginning to trade.

On the broker's application, you will be asked to provide information about your investment objectives, level of trading knowledge and experience, employment, net income, etc. Based on the information, especially your level of experience with options trading, a Registered Options Principal, ROP, will then approve your account up to a certain level. An ROP is a person who is responsible for monitoring option trading accounts for the broker and must pass FINRA Exam Series 42 to demonstrate a high level of knowledge in the area. There are five levels of approval, from most conservative to most speculative. Approval at each level represents approval for all the lower levels as well.

Level 1 allows for writing covered calls only. Level 2 adds approval for purchasing options. Level 3, which requires a Margin Agreement in conjunction with the Options Agreement, allows for trading equity spreads and writing puts. Level 4 allows for uncovered strategies. Level 5 adds uncovered index option strategies. The terms used to define these levels will be explained shortly. Needless to say, the higher the level, the greater the risk associated with that type of option trading.

The conventional method of describing an option contract, called an option **series**, requires a four-part description. The conventional order for these parts is: the **name** of the security to which the contract applies, the **month** that will include the contract's expiration date, the **strike price** at which the option can be exercised, and whether the option is a **call or put**. An option series on Unique Inc, for example, might be "UIQ July 35 Call". This describes a contract on Unique Inc. (name), usually expiring on the third Friday in July (month), at 35 per share (strike price), and gives the holder the right to buy 100 shares (call).

The cost of the option series, whether it is a put or a call, is called the **premium**. As stated earlier, a put contract represents the right to sell 100 shares, and a call represents the right to buy 100 shares. All regular option contracts are for 100 shares of the underlying security. The premium, cost of the contract, is expressed in $100 increments. Thus, a contract premium of 1 equals $100. This price represents the dollar value of the added cost for 100 shares of stock.

One of the few times a listed option contract would not represent 100 shares would be when a stock splits and the post-split shares cannot be adjusted into 100 share lots. In that case, the option contract would be adjusted to represent whatever number of shares the original contract would change into. If the option is for an amount of shares different from 100, there will be a unique symbol.

The option premium may look the same, but it will represent an amount different from $100 for each point in the premium.

For example, if Unique Inc. stock splits 3-for-2, the July 35 option would be adjusted to a new contract representing 150 shares at a strike price of 23.33. The new contract would be for 3/2 more shares, but the strike price would be at 2/3 of the original. The symbol for this option contract will be different from the regular stock options for UIQ. Also, the premium for that post-split option will be 3/2 times the quote. An option premium of 1 after the split will represent $150 because it is for 150 (rather than 100) shares.

Keep in mind this is only the case if the stock split cannot be adjusted to round lots. If UIQ were to split 2-for-1, instead of 3-for-2, each UIQ July 35 option (call or put) you own will be exchanged for 2 UIQ July 17.5 options. Likewise, any split ratio such as 3-for-1, 4-for-1, and so on, would not result in any necessity of adjusting the size of the option contracts from the 100 share norm. Only the number of contracts and the strike price will be adjusted.

Barring certain events, such as stock splits with uneven ratios or mergers or spin offs that create odd lot quantities, option contracts will be for 100 shares of the underlying security. So, 2 contracts would represent 200 shares of that security; 10 contracts, 1000 shares, and so on. Also, the premium you would pay for each contract will be 100 times the price quote. If an option premium is quoted at 0.5, it will be $50; 1.25, $125; 12.80, $1280; and so on. Thus the option premium represents the price per share of the underlying security, and the dollar amount of that premium represents the price of 100 shares.

For most options, only the month of expiration is needed because the last trading day for regular cycle options is the third Friday of that month. However, for companies that are very actively traded, the exchange may make available contracts that expire on a weekly basis, every Friday, rather than just once a month.

The strike price represents the per share amount the **holder of a call** would pay to *buy* the underlying security. The **holder of a put** owns the right to *sell* the underlying security at that price. The options exchanges will make available a new option series with strike prices close to the market price of the underlying security. Thus as the security moves away from those strike prices, new contracts will be created closer to the changed price. This is done to satisfy market demand. Since the time length for options can be as long as about two-and-a-half years, the price of the underlying security could change dramatically. That is why when you sometimes look up options, you might find strike prices listed that are far away from the current market price. At some point during that option's life, the price of the underlying security was close to that price.

An **option chain** is a list of all option contracts that are available on one security. Usually when you click on the price quote for a security there will be a link labeled "options" associated with it. When you click on it, you will get a list of all the options available for that security (chain). They are organized on a chart, horizontally by month and vertically by price. So the first page will give you the quotes for all the strike prices associated with the shortest term. A horizontal list of the other months available will link you to all the strike price quotes for subsequent months.

The longest options are called Long-Term Equity Anticipation Securities, **LEAPS**. They are **contracts that will expire two or three years beyond the current year**. LEAPS expire on the third Friday of the month of January. The shorter-term contracts are usually organized to expire in the current month and the closest two or three months. After that they will usually expire in three month increments.

The quotes on options are similar to stock quotes. They will report the current bid and ask prices, as well as the last trade. They will also record the day's volume and the *open interest*, which will be explained shortly. The volume information, however, will almost always show you that the contracts whose strike price is closest to the current market value are the most active.

You may also note that the some of the quotes in the chain are highlighted and some are not. The highlighted ones will be those contracts that are **in the money**, which means there is some intrinsic value in the option. Intrinsic value for a call option would mean that the strike price of the option is lower than the current market price of the underlying security. For a put option, intrinsic value would mean the strike price is higher than the current market price.

Consider the option series UIQ July 35 Call, when the price of Unique Inc. is at 35.50. This option is "in the money" by $0.50 because the strike price is 0.50 lower than the stock price. The option will be priced at a premium higher than that. The amount of the premium over 0.50 will be the time value of the option. It already has an intrinsic value of $0.50. The call option gives you the right to buy the stock at a price $0.50 lower than the current market price.

So, if there is about six months left before expiration, the amount of the premium over $0.50 will represent the speculative value for that length of time. Since UIQ has been a volatile stock (if you remember a few chapters back it was at $40), the time (speculative) value of the premium might be something like $1.50. Thus, the total option premium will be $2.00—$0.50 intrinsic value and $1.50 time value.

Keep in mind that the price of the underlying security is a moving target. If UIQ drops under $35, the option will then be **out of the money**. That means it will have no intrinsic value, only speculative or time value. The premium will drop to whatever the market values the speculative value of the six months remaining on the contract. This will usually be based by the volatility of the underlying stock.

If you are going to speculate with options, I would generally advise you not to buy deep in the money contracts. Often those premiums look cheap because they will have a large intrinsic value and a small speculative one. However, keep in mind that one hundred percent of your option premium is at risk. If the underlying security moves against your position, the loss from a high premium will be greater than the one from a smaller one. Speculating with less money will generally give you a better percentage return than one that costs significantly more because of the intrinsic value amount. The most active contracts will almost always be at or near the current market price.

Most of this past discussion has been around the prospect of speculating by buying options. However, options were originally created with the concept of offering stock investors a means of hedging market risk, essentially a partial insurance on their portfolios. Thus, many of the terms used for options are terms associated with the insurance industry. When you *write* an insurance policy, some of your risk of loss is *covered*. The cost of the insurance policy is the *premium*. So, remembering the source of these terms may help you to understand the significance of the options strategies referred to as "covered writing".

Stock owners can **write** (sell) a **covered call** on the amount of shares they hold. That contract will obligate them to sell the shares at a predetermined price within a fixed period of time. Usually this price is set higher than what the shareholder originally paid for those shares. Thus, these shareholders assure themselves a profit on the stock if the option is assigned. So, they must stand ready to deliver the shares if the price rises above the strike price before the option expires.

When stock owners write covered calls on their shares, they receive the **premium**, the price paid by the one who bought the calls, the **holder**. The writer has a short position, and the holder is long. The holder owns the right to exercise the option. As there is with shares of stock, there is always a counter-party on the opposite side of every option position. For every option sold, someone bought it. For every writer, there is a holder—and vice versa. Often the counter-party is an option market maker, an institutional trader who functions like the market maker on securities exchanges.

Thus, a covered call writer receives income from the trade, the premium that the holder of the option paid. That premium can be viewed as reducing the cost of buying the shares of stock to the writer, but it also increases the cost of buying the stock to the holder. The holder owns the right to exercise, to buy the stock at the strike price. The covered call writer will be the one whose shares will be sold, if assigned.

If the market price of the stock stays under the strike price of the call, the option will probably not be exercised. Holders who can buy the stock on the open market at a cheaper price than the option strike have no incentive to exercise the option. They were speculating that the price of the stock would rise higher than the strike price within the timeframe of the option contract.

Writers, on the other hand, hope the price of the stock remains under the strike price for that time period. However, even if it does not, a covered call written with a strike price higher than the price paid for the stock will generate a profit. In that case, the covered call writer has properly hedged the security by mitigating potential loss on the downside and insuring a profit on the upside. The only way covered writers could be in a disadvantageous position is if the price of the stock rallies above the strike price plus the amount of the premium they received at the time of sale. If that happens, the covered call writers could be forced to sell the underlying shares at a lower price than what they could have received if they had not written those contracts.

When holders exercise call options, they are committing themselves to buy the underlying security. So they must have available the amount of money to pay for the shares. In the previous example that would be $35 per share, the strike price. To exercise one UIQ July 35 call is going to cost $3500 ($35 × 100 shares). However, the real net amount of money being invested to establish that position must also be adjusted by the cost of the option. When holders exercise their contracts, they also need to add on the premiums. So if the premium paid for the option was $100, the actual cash investment for 100 shares was $3600, or $36 per share.

Likewise, writers will receive the strike price of the option at the time it is exercised, but keep in mind, they had previously received the option premium. Thus the actual amount of money the writer will receive from the sale of the 100 shares of UIQ in this example was $35 per share, the strike price, plus the $100 premium that had already been received at the time the covered calls were written. The holder paid a total of $3600 for the 100 shares of UIQ, and the writer received that same total amount.

Regardless of whether or not you are a holder or a writer, your initial option transaction will be identified as an **opening** transaction. The total number of open trades for any option series will represent the **open interest** for that contract. If you decide to sell a contract you bought or buy back an option you wrote, that will be a **closing** transaction. When you close your open position, it will reduce the amount of open interest.

What Happens When You Buy Options?

Regardless of whether you are a holder (buyer) or a writer (seller), your initial option transaction will add to the open interest of that option series. Open interest is sometimes confusing to new options traders because it would seem that as the volume of trading increases in an option series, the open interest should increase by that same amount. That is not the case.

Remember, when someone buys an option, someone sells it. Buying usually adds to open interest, for it is clear that at some point between that opening purchase date and the expiration date, the position will be closed. The option will either be sold, exercised, or expire. All long positions will eventually be offset by whoever owns the offsetting short position. Long and short are terms synonymous with buying or selling. Less clear, however, is that a writer, who has a short position, also adds to the open interest total for the option series. Some other trader bought the option you wrote.

Unless or until you close the short position for the option you wrote, it will remain part of the open interest total. So, the reason why a high volume of trading on an option series may not result in an equivalent increase in open interest is that some of that high volume may have been closing transactions.

Usually options traders prefer options series that have a high open interest. That means that there is likely to be more volume of trading on that contract. More volume usually means narrower spreads, that is, a smaller difference between the bid and ask quotes. Thus, tight spreads often mean a better price execution, whether you are a buyer or a seller. Options series that have small open interest will not be as liquid as those with a larger number. It is more likely that the market makers will widen the spread between the bid and ask quotes for that series. Supply and demand affects prices of all securities, including options.

"Large" and "small" are relative terms. So, to put them in some context, actively traded securities such as SPY and QQQ may have an open interest of over 100,000 for near term options where the strike price of the contract is close to the market price. Those options will have narrow spreads. However, some small cap stocks that trade fewer than 50,000 shares per day may have open interest on their most active contracts of some double digit number, or less. The spreads on those contracts will consequently be wider.

Open interest is also a popular technical market indicator, especially the open interest on market index calls and puts. Although it was not covered in the chapter on technical analysis, there is a good deal of interest in it, especially regarding options trading on market index ETFs. It is a corresponding indicator. The higher the open interest in calls or puts, the more bullish or bearish the indicator.

Up to this point the discussion on options has generally centered on stocks, but the fastest growing market for options is on exchange traded funds, particularly ETFs on market indexes. That type of trading will be covered later in this chapter.

Speculators are usually more attracted to buying options than writing them, because of the leverage potential inherent. A speculator can benefit from the price movement of 100 shares of the underlying stock without having to invest the entire amount of money it would cost to purchase those shares.

In the previous example, an investment in a UIQ July 35 Call would make the same amount of money as that of a shareholder who owned 100 shares of stock. However, the cost to purchase 100 shares would be $3500, if the stock was at 35. The cost to the options investor, on the other hand, was only the amount of the premium—$100 in the example. If the stock goes up about five points, both the investment of the stock owner and the option holder would appreciate about the same amount of money—$500. But the stock owner invested seven times the amount of money the options speculator did. That is a tremendous amount of leverage, which is defined as a smaller amount of money benefitting an investor by the same dollar amount as a higher priced investment.

The term leverage was first introduced in the discussion on margins. In a margin account you could put up half the market value of investments with your own money and borrow the other half from the broker. However, whether you paid for half the security or the whole, you made—or lost—the same amount of money as if you paid the entire amount. The use of leverage is a wonderful feature when the security is going your way. However, if the value of the underlying security is moving against your position, you will lose a greater percentage of your investment than if you were not leveraged. By speculating with options you could make a much greater percentage than you could on margin, because the option premiums are generally much less than half the market value of the underlying security, the margin requirement.

Option speculators should be forewarned that what they own is a *time decaying*, or *time wasting*, asset. That contract is going to expire after a predetermined period of time. If the underlying security has not gone the way you want it to, the option is going to expire worthless. You are going to be left holding an empty bag—actually, not even a bag. It is gone too; the term of the option contract has expired. There is nothing there.

Professional traders have made studies on how quickly the speculative part, the time decaying part, of option premiums declines. The intrinsic value amount of the premium should remain at whatever value the price of the underlying security is in relation to the strike price. A typical chart pattern of time decay shows a fairly steady downward slope that accelerates dramatically in the last month of the contract's life.

However, equity margin investors do not have to worry about time decay. They will continue to own the asset and thus have the potential for appreciation, even though the equity is currently going through a declining market cycle. Equity investments usually do not expire. There are a few finite term equities, but most are not. However, options and futures contracts are finite term contracts. Those investments by definition have a limited life span.

Thus, as a general rule, speculators would be well advised to buy options contracts with long-term horizons. All you really own with an option is time. You own the right to participate in the gains or losses of an underlying security for a limited period of time. Nothing more. So, even though the premiums for long-term options will be higher than those for equivalent short term ones, you are generally better off paying a higher premium for more time.

The tradeoff of money for time is a judgment call. There are no rules covering all situations in option speculation. You need to decide how much money you may want to risk versus how much time you think you will need for the underlying security to move in the direction you expect it to—higher if you buy a call, lower if you buy a put. Keep in mind that you are always risking 100% of your option premium for a limited amount of time, so the higher the premium, the more money you are risking. Since options are finite contracts, you should keep in mind that you can hedge your speculation a bit by buying more time than you think you will need. Over short periods of time, the market can be rather unpredictable.

One last note of caution regarding option buying: estimates are that about 80% of all option contracts expire worthless. Some commentators have suggested it is as high as 90%. Regardless of what the actual number is, the odds favor option writers. They are the ones who benefit from worthless expirations. The odds certainly do not favor the speculative holder who purchases calls and puts. Option premiums are debits to holders, but credits to writers.

When options expire, the writers' potential liability is eliminated. After expiration, option writers no longer have to worry about closing the short position by buying the option back or having it assigned. After the covered calls expire, writers are free to write more options. Additionally they can repeat this strategy over and over, for as long as they own the underlying security. Thus, writing covered calls is a conservative strategy. Buying is more speculative, and next up on the risk scale of option strategies is writing puts.

What Happens When You Write a Put?

Before discussing the strategy of writing puts, a few comments on buying puts may be in order. Most new option investors might automatically assume that the most common reason for buying puts would be to insure the downside risks for their stock portfolios. However, writing covered calls is a much better hedging strategy for minimizing risk than buying puts.

When you buy puts that could be exercised for the same amount of shares of stock you own, you will be able to sell those shares at the strike price of that put. However, the premium of that put will offset some of the proceeds of the sale if you decide to exercise. When you write covered calls, on the other hand, you increase the net proceeds you will receive if the calls are assigned.

Buying put options protects you from the maximum downside risk of owning the underlying security. Technically, all securities have the potential to drop to zero, but you would still own the right to sell them at the strike price. It should be pointed out, however, that the chances of an optionable stock dropping to zero is also nearly zero. Option strategists often use zero to illustrate the downside risk potential of stock ownership, but that is a purely hypothetical assumption. There will be plenty of warnings if a stock is a potential candidate for bankruptcy, and there are many checks and balances in place to protect shareholder rights before that action is taken. Companies can go bankrupt and forced to liquidate all assets, but there is a much greater risk of losing all your money buying put options than of seeing your stock become worthless.

Writing covered call options, on the other hand, only mitigates the risk by the amount of the premium. It will not cover your entire downside risk. But if you are that concerned about losing your entire investment, a better strategy would probably be to sell the security. Perhaps you do not really have the risk tolerance level you thought you had. If you are uncomfortable holding a security position and are willing to pay a put premium over and over again to be able to sleep at night, you may sleep better if you get out of that position.

Keep in mind that if the underlying security does not drop, and you keep buying puts to insure that position, the premiums you are paying keep adding up. You will lose all those premiums and should probably just get out of the stock. You might also want to reevaluate whether or not you really have the emotional makeup to be in the market. There is inherent risk in securities markets—as there is in life. That risk is not going to be eliminated by pursuing a strategy of spending more and more money to make you feel secure.

Buying puts is a much more appropriate strategy for speculators than for conservative investors looking for insurance. Buying puts offers the speculator the potential to benefit from the leveraged potential of capitalizing on a bearish market move in the underlying security. Writing puts, however, changes the nature of the speculation considerably.

Remember that for every option position there is a counterparty. If you buy a put, you own the right to sell the underlying security. But to whom do you sell it? To the one who sold the put. So, if you write a put, the risk you are taking is that you may be in a position where you could be required to buy the underlying security at the strike price from the put buyer.

Keep in mind that when you write a put, you get to keep the premium. Put writers, like covered call writers, receive the premium as a credit balance in their account at the time of the sale. When a covered call writer's position gets assigned the premium is essentially added to the sale price of those shares. So, the covered call writer actually sells the underlying security at the strike price plus the premium.

Likewise, the put writer buys the underlying security at the strike price minus the premium. When the put is assigned and the put writer buys the underlying security, the out of pocket expense will be the strike price minus the put premium, which has already been received. Consider the following example. Unique Inc. has dropped back to around 30. The UIQ July 30 Put premium has gone up to 2. You may be thinking to yourself, I'd like to buy UIQ at 30. That's a good price; I remember when it was 40 a few chapters ago. I could jump in and buy the stock with a limit order at 30.

However, if I were a knowledgeable options investor who was approved for Level 3 Option trading and understood writing puts, I could sell a UIQ July 30 Put at 2 and receive $200 in my account immediately. My risk would be that if UIQ dropped under $30 per share, my short put position could get assigned. In that case I would have to buy 100 shares of UIQ at $30 per share. But my actual out of pocket cost for the stock would be $30 minus the $2 premium I already received, or $28 per share. I was willing to buy the stock at $30, but with this strategy, I might end up buying the stock at a better price, $30 – $2 = $28.

What happens if the stock goes up and doesn't get assigned? I keep the $200 as consolation for not getting to buy the stock. In reality, if the stock goes back up to $32, I could buy it there, and my out of pocket expense is still only $30; for I kept the $2 premium. The proper time to write puts is when the underlying security is one that has come down to a level where you would like to buy it. Then the put premium is usually the highest, and the net cost to you, if put gets assigned, will be the lowest.

Remember that for Level 3 options trading and higher you need to also sign a Margin Agreement. The reason is that your risk with this short put position is you must stand ready to buy the stock at any time if the holder of that option decides to exercise. Consequently you must maintain a credit balance in your margin account.

The exact amount of margin equity required for a short put option is set by the brokerage firm. The minimum margin requirements that are set by the Chicago Board Options Exchange, CBOE, is explained in the booklet *CBOE Option Manual*. A downloadable version is available on the CBOE website. The margin amount set by the broker will be slightly higher than that of the CBOE, so that the broker will not be in violation of exchange requirements.

Suffice it to say that the amount of equity required for the short put position will be substantially less than the 50 percent you would be required to deposit to margin the equity position. The equity requirement for short puts generally runs at 20 percent of the market value of the underlying stock. However, the put premium you received from the sale applies to that margin requirement. Also, the requirement could be reduced by the out of the money amount of the strike price. There are other details and minimums that apply to the margin requirements, but you should get those from your broker. The firm where your account is established is responsible for making sure you comply with their policies.

There are also other option strategies involving establishing two put and/or call positions simultaneously. One is a **straddle**, an option position where the speculator either buys or sells the same number of puts and calls on the same security with the same expiration date. If you are long a straddle, you would buy both a put and a call; if you are short, you would sell them.

With a long straddle your hope is that the underlying security will be volatile enough that the profit on one side, either the put or the call, will be enough not only to cover the premium of the winning side but also the premium of the losing side. One of those positions (either put or call) is likely to expire worthless, for the underlying security will either go up or down. So it will have to go up high enough or down low enough to cover the cost of both premiums before you will realize a profit for the position.

A short straddle might be used by a speculator who thinks the underlying security will be stable enough to stay between the two strike prices. In that case, the speculator would probably keep all of one premium and perhaps some of the other.

Another multiple contract strategy is called a **spread**, an option position whereby a speculator buys and sells calls or puts on the same security at different strike prices and/or at different expiration dates. A vertical (or price) spread involves different strike prices and a horizontal (or time) spread involves different expiration dates.

The reason for establishing a spread position is to speculate on short term movements of the underlying security. You might expect it to go up before the long call side of your spread expires and then down before the short side does (or vice versa). Some option speculators who own shares of the underlying security use the short side as a covered write and the long side as a hedge to be able to reestablish the position if the short side gets assigned, or called away.

Variations of straddles and spreads are called combinations. There are countless combinations that can be created by changing the number of contracts on each side of a position or by using multiple strike prices or expiration dates. Remember that all these option strategies require that you be approved by a Registered Option Principal at risk level three or higher. The last two levels of risk, four and five, involve strategies associated with ETFs and ETNs. Most of those strategies are so highly speculative they should more appropriately be referred to as gambling.

How Do You Trade Options on ETFs and ETNs?

Exchange traded funds, ETFs, and exchange traded notes, ETNs, have not only revolutionized the investment company industry, but the options industry as well. Many ETFs were created for the primary purpose of facilitating options trading on them. If the motivation behind their creation was to reinvigorate the options market, they certainly have done that.

As mentioned earlier, the ETF market began as a convenient way to trade indexes, such as the Nasdaq 100 or the S&P 500, rather than individual securities. Trading indexes had been popular long before options on them were available. The trading of indexes is often associated with program trading. **Program trading** is a term used to describe the use of computer algorithms for entering orders. It is usually done by institutional investors who run a computer program for monitoring the continuously changing market prices of the equities or commodities that make up an index with nearly instantaneous speed. There is virtually no time lag between the change of the index and the computer calculation of that change. The computer program is designed to continuously monitor small inefficiencies between the price of an index option or futures contract and the real time market value of that underlying index.

When the computer program sees a price difference large enough to capitalize on, it will automatically generate simultaneous (or nearly simultaneous) buy and sell orders for the two equivalent investments to take advantage of market discrepancies. This type of trading is called arbitrage, and a brief description of the style of trading of arbitrageurs was given in the section on ETFs in the last chapter. The type of strategy just described is called risk arbitrage.

On October 19, 1987, Black Monday, there was a dramatic market drop of over 500 points on the Dow. It was the first time in history that the market had dropped that many points in one session. Some of the ramifications of that event will be discussed in the next chapter, but its importance in mentioning it here is that many commentators blamed the market crash, in whole or in part, on program trading. As a result, restrictions were imposed on program trading during highly volatile market sessions.

Usually high market volatility is a result of some unexpected news event. However, traders have come to routinely expect high volatility on what has come to be called **quadruple witching days**. These days are either on or a few days prior to the third Friday of the months of March, June, September, and December. They are the days when not only equity and index options expire, but also commodity contracts on indexes and individual equities. So you have somewhat equivalent contracts on four different exchanges expiring on the same day.

The high volatility of quadruple witching days is often due to a large number of institutional and program traders moving out of one contract and into another one, usually further out. The volatility does not happen on one day, but rather on the several days leading up to that third Friday in the quarterly cycle.

There are currently several hundred options or commodity contracts for an equivalent underlying security available. Remember from the discussion on ETFs and ETNs that these funds were modeled after mutual funds and institutional traders could create or redeem shares of ETFs by delivering a package of the underlying securities that made up the index to the market maker. So the options on ETFs could be subject to physical delivery of the market basket of securities at expiration. ETNs, on the other hand, are debt instruments, and on the expiration date those contracts can only be settled with the cash value of the underlying security. There is no physical portfolio of the underlying value of an ETN.

Options that can be settled with physical delivery of the underlying security are called American style. Options that are settled only with the cash equivalent of the underlying security are called European Style. Stock options are almost always American Style; ETFs may be either one, depending on the issuer; and ETNs will always be European Style because there is no physical security.

American style options can be exercised anytime from the initial opening transaction date to expiration. European style options can only be exercised on the expiration date. But for most individual investors, this is irrelevant, as they seldom exercise contracts until the last week before expiration anyway. One possible exception to this, however, could be if a company pays a particularly high yielding dividend.

As is the case with stock options, holders of American style ETFs may want to capture a dividend by exercising their contract before an ex-dividend date. Dividends are not paid to option holders, only stockholders. Thus, some critics of American style options claim they carry an added risk factor because they could be subject to assignment, necessitating the delivery of the securities that make up the underlying index.

Index:	**ETF:**	**ETN:**
Dow Jones Industrials	DIA	DJX
S&P 500	SPY	SPX
S&P 100	OEX	XEO
Nasdaq 100	QQQ	NDX
Russell 2000 Small Cap	RUT	IWN
CBOE Volatility	VIX	VZZB

Some popular categories of ETFs or ETNs are:
Domestic Indexes (some leveraged 2 or 3 times—up or down)
Foreign Stock Indexes (Brazil, China, EU, India, Japan, etc.)
Specialized indexes (large- mid- and small-cap, growth, value, sector, etc.)
Currencies (euro, yen, pound, etc., vs. U.S. dollar or other currencies)
S&P 500 SPDR sectors (Information technology, financials, health care, etc.)
Commodities (precious metals, energy, food, index, etc.)
Bonds (U.S. Treasury, corporate, muni, international companies, foreign sovereigns, etc.)

Those are short lists of a few comparable ETFs, ETNs, and their related indexes. A complete list of all available funds would not be practical, as it would be quickly outdated. If you are interested in investing in any specialized segment of the market, the investment companies that underwrite those contacts will probably introduce a way to invest in it.

Most options on CEFs, ETFs, and ETNs are fairly straightforward. However, the CBOE Volatility Index, generally referred to as the VIX, is an exception. The VIX, also referred to as the fear index, is designed to be a predictive approximation of the volatility in the S&P 500 Index over the next 30 days. It is a calculation of the percentage change in the market as an APR, annual percentage rate.

There are several different mathematical models, or algorithms, designed to predict the theoretical relationship between index option premiums and the underlying index's future price probabilities. These models allow their users to capitalize on situations where there is a price discrepancy between the actual option contracts and what the algorithm predicts the discrepancy should be based on volatility.

If you want to study these mathematical models, there are many online sources. However, in most cases this is not the approach individual investors should take toward the market. You should realize that you would be competing with some very powerful computer models searching for market inefficiencies in *your* strategy. *Caveat emptor*—buyer beware.

Speaking of *caveat emptor* and mathematical models, the options market is constantly on the prowl for new ways to appeal to the greedy side of human nature. The most recent product to tempt gamblers is binary options. These are option contracts that expire within a few days, or even on the same day they are issued. It is the gambler's equivalent to the over-under (binary) bet. They are contracts where the payoff is either a fixed amount well in excess of the bet, or nothing. The outcome of your bet is not reduced by the amount of the premium. You could win a large amount of money if the bet is over a benchmark or lose your premium if it is under.

Binary options may also be referred to as all-or-nothing, fixed return, or digital options. You can trade binary options on several ETFs, including those on the S&P 500, Nasdaq 100, and the VIX.

They are also available for several forex trades, such as the U.S. dollar/Euro exchange rate. An example of a contract on the SPY might look something like the following scenario. If the index is trading at 119 you could buy a contract with a few hours left in the trading day betting that the index will be over 120 on the last trade of the day. The premium for that contract may be $200. If SPY closes over 120, the binary option will pay out $1000, and if it does not you lose your $200.

This is a book on investing, and binary options have nothing to do with investing. So, they will not be explained in detail. However, you should realize that the counter party in these trades will always be a market maker armed with access to more information than what is available to you and with proprietary mathematical algorithms designed to predict the probability of the outcome. In every for-profit game of chance, the odds will favor the house. Binary options are no different.

As with any gambling game, the draw is that you could win a great deal more than would normally be possible with most investments. But you should also be aware you could lose it all. Gambling always appeals to everyone's greatest weakness—greed. Before participating in this market, go back and reread Chapter 1. Greed is the greatest hindrance to making reasonable investment decisions.

What Are Commodity Futures Contracts?

Futures contracts are similar to listed stock options in that they give the speculator the right to buy or to sell a specified quantity of a commodity within a limited amount of time. A **commodity** may be broadly defined as an asset used to meet human physical needs or a financial asset used to meet economic needs. There are many major differences between commodity futures and equity put and call options.

First, **futures** contracts may be either purchased or sold, giving the speculator the right to buy (a long position) a specific amount of the underlying commodity or the right to sell (a short position). Futures contracts are not equity securities. They trade on separate exchanges from the equities markets. The exchanges generally specialize in a certain type of commodity, such as energy or metals.

Commodities may be separated into five categories: metals, agricultural products, energy, financial, and forex. Metals may be precious, such as gold, silver, or platinum; or industrial, such as copper, steel, aluminum, titanium, etc. Energy may be oil, natural gas, heating oil, electricity, etc. Agricultural products include wheat, soy beans, cocoa, sugar, coffee, orange juice, lumber, livestock, and many more. Financial contracts could be interest rate futures, such as T-bills, notes, or bonds, GNMAs, or the S&P 500 Index. Forex is foreign exchange, and involves trading one currency against another, or against an index, such as the U.S. dollar index.

Each contract on these commodities represents a specified quantity that varies from one commodity to another. The quantities are not standardized as they are with listed stock options. A T-bill contract is for $1 million in principal. A gold contract is for 100 troy ounces. A coffee contract is 37,500 pounds; sugar, 112,000 pounds; wheat, 5000 bushels. A commodities speculator must learn the quantity of a contract and the unit price at which it trades. Also, the time periods for commodities are not uniform as they are with listed options. Some commodity exchanges offer contracts expiring every month of the year and can go out two years. Others offer periods expiring in two- or three-month increments.

The actively traded short-term contract is referred to as the **spot contract**. The spot price, frequently quoted by business reporters, is the price of the contract for near-term delivery of the commodity, usually the following month. In other words, the one buying a contract at the spot price is likely expecting to take delivery of the underlying commodity.

Usually traders who plan to take delivery of the commodity use the future's market for hedging. **Hedging** is the strategy whereby producers or users of the commodity can lock in a fixed price for the commodity months in advance of taking delivery. Hedgers can work out a financial plan for the sale their product to insure a certain profit margin based on the cost of the raw materials they will need to produce that product.

Wheat farmers, for example, might hedge their future harvest from loss by establishing a *short* position, or selling a commodities contract approximately equal to the anticipated size of their harvest.

By selling these futures at an acceptable profit margin, they can prevent a loss if the price of wheat drops by the delivery due date. They essentially have presold their harvest. However, if wheat appreciates on the commodities market, the farmers will not realize as much of a gain as they would have without the commodities contract. Regardless, farmers have locked in a predictable profit margin. Without the hedging contract, they could have lost if the price of wheat dropped below their overhead costs.

On the other side of the farmer's contract, a buyer, who might be a baker or breakfast cereal company, would lock in a fixed price by going *long* wheat futures. Thus the company can calculate the profit margin of the retail price by knowing wholesale costs for producing their product. They can determine what they will need to sell a loaf of bread or a box of cereal for based on what their manufacturing costs will be, including the cost of the wheat. If the price of wheat drops, the company can close its futures position, so they won't have to take delivery. Then they can buy what they need at a lower price than they would have been contractually obligated to pay if they took delivery of the future's contract. They will lose money on the commodities contract, but they will make up for it on the open market. So hedging could work both for the farmer and the manufacturer.

Hedging is not a strategy limited to consumable products. Interest rate futures are frequently used by banks and other financial institutions to offset the interest-rate risk on loan portfolios. A bank, for example, that has a portfolio of mortgages paying an average of five percent, could hedge that portfolio by selling GNMA futures. If interest rates rise, although the value of the portfolio of mortgages will decline, the value of the GNMA contracts will appreciate at an approximately offsetting pace.

One of the main differences between commodities and stock options is that with an option you cannot lose any more than the premium, what you invested. With commodities futures, however, the speculator has undefined risk. Speculators deposit only a small fraction of the market value of the contract when they buy or short on the future's exchange. If the price of the commodity moves against that position, that is, if the speculator is long and the price drops or short and the price rallies, speculators will have to deposit additional equity to meet margin calls.

Speculators could theoretically have to continue adding money to meet margin calls many times, if the commodity keeps moving the wrong way. So, most commodities exchanges have introduced trading in options contracts as an alternative to futures. The options have the same or a similar structure to the corresponding futures regarding the size and delivery date of the commodity, but they limit the risk to the amount of the investment. In that sense, commodities options are similar to equities options.

The commodities exchanges are regulated by the Commodity Exchange Authority, which is part of the Department of Agriculture. But commodities speculators should be forewarned there is no regulation of trading risk. A frequently quoted statistic, whose accuracy may be called into question, highlights the inherent risks in the commodities markets. It is estimated that 90 percent of all commodities speculators lose money. Your odds may be better on the casino floors in Las Vegas than on the floors of the commodity exchanges.

What Are Stock Rights and Warrants?

This chapter has so far covered various types of derivative securities traded on several different markets. The last two securities that fit in this category are stock purchase rights and warrants. They are similar to options in that they are relatively low priced securities that can be converted into shares of stock, but there are significant differences between these securities and options.

Stock purchase rights are issued if a company is planning to issue more shares in the primary, IPO, market. Prior to the issuance of these shares, the company will make available to its current shareholders the right to purchase enough additional shares to counteract the dilution from the new IPO shares.

Rights are credited to current owners of a company about a month or so in advance of the offering in the proportional ratio of what the dilution will be to the outstanding shares after the new issue shares begin trading. This allows current shareholders to maintain the same percentage ownership of the company that they had before the offering.

The exercise price of these rights will approximate what the price of the shares will drop to after the dilution. In other words, if the company is planning to issue approximately 10% more shares, the current market price of the stock will likely drop about 10%. If the company has 100 million share outstanding, a 10% dilution would be the issuance through the primary market of an additional 10 million shares So, the exercise price of the rights will be set at a price at least 10% below the current market price of the stock. The exercise price could be set at a larger discount if analysts or market forecasters predict the price could drop more than that.

For example, if the price of the stock is $25, and the new issue offering will increase the number of outstanding shares by about 10%, the exercise price of the rights would be about $22.50. If the dilution is 5%, the exercise price would be $23.75, and so on. Keep in mind that the price of the stock is a constantly moving target and may drop more than the amount of the dilution. So, depending on the market conditions, the exercise price could be set slightly lower than the dilution.

Investors are going to give the company an indication of what they think of the offering with their buying and selling activity following the IPO announcement. The management of the company has to do a good job of convincing their shareholders that what they are going to do with the proceeds of the sale will result in greater growth in the future to make up for the loss in share price that their shareholders will endure.

Typically current investors will be issued one right for each share they own. So, if you own 1000 shares you would be issued 1000 rights. However, if the dilution is 10 percent, it will take ten rights to buy one share of stock. Each right represents a contract to buy one-tenth (1/10) of a share. So, 1000 rights would give you the possibility of increasing your number of shares owned by 100, ten percent of 1000. Likewise, if the dilution were five percent, it would take 20 rights to buy one share. A two percent dilution would take 50 shares, and so on.

The rights would have a nominal cash value, and shareholders are able to sell them if they decide not to exercise them. The price of the rights will not be anywhere near the dilutive amount for the stock. It is usually only a few cents. Often these rights are bought by institutions or large shareholders who want to increase their ownership of the company to a higher percentage than they would have by exercising the rights they receive. They may like the company's plans for the additional capital they will receive from the offering and will want to increase their position while the price is relatively low due to the dilution.

Warrants are quite different from rights. They are long-term contracts that allow the holder to convert them into shares of stock of the underlying company. However, whereas rights will be priced below the market price due to dilution, the exercise price of warrants will usually be set at a price higher than the current market. They are like long-term call options, except that they trade on an equities exchange rather than an options exchange.

Warrants are issued by the company, not by a separate exchange as is the case with options. The company sets the warrant's features. Typically the exercise price will be at a slight premium, such as 10% and the length of time will be for perhaps ten to fifteen years.

The issuance of warrants has a negative effect on diluted earnings per share (EPS), so companies are often reticent to issue them. The SEC requires that companies report their earnings not only on the basis of current shares outstanding, but also on a fully diluted basis. So, if the company has issued securities, such as warrants or preferred stock, that can be converted into shares of stock, it will need to report what the EPS would be if all those securities were exercised. Also, the company receives no capital benefit from the issuance of the warrants other than their cost, which is analogous to the premium for an option.

Warrants are sometimes used as an added perk to an IPO to make the offering more attractive to investors. The warrants may become valuable to investors if the price of the underlying stock rallies past the exercise price. So, these can be attractive investments due to the leverage potential. The leverage from rights and warrants, however, pales in comparison to the leverage from commodity futures contracts.

248 ◊ Put and Call Options

Quadruple witching days, when four types of options and futures expire on the same day, can cause unusual market volatility.

Chapter 10

How Are Investors' Rights Protected?

All investments in accounts with brokers that are members of the **Securities Investors Protection Corporation, SIPC**, are insured up to $500,000 and up to $250,000 for cash balances. The SIPC is a corporation similar to the Federal Depositors Insurance Corporation, FDIC, which insures member banks accounts up to $250,000—per depositor, per bank. Neither of these are government agencies, but they are both federally mandated private corporations owned by their members.

It is important to note that the insurance provided by both these agencies, the SIPC and FDIC, cover investors' or depositors' account balances in the event of the failure of the financial institution. There is no insurance that covers market risk. The FDIC insures the amount of money deposited in member banks, but not what the purchasing power of that money will be. One dollar will always equal one dollar, but what you will be able to buy with it is unknown. You cannot insure what a product is worth. FDIC insurance does not guarantee what you can buy with your deposits.

In the same manner, SIPC insurance covers the amount of the securities in your brokerage account, but not what those securities will be worth. Since the market value of securities is constantly changing, the insurance coverage of the SIPC for brokers simply covers the identity and quantity of the investments. Insurance only covers what the securities are, not what they will sell for. If the brokerage firm goes bankrupt, you are guaranteed by SIPC to have your same securities intact.

The structure of the banking business and the brokerage business is completely different. Banks are prone to go bankrupt because of investment losses from risky investments they made with depositors' money. In 2008 when the economy was rocked by the real estate crisis, many banks went bankrupt or were bailed out with U.S. government guaranteed loans.

However, the business model for most securities brokers does not assume risks with their clients' accounts. They lend their own capital to fund margin accounts. But if a margin account falls below the 30 percent minimum maintenance requirement, the broker can automatically force liquidation of assets to bring the account back into compliance with the firm's guidelines. So, margin accounts are almost never a factor in a brokerage firm's financial distress. Margin loans are structured to be backed by more equity than the amount of the loan for which they are being used as collateral.

That said, it is important to note that brokerage firms can go bankrupt. Usually this is because of risky investments they assume with their own capital, not their clients'. This can be a problem when brokers over leverage their own firm's trading accounts with speculative securities. The cautions cited in the last chapter about the dangers of trading CEF, ETF, and ETN derivatives is applicable to brokers as well as individual investors. Corporations are made up of individuals, and everyone is vulnerable to the temptation of greed. Greed is not just a characteristic of the Small Investor Syndrome. Persons employed by financial institutions are equally as vulnerable as individual investors to making decisions on the basis of greed, if not more so. Corporations usually handle much larger sums of money.

Both the FDIC and the SIPC are private corporations (like the Federal Reserve Bank). They are owned by their members. However, because they were created by acts of Congress, they function as quasi-governmental agencies. Both agencies can borrow money from the U.S. government if necessary to pay insurance claims that exceed their financial reserves. However, the risk factors covered by the FDIC and the SIPC are for two industries with completely different business models—commercial banks and investment banks.

Commercial banks receive investor funds and deposit them into lower yielding savings accounts, certificates of deposit, or other products. The banks pay the interest on those accounts from the profits they make on the higher interest rate they charge on long-term loans, such as mortgages, business loans, etc. The difference between what the bank charges for its loans and what it pays out to its depositors represents much of their profit margin. Of course they also make much of their profit from fees.

On the other hand, investment banks, that is, securities firms, simply warehouse your investments and operate primarily on a fee-based business model. However, they too benefit from the interest rate spread by borrowing from banks at the broker loan rate and lending at the margin interest rate.

The FDIC insures bank accounts up to $250,000. This coverage limit would apply to the total of all accounts in one bank held in the same name. So, if you had a $175,000 certificate of deposit (CD or time account), $85,000 in a passbook savings account, and $5,000 in a checking account (demand deposit account), the total amount you would have invested with that bank would be $265,000. Therefore, $15,000 of your deposits would not be insured if the bank failed.

Additionally, if you invested in a $250,000 jumbo CD, any interest that you would earn on that CD would not be insured. You would be well advised to move some of that money to a different bank—not a different branch of the same bank. Only if the amount of your money that exceeds $250,000 is on deposit at a different bank can you ensure that all your deposits are covered by FDIC insurance. Any bank account in the same name or identified with the same Social Security number would be subject to the FDIC insurance limit.

Regarding brokerage accounts, SIPC insurance coverage for *cash* balances has the same limit as the FDIC—$250,000. That coverage is in addition to the $500,000 limit for securities. However, money market funds, described in Chapter 4 as the brokerage industry mutual funds that function similar to bank savings accounts, are defined by the SIPC as securities. So they would be included in the $500,000 limit. You would seldom have a cash deposit in a brokerage account, since most brokers automatically sweep any credit balances into a money market fund.

Also, in addition to SIPC insurance, most brokers purchase additional coverage from outside insurance companies. Accounts whose value is above the SIPC limit are usually covered up to $2 million; some brokers cover accounts up to $10 million. Check with your broker if you want to know exactly what the coverage limits are at your firm. Remember that to a private insurance company, brokerage accounts would generally be considered low risk, as they should be usually covered by more equity than debt.

The FDIC was created as part of the Banking Act of 1933. It was one of many legislative attempts to reform the U.S. economic environment that had led to the Stock Market Crash of 1929 and ushered in the Great Depression. The sponsors of the Banking Act were Senator Carter Glass of Virginia and Representative Henry B. Steagall of Alabama. So, the law is usually referred to as the Glass-Steagall Act.

However, when you hear people refer today to Glass-Steagall, they are not usually referencing the formation of the FDIC, but another provision of the bill, the one that separated the business activities of banks and brokers. A so-called "Chinese Wall" was created by Glass-Steagall to separate commercial banks from investment banks. That wall eroded away in the 1990s and was formally repealed in 1999. However, because of the upheaval in the banking industry after 2008, there is often talk of reviving those Glass-Steagall provisions.

Some market commentators opine that commercial banks should not have been allowed to participate in the derivative mortgage markets, Fannie Mae and Freddie Mac. However, the banks seldom "participated" in those markets. They simply created the mortgages that went into them.

The Federal National Mortgage Association (FNMA) and the Federal Home Loan Mortgage Corporation (FHLMC), better known as Fannie Mae and Freddie Mac, were agencies created by Congress and subject to the regulation of the Securities and Exchange Commission (SEC). "Fannie" and "Freddie" were publicly owned corporations with shares traded on the NYSE, and thus only quasi-governmental agencies. They were not under the regulation of the Federal Reserve Board (FRB).

There is a common belief that banks would not have gotten into the financial distress following the real estate market meltdown if they had not been allowed to generate a flood of derivative securities. However, all the mortgage loans that banks were issuing before and after the real estate crisis were already under the supervision of the FRB. The banks simply issued mortgage loans in many cases regardless of whether they met conformity requirements or not.

Many banks simply failed to follow their own standards for conforming loans because of government policies that encouraged FNMA and FHLMC to purchase loans even if their quality was questionable. Thus, it was common practice during the real estate market bubble that was created leading up to the 2008 crash for most banks to issue mortgages with a zero down payment and based on unverified, or *stated*, income. The borrower did not have to provide documented proof of income, but could simply declare, or state, what it was. This was a politically correct policy probably aimed at protecting those whose main source of income was "under the table", without taxes being withheld or reported to the IRS.

Those who supported this change of lending policy justified it by saying it was benefitting many low income individuals who might not otherwise be able to get into the housing market. However, the net effect of that change of policy did not benefit anyone. The low income homebuyers who could not afford their mortgage payments lost their homes anyway. Consequently, many well-qualified buyers did not want to continue making payments when the resale value dropped below their outstanding mortgage.

The flood of inventory of houses on the market caused prices to plunge dramatically. Every location in the U.S. was hit, and global markets were affected. In some of the hardest hit areas, housing prices fell as much as 60 to 70 percent. Homebuilders stopped building, and the number of filings for personal bankruptcies hit new highs. Virtually everyone who purchased real estate in the years prior to 2008 was *underwater* on their mortgage.

The cause of this crisis was that the function of government had switched from regulating fair and just economic policies into one where the government attempted to act as market manipulator. In their attempt to pursue a mandate that everyone should be able to own a home, they destroyed the competitive forces that maintained real estate prices. Government had lost sight of the fact that its job should not be advocacy, but governance.

Much of the world economy felt the effects of the U.S. housing bubble bursting. U.S. foreign relations with many countries that invested in Fannie and Freddie CMOs was strained for many years because of that fiasco. Not only U.S. citizens, but many foreigners and foreign sovereigns had purchased Fannie Mae and Freddie Mac debt securities believing they would be backed by the full faith and credit of the U.S. government. Although the principal was backed, the strange configurations of these debt instruments made it difficult to determine who actually owned the principal.

The Big Short (2015) is an interesting film about that crisis. It creatively exposed the role of inane brokers and bankers leading up to the housing market crash. Those people are being called into account by a few autistic financiers who have figured out the fraudulent game being played. But the film fails to accurately represent government's responsibility in fomenting the fraud. It implied capitalism is to be blamed for a problem created by socialism. The real villain was (and is) the government, which ignored its own rules in order to allow ignorant and greedy people to destroy the lives of millions—as well as themselves.

What began under the George W. Bush administration as a misguided plan to stimulate the housing market was completed under the Barrack Obama administration to "fundamentally change America" from capitalism to socialism. The movie ends with the statement, "When the dust settled from the collapse, 5 trillion dollars in pension money, real estate value, 401k, savings, and bonds had disappeared. 8 million people lost their jobs, 6 million lost their homes". However, money doesn't just disappear. It was confiscated by government officials who have never been held accountable. The government surreptitiously took control of the profits from the real estate industry—and it hasn't stopped yet.

Government abuse will not end until we put people in power willing to subvert their love of self for a love of the values on which this country was founded—especially freedom and escape from totalitarianism. Is it possible to find people willing to serve principles greater than themselves? That remains to be seen. But this country was founded by men and women who put their lives on the line for our sake, and we owe it to them to preserve their legacy.

What Has Been Learned from Past Events?

Prior to the Stock Market Crash of 1929 there were virtually no federal government regulations for the securities industry. Public companies were under state security regulations only. State regulatory laws, as opposed to federal, are known as **Blue Sky**

Laws. State securities laws were so diverse someone once described them as having nothing in common except that the sky is blue. Now most state laws conform with federal regulations, but each state still sets the requirements for trading new IPOs there.

Companies were not required to file public financial statements or report earnings on a regular basis prior to 1929. Consequently, the illegal or unethical trading of many securities went uncaught and unpunished. Most states did not have the capability of enforcing their laws. Manipulation of some securities was commonplace because a few wealthy individuals were able to corner the market on specific commodities and even industries.

By controlling all, or most, of the business of a particular industry, executives had the ability to set artificially high prices on their products. They had a monopoly. In 1929 there were several companies that operated with near monopolistic power. The oil, steel, utilities, railroad, and banking industries, among others, were examples of industries where a handful of companies controlled nearly the entire market for their products or services. Most of the economy of the U.S. was under the control of a few wealthy individuals.

Manipulative, sometimes fictitious, trades of shares in these monopolistic companies were often recorded. They were called wash sales. Such trades were direct attempts to misrepresent market prices or conditions. Wash sales were arranged transactions usually between parties in collusion who would broadcast the execution prices to floor brokers. These trades would often be much higher than the current market. Other traders would then be misled into believing that the price of the security was rising. Often in those cases no money would actually change hands.

As a result of this ruse, traders would scramble into the security *en masse*. The frenzied buying activity drove the price higher. Then the market manipulators who had started the panic buying through wash sales, would begin selling their shares at inflated prices. Of course, when the traders became aware of the identity of the sellers, the buying frenzy turned into a selling frenzy; and the market crashed.

Today the term **wash sale**, as generally used, is in an entirely different context. The Internal Revenue Service refers to the sale of a security for a capital loss followed by the repurchase of the same security within the next 30 days as a wash sale. If an investor does repurchase the same or equivalent security within that 30-day period, the IRS will disallow using the capital loss as a tax deduction. To the Internal Revenue Service, it is a *wash sale*. In order for you to qualify to receive a tax deduction associated with that capital loss, you must wait over 30 days before repurchasing the same security that was sold.

Note that wash sales only apply to capital losses. If you sell a security for a capital gain, you can buy the same security back immediately. You will owe income tax at the applicable capital gains rate on that sale. There is no tax benefit for selling and buying the same security when you have a capital gain. The IRS is happy to receive taxes, but not so happy about giving you a tax break for fictional capital losses.

Also, speculators in 1929 could borrow up to 90 percent of the market value of their securities. The initial margin requirement was only 10 percent, whereas today it is 50 percent under Reg. T, explained in Chapter 3. So, ten thousand dollars back then could buy $100,000 worth of stock. Thus, if the market dropped 10 percent, speculators lost 100 percent ($10,000) of their money. If the market continued dropping, the brokers who had loaned the margin funds began losing their money. The Great Depression following the Crash of '29 rendered most margin loans uncollectable.

From peak to trough, the Dow Jones Industrial Average saw nearly a 90 percent drop over a three year period. It topped out at 381.17 on September 3, 1929, and hit 41.22 on July 8, 1932—a 339.95 point drop. Today the Dow can move that many points in a trading session, and most traders will not think much about it. That is because a 340 point move now amounts to around 1 percent, not 90. The market has come a long way since 1929.

There were three days that were each labeled "Black" in less than one week near the end of October 1929. The first was Black Thursday, October 24, 1929. On that day the Dow lost about 11 percent in a panic selloff. The next day a group of six prominent New York bankers each put up about $40 million apiece and attempted to stabilize the market by putting in buy orders, generally at higher than market prices. This tactic had worked in 1907, staving off a panic selloff. However, that was twenty years ago.

After most of the rest of the nation became aware of the market gyrations over the weekend, the selloff continued on Black Monday, October 28. The Dow dropped nearly 13 percent. The bankers had run through their millions and were completely unsuccessful at stabilizing the market. On Black Tuesday, October 29, the floodgates were opened. In a record-setting session for volume about 16 million shares changed hands, and the Dow dropped another 12 percent. That record for volume trading would last about forty years.

The market had lost over 30 percent of its value in just a few days. The wealthiest men in America and innumerable average citizens lost about $40 billion in what seemed like the blink of an eye. Although most people were not aware of it yet, the Great Depression had officially arrived and would last for nearly two decades. It would not end with any of Franklin Roosevelt's efforts to implement the Great Society, but only with the economic impact of America's impending entry into World War II.

Over the next few years following the stock market events of 1929 the government enacted several pieces of legislature trying to find a way out of the problem and prevent it from ever happening again. One of the first acts of federal legislation to address the problems of the securities industry was the Securities Act of 1933. This act specified that companies that conducted business across state lines would be required to file a registration statement or prospectus for all new issue shares. The act mandated that every investor in an initial public offering (IPO) of a company be provided with a **prospectus**, a booklet that represented full disclosure of the company's business. It also made corporate officers accountable for any misrepresentations or omissions in the prospectus.

The Securities Act of 1933 was followed shortly by the Securities Exchange Act of 1934. It expanded some of the rules governing new issues to include securities trading on secondary markets, such as the New York Stock Exchange. To enforce these new laws, it legislated the creation of the Securities and Exchange Commission (SEC). This act required publicly traded companies to file quarterly financial reports, Form 10Q, and annual reports, Form 10K, on a timely basis. In addition, it authorized the Federal Reserve Board to set initial margin requirements, thus expanding the bank regulator's fiscal powers to include the securities industry.

Other provisions of the Securities Exchange Act of 1934 included the requirement to send proxy solicitations to all shareholders allowing each the right to vote on any material changes to the company's charter. **Tender offers**, attempts by an outside party to buy shares directly from current shareholders, had to be filed with the SEC. Often tender offers are made with the intent of gaining voting control of a company, or of using a voting block of stock to influence the policies of the Board of Directors. Minority shareholders who use the voting power of their shares to influence corporate governance are referred to as activist shareholders.

Perhaps one of the most important parts of the Securities Exchange Act was defining and allowing for prosecution of **insider trading**. Anyone who has information about a company that has not been made publicly available is considered to be an insider. So, the act made it illegal for anyone who had access to non-public information to profit from it. An insider did not necessarily have to be an employee of the company. It could be anyone who happened to overhear a private conversation between corporate officers or who came across corporate documents before they were released.

There have been many scandals involving trading securities on the basis of insider information, and the SEC has a department dedicated to catching and prosecuting those who try to profit from such access. Insider trading has always been illegal, but for many years white collar crime had been given a low priority because it was considered a victimless offense. However, the Great Depression changed all that. There were far more victims of white collar crime than of all other felonies.

Several other securities regulations followed the two milestone acts of 1933 and 1934. The Public Utility Holding Company Act of 1935 laid down regulations governing electric and gas utilities. The Trust Indenture Act of 1939 clarified the legal obligations of debt security investments. The Investment Company Act of 1940, amended in 1970, expanded the powers of the Securities Act to include mutual funds and other types of investment companies.

Many other pieces of legislation have expanded the oversight powers and authority of the Securities and Exchange Commission and the Financial Industry Regulatory Authority. The one common factor that all security regulations share is that they all are a result of the Great Crash of 1929. Today the securities industry is perhaps the most heavily regulated of all. Brokers are accountable to the regulatory authority of the Securities and Exchange Commission, the Financial Industry Regulatory Authority, the Department of Corporations in the state where they are located, as well as the broker's own internal auditing practices.

However, it is important to note that honesty and integrity cannot be regulated. Ethics can be mandated, and rules can be enforced; but dishonest people cannot be made honest by legislation. At best, they can only be made to comply with the law.

People are greedy, and money can make people do strange things. That will probably never change. It is basic human nature. Business ethics is an exercise in cross purposes. Everyone wants wealth, and most are willing, at some level, to violate their inherent sense of right and wrong to get money. Most people are willing, at some time in life, to do what they know in their hearts is wrong if they think it is in their own best interests.

A complete discussion of all of the issues that business ethics covers would be another book. A small section of this brief introduction to investing will certainly not cover the topic of business ethics adequately. For that matter, every chapter covers topics that would probably fill volumes of other books.

Business ethics covers a wide variety of diverse topics: employer/employee relations, product safety, sales and advertising, workers' rights, human resources, financing activities, and so on. These are all topics that are well worth studying. However, since this is a book on investing, it will only briefly cover the philosophical foundation that business ethics plays for an investor. Since investors are primarily concerned with a company's earnings, the discussion will be limited to how corporations relate to their shareholder owners.

At the beginning of this book, it was noted that securities markets are the free market capitalism—not just representative of it. For a free market capitalist economy to work properly, there must be adherence to ethical standards and strict enforcement of penalties for unethical practices. Without a foundation in ethics, the free enterprise economic system will fail. If a business is built on lies and deceit, it should fail; for if it succeeds, the markets will not be free. Lies and deceits are the tools of totalitarians, not of free market capitalists. If corporations are built on ruthlessness and lies, the economic system that follows will reflect those same traits.

Economic systems generally fall into two basic types: government or state controlled systems, which would include socialism and communism, and free market capitalism. Under a government controlled system the productivity of workers is primarily meant to benefit the state. Under a free market capitalist system, workers are allowed to benefit themselves.

Government run systems are usually founded on a utopian vision of society. Everyone works for everyone else in a mutually beneficial manner. Ideally there is no class structure, neither rich nor poor. The often quoted tenant of Karl Marx's Communist Manifesto is, "From each according to his means to each according to his needs." This seems like a very reasonable ideology. However, it has never played out so idealistically in the real world. It assumes the best in people, but neglects to make provisions for the worst.

The most prominent social experiment in communism was the former Union of Soviet Socialist Republics, U.S.S.R. It illustrated the approximate limit to the life span of that economic model. From its founding as a result of the Bolshevik Revolution that began in 1917 to its symbolic collapse with the tearing down of the Berlin Wall in 1989, soviet communism lasted about 72 years. That is not a very long time in economic terms.

Why did communism fail? Because its approach to economic equality contradicted human nature. Communism banned free enterprise, labeling it imperialistic capitalism. It took away most of the incentives for individuals to raise their own economic status. As a result, the Soviet Union reached a point where it could not produce enough food to feed its citizens or to manufacture a product that could be sold at a competitive price to the rest of the world. There were, of course, droughts and Cold War expenses contributing to the collapse of communism, but the primary flaw in the system is that it took away people's rights to benefit themselves from their own labor.

A good standard for judging the economic success or failure of a nation is to observe how many people want to move there. The Soviet Union erected an Iron Curtain to keep people from leaving. There was no need to keep immigrants out; almost no one wanted to get in. But the reason why so many people want to immigrate to the United States is that they believe they will have greater economic opportunities. Although there is much debate over free market capitalism in the U.S., this is still a country where citizens know if they work hard, they can prosper. That was not the case under Soviet communism.

The reason communism, or any state-run economic system, fails to prosper a nation is because it doesn't acknowledge basic human nature. People are greedy. The people who have the most money have the most power, and power corrupts. The Soviet politburo, the communist government bureaucracy, became the upper class bourgeoisie they were so quick to denigrate at the beginning of the revolution. They could only hold on to their power by brutal threats and brainwashing. That was not part of Marx's Manifesto, but it was the inevitable outcome of that economic philosophy.

The proper function of government should be to maintain a fair and equitable economic environment. Government should monitor the wealth of the nation, not *be* the wealth of the nation. If corporations are rich and powerful, their business practices can and must be kept in check with government oversight. However, if government overseers themselves become the rich and powerful, who has oversight over them? If a socialistic economic system replaces free market capitalism, it will lead to economic ruin as surely as Soviet communism did.

So, the job of government is to protect free market capitalism, not to become it. If they become it, the system is no longer free. A workable economic system must be built on a solid foundation of ethics. Free market capitalism acknowledges the inherent weaknesses of human nature and has a system in place to keep it in check. State-run economic systems put the power in the wrong hands, and there is no provision for checks and balances.

How can businesses operate on ethical standards if the people who set the policies of ethics are themselves unethical? That is the dilemma of business ethics. Only a system that addresses the issue of the human tendency toward unethical behavior will allow for economic prosperity. State-run systems virtually guarantee that there will not be a level playing field in which corporations will be able to compete.

Free market capitalism functions well because it usually allows the company that produces the best product at the best price to prosper. If the competitive nature of capitalism is removed, the system becomes increasingly inefficient. Government regulation is necessary to maintain capitalism; government intervention in the competitive nature of capitalism will destroy it.

Regulation is what all the securities industry legislation was originally intended to accomplish. Corporations are required to file accurate financial statements in a timely manner. They are required to maintain nondiscriminatory employment policies and provide safe work environments. They are prohibited from profiting from insider information. These, and many more, are necessary functions of government oversight. However, allowing government to own and profit from the labor of others will inevitably lead to abuse of power. It will produce an economic system that is doomed to fail.

If the information that companies release cannot be counted on to be reliable, free market capitalism will collapse. A common euphemism used to describe a company's manipulation of financial data is *creative accounting*. It means that the accountants or comptrollers who manage a company's financial records have used non-traditional, and often illegal, methods of reporting the financial statements to manage their earnings. Such manipulation could either be used to report higher earnings to shareholders or lower earnings to the tax collector.

A common example of creative accounting is adjusting the basis for reporting the cost of sales, such as from LIFO to FIFO or vice versa. LIFO is an acronym accountants use for *last in-first out*, and FIFO is *first in-first out*. FIFO is the usual way of recording the cost of sales. It means that the cost of goods that were sold was based on the cost basis for the oldest products in the inventory. They were the first in. These products usually cost less than those more recently added to inventory because inflation usually causes prices to rise.

Thus, corporations usually report the highest profit margin on goods sold using FIFO accounting. This method impresses shareholders or potential investors. However, corporations could benefit from a lower tax bill by reporting smaller profits using LIFO accounting. Changing the cost of inventory to a higher basis would lower the profit margin. So, the method of determining the earnings that corporations report to the tax collector might be based on LIFO, but to their shareholders, FIFO.

Other common methods of creative accounting could be to use accelerated depreciation and amortization schedules, deferring the reporting of sales into the subsequent quarter, or perhaps transferring sales from one division to another in a lower tax bracket. These methods are not usually illegal. However, they only delay taxes due; they do not eliminate them. Creative accounting methods like these are quite common in corporate financing. Problems arise when accounting practices move from creative to fraudulent. Good creative accountants are in high demand. The euphemism used to characterize corporations that falsify the data on financial statements is *cooking the books*. Falsifying financial data is fraud and will result in legal action.

If the Securities and Exchange Commission, SEC, suspects a company of any questionable activity, they could issue a **Wells Notice**. It is a letter warning companies or individuals that the SEC (or FINRA) may be about to bring a civil action against them. It was named after John Wells, the chairman of the SEC committee responsible for taking action in those cases. A Wells Notice is not required before legal action is taken, and it is commonly used when the nature of the offense is considered relatively minor. It allows the company to respond before a lawsuit is filed.

Investors should take notice of companies that are issued a Wells Notice. In common use today, its intent is often to warn shareholders of potential legal action pending. Investors could have a window of opportunity to sell their positions in such companies before the situation escalates. Shareholders are often the innocent victims of corporate crime. This is an important safeguard.

However, shareholders can sometimes be harsh taskmasters. They can quickly and severely punish a company whose managers do not produce their earnings forecast, or even if they do, still miss their sales growth projections and net profit margins. Investors are accustomed to expect results, not excuses. Additionally, activist shareholders may apply pressure on a company to meet or exceed earnings projections.

Several cases revealing the failure of corporate governance came to a head in 2002. In that year several companies filed for bankruptcy following the disclosure of financial irregularities. The most noteworthy of these was Enron. At its peak it was the fifth largest company in the U.S. by market capitalization. It had started out as an energy trading and brokerage company, and had expanded into trading several non-energy commodities. Accusations of accounting irregularities finally caught up to it, and the company came crashing down. It ruined most of its employees' retirement accounts and most of its shareholders' investments in the process.

Enron was not the only casualty of fraudulent accounting at that time. Other large companies that also went bankrupt primarily because of accounting irregularities were WorldCom, Global Crossing, and Calpine. K-Mart also went bankrupt, but not because of their accounting. The company declared its stock worthless and arranged for a buyout by Sears Holdings. After the buyout, the new stock went from about $15 per share to about $180 over a three year period, as Sears sold off marginal stores to real estate developers. However, the original K-Mart shareholders were left holding worthless securities.

Nevertheless, Enron remains the poster child for corporate corruption, not only for their abuse of shareholders, but for the abuse of their employees. Upper management had publicly advocated that employees keep their 401k Plans invested in Enron stock right up until the announcement of their demise. It is hard to imagine how people in such high positions of corporate governance could demonstrate such sociopathic behavior.

The management of Enron allegedly worked in collusion with their supposedly independent auditing firm to misrepresent the company's fiscal position. This was done by creating a maze of limited partnerships to which losses in the company's business were transferred. These limited partnerships became separate legal entities. Thus, profitable segments of Enron remained on its books, while the losses of unprofitable ones were scattered around several partnerships. Enron had been speculating on highly leveraged commodity trades for its own account and had lost more money than the company was worth.

The legislative response to the Enron situation was penned in record time, less than six months following the bankruptcy. It was the **Sarbanes-Oxley Act** and has been called the most comprehensive reform of securities law since the Securities Exchange Act of 1934. First and foremost, Sarbanes-Oxley required

CEOs and CFOs to personally certify the authenticity of their company's financial statements. They could no longer plead ignorance and blame accountants when called on to testify in legal proceedings. The chief corporate officers of all companies subsequent to Sarbanes-Oxley are required to understand their company's accounting practices as well as their auditor s do.

The heart of the Sarbanes-Oxley Act was to increase the stringency of accounting regulations across the board. It required full disclosure of accounting methods and ongoing investigations of anything that was deemed irregular. The act also shortened the allowable lag time between when the fiscal quarter, or year, ended and when the financial report was due to be filed with the SEC.

Although many corporate officers were ill prepared for such a rapid reformation of their accounting methods and practices, shareholders breathed a sigh of relief. They could finally feel confident in the numbers that were being reported. The Sarbanes-Oxley Act did much to restore investor confidence in the stock market. It came at a time when reform was sorely needed. However many corporate officers were critical that some provisions of the bill were so onerous as to be nearly impossible to comply with.

What Does FINRA Do?

The **Financial Industry Regulatory Authority**, **FINRA**, is a self-governing professional organization of securities broker/dealers. It was formed in 2009 with the merger of the National Association of Securities Dealers, NASD, and the New York Stock Exchange Regulatory Authority. FINRA sets legal and ethical standards of conduct for professional securities brokers. It is the agency responsible for administering the broker tests required for membership in the organization. It also administers other tests and continuing education requirements for members.

FINRA is to the financial services industry what the American Bar Association is to the legal profession. The ABA is responsible for testing and granting membership to attorneys. The examination administered by FINRA for qualifying individuals to become stockbrokers is called the General Securities Exam, usually referred as Series 7. It is copyrighted by FINRA. Like the ABA, FINRA can discipline members who violate its rules or ethics by revoking membership. This makes it impossible for brokers to continue to conduct securities transactions. Brokers need to be members of FINRA in order to act on behalf of their clients.

FINRA also maintains arbitration and mediation committees to adjudicate investor complaints against broker/dealers. The FINRA arbitration process is in lieu of the courtroom legal process. Arbitration is usually far less costly than the legal system, and FINRA arbitrators are more knowledgeable on specialized aspects of security law. There is a very small filing fee for customers with small claims, up to $1000, and claims with monetary damages over that follow a sliding scale that can be accessed on the FINRA website. Arbitration filing fees are likely significantly lower than attorneys' fees would be.

A few of the common investor complaints about brokers are unauthorized trading, churning, and recommending inappropriate investments. **Unauthorized trading** is the practice of brokers making investments on behalf of their clients without the client's permission. If your broker charges a wrap fee to manage your account, you would have authorized him or her to make trading decisions on your behalf. But if have the type of account where the broker charges a commission for entering your trades, unless you sign a Power of Attorney giving your broker the right to enter orders without your authorization, the broker must always get your permission before entering any trade

Churning is the practice of a broker making frequent changes in securities positions in a client's account that do not benefit the investor. Even if your broker calls you and gets your authorization to enter trades, it could still be considered unethical by a FINRA arbitration committee. If you can demonstrate that the broker recommended buy and sell orders to generate commissions and did not improve your account, you may have the right to recoup damages from the broker. It should be noted that churning is an issue only if the brokers appear to be recommending trades that only benefit themselves. Most full-service brokers now rely on wrap fees to avoid being accused of churning.

If you are an online trader making your own buy and sell decisions, you cannot sue yourself for churning. This is probably a greater danger to investors than old fashioned churning. With the rise in popularity of day trading or high-frequency trading, many individuals churn themselves to death without any help from a broker. So, unless a broker has some role in your high frequency trading, there is little legal recourse for that behavior. It has become common for online brokers to try to screen out customers who may pose a potential liability by asking questions on the New Account Application such as, "Do you have a gambling addiction?"

Brokers recommending **inappropriate investments**, such as high-risk ones to a conservative investor, can also often result in penalties being assessed against brokers. If you are retired, living on a pension, and do not have the means of earning more income, it is always inappropriate to recommend speculative investments.

However, keep in mind that in cases of inappropriate investments what FINRA arbitrators will look at first is your primary investment goal on the New Account Application Form. If speculation was your primary goal when you opened the account many years ago, but now you are retired, you need to remember to amend and update that designation. Unless you can truly afford to lose money through speculation, do not make that your primary objective. Remember, brokers are trying to limit their legal liabilities, not necessarily yours. Update all information to represent your current situation.

Even if your application information has not been updated, you may still have a case. The merits of any legal action are based on more than one criterion. Arbitrators are very reasonable and look at all the surrounding circumstances of a dispute. If you feel you have been taken advantage of, there are convenient means in place for resolving your disputes.

Quite often disputes are resolved on the basis of the **Prudent Man Rule**. This has rather broad applications and interpretations, but the Prudent Man Rule assumes that a financial advisor should make investment decisions in the manner that an intelligent and knowledgeable person would. If you are retired, would a prudent man advise you to speculate with index options, even if you hadn't updated your investment objectives when you filled out your account application over 20 years ago? I don't think so.

As an investor, it is important that you realize your legal rights are protected and that securities laws are strictly enforced. You have several resources available if you should have a complaint against your broker. However, it is better if you are able to avoid the need for resolving a complaint in the first place. If you are a well-informed investor (and you are if you have read and understood this book so far), you should be able to avoid the need for arbitration, mediation, or legal action in most cases.

Most broker-client disputes arise from miscommunication and misunderstanding. A knowledgeable investor knows how to avoid inappropriate investments. You should already have the ability to discern imprudent advice and the means to resolve any potential dispute before it becomes necessary to take legal action. Ideally, you will never need to use the resources and information presented in this chapter. But in such a litigious society, it is nice to know the resources for resolving problems is readily available.

FINRA is the watchdog for the securities industry, responsible for bringing action against members who do not follow professional standards of conduct and protecting investors from abusive activity.

Chapter 11

What Types of Investments Offer Tax Advantages?

When Albert Einstein was reportedly asked the question what is the hardest thing in the world to understand, he is said to have quipped, "Income tax." It has been over half a century since he spoke that oxymoron. Income tax, if anything, has gotten even more difficult to understand than it was in Einstein's time. Grasping the concepts of the Special and General Theories of Relativity is easy compared to the task of comprehending the Internal Revenue Code.

The Theory of Relativity altered the way people viewed the universe only once. But the Internal Revenue Service has altered it thousands of times. Einstein's book explaining the space-time continuum is 157 pages, written at a high school reading level. The U.S. Internal Revenue Code is an over 72,000 page tome, and it was not written to be understood at any reading level. Relativity is a relatively constant idea, but tax code is comprised of questionable concepts in a constant state of flux. Relativity is theory, but tax code is concrete law. Something is wrong with this picture. Can you understand why trying to explain taxation in a short chapter like this is an impossible task?

Any book about tax-planning strategies is bound to have a short shelf-life. Tax code is revised so frequently that anything put into print about it had better be written in morphing ink, for it will quickly become obsolete, inaccurate, and potentially a trap for a costly IRS audit. So, the information presented here is not going to be specific regarding particular tax strategies. It is going to be general in nature, hopefully on aspects of the tax code that are likely to remain unchanged for a few years.

Whenever you read something offering tax advice, it is usually preceded by a standard disclaimer that goes something like, "The information presented here is for general information purposes only and is not intended to be taken as advice for your particular needs. Consult a qualified tax professional about your situation". So, realize that information presented here is subject to change without notice, and consider its applicability to your tax situation properly disclaimed.

The information in this chapter was current and accurate as of the day of its writing. However, none of the information can be guaranteed to still be accurate and pertinent at the time you read it. In recent years, lawmakers have become increasingly more active in rewriting tax code.

Revisions of tax laws are happening so rapidly because taxes are often used by politicians to gain political favor, not just as a means to regulate revenue income for the government. Politicians are well aware that the regulation of economic activity can enhance or end their political careers. Tax cuts have been used to stimulate consumer spending and thus economic growth. Tax hikes have been used to slow the rate of inflation that naturally results from too much consumer spending.

Note that the problem of regulating the economy through tax rate manipulation is fraught with inherent problems. High tax rates, by their very nature, will slow economic growth and can create disinflation or recession. Because growth in the economy is often achieved through consumer spending, anything that reduces the consumer's availability of cash reduces spending. With higher taxes, consumers have less money to spend.

However, that does not mean if taxes are lowered, consumer spending will increase. Although that is certainly the hope, people do not always respond as expected. If the psychological motivation of most consumers is primarily based on fear and concerns about the economy, most will still put a high priority on saving rather than spending. So, such simplistic reasoning that tax incentives can achieve economic results does not necessarily follow. Economists are constantly faced with the dilemma of trying to solve psychological problems with non-psychological means.

One of Benjamin Franklin's famous quotes is, "The only things certain in life are death and taxes". Few would disagree with that, although some anonymous online source opined that taxes are worse than death because a taxpayer doesn't die every year. Although taxes may be certain, how much they are is anything but certain. In recent years few things have been more uncertain than how much you will owe in taxes. Even when your tax bracket remains the same, the changes in methods of allowable deductions or methods of computation can dramatically affect the amount of taxes you owe.

Your marginal tax brackets may be creeping up, even if your income isn't. So, you need to keep a watchful eye on the effects your investments have on your tax situation. You should be aware of the level of taxable income that will bump you into the next higher bracket. But there is often no way of determining what that number will be, because it is a constantly moving target. However, keep in mind that even if your income doesn't rise, your tax liability very well could.

Because of the complexity of the tax code, several proposals have been considered to reform the way taxes are paid. Before this book is out of print, some legislature will likely have been enacted completely changing extant tax law. There are several proposals currently under consideration that call for the complete elimination of the current IRS income tax code, and replace it with another method. The most noteworthy proposals generally fall into two categories: (1) a flat tax, modified flat tax, or marginal flat tax; and (2) a consumption tax, such as a sales tax, value added tax (VAT), or expenditure tax.

Flat tax proposals usually involve repealing most, or all, deductions and charging all taxpayers a set percentage of gross income. A flat tax would probably be set at about 20 percent, and in theory, should be revenue neutral, maintaining about the same amount of revenue income as the existing tax code. In other words, it would not increase or decrease the total amount of annual tax revenue received by the government. A modified flat tax would be one for which some deductions are allowable, such as mortgage interest and charitable contributions. A marginal flat tax would be one for which the rate would be scaled higher for higher income earners, similar to the tax brackets in the existing tax code.

Proponents of flat tax proposals argue that it is fairer than the current system because the rich would pay at least the same tax rate as those less wealthy. They would probably pay more money in taxes than they do under the current system with all its loopholes and deductions. Also, a flat tax would eliminate all the time spent filling out the complex forms usually needed to calculate tax liability. This could save literally millions of lost work hours.

Critics of flat tax proposals say the hang up would be over what, if any, common deductions might, or might not, be eliminated. If all deductions were eliminated, that could severely depress the real estate market and greatly reduce charitable giving. Many taxpayers plan their deductions around those areas. Charities and non-profit organizations would undoubtedly see a dramatic reduction of contributions if donors were no longer able to use contributions to reduce taxable income.

Also, a primary tax benefit of home ownership is the allowance for deducting the interest portion of mortgage payments. For home buyers, most—sometimes all—of the mortgage payments are applied to interest only and none to principal because of the way compound rates are calculated. However, if the real estate mortgage interest deduction is allowed under a flat tax structure, the government could potentially lose hundreds of billions of dollars. Then the flat tax rate would probably have to be raised.

The most common type of **consumption tax** being considered is a sales tax. It would be a tax paid by consumers at the time of purchase at the point-of-sale, POS. Many states, and some counties or other municipalities, already have sales taxes. An expenditure tax would be one in which the total amount of money spent on consumption would be taxed, but not at the time of sale. Also, the amount put in savings or investment accounts could be used to reduce tax liability, thus incentivizing saving.

Like the flat tax, a consumption tax would generally mean that the rich would pay more because they spend more, and the poor would pay less because they spend less. Also, much of the money that goes unreported to the IRS, such as from undocumented laborers, would be taxed as that money was spent.

The popular argument against a consumption tax is that it would be inflationary. The cost of everything would go up simply because of the tax. The rebuttal to this argument is that, theoretically, the increased cost would be offset by the extra money most people would have by not paying any other income tax. Of course, the problem with this type of tax would be in the execution of the transition from an income tax to a consumption tax. Too rapid a transition could cause a period of economic chaos.

Probably the most valid criticism of a consumption tax is that it would likely cause an active under-the-table economy—barter system or black market. Retailers may attempt to develop untraditional means of recording sales to avoid reporting normal retail transactions. In countries where a national sales tax has been established, a very active black market has inevitably followed. Governments that have converted to a sales tax have become even more intrusive into monitoring business transactions than they were with the current income tax model.

Needless to say, there is no simple answer to the current problems with income tax code. The flat tax would probably punish the rich more by taking away many of the tax deductions they can use. The consumption tax would probably punish the poor more, because they usually pay no income tax. Low income wage earners would be forced to pay into the system as they need to spend most, if not all, of their money.

Some combination of these proposals is the likely outcome. Many countries around the globe have adopted a flat tax system, and many more are debating plans for implementing one. Most of the countries that have a flat tax have seen lower unemployment follow in the years after adoption.

The predominant economic theory that lowering taxes brackets can result in decreased unemployment is the **Laffer Curve**, a counterintuitive economic theory that in the right proportion lowering tax rates can increase tax revenue. In countries that adopted a flat tax system, when the rates were lowered, unemployment also fell, generally at a rate consistent with the predictions of the Laffer Curve. Lowering taxes could stimulate economic growth by increasing corporate profit margins. Thus, as corporations earn more, they can afford to hire more workers and increase production. In this manner, and within certain parameters, lower tax rates result in increased tax revenue to the government. A lower unemployment rate means more workers are paying taxes.

However, talk about revamping the tax code is a distraction from the real issue of how much money the government needs. Focusing the debate on how tax law should be changed takes the focus away from the more important discussion of how the government has managed to constantly overspend and waste trillions of dollars more than it takes in. If government is not held accountable for its abuses and excesses, no tax law changes will ever result in a healthy economy. Every time the government has increased its revenue income, it has increased its spending at an even higher rate.

So, the reality is you must plan your investment strategies around the tax ramification of those investments. In addition to the taxes you would have to pay on taxable bond interest or on equity dividends, you will also owe taxes on capital gains. A capital gain is the difference between what you pay for an investment, or its adjusted cost basis, and what you sold it at if the price is higher. A capital loss would be created when you sell and investment at a price lower than your cost basis.

Capital gains and capital losses are reported on Schedule D of the 1040 Tax Form. The net amount of losses minus gains is transferred to the 1040 Form. At the time of this writing, a long-term gain or loss is generated from investments held over one year. Since changing the tax status of capital gains is a frequently discussed topic in the tax code, you should check a current source to know how your capital gains or losses will affect your tax liability. However, at the time of this writing, there was a lower tax rate on long-term gains than there was on ordinary income.

Should You Have an IRA?

There are several investments designed to supplement retirement income that offer tax advantages. One of the most popular of these is the **Individual Retirement Account, IRA**. IRAs must have a custodian separate from the owner of the account. Custodianship will usually be a service offered by the securities broker, commercial bank, or investment company where the account is established. Investments in an IRA must be kept separate from assets in other accounts you may have with the same financial service company.

The **custodian** is responsible for filing the proper paperwork with the IRS. All income and capital gains received from investments in an IRA are exempt from current income tax. However, the Custodian is responsible for ensuring that the account conforms with the tax code. Typically the custodian will be the financial institution with which you established the IRA. However, it could be another entity the financial institution uses to facilitate those services.

If you establish an IRA at a bank, the custodian will probably be the trustee department of the bank. Also, the IRA will usually be a certificate of deposit, CD. Thus, your account would be subject to the illiquidity features of a CD. Banks do not usually charge a custodian fee for a bank IRA.

If you set up your IRA with a mutual fund, the custodian will probably be the trust department for that investment company. Your investment options with a mutual fund IRA will probably be limited to the family of funds managed by that investment company. A common custodian fee some mutual funds charge is $5.00, and many charge no custodian fee.

IRAs set up with a brokerage firm as custodian will usually be a self-directed account. That means you will be able to choose from almost any investment available from that broker. A self-directed IRA allows you to invest your contributions in stocks, bonds, mutual funds, CEFs, ETFs, ETNs, Limited Partnerships, and so on. Because there are more complex reporting requirements for a self-directed IRA, the annual custodian fee usually runs between $25.00 and $50.00 per year. You will have to check the IRA Account Application for the exact amount your broker will charge.

There are several self-directed IRA custodians that allow for direct investing in real estate, real estate options, contracts, notes, mortgages and trust deeds. These companies usually charge hundreds of dollars in fees: set up fees, annual fees, termination fees, etc. Also, there would be real estate commissions applicable for the number of transactions per year. It is not unusual for these custodians to charge thousands of dollars in fees and commissions each year. However, for those who want to participate in real estate with their IRA contribution, this is available.

In addition to various custodians and levels of service, there are also several different types of IRAs. The two most common individual retirement accounts are a Traditional IRA and a Roth IRA. Additionally, a Spousal IRA allows for a wage earner to contribute to a retirement account for a non-working spouse. The type of IRA specifically designed for self-employed individuals is called a Simplified Employee Pension Plan, or SEP-IRA. There is also a Rollover IRA into which you can transfer funds from another retirement savings account, such as a 401(k) plan or pension fund. Finally, businesses can establish IRAs for their employees under a plan called a Savings Incentive Match Plan for Employees, or SIMPLE IRA.

One of the primary differences between a **Traditional IRA** and a **Roth IRA** is the tax status of contributions made to each. You may be able to deduct contributions to a Traditional IRA from your taxable income. The term **qualified** is used to describe non-taxed funds used for retirement account contributions. However, contributions made to a Roth IRA are made with after-tax, or non-qualified, funds.

If you are already participating in a retirement account through a source other than an IRA, such as through your employer, you will probably not qualify to make additional contributions to a Traditional IRA with qualified, pre-taxed, funds. If you participate in a 401(k) plan or pension plan at work, the IRS does not generally allow addition tax sheltered contributions. However, you will probably still be able to contribute to a Roth IRA.

At the time of this writing, the contribution limit for both Traditional and Roth IRAs is $7,000 per year of earned income, but check with your broker to see what the limit is at the time you read this. The source for all contributions to either of these IRAs must be money that has come from *earned* income. If you only have unearned income, such as from Social Security, stock dividends, or pension fund distributions, that money will not be considered earned income and is not eligible for an IRA contribution. Also, you have until the tax filing deadline, usually April 15, to make a contribution to either type of IRA for the previous tax year. This is different from most other tax deductions, which must be made in the same year as the one for which the deduction is allowed.

You can contribute 100 percent of earned income up to the maximum allowed, but no unearned income. So, if you had a part-time job or short term employment and earned only $3,000 in one year, you could only contribute $3,000 to an IRA for that year. If all your income came from unearned sources, you would not be able to make any contribution to an IRA.

Also, if you are age 50 or over, you can contribute an additional $1,000 of earned income as a "catch up" contribution, for a total of

$8,000 per year. This provision was added to allow for larger contributions as you near retirement age. It is meant to help people who have not contributed enough money in past years to meet, or come closer to, their retirement income goals.

There are income limits over which you will not be allowed to contribute to an IRA. However, these are adjusted each year. So, check a reliable website that updates its information to verify if you still qualify to make an IRA contribution, particularly if you are in an upper income tax bracket.

Since the tax status of contributions to Traditional and Roth IRAs is different, so is the tax status of the distributions. Under normal circumstances, you may not be able to withdrawal funds from a Traditional IRA without a penalty before the year you reach age 59½. You must begin taking annual withdrawals from your IRA beginning for the year in which you reach age 70½. Also, you may not continue to make contributions to a Traditional IRA after age 70½, even if you still have earned income. Normally the penalty for a premature withdrawal is 10 percent of the amount. Keep in mind you will also need to pay taxes on that distribution. So, the 10 percent penalty plus the tax liability on the distribution usually makes a Traditional IRA a poor source of funds before you reach retirement age.

There are a few exceptions to this early withdrawal penalty. Funds may be accessed from a Traditional IRA before age 59½ for purposes of meeting medical or other emergency expenses. Also there is an exemption for first time home buyers. Of course all the funds withdrawn from a Traditional IRA are subject to normal income tax, since these funds have never been taxed.

The rules regarding distributions from a Roth IRA are different from those applicable to a Traditional IRA. Withdrawals from a Roth after age 59½ are usually tax free and penalty free. So the earnings from income and capital gains accumulated in a Roth IRA over the years, which will probably be significantly higher than your original principal, might never be taxed. Also, withdrawals of principal before age 59½ can usually be made without being subjected to penalty or tax. Remember that taxes have already been paid on the principal contributed to a Roth IRA.

One last difference between Traditional and Roth IRAs is that wage earners over age 70½ may still continue to make contributions of earned income to a Roth. Since Roth contributions are non-qualified, the IRS does not mind that you continue to pay taxes. However, wage earners over age 70½ are not allowed to make any additional contributions to a Traditional IRA.

Traditional IRA participants are required to take annual distributions beginning in the year at which they turn age 70½, but the original Roth IRA owners are not. The calculation for an IRA **required minimum distribution, RMD**, is based on actuarial tables of life expectancy. For example, if you are age 70, the divisor for your RMD might be 27.4 based on the uniform life expectancy table. So the minimum required distribution from your IRA would be the market value of your IRA on December 31 of the year in which you turned 70½ divided by 27.4.

You are required to take a RMD before the end of the year for the distribution to be applicable for that tax year. If you fail to do so, you will be charged a penalty. Also, you should realize the RMD divisor becomes a smaller number each subsequent year, increasing the percentage of your IRA you will need to have distributed. Because average life expectancy continues to grow, the RMD tables will probably also be adjusted. There are several websites that offer updated RMD calculators.

Spousal IRAs were introduced during a time when the nuclear family was the norm. The term nuclear did not refer to the atomic bomb, rather it implied a family structured like an atom. The nuclear family had a parental nucleus—one husband, one wife, and 1.7 average kids. One spouse had a career and one stayed home to raise the kids. The idea of the nuclear family is vanishing with cultural changes, but the Spousal IRA remains.

The wage-earning spouse can contribute his or her earned income into a Spousal IRA up to the same maximums applicable to the employed individual. That would be $7,000 per year, or $8,000 if the spouse qualifies for the catch up provision. A Spousal IRA can be established either as a Traditional or a Roth IRA.

The next type of retirement account is the **Rollover IRA**. It is established only by transferring assets from another retirement account, such as a 401(k) plan or pension fund. This is usually done when you leave a company and are no longer eligible to participate in their employee retirement plan. However, most fund managers no longer require former employees to transfer their assets out, or at least have generous grace periods.

The key word regarding a Rollover IRA is *transfer*. If you take a full distribution and then deposit it into an IRA, the IRS will disallow the tax deduction and consider your distribution fully taxable. A Rollover contribution must be transferred from one institution to another without going to the individual in order to avoid being fully taxed. Keep in mind, however, this transfer could be done just as well into a Traditional IRA (for qualified funds) or a Roth (for non-qualified funds), as well as into a Rollover IRA.

The primary purpose of a Rollover IRA is to provide a place to park your retirement savings where you could later transfer them back to a new company's 401(k) or pension plan when you change employers in the future. However, you cannot commingle new IRA contributions with your Rollover funds, or else the fund will be ineligible to transfer back to a new 401(k).

When you leave a company, it might be better to simply transfer your old 401(k) account into a Traditional IRA, rather than a Rollover IRA. With a self-directed Traditional IRA, you have many more investment choices than you would have in a 401(k). Also, you won't end up paying extra fees if you have more than one IRA. Although you lose portability, that benefit may be offset by other disadvantages.

If you are a self-employed individual, you are eligible to establish a **Simplified Employee Pension** or **SEP-IRA**. A SEP-IRA allows you to contribute up to 25% of annual adjusted gross income (AGI) to a maximum of $54,000. That maximum amount is significantly larger than for other individual retirement accounts, and it is all with qualified, or pre-taxed, earnings.

Since one of the adjustments to your AGI is the SEP contribution, you can earn up to $345,000 (at the time of this writing) and still make the maximum contribution. The calculation looks like this:

```
  $345,000   total self-employed earned income
 - $69,000   SEP-IRA contribution
  $276,000   adjusted gross income (AGI)
      × .25  max. allowable percentage SEP-IRA contribution
   $69,000   max. allowable contribution
```

You will not be able to shelter any additional income over $345,000 in a SEP-IRA.

This might be a good time to remind you that all the numbers cited here are subject to frequent annual adjustments. Check with a reliable source to confirm you tax information at the time you file your return. Heed the comments at the beginning of this chapter. The tax code is rewritten almost every year. Taxes may be certain, but how much they is anything but.

A **SIMPLE IRA** is one that small businesses or self-employed individuals, anyone with 100 or fewer employees, can set up. In it the employer can establish separate retirement accounts for each participating employee, and it can be funded either with employer contributions or employee salary reductions. Employer contributions can be non-elective, meaning the employees do not need to fund the retirement account with their own money; or employer contributions can be matching.

SIMPLE is an acronym for **Savings Incentive Match Plan for Employees**. The *match* part of that acronym means that employers can make contributions equal to all or part of the amount of employees' contributions. The limits on the matching amount can be between one and three percent of the employee's salary up to certain limits. This means that if employees elect to have two percent of their salary contributed to a SIMPLE IRA, the employer will match that amount.

Additionally, employees are allowed to take pre-taxed salary reduction contributions up to $16,000 per year (at the time of this writing) if they participate in the plan. The catch up provision for employees age 50 or older to SIMPLE IRAs was an additional $3,500. So, that would increase the total contribution limit to $19,500 per employee per year in salary reduction. Of course, you have to be a well-disciplined budgeter to be able to meet your normal living expenses while taking that much of a salary reduction. At the time of this writing, the total maximum amount that could be contributed per employee, that is, to a SIMPLE plus other retirement funds, was $23,000.

In addition to the types of IRAs described so far, there are two more variations of the Traditional and Roth IRAs. They are 401(k) IRAs and 401(k) Roth IRAs. These are basically structured like Traditional and Roth IRAs, but the contribution limits are like those of 401(k) Plans. Corporate 401(k) Plans are the most common type of retirement account available to most employees. To understand the IRA versions of 401(k) Plans, you first need to understand the original version.

Should You Participate in a 401(k) Plan?

The answer to the question of participating in a **401(k) Plan** is almost always, "Yes." For most employees, the tax advantages and retirement benefits available to them through participation in employer-sponsored 401(k) plans outweighs most other alternatives. The similar type of account for nonprofit organizations is identified as a **403(b) Plan**. For employees of state and local government entities the equivalent retirement account is a **457 Plan**.

Some organizations, particularly in education, identify this type of plan as a tax-sheltered annuity, TSA. Many features of these plans, such as the investment choices offered, are designated by the plan's sponsors. Consequently, some are better than others. However, as a general rule, employees will have more flexibility and more generous tax benefits by participating in their 401(k) plans or equivalent payroll-deduction programs.

Most companies offer 401(k) plans, but the majority of the plans available to some professional organization, especially teachers and nurses, are Defined Benefit (DB) Pension Plans. Some companies still offer Defined Contributions (DC) Pension Plans, but the majority have adopted 401(k)s. The custodial and management requirements for such plans are much less cumbersome than the other pension funds. However, whatever your employer offers, you should probably take advantage of it.

One of the most important benefits of retirement plans is they allow you to contribute pre-taxed dollars to an account that will grow on a tax-deferred basis. Also, contributions are made as payroll deductions, so you cannot be tempted to spend the money before it gets invested. To those who have trouble being disciplined savers, who are easily tempted to spend every paycheck (and then some), this can be an beneficial feature.

As was implied previously in the section on Rollover IRAs, one beneficial feature of 401(k)s is portability. If you leave one company, you can transfer the vested amount in your account to your new company's 401(k). On average, employees change jobs five or six times during their careers, so portability can be useful. Also, if you go through a period of unemployment, you can transfer the value of your account into a Traditional IRA for pre-taxed contributions or to a Roth IRA for after-tax contributions, as well as a Rollover IRA.

Like contributions made to IRAs, a withdrawal from a 401(k) Plan, or other pension plan, is usually subject to a 10 percent penalty if withdrawn before the year in which you reach age 59½. However, participants can take out a loan from their 401(k) account before that age. Typically, such loans can be taken for any reason. Participants are, in effect, lending the money to themselves with a commitment to pay it back in the future. Thus the tax status of the funds remains as if it were still in the 401(k).

By having pre-taxed dollars taken out of your paycheck, you reduce the amount of current income tax you would owe. For example, assume your monthly paycheck is $10,000, and you have 10 percent ($1,000) withheld as a 401(k) contribution. If you are in a 28 percent tax bracket (combined federal and state), instead of owing $2,800 in taxes (28 percent of $10,000), you would owe $2,016 (28 percent of $7,200, that is $10,000 – $2,800). That represents a $784 monthly savings, or $9,408 per year. These are hypothetical numbers, but crunch the numbers for your particular situation, to see what you could save.

Of course, you will have to pay taxes on the money accumulated in your 401(k) when you begin taking withdrawals, presumably at retirement. However, the benefits of earning tax-deferred interest on retirement account contributions are significant. Imagine how much the $9,408 per year, used in that example, can add to your retirement savings over the time you remain with that employer. Typically it could amount to hundreds of thousands of dollars.

Also, you should realize that for those people currently entering the work force, Social Security benefits will likely be much lower (or nonexistent) when they retire. The Social Security Administration currently predicts that it will not be able to fund mandated benefits after the year 2034. So yes, you should absolutely participate in whatever retirement account you can. Take control of your future; do not rely on politicians to be there for you.

There are several online services that provide retirement fund calculators. This may or may not be particularly useful for individual retirement planning. One of the weaknesses of financial calculators is that they base your projected retirement benefits on assumptions that may or may not be accurate in the future. Whatever you input is probably not going to be what you will actually realize.

First, the amount of your contributions will not likely remain the same throughout your lifetime. Most people change employers several times, especially during their early years. Also, your investment choices probably will not be able to guarantee a constant rate of return for your entire length of employment. An accurate calculation for a specific situation would need to be based on the exact amount of money you will contribute and the exact rate of return you will realize on it, and that is impossible. However, the calculator will illustrate how much more money you could accumulate from tax-deferred compounding versus a taxable alternative. This can be very dramatic, especially over long periods.

If you contribute $1000 per month in pre-taxed, or qualified, dollars to a retirement account earning 8 percent, over a 20-year period your total contributions would be $240,000. However, the value of your retirement account would grow to about $1,468,153. As a result of a compound rate of return on money that would have otherwise gone to pay taxes, you would make $1,228,153 on your investment. But if you were to invest $1000 in a taxable account over the same period of time, and you were in a 25 percent tax bracket, the account value would only grow to $1,005,622. You would earn nearly half a million dollars more in a tax-deferred account versus a taxable account.

Although most companies offer 401(k) Plans, not all employees enroll in them. However, most do. It is estimated that about 90 percent of eligible employees participate. Some companies automatically enroll all employees who meet their eligibility requirements. With some plans, however, you need to opt in. Most companies have an Employee Benefits Department where you can get information on retirement savings.

Now that you understand the benefits of investing in a 401(k), is there a downside? A worst case scenario for 401(k) investors was played out in 2001 with the collapse of Enron Corp. Prior to its failure Enron was the largest energy trading company in the world. The upper management of the company had publicly been advising employees to keep their 401(k) assets in Enron stock, and most employees took that advice to heart. However, at the same time upper management was in collusion with the company's auditors to release misleading financial statements, and they were liquidating their own personal holdings of the company.

At the time it seemed inconceivable that corporate management could have gotten away with so much while so many regulators were watching. However, that situation, and other corporate bankruptcies around the same time, resulted in the stricter enforcement powers of regulators through the Sarbanes-Oxley Act. This was discussed in the last chapter. Some would say that justice was served; the guilty parties were convicted. But the innocent victims of the corporate fraud committed by Enron's management were the 401(k) Plan participants. Many saw their entire retirement savings accounts completely disappear while they were unable to do anything about it.

Although that scenario could probably not be repeated, the memory of that event is a lesson never to become too complacent with your retirement assets. You are at far greater risk of living in financial distress at retirement by not planning for it than you are by mismanagement of your 401(k). The federal government is telling you by giving you tax breaks on retirement account investments that you need to act to prepare for your golden years.

The federal regulatory oversight of these plans is the responsibility of the Pension and Welfare Benefits Administration, PWBA. It is a division of the Department of Labor. You can check their website for current information regarding general rules changes in 401(k) Plan.

In addition to tax-free or tax-deferred plans to help people with the cost of retirement, there are other plans for helping with other major expenses. One of these other expenses is the cost of your children's college education.

What Investments Are for Education Expenses?

The total cost of a four year college education at a private university can easily run over $200,000. At an in-state public school the tab usually runs about $100,000. Of course, those amounts are broad estimates, not accurate statistics. The actual costs of attending any particular college are different. Nevertheless, the cost of a college education has been rising faster than the consumer price index for several decades. Also, keep in mind that those approximate costs are for an undergraduate degree only. If you pursue postgraduate studies, the cost would likely double or triple, and for most high paying jobs, a postgraduate degree is a necessity.

The total amount of student loan debt outstanding recently surpassed the total amount of credit card debt. It is likely that the rate of the growth of student loan debt will outpace all other types of debt for many years. Most people simply cannot afford the cost of a college education without some form of financial assistance—loans, grants, scholarships, or savings.

For many (probably most) college graduates, the joy of receiving that diploma is almost immediately squelched by the prospect of being unable to get a job that pays well enough to meet living expenses and still make payments on those student loans. If you want to avoid putting your children in a position of beginning their careers where most of their paycheck will be applied to paying off student loans, there are some investments available to help out.

Anyone who wants to help pay for a child's future college education—parents, grandparents, or others—can set up a **529 Plan**. These plans were written into the Internal Revenue Code, but they are enacted and regulated by the states. They are designed to provide federal tax-free rate of return, which in most cases is free, or partially free, of state income tax as well. Also, under most circumstances, these funds may be withdrawn tax-free to meet qualified college expenses. In that regard, they are similar to after-tax contributions to a Roth IRA or 401(k).

An important feature from the donor's point of view is that funds in a 529 Plan are not considered to be the property of the minor, as funds in a custodian account would be. Thus, if the child does not go to college and use those contributions for qualified education expenses, the funds will revert back to the donor.

Some form of a 529 Plan is available in each of the fifty states, and most have similar features. However, you should check a website providing state specific information on 529 Plans to make sure all general information presented here is applicable to your particular state. Many investment companies or financial institutions provide account designations that conform to state-specific 529 Plans.

There are two general types of 529 Plans: prepaid tuition plans and college savings plans. Prepaid tuition plans allow you to pay for future college expenses at current prices with a guarantee that all funds will grow at the rate of college expense inflation to meet actual college education costs at the time the student will be attending. College savings plans allow you to contribute after-tax dollars into a mutual fund, or similar investment, and thus will grow at the rate of that investment.

Because the rate of inflation for the cost of education has been running at about twice that of the overall rate of inflation, you might think prepaid tuition plans would be the more popular of the two types of plans, but they are not. In most states, prepaid tuition plans can be set up through a specific educational institution as well as through other sources such as investment companies. Of course, if you set up a plan through a particular institution, you will probably not be able to use those funds at another college.

Also, prepaid tuition plans allow you to make contributions on the basis of the cost for a full-time college student for each term—semester or quarter. Thus, you can pay for eight semesters or twelve quarters and hopefully give the student an incentive to finish school in a timely manner and not procrastinate. Although, since that is not the student's money, but yours, it may not be as much of an incentive as you intended.

Most financial institutions have master 529 Plans that comply with the applicable state laws. The amounts being contributed to these plans have been growing exponentially. These plans offer more benefits and flexibility than some of the alternative plans in the past. The sponsoring state will maintain income tax records. When students make withdrawals for college expenses, they will receive a 1099 Form itemizing the amount they need to report.

One other important consideration regarding tax-advantaged plans for college education, you should be aware that many college expenses may be tax deductible as a result of American Opportunity, Hope, and Lifetime Learning Education Credits. If you take advantage of those credits, using some of your college savings plan funds may not be tax-free as anticipated. The IRS does not allow a double deduction for such expenses.

For information about the IRS rules regarding these credits visit the website irs.gov. It covers all the frequently asked questions about the subject. Also, Publication 970 *Tax Benefits for Education* is available in print or online and covers all the information on the topic. This is one of those areas where you should check with a professional tax consultant about your particular situation and how IRS regulations may have changed.

For more information on 529 Plans check out the site collegesavings.org, which is sponsored by the College Savings Plan Network and affiliated with the National Association of State Treasurers. Many financial institutions and investment companies maintain websites with a wealth of information on 529 Plans.

What Is an Annuity?

Another type of tax-advantaged investment is an **annuity**. It is a contract issued by an insurance company that allows returns on investments held in it to accumulate on a tax deferred basis until withdrawn. Like other tax-advantaged investments, an annuity is also subject to a 10 percent IRS penalty if withdrawn before the year in which the insured turns age 59½, under most circumstances.

Both annuities and life insurance policies are products offered by insurance companies. However, there are distinct differences between these two products. One of the primary differences is that the annuity is designed to pay out income while the insured is living. A life insurance policy is designed to pay out to the insured's beneficiaries after he or she is deceased.

When you begin withdrawing from an annuity, you will owe income taxes on any untaxed earnings or capital gains, but not on the original principal. Since you already paid taxes on the amount of money you contributed, you will not have to pay taxes on the same funds again. In most cases you can take principal withdrawals under qualified circumstances, and thus manage the tax consequences of your annuity distributions.

Unlike most other tax-advantaged investments, the contribution limits on annuity contracts are not limited by government regulations. The insurance company may set limits on the amount of individual contracts, but those are usually set at a much higher amount than IRAs or 401(k)s. Typically some insurance companies set contribution limits at one million dollars, but others may set no limits at all.

Some insurance companies set an age limit for annuitants. This is usually because the annuity may include a guaranteed death benefit to the beneficiary. Typically the age limit is set between 70 and 85 years old. The death benefit is a payout to the beneficiary in the event of the death of the annuitant. That amount could be higher than the current value of the annuity at the time of death. This will be explained later.

First, you need to understand that there are three designated parties associated with an annuity: the owner, the annuitant, and the beneficiary. The **owner** is the one who purchases the policy and has the authority to make investment decisions regarding it. The owner of an annuity is usually an individual, but it need not be. It could be a Living Trust or some other legal entity. The **annuitant**, however, must be an individual, because he or she is the one upon whose life the duration of the distributions will be calculated if the contract is annuitized. Often the owner and the annuitant are the same individual, but in some cases, they may be different. The **beneficiary** is the one who will receive the distribution of the assets upon the death of the owner, or in some cases the annuitant.

The death of the annuitant will result in the necessity of distributing the equity value of the annuity to the beneficiary. The transfer of the value of an annuity avoids probate, the legal process of distributing assets through the court system after the owner is deceased. Usually all that is necessary is to supply the sponsoring insurance company with a certified copy of the Death Certificate of the owner (or annuitant) and sign the proper form. The distribution should follow shortly. The ease of transfer of assets is one of the primary benefits of investing in annuities.

There are two phases to an annuity contract: the deferral phase in which income is added or investment returns are accumulated, and the annuity, or income, phase in which the annuitant receives income. For the deferral phase, the owner of an annuity may select either a fixed or a variable return. A fixed return will guarantee a rate of interest for a predetermined period. Most insurance companies offer several options for fixed annuities, such as five or ten years. The interest rate will be similar to the rates available on U.S. Treasury notes or bonds.

A **variable annuity** is usually set up as a subaccount with an investment company. The insurance company underwriting the annuity will offer a variety of mutual fund portfolios designed to match those available with the same name from the investment company. These subaccount portfolios are designed to closely resemble the portfolios of the mutual fund, but they are separate accounts. In other words, the annuity subaccount will be a separate from the mutual fund, but it will invest in the same, or similar, securities as the corresponding fund.

Also, the annuity investor will be allowed to transfer between subaccounts in the same family of funds, in a manner similar to that of the mutual fund family. Annuity owners can also change the percentage mix of funds in a manner similar to that offered by most retirement accounts, such as 401(k) Plans. For example, the owner could designate 50 percent in a growth fund and 50 percent in an income fund.

The annuitant may begin taking distributions that would not be subject to an income tax penalty in the year he or she reaches age 59½. There are two general methods of taking distributions. You may either take periodic withdrawals or annuitize. Periodic, or systematic, withdrawals may be taken as a one-time lump sum distribution or as fixed amounts on scheduled dates. Many annuity holders set up distributions to supplement their retirement income on a monthly or quarterly cycle.

To annuitize is to set up distributions in a predetermined amount for a period-certain length of time. There are several annuitization options based on the value of the contract at the time the distributions begin. Annuitants can select a periodic fixed amount distribution based on a certain number of years, or they may select a fixed amount guaranteed for the life of the annuitant. There are also usually options available to guarantee income for the life of a spouse, as well as that of the owner. It is usually more popular to take periodic distributions rather than to annuitize because once the contract is annuitized, there can be no further changes to the distributions.

A third type of investment that is frequently used for tax strategies in a limited partnership. Probably because many limited partnerships were designed primarily for tax benefits, many of them have turned out to be investment nightmares. Indeed, the term limited partnership has taken on such a negative connotation that it is usually identified by a euphemism.

What Are Limited Partnerships?

You will often hear limited partnerships referred to as private investments or direct investments. The term limited partnership is often avoided because it has a negative connotation to some people due to past investment fiascos. Several brokerage firms were named as defendants in class action lawsuits over partnerships they sponsored or endorsed. For a period of time, an unusually high number of partnerships reported substandard investment returns.

First, it should be noted that there is nothing inherently wrong with the legal structure of a **Limited Partnership, LP**. It is nothing more than a business partnership structure in the traditional sense of the word, as discussed in Chapter 2. A limited partnership will be managed by a **General Partner, GP**, who will usually have all managerial responsibility for the partnership and make all investment decisions. The limited partners are generally limited as to their ability to influence management decisions. They will also have limited liability in their investment. Like common stock investors in public corporations, that liability is limited to their invested capital. Also, most limited partnerships are structured to liquidate remaining assets after a certain period of time, such as ten years.

There are many popular types of Limited Partnerships. Probably the most popular investment would be real estate. These partnerships can be structured as investments in equity or mortgages. A couple popular variations of real estate partnerships would be purchase and lease back arrangements with existing tenants and purchase of raw land for future development.

Oil and natural gas production and distribution would be another common type of LP. These generally fall into the categories of drilling exploration and development or construction of pipelines or other infrastructure for the energy industry. Also, equipment leasing has been a popular investment option. One popular leasing option has been for commercial or private aircraft. Mainframe computers, servers, or other high tech hardware have been used in some leasing partnerships. Also, some film production has been financed through LPs.

One obvious advantage of a partnership structure over a corporation would be the avoidance of double taxation on most distributions. Remember that corporations pay taxes on their earnings, and the shareholders pay taxes again on the share of those earning they receive as dividends. Thus, the same dollar of corporate earnings is taxed twice. However, a limited partnership investment functions as a pass through agency, and the earnings are not taxed before distribution. Consequently, the limited partner investor receives pre-taxed distributions, which would naturally be higher than a comparable corporate distribution.

Limited partnership distributions will be higher approximately by the amount of tax that would need to be paid if the business were structured as a corporation. In other words, if a corporation and a partnership both have the same net profit, the partnership would be able to bring more net income to the bottom line than the corporation because of the income tax savings. Only the limited partner investor would be liable for income taxes due on that distribution.

Additionally, as mentioned earlier, tax advantages are often an important feature of limited partnerships. Many limited partnerships are structured to include a means of sheltering some of the tax liability with their distributions. Real Estate LPs often shelter some of the tax liability of their distributions through accelerated depreciation of their assets. Oil and Gas LPs shelter distributions through amortization, which essentially means you are receiving return of your capital. In other words, you are simply receiving back money you paid for an asset in the ground as it is extracted and sold.

Some LPs are also structured to offer income tax credits, which, rather than simply sheltering part of the distribution, provides a fixed dollar amount to offset income tax owed from other sources.

Tax credits are sometimes offered for Oil and Gas LPs that drill in shale formations or other geographically difficult development sites. Real Estate LPs may offer tax credits for investments in government subsidized low-income housing. Income tax credits are only available because of legislative action, and these types of investments are becoming less common. Be aware that what legislators create, they can also take away, so check with a tax consultant regarding investments in these types of LPs.

Now that you are familiar with some of the positive aspects of investing in LPs, consider some possible negatives. One is that if you invest in a partnership in a retirement account, such as an IRA, your distributions may be subject to a peculiar tax known as unrelated business income tax, UBIT. Since such a tax defeats the tax-free benefits of investments in a qualified retirement account, you should address these issues with a qualified tax consultant.

Another notable negative is that LPs are generally illiquid. It is usually very difficult to transfer ownership if the limited partner investor needs to liquidate prior to the termination of the LP. Most brokers maintain a secondary market for partnerships they sponsor. However, that market is not usually on an exchange, so the partnerships are seldom priced at full market value. Anyone who might be willing to purchase a limited partnership in a third market transaction, will probably also be thinking that the seller must be desperate to liquidate, since the program would have a scheduled termination date. So, buyers generally offer lower than market value for these LPs, being aware the seller may be more willing to accept a low bid.

However, there is a type of limited partnership that avoids problems of illiquidity. A **Master Limited Partnership**, **MLP**, is one that trades on an exchange, as shares of common stock do. However, the shares traded for an MLP are not common stock. They are limited partnership units, often referred to as **shares of beneficial interest**, **SBI**. MLPs are available in several industry groups, as they are created by government legislation. They tend to be concentrated in commodities or financial services. To most investors, MLPs are attractive because of the high cash flow from quarterly distributions, and there are often tax advantages attached to these distributions. There are hundreds of MLPs in a wide variety of products. The distributions from MLPs are generally at a higher annual percentage rate, APR, than dividends for comparable corporations.

Brokers may also offer limited partnership investments designed as **Private Placements** to some of their accounts. These are partnerships offered to a small number of accredited investors. The SEC defines **accredited investors** as those with a high degree of knowledge and sophistication regarding financial matters. Accredited investors must also have a net worth of $1 million and annual income of over $200,000 (or $300,000 jointly). These types of partnerships are usually similar to venture capital investments. They often involve seed money for a new product or idea whose end market potential may not be fully realized. Obviously these are for high risk investors only.

You need to be aware of tax consequences on your investments to determine your real return. Uncle Sam may give you a break on some.

Chapter 12

What Issues Will Affect the Economy in the Future?

In this chapter I am going to leave the world of facts and enter the world of opinion. I do not wish to imply that opinions are not based on facts, only that conclusions may or may not be realized. Events happening today are going to have consequences in the future. I am going to evaluate where they might lead and present some thoughts about what you might want to do. You might hear a point of view you have not considered before. The topics will probably be familiar, but I am not going to approach them by rehashing what other prognosticators have said. I want to present some fresh ideas and viewpoints.

Successful investors should always be looking around the corner to see what is coming. They should not make kneejerk reactions to current headlines. Reacting to what has already happened is a strategy guaranteed to lose money. You should be constantly anticipating what could happen and plan accordingly. No one knows the future, but prepare for potential trouble beforehand.

I strongly recommend you never stop studying. Read everything that interests you—and even some that doesn't. You will not only be better informed, but you will also be in a better position to evaluate current events. Always be on the lookout for a bias or self-serving agenda. Not everyone is a truth seeker. Most people tend to taint their comments with personal issues, often unawares.

The first issue I would like to address is that investors are currently being held hostage in a feud of monumental proportions. This feud has been waged over a hundred years and continues to this day. Most people are not paying attention to it, because few people understand the issues behind it.

It is an economic feud, not being contested *among* nations, but rather *with* and *within* nations. Countries are the pawns in this global game, and the U.S. is no less a pawn than any other sovereign country. This feud is being waged in boardrooms and the weapons of war are often nothing but gargantuan egos. On one side are government officials and on the other, bankers.

There is supposed to be a symbiotic relationship between governments and their central banks. In the U.S., the central bank is the Federal Reserve System. But in recent years this relationship could be described as more of a strained *frenemy* one. This may not be noticeable by outward appearances. Politicians are adroit at smiling in the face of adversity, and bankers seldom smile at anything. In fact, top bankers are seldom seen in public, except perhaps for a photo op with influential people in the public and private sectors at the annual Economic Forum in Davos, Switzerland or the Economic Summit in Jackson Hole, Wyoming. Nevertheless, each side is pitted in a high stakes struggle for power and control.

First, you need some background on the relationship between the government and banks. It is not a long history. Yet most people assume it has always been as it is today. The creation of a Federal Reserve System became a hot topic of discussion around the turn of the 20th century. The U.S. had endured decades of economic crisis. Unemployment topped 18 percent in 1894, and the NYSE fell about 50 percent in 1907. There was a general lack of confidence in banks, which were largely unregulated; and *runs* on banks were frequent.

Congress considered several proposals for the establishment of an organization to regulate the banking industry. But the political parties were divided as to how best to accomplish this. The Republicans favored a private banking system in which the government was not involved. The Democrats wanted a government controlled system.

The debate eventually resulted in the Federal Reserve Act of 1913, a compromise allowing the creation of the Federal Reserve System. The FRS is a study in contradictions on many levels. It is a private bank for the public good; independent, yet regulated; centralized, yet composed of thousands of member banks. The bank is run by Congressional appointees, but the committees responsible for making those appointments are not very involved in its regulation. They rely on testimony from the Fed to explain what courses of action the central bank is pursuing—not a very good strategy for an oversight committee.

Since its inception, the **Federal Reserve System** has had a love-hate relationship with the government. The Fed is tasked with the responsibility of regulating a relatively low inflation rate for the economy, while at the same time maintaining a high percentage employment, which causes inflation. But most of  the time, the Federal Reserve is kept busy trying to bail the government out of the problems it creates with excess spending.

The U.S. Congress is tasked with setting *fiscal policy*, and the Federal Reserve with *monetary policy*. Public servants are in charge of government spending, and the Fed is in charge of the supply of money in the banking system. The Fed cannot control government spending; they can only regulate the supply of money. Yet the fiscal policies instituted by the government often conflict with the Fed's monetary ones. Bankers do not govern, nor do they want to govern. But they would probably prefer to have more influence over those who do, especially when the government initiates policies that undermine the goals of the Fed—thus the feud.

The Fed used to issue one time quantitative easing (QE) programs. QE is a term some refer to as printing money, but it is really a process of putting more fiat currency in circulation. The Fed sells government bonds to member banks to take money out of circulation when it wants to reduce money supply. Then it buys bonds from member banks when it wants to increase money supply. Buying bonds gives banks more cash with which they are supposed to issue more loans.

Today the Fed's QE Program is open-ended. Member banks purchase U.S. Treasury securities *every month*. This would add constant liquidity to the banking system and would continue until the banks started lending more of that money being forced into their vaults—or until the U.S. dollar collapses or the economy implodes, whichever came first.

Today, instead of buying the normal Treasury securities, the Fed focuses purchasing activities on mortgage backed securities

(MBS). This was an expansion of an earlier Fed program called Operation Twist in which it was already committed to purchasing long-term debt and issuing short term.

The combined programs meant that the Fed was infusing money into the banking system at an alarming rate. It also resulted in a situation where the Fed was holding the majority of mortgages in the U.S. Member banks, on the other hand, always reticent to lend money in a bad economic environment, invest most of that cash into more U.S. Treasuries securities.

The Federal Reserve Bank currently owns over $2.3 trillion worth of mortgage backed securities. At an average interest rate of 7 percent, the amount of interest paid on those mortgages would be over $160 billion, most of which would go into the government's coffers. Also, the member banks of the FRB continue to make more mortgage loans and their profitability is guaranteed, courtesy of U.S. taxpayers. Yes, federally chartered *private* financial institutions—such as JPMorgan Chase, Bank of America, Citigroup, Wells Fargo, and Goldman Sachs—are guaranteed to make a profit in a backhanded way by U.S. taxpayers. The banking system and the government have a symbiotic relationship. Taxpayers are underwriting both.

But buying mortgage backed securities is just the tip of the iceberg. Total national debt will reach $50,000,000,000,000 in 2025. The Fed continually refinances maturing debt with new. Thus, the U.S. government competes with all other bond issuers for investors' dollars. If the government must raise interest rates to attract more investors to fund its bonds, other bond issuers must do the same. The annual interest expense on that debt is one of the largest components of budget expenditures. Just to give you a general idea about how much costs, without adjusting for compounding, the interest on $50T at 4% would be approximately $2T/year, $167B/month, $38.5B/week, $5.5B/day, $228M/hour, $9.5M/minute and $158,000/second. Up to the minute information on government finances can be found at usdebtclock.org.

The money the Fed earns is returned to the U.S. Treasury, and the Fed is paid a six percent flat rate on the assets it controls. Since the total balance sheet of the Fed now runs about $8 trillion, the Fed is likely paid about $480 billion a year with tax dollars. I doubt they pay taxes on that income because that is tax money. The balance sheet of the FRB is updated weekly at the website federalreserve.gov. But it has never been audited by an outside independent source. Now back to the feud. No one knows where all that money goes.

The Fed seems to have the upper hand in this ultimate high grudge match. Furthermore, they have always had the upper hand. The central banks of most nations around the world are now working together to coordinate their monetary policies because of interdependent economic relationships of global trading partners. Other central bankers around the world can punish any sovereign participant who is not a team player.

The leaders of the central banks of 63 nations, representing 95% of the world's economy, meet every two months in Basel, Switzerland, at the headquarters for the **Bank of International Settlements**, **BIS**, the world central bank for the national central banks. At these meetings central bankers secretly discuss plans for coordinating money supply on a global scale. No one knows what is discussed; some meetings are so secretive not even the bankers' aides are allowed to attend.

International Bank of Settlements building, Basel, Switzerland

There is probably not much real debate going on at these meetings. Most of the members of that elite group are associated with one college, Massachusetts Institute Technology, MIT. The influence of that school on global economics is astounding, and it favors a Keynesian bias, involving greater government intervention. There are so many central bankers with backgrounds at MIT that meetings probably sound more like a fraternal organization, than a forum for debate. MIT and other primarily Ivy League schools profess a philosophy referred to as saltwater school economics, because of their proximity to the oceans.

In the world of economic theory, the chief rival to MIT is the University of Chicago, where Milton Friedman taught. He is one of the most influential economists in the 20th century, and his book *Methodology of Positive Economics* lays out an approach to solving economic problems that favor Austrian School with less government intervention. At the beginning of this book, I also mentioned F.A. Hayek as a chief spokesman for Austrian School. However, there are not many voices representing the Austrian School among the central bankers meeting in Basel.

It is important to note that central bank policy decisions are made on the basis of secret talks and can be changed or adjusted with a simple phone call. Since central bankers are now pursuing policies that have never been tried before, this is a very dangerous precedent to set with virtually no voice expressing a contradictory point of view. One would think that a little more open debate on the feasibility of these policies would be in order.

The power the Federal Reserve has assumed, with little accountability and oversight, continues to be largely unnoticed by most people. That is by design. The Fed has the power and authority to create fiat currency and obligates U.S. taxpayers to pay interest on it. Someone who has the ability to create something from nothing and obligate someone else to assume the financial responsibility for it might want to minimize the scrutiny to which they would want to be subjected.

The job of the U.S. Federal Reserve is one where accountability is needed most. Steering the economy is the most important job not just in the U.S. but in the world. Yet, there is an obvious inherent conflict of interest. The Fed and its member banks stand to profit from the more money it speaks into existence. I suspect the Fed's propensity to create money will ultimately lead to its undoing. There are many voices currently calling for its dissolution. That is a plank in the Libertarian Party platform and advocated by many independents. However, I would not be one to make such a call. To deconstruct the banking system would probably create far more chaos, compounding the current problem. The simplest solution would be to take away the profit incentive for creating money. I believe the profit incentive is a major hindrance to finding a resolution.

Additionally, the U.S. is in deeper economic trouble than its immediate debt obligations. Government commitments to unfunded and unbudgeted future expenditures (such as Social Security and Medicare) is well over $200 Trillion! Check the usdebtclock.org website for current numbers. Excessive spending is the real problem, and an interest bearing monetary system is compounding it. There is little oversight on the actions of the Fed, and the people in government responsible for allocating debt have no cap on their spending. No one is going to stop irresponsible spending if they have a profit incentive to keep it going.

Any solution to the current fiscal problems is going to be painful, but to ignore the situation and continue down this path of ignorance will be a death sentence. Neither the U.S. nor the world can endure a monetary system that allows a profit incentive for those who control it with no accountability. If the U.S. took the lead in resolving this problem, the rest of the world would follow. But I imagine the World Bank and the BIS are there to bail them out.

The Federal Reserve System needs to be revised, and its charter rewritten. The U.S. economy is certainly doomed if it continues to rely on a system created only with interest-bearing fiat money—U.S. Treasury bills, notes, and bonds—enriching those who create them. The taxpayers who are responsible for paying the interest and principal on this debt have no control over it. Those who mandate the debt are not held accountable to those who must fund it.

Is it such a radical idea that banks should be required, like all other businesses in a free enterprise economy, to *earn* a profit from the products and services they provide? It seems a far more radical idea that the richest corporations in America—the federally chartered commercial banks, the members of the FRS—are supported by a surreptitious public welfare policy—taxes. There is no logical reason why banks should be afforded the clandestine support they receive. No other business gets that privilege.

The solution to this problem is to remove the profit incentive from financial institutions to do nothing and put the incentive back on them to do their jobs. The unregulated environment that existed in banks when the Federal Reserve was created a hundred years ago has been replaced with another unregulated environment that masks itself as being regulated. The pendulum needs to swing to the middle where proper regulation and oversight will maintain the competitive environment inherently necessary for a functional free market capitalist system.

Note that this should be an easily accomplished solution to an obvious problem. But it will be far from easy. Those in power, especially those wielding sovereign power, will not willingly surrender it. Correcting the problem will be like taking drugs from an addict. The need is obvious; the solution simple; but the execution seemingly impossible.

Many Fed critics advocate a return to the gold standard, or some commodity-backed money supply. Although that is a popular position, I do not see it as a pragmatic one. Reverting to a gold standard would simply put the power back into the hands of those who hold the gold. Again, there is an obvious profit incentive for a few to pursue this course of action, and that is what created the problem in the first place.

What is needed to prevent a fiscal crisis from becoming a financial meltdown is to put the power of controlling money supply into the hands of someone who does not have a motive to profit from it. Money supply needs to be under the authority of an agency that has no other incentive than to maintain economic equilibrium.

Again, at the heart of every economic problem is greed. It is everyone's undoing. Greed is not confined to any one group; politicians are just as greedy as bankers. Unless you are an extremely rare individual, you are motivated by greed. But if the incentive to profit from the creation of the money supply were removed, the economy would be on a much more solid foundation. What is needed to keep greed in check is an economic system based on high ethical standards. That is the next topic.

What Causes the Wealth of Nations to Rise and Fall?

I am going to conclude with some thoughts about the interrelationship of ethics, particularly regarding free market capitalism and a workable worldwide economic system. Some may consider this discussion controversial. Ethics itself is not controversial, but the source of ethics can be. It is a sad state of affairs when there are many people who claim they cannot recognize the difference between right and wrong, who deny they have an internal moral compass to tell the difference.

Some people say *business ethics* is an oxymoron—in the same category as words like student teacher, black light, jumbo shrimp, or Civil War. Business ethics, however, should not be an oxymoron.

Those words need to be related; ethics is necessary for *any* economic system to function properly. If any of the components that make up an economic system—public businesses, private enterprises, or governments—do not conduct economic activity on an ethical basis, they will self-destruct and produce economic chaos.

A public business or private enterprise built on lying, cheating, and stealing will have to continuously wage a propaganda war or a sabotage campaign on potential competition to remain functional. Additionally, any government system not founded on a basis of ethics must keep escalating its threat of violence to retain its grip on power. If one's power depends on intimidation and threats of violence, it will not last. People will not continuously endure abuse. They will inevitably choose either flight or fight.

In a free market system, unethical business practices can prosper for a time. But if any economic model is not founded on ethical standards and does not have a system in place for addressing unethical business conduct, it will collapse. Those participating in economic activity will not function effectively in a financial framework that takes advantage of them or treats them unfairly. In a free market capitalist system, there is always an alternative, or potential alternative, to an unethical one, and the collapse will happen quickly. But even in a system where there is nowhere else to go, that economic model will fail due to inherent inefficiency.

Free market capitalism is the best path to prosperity. By definition free market capitalism is an economic system wherein competition in the marketplace determines the price of the product. Consumers pay what they think a product or service is worth. Prices are not manipulated by outside intervention, such as government actions that might favor a political agenda.

A closed economic model that does not allow for competition in the marketplace will always implode. It will not work because there is no economic incentive to continue to improve products and keep prices competitive. So, a competitive market is inherently the only system that rewards ethical conduct. If a business wants to keep its customers, it must treat them fairly.

Businesses built on unethical practices may prosper for a time, but if their governance policies assume lying, cheating, and stealing are acceptable, it will become a victim of its own values. It will produce an increasingly substandard product or service. In a competitive capitalist marketplace such a business will usually fail quickly, because of readily available of alternative products.

However, even in a closed or subsidized socialist economic system, a business model without an ethical foundation will still collapse. It will just take longer. When people are forced into survival mode, they can become very creative capitalists. The world is shrinking so quickly that there will always be someone who is able to fill a competitive market need.

Ethics is necessary for every component of a workable economic system—governments and private businesses, producers and consumers, employees and employers. There is always more than one party involved in any economic activity; thus ethics is always a multifaceted issue. Regulators must have someone to regulate; management must have labor; sellers must have buyers; and arrangements between all parties must be fair.

Consider the manifold complexities of economic relationships. Workers who are mistreated are likely to produce a product of inferior quality. So, management needs to be sensitive to the attitudes and opinions of their employees and simultaneously aware of the attitudes and expectations of their customers and investors. Thus, corporate governance issues are always a priority.

In a capitalist system, major corporations are required to maintain a Human Resources (HR) Department whose function is to ensure employees are treated fairly. Whether or not all disputes are settled to everyone's satisfaction is a different question. Any system will only be as good as the people who implement it, but suffice it to say, there is a system in place with the stated goal of striving for a fair resolution to employees' complaints or disputes.

Also, corporations maintain a Customer Relations Department that ensures procedures are in place for dealing with consumer complaints. For corporations to survive and thrive in a capitalist system, they must constantly reassure their customers they will do everything within their power to settle all disputes in a fair and equitable manner. If they don't, they will lose customers; and ultimately, their business.

I am not making a claim that free market capitalism is a perfect system. I am only saying that it is better than any other alternative. It has better provisions of checks and balances than any other economic model. There will always be problems; people are imperfect. But problems are likely to be addressed with a better resolution in a competitive market environment.

With that said, I also need to point out that size matters. Becoming more powerful and influential creates more opportunities for corruption. Only free market capitalism keeps one's tendency toward unethical activities in check. If you have a complaint against a large corporation, you may feel like David fighting Goliath. In that case, however, you have a fighting chance. David won.

But if a sovereign government is running a corporation, you have virtually no legal standing for action. An individual cannot file a legal dispute against a sovereign. You can sue government agencies or individual government employees, but not the federal government itself. Every type of federal government has unlimited power—even a democracy as much as a dictatorship.

Thus, freedom of choice is limited when a sovereign government controls the economic system. If a socialist form of government is in complete control, operating as a monopoly over the economic system, there would be little or no legal protection for individuals. An economic dispute with a sovereign simply means you have no rights. You have no legal protection; there is no court to which you can appeal.

All governments are monopolies by definition. Countries do not function well with more than one government. Thus, businesses run by the government would be a monopoly by proxy. The most extreme example of this would be a Marxist communist system.

Under capitalism, corporations may sometimes operate as a partial monopoly; but there are checks and balances on power in those situations. An electric or natural gas utility, for example, needs to be a monopoly. You do not want competing electric lines or natural gas pipelines running into every house. These businesses are necessarily regulated by a government agency, in this case, the Public Utilities Commission. They ensure that utilities cannot charge exorbitant rates for their services. This example also illustrates that the proper role of government in businesses, not just utilities, is to be a *fair* regulator.

The struggle between the two primary economic philosophies is far older than Keynes and Hayek. It is, broadly speaking, socialism vs. capitalism; and it is as old as the concept of an economy. Socialists would say that the fruit of one's labor should go to prosper all. Capitalists would say that one's labor should benefit those who buy the product of that labor. The more your work benefits others, the more likely you are to benefit yourself.

Thet free market capitalism is the best economic system. If you take away the profit incentive to work, why would anyone work? If you are given the choice of working hard to earn something or being given it without having to work hard, of course, most people would take the easy road. But if that is the case for all, why would the economy grow? There is no incentive, because the quality of your work output does not correlation to the quality of your labor.

Consequently, any incarnation of a socialist economic system will inevitably digress to inefficiency and ultimately failure. Governments involvement in the free market process will inevitably reward bureaucrats who profit from the labor of others. Simultaneously, it will create a workforce that has no incentive to maximize productivity. Again, if there is no reward for hard work, why would anyone work hard?

Nevertheless, the struggle between the economic philosophies of capitalism and socialism plays itself out continuously around the world. In some cases, government officials consolidate their power into a monopolistic framework—some incarnation of socialism. In others, the government exists to prevent the monopolistic tendencies of the most powerful of its citizens. The U.S. is currently in the throes of such a struggle. But I do not believe there is anything unique about its situation. All nations—including the U.S.—are continuously facing such conflicts of ideologies. The debate may wax and wane, but it never ceases.

Because of the influence of the U.S. on global markets, shifting economic philosophy will affect much more than just the Western Hemisphere. Sovereign states need policing as much as corporations, and the most economically powerful nations are the most likely to be in a position to expand their sphere of influence.

The U.S. is the most influential arbitrator of human rights abuses in the world. It has consistently favored the abused over abusers. Critics of U.S. foreign policies are usually quick to claim the involvement of the U.S. is in its own best interests. That is true, but it is also in the best interests of the victims of abuse. The benefits of U.S. involvement in addressing global issues of ethics violations, goes far beyond its borders. Historically, the world has been made a better place because the U.S. was willing to defend it from abusive tyrants, not only with its abundance of wealth but also with the blood of its patriots.

The U.S. role as arbitrator in the world has been greatly diminished in recent years as a result of poor economic management. Much of its wealth has disappeared into a black hole of debt, and its commitment to peace through strength has been undermined. The U.S. has set itself on a course of socialism that has rendered it impotent on a global scale. This has been done freely and willingly—the people's choice.

Nevertheless, the absence of the U.S. leaves a void at the top of the global power pyramid. It is a void that will likely be filled by another nation that will not share the same standards of morality regarding human rights and freedom.

There is, and always has been, a constant struggle among the powerful nations of the world to increase their influence over the rest—and to capitalize on it. At the time of this writing, the European Union and the United States remain the two largest economies. However, both are in economic decline because of unrestrained government spending, the cost of socialist policies.

The other countries that are rising to positions of power on the global scene are Brazil, Russia, India, China, and South Africa referred to by the acronym BRICS. They are the largest and most likely countries to emerge as global leaders.

At the time of this writing, the EU was still the largest economy in the world, but it was also the weakest of the major players. The EU will be tied up in internal turmoil for many years. It is doubtful that it will be in a stable enough position to pursue global ambitions. This is in stark contrast to the history of its individual members.

It is important to note that what has weakened the economy of the EU is the prevalence of socialism. The debt incurred by most of the sovereign nations of the EU is a direct result of excessive spending tied to the redistribution of wealth. That will likely keep the EU in a weakened economic state for decades. As the EU attempts to renegotiate and police the irresponsible spending and accumulated debt of its weaker members, the stability of its stronger members will be undermined.

For the last century, the U.S. has been the most powerful force for peace and stability in the world. However, the role of the U.S.

in global politics has declined lately as it has pursued spending policies far more catastrophic than those in Europe. When the U.S. totally relinquishes its role as moderator in the world, the most likely country to rise up and fill that void would be China, the country with the largest army.

China is an interesting study in contrasts. Its government was firmly founded on traditional communist principals. The conflicts in China that led to a communist dictatorship spanned over two decades from 1927 to 1950, including the Second Sino-Japanese War (1945-9). Mao Zedong proclaimed rule over mainland China by the Communist Party in 1949. The wars had resulted in the deaths of an estimated 40 million people.

Mao took to heart Karl Marx's dictate, "Religion is the opium of the masses". He officially declared China an atheist state, and under communist atheism it took less than two decades for those utopian economic ideologies to lead China to near self-annihilation. Another estimated 40 million people died, and there were probably more Christian martyrs included in that number than have been killed in any other nation. After decades of death and starvation, Mao declared the Cultural Revolution in 1966, attempting to transform many rural agrarian regions into manufacturing industrial centers. This too failed miserably, resulting in the deaths of perhaps as many as 20 million more people.

All totaled, the communist experiment and the misguided attempts to rectify it may have resulted in the deaths of about 100 million people. Sometimes the impact of statistics diminishes the reality of the events. It is easy to lose sight of the fact when transferring death tolls into statistics that everyone included in that toll was a human being. Each was someone who was loved by and connected to someone else.

Communism in China resulted in more destruction of human life than any other event in history. The only other that comes close is the communist takeover in Russia. Between the deaths resulting from the Bolshevik Revolution and the ensuing 60 years of communist rule, there are estimates of about 60 million lives lost due to war and economic hardship. Stalin's infamous gulag archipelago could have been responsible for almost two-thirds of that total, 39 million lives.

How can anyone continue to advocate a government-controlled economic model in light of such overwhelming and gruesome proof of the failure of that ideology? For documentation of this information check out the many websites on the topic. The information should be a must read for everyone, as a reminder of how depraved the human condition can become when big government ideologues fulfill their ambitions.

Both the Chinese and Russian experiments in socio-economic engineering should have clarified for everyone the folly of trying to create an economic system so opposed to logic. In both cases what began as an idealistic dream turned into the most horrific nightmare imaginable. However, as with any dream, we wake up.

In the case of China, Mao's successors, notably Deng Xiaoping, was in a good position to observe the catastrophic effects of communism. He was born to a peasant family in a rural area of central China, where communist economic policies had the most devastating impact. Thus, when Deng had the opportunity to do so, he guided the country toward an economic policy of free market capitalism—even while some hardliners remained in power. His capitalist policies saved China.

In the 1970s Deng was instrumental in tearing down China's bamboo curtain and opening the country to foreign investment. He initiated policies of "limited capitalism". Whereas communism utterly destroyed China in about 50 years, it took less than 30 years for free market capitalism to reverse its effects. Today China is the third largest economy in the world—and the leading contender for number one.

Capitalism in China allowed individuals rather than the state to profit from the people's labor. China will probably surpass the EU and the U.S. as the largest economic power in the world within a few years, based on current growth projections.

However, what happens after that is unclear. If there is still a communist politburo governing China, it will be able to wield a mighty big stick. If state-sponsored companies compete with private enterprise, the nation will probably revert back to the communist system, and a depression will inevitably follow. Also, China does not have an admirable reputation regarding ethics. Former ambassador Jon Huntsman described China as the worst offender for stealing intellectual property and patent infringement, manufacturing products with copycat designs. He estimated that about 80 percent of that type of theft worldwide could be attributed to China.

Also, it is a popular political stance in the U.S. to label China a currency manipulator. That means the government has a policy of keeping the exchange rate of the Chinese yuan vs. the U.S. dollar, as well as the euro and other currencies, at a relatively low level. This is a manipulative means of making Chinese manufactured goods cheaper in the U.S. because the dollar can buy more yuan-denominated goods than it could if the currency were allowed to rise in an open market.

Few would characterize China as saintly, but there is never just one side to a story. Despite the fact China remains under communist control, it is certainly a much more moderate nation than it was under hardline communist rule. Religion is on the rise there at a much more astounding rate than any other nation in the world. About 80 percent of the population identifies with a religion, an amazing development for a country with an official atheist policy for over half a century.

China is the most likely country to replace the U.S. on the global scene, but how they will wield their power is more difficult to predict. Internally China is headed toward a conflict of monumental proportions. The tenants of religion influence a culture toward greater conformity to the ethical principles it espouses. So, this could be a positive influence on China's economic policies. The leadership tolerates religious practice, but most of those holding power appear to be steadfastly committed to atheism.

If you want to know where a country is going, you need only look in the direction its moral compass is pointing. In the U.S. it is turning downward, but in China it may be turning upward. The other BRICS countries are in less competitive positions to be a major influence on the global scene.

Russia has the largest untapped petroleum reserves in the world and significant quantities of other natural resources, especially rare earth commodities. They also have a history of inserting themselves into regional conflicts around the world—the Brezhnev Doctrine. However, Russia is trying to revert back to communism. The government has been seizing and privatizing some of its most successful public companies. This path has already failed the country once, due to the same political corruption that is currently doing the seizing. Russia's economic model is likely to cause it to fail again. Governments cannot run companies as efficiently as private enterprise.

India is the second largest county in the world by population. It has a stable democratic government and adequate corporate governance policies. However, it also has the greatest need for improvement to its infrastructure of the major countries. India will likely be economically tied up in internal projects—improving roads, bridges, the electricity grid, mass transportation, and so on—before it can pursue external economic expansion.

Brazil also has a vast amount of natural resources. Its rise to global prominence, like that of China before it, was tied to hosting the Summer Olympic Games. That focused the eyes of the world on its positive assets. But Brazil is battling its own communist dictators and does not have a strong military. Also, it seems to have little interest in becoming involved in global affairs.

There are, of course, other countries or regions that could rise to the top of the global economic pyramid. I have not included alliances of predominantly Muslim nations, or others rich in natural resources, such as Australia and Canada. However, as the U.S. relinquishes its position as global economic leader, it will also relinquish its role as chief global arbitrator. These are the likely contenders to fill that void, and the ones with the most aggressive leadership are not likely to be the fairest arbitrators.

Why has the U.S. failed? There is an economic principle that the company that rises to the dominant position in its industry group will not maintain that status for long. Consider this list of companies that were all at onetime at the top of their industry: Sears Roebuck (and before that Woolworth), Eastman Kodak, Pan Am, Xerox. Does anyone remember Arbuckle Coffee? It popularized coffee drinking in America; for decades Arbuckle was a synonym for coffee. What do you think the Starbuck's barista would think if you ordered a cup of Arbuckle? The company that launched the video gaming industry is Atari. Where is it today?

There are two reasons why top dogs are unable to maintain their status. Companies at the top are more inclined to rest on their laurels and lose their competitive edge. Also, competitors are much more motivated to compete for their business. To use a sports analogy, the underdog team is far more likely to play its best game when it is trying to knock off the number one seed, and the number one is unlikely to consider a win over an unworthy opponent as such a great accomplishment.

Back to the global perspective, the underdog that will rise to fill the power void at the top of the economic pyramid is uncertain. But whoever it is, they will *not* likely have the same commitment to human rights as the U.S. That is a sad state of affairs.

It is easy for the U.S. to blame its distracters, but I know it is a natural consequence of economic evolution. The U.S. has been resting on its laurels for too long. It is a generous nation, and true to that nature, has committed itself to excessive deficit spending. The accumulated debt has become so large and so onerous that the bureaucratic infrastructure managing it has lost all semblance of accountability. The government no longer bothers passing (or usually proposing) an annual budget, even though it is required by law to do so. If our government representatives cannot live by their own standards, can they force their constituents to do so?

The U.S. was built on a foundation that everyone has equal *opportunity* for success, not that they are all *guaranteed* economic equivalency. Success must always be earned; it is not something that can be bestowed as a birthright. The expectation that all will have the opportunity to pursue their own path is what draws millions of immigrants to this country every year. But today, the U.S. is about to be overrun by "dreamers" and many others who are coming in illegally to destroy those dreams.

The massive amount of national debt is the greatest hindrance to dreams. Ironically, the financial commitment in the name of economic equalization will only make worse the plight of those they are trying to help. It will bankrupt the nation—everyone will be hurt, but the rich far less than the poor. Despite the fact that taxing the rich is a mantra for the solution to the debt, the size of the spending problem has escalated far beyond that. Seizing all the assets of the rich would not even amount to a sufficient down payment for a $40 trillion loan.

With that rather negative assessment, I would leave you with one thought. The human spirit is indomitable. Everyone is endowed with unique talents and abilities. Everyone has something to contribute to society. Life is precious. Everyone's story matters.

There will always be obstacles in life; some may seem insurmountable. But the U.S. was built by those who believed in overcoming insurmountable obstacles. Everyone in the U.S. is assured of having the opportunity to pursue dreams—if they chose to do so. The U.S. remains the land of opportunity, where dreams can still be realized. The economy is resilient because of the indomitable human spirit.

The U.S. was created by men and women no different from you. But consider what they resolved to do in bringing this country to where it is today. They defeated the most powerful army in the world to win independence. They fought a Civil War to abolish slavery and keep the Union from being torn apart. U.S. doughboys were subjected to the first use of chemical weapons of mass destruction while huddled in trenches during in the Great War "to end all wars". A few years later, the people referred to as the "greatest generation" saved the world again from total dictatorship in WWII, which everyone knew would not end all wars. The U.S. has survived depressions and Presidential assassinations. It can survive political turmoil. But it needs the resolve to do so.

I hope that common sense will ultimately prevail. I believe the United States of America will remain the country that most people will continue to want to come to legally. Opening our borders to immigrants without knowing who they are or what they intend to do here will result in the worst case scenario for this country. It will likely be the death of America—either through terrorist attacks, illegal voting, or government expenditures on them resulting in bankruptcy. What made America great in the beginning was its freedom. What threatens it now is the socialist agenda to take our freedom away and become slaves of the government. I hope and pray we are a better people than that.

But everything depends on preserving our system of free market capitalism. Opportunity for success is what drew people to this country when it was growing. If government acts fairly and equitably to preserve our freedom, the U.S. will continue to prosper. But we will only decline if we lose that vision. Protecting the American dream is not easy, but that is the point. The easy path does not lead in the right direction.

The stock market *is* free market capitalism. As long as it exists, you are assured you have the freedom of choice to pursue economic opportunities. Work hard and work smart. You will not only be a successful investor, you will be successful in life. Your road to success begins by learning what you need to know before you invest.

~$ $ $~*Investing Tip*~$ $ $~

You should always be looking around the corner and preparing for what you see coming. You might avoid an economic mugging.

Glossary

This glossary presents definitions of key investment terms in a nontechnical way. In many cases, it will also give you the reason why you should understand them. It will explain the relevance of words and phrases to real world investing. Hopefully you will be better able to comprehend what you hear on business reports or read in financial publications or websites. Many of the words included in this glossary were chosen because they are terms you might often hear or read in business reports. For beginning investors there is a steep learning curve regarding the language of the financial services industry. This is not a comprehensive list of terms, as that would take another entire book. But the words and phrases included here will lay a foundation, making it easier to understand business speak. You must begin somewhere.

Accredited investor: designation the SEC uses to describe someone, either an individual or another legal entity, who is knowledgeable and experienced regarding financial investments and thus qualifies to assume a high degree of risk, such as is characteristic of some private placement partnerships. Individuals generally must have annual income of $200,000 ($300,000 jointly) and a net worth of at least $1 million excluding primary residence.

After-market (or after-hours) trading: the four hours, 4:00 – 8:00 p.m. East Coast Time, that electronic communication networks continue to execute trades after the regular markets are closed. The NYSE and Nasdaq are open 9:30 a.m. to 4:00 p.m. ECT. See **Pre-market (or pre-open) trading**.

American Depositary Receipt (ADR): a designation for shares of foreign companies that trade on U.S. Markets. The foreign company deposits shares of its stock with a U.S. financial institution, which will reissue new ADR shares with certificates printed in English and dividends or distribution converted to U.S. currency.

GLOSSARY ◊ 315

Annuitant: the individual who is designated to receive the distribution from an annuity and upon whose life the insurance benefits will apply. The annuitant may be different from the contract owner. For example, the owner could be a living trust, and the annuitant the trustee.

Annuity: a contract issued by an insurance company that allows investments held in it to accumulate on a tax deferred basis. Annuities are generally used to supplement retirement income, and there could be a 10 percent IRS penalty on withdrawals from earnings or capital gains made before the year in which the annuitant turns age 59½. The transfer of an annuity to a beneficiary can be accomplished without going through the probate process.

Arbitrage: an investment strategy of buying and selling the same or similar securities (usually on different markets) in order to take advantage of price disparities. Riskless arbitrage might involve buying a convertible bond selling at a price below the conversion parity for the underlying stock, and simultaneously selling the shares of stock realized from the bond conversion. Risk arbitrage involves trading two equivalent positions that are constantly changing in value, such as a large block of stock on one side and an index option or futures contract on the opposite side. See **Program trading**.

Arbitrageur: one who participates in arbitrage trading.

Ask price: the lowest price at which someone is offering to sell an investment on an auction market; also called offer price. See **Bid price**.

Asset: a resource that a company can use to operate its business and whose monetary value is included on the balance sheet. Assets are separated into current, fixed and intangible categories. Current assets can be easily turned into cash; fixed assets include property, plant, and equipment; and intangible assets include goodwill, patents, copyrights, etc.

Back-end load fund: A class of mutual fund shares, class B, that may be purchased with no sales charged but are subject to exit charges within a certain time period. This charge declines to zero after a few years. It is referred to as a contingent deferred sales charge, CDSC. (See **front-end load fund** and **no load fund**.)

Balance sheet: a financial statement that expresses the current financial condition of a company, or some other financial entity. It follows the formula *assets minus liabilities equals equity* (or net worth). For corporations it is reported quarterly and totaled for the company's fiscal year.

Bear market: a period of time when major market indexes decline by at least 20% for an extended period of time, with a larger than normal number of stocks hitting new lows. Bear markets generally imply a period of months or years. See **Bull market**.

Beta: a method of measuring the market risk of equity investments, usually stock or mutual funds. It compares the volatility of the investment with the volatility of the S&P 500 Index over the same period of time. If the percentage change in the price of the investment is the same as the percentage change in the S&P, the investment would have a beta of 1.00. If it changed 50 percent more than the S&P, it would have a beta of 1.50. The higher the beta, the greater the perceived risk of owning that investment because of what it implies in a down market. If a stock has a beta of 2.00 and the market drops 15 percent, one would expect the stock to drop about 30 percent.

Bid price: the highest price at which someone is willing to buy a security on an auction market. See **Ask price**.

Bitcoin: The unit of digital financial currency that started the cryptocurrency industry outside the regulatory agencies that govern most bank activities.

Blue chip: a term used to describe a large company recognized as a leader in its industry. Usually, Blue Chip stocks pay dividends and are considered to be less volatile than stocks of smaller companies. The term refers to the gaming chip with the highest value. See **Dow Jones Industrial Average (DJI or Dow)**.

Bond: a debt security representing a loan, the terms of which are set by the bond issuer. The bond issuer agrees to pay a fixed rate of interest to the investor, usually in semiannual payments, and guarantee the return of the investor's principal on the due date (maturity). As a lender, a bond investor has a senior position over equity investors regarding legal claims to the issuer's assets in the event of bankruptcy.

Book value: a calculation of a company's equity value expressed on a per share basis. The net equity of a company is adjusted by subtracting the value of intangible assets, because they are not marketable. Then that adjusted net equity is divided by the number of shares outstanding. Book value gives an investor a means of evaluating what a company would be worth if marketable assets were sold at their accounting value and all its liabilities paid off. Conservative investors might look at book value as an approximation of the downside risk of owning that stock. Most companies will not likely sell at much of a discount to book value.

Breadth of market: the measure of the total number of companies that closed at a higher price than the previous day's close versus the number that closed lower, also referred to as the Advance/Decline Line (ADL).

Broker loan rate: the rate that commercial banks charge brokerage firms to borrow money for the purpose of issuing margin loans.

Call option: a derivative security contract giving the purchaser (holder) the right to buy one hundred shares of a security from the seller (writer). Call options for a particular security are identified by the length of time it will remain in force and the price per share at which it may be exercised. See **Put option**.

Capital asset: a long-term asset, usually one with a useful life of over one year.

Capital gain (or loss): the difference between the purchase price, or some other adjusted cost basis, and the sale price, or redemption price, of an investment. Long-term capital gains may qualify for favorable tax treatment.

Capitalization: the term used to describe how a company has funded the purchase of its assets with liabilities and equity, the right-hand side of the balance sheet. This term is often confused with market capitalization, which is the price of a stock multiplied by the number of shares outstanding.

Cash flow statement: the financial statement concerned with the source of funds coming into a company (in flow) and going out (out flow). It is separated into Operating Activities, Investing Activities, and Financing Activities. It is useful to investors for evaluating the quality of earnings, who expect most of the cash inflow for a company to come from operating activities.

Cash settlement: a special request from an investor to have a trade settle on the same day the order is executed, rather than with the normal three day settlement period. This is sometimes used by sellers who have an immediate need for cash. Another common settlement option is next day, ND.

Churning: the illegal and unethical practice of a broker generating multiple trades for a client, creating a large number of commissions for the broker with little or no benefit to the client.

Closed-end fund (CEF): an investment company with a fixed number of authorized shares that trades on an exchange. This is different from an open-end mutual fund that can issue an unlimited number of shares. Closed-end funds usually represent equities or bonds and should not be confused with exchange traded funds or notes, ETFs or ETNs, which usually represent indexes or commodities rather than equities.

Commercial paper: short term corporate unsecured loans having maturities of less than 270 days, but most frequently averaging about 30 days. Commercial paper is usually the most common investment in money market funds offered by brokers.

Common stock: the most popular method of public ownership of corporations. Each share of stock represents a share, or percentage, ownership of the corporation.

Compound interest: the principle that interest paid also begins earning interest as it is credited. If the interest rate paid on the interest is the same as the rate paid on the principal, the formula for compound interest is $F = P(1 + i)^n$, where F is future value, P is present value, i is interest, and n is the number of years to maturity.

Consumer Price Index (CPI): the monthly measure of the changing prices of a market basket of goods and services, representing the inflation rate at the retail level. It is compiled by the Bureau of Labor Statistics (BLS) and is usually used as a basis for the cost-of-living adjustment index (COLA).

Convertible securities: usually either bonds or preferred stock that have a special feature allowing for exchange into another security, usually common stock, at a predetermined price.

Corporation: a legally created entity for conducting business that is granted most of the rights and obligations associated with individuals. A corporation may own property, pay taxes, file lawsuits, or enter into other legal contracts. Public corporations are owned by shareholders, and there is a readily available market for the exchange of ownership. Private corporations are owned by a small number of investors and exchange of ownership is handled in private transactions.

Coupon interest: the annual rate of interest quoted in a bond's description. This rate is the yield that a bond would pay if it were purchased at par value ($1000). Thus, a five percent coupon bond would pay $50 per year ($25 semiannually). The word coupon is a carryover from old bonds that had coupons attached to the certificate. They had to be cut off and redeemed on or after the due date printed on the coupon.

Cryptocurrency: a general term for a means of making financial transactions that bypass government monitoring and regulations. Bitcoin is the most popular cryptocurrency and was invented in 2009.

Current ratio: from the Balance Sheet for a company, it is the computation of current assets divided by current liabilities. It reveals whether the company has enough liquid assets to meet its fixed expenses due within the following fiscal year.

Current yield: the amount of annual interest an investor in a fixed-return security receives divided by the cost of that investment. If the price of a bond is below par value, the current yield will be higher than the coupon rate. If the price is higher, the current yield will be lower. See also **Yield-to-maturity**.

Debenture: a bond for which no specific asset, or collateral, has been pledged as a guarantee for the repayment of the bond. In the event of bankruptcy of a bond issuer, all collateralized bonds, such as mortgage bonds, have seniority over debentures. Most corporate and municipal bonds are debentures.

Designated Market Maker (DMM): an individual or institution that maintains an inventory of shares of a security and is ready to buy or sell those shares to other investors on an exchange. The DMM posts a bid and ask quote for that security and must compete with other market makers and brokers that act as principal on an equal basis so as not to unfairly benefit from a foreknowledge of order flow. DMMs on the NYSE succeeded the old designation of *specialist*.

Derivative securities: any investment whose underlying value is based on that of another investment. Common derivative securities are call and put options, exchange traded funds and notes, and equity futures contracts. The term mortgage derivative is a reference to securities issued by a government sponsored enterprise (GSE) such as Government National Mortgage Association (GNMA or Ginnie Mae), Student Loan Marketing Association (SLMA, Sallie Mae). The two largest GSEs, Federal National Mortgage Association (FNMA or Fannie Mae) and Federal Home Loan Mortgage Corporation (FHLMC or Freddie Mac), went bankrupt in September 2008 with the collapse of the subprime mortgage market. However, both corporations continue to trade under the tickers FNMA and FMCC.

Discount rate: the interest rate set by the Federal Reserve Board at which the banking regulator will lend money to member banks for overnight loans. Most other bank rates are set at premiums to the discount rate, making this one of the most powerful tools the Fed can use to regulate economic expansion and contraction.

Diversification: the strategy of reducing risk by selecting investments that are not correlated, such as companies that are not in the same industry. Many advisors recommend including global investments in portfolios for this reason. Even though individual foreign markets may be riskier than the U.S. markets, this strategy could reduce the overall risk to a portfolio because they are not correlated.

Dividend: a payment to shareholders of a company representing a portion of the company's earning for that quarter. So investors would be wise to compare the quarterly earnings per share with the quarterly dividend to make sure the payment of the dividend is covered by earnings. The amount of the dividend is expressed on a per share basis and is annualized. Thus, a $1.00 dividend would be paid at the rate of $0.25 per quarter. A shareholder who owns 100 shares would be paid at $25 per quarter, adding up to $100 for the year. The Board of Directors must declare each dividend payment. See Ex-dividend Date and Record Date and compare to Trade Date and Settlement Date for information about dates pertinent to dividend payments.

Dividend reinvestment program (DRIP): a service most companies offer that allows investors to have their dividend payments reinvested into additional shares of the company instead of being paid out in cash. This program is managed by the Transfer Agent for the company and most allow investors to deposit addition funds into the DRIP. Most companies do not charge any fees or commissions for this service.

Dividend yield: the annualized dividend amount divided by the price per share of the security. The dividend yield is analogous to the annualized interest rate on fixed-return investments; but the dividend rate is not fixed.

Dogs of the Dow: the companies in the Dow Jones Industrial Average that have declined the largest percentage, usually the bottom five. Investing in them is a popular strategy, and several investment companies offer products using them. Often the worst performing stocks one year will outperform the market average the next.

Dow Jones Industrial Average (DJIA or Dow): a stock market indicator published by Dow Jones Corp, a subsidiary of News Corp. The Dow is the adjusted average of 30 Blue Chip stocks. The adjustment is accomplished by changing the divisor. A true arithmetic average of 30 items would be the total divided by 30. However, because of stock splits and company changes, the divisor has been adjusted to about 0.4. One can determine how much any one company in the Dow is affecting the total Average by dividing that company's price by the divisor.

EBITDA (earnings before interest, taxes, depreciation, and amortization): an acronym from the balance sheet entry representing the gross earnings, total sales minus the cost of sales and the administrative and operating expenses, also referred to as operating profit.

ECN (Electronic Communications Network): a computer network programmed to maintain a liquid market for securities trading. All major exchanges trade electronically and the ECNs that formerly operated independently are now integrated with one of the exchanges (NYSE or Nasdaq). ECNs offer premarket trading for two and half hours before the market opens, from 7:00 a.m. to 9:30 a.m. Eastern Time. They also offer after hours trading for four hours after the market closes, from 4:00 p.m. to 8:00 p.m., East Coast Time. However, trades made before or after the regular market hours have much less liquidity than during normal hours.

Earnings per share (EPS): the net annual income of a company divided by the number of shares outstanding. It is the bottom line entry on an Income (or Earnings) Statement.

Economics: the study of the creation, distribution, and transfer of wealth.

Exchange traded note (ETN): a hybrid type of investment company product characterized by an open end capitalization and tradeable as shares on an exchange. It differs from exchange traded notes because ETNs do not need to hold the underlying investments physically for which they are being traded. Thus, they avoid annual tax reporting on some capital gains for trades within the fund.

Exchange traded fund (ETF): a hybrid type of investment company product characterized by an open end capitalization and tradeable as shares on an exchange. ETFs are derivative securities that are frequently created for the purpose of trading options on a market indexes, commodity prices, industry sectors, and others.

Ex-dividend date: the date on which an investor who purchases a stock will not (*ex-* means without) receive the next dividend payment. The settlement date for the purchase will be the day after the record date for the dividend payment. See **trade date**, **settlement date**.

Fannie Mae (FNMA) and Freddie Mac (FHLMC): two government sponsored enterprises (GSEs) seized by the government in 2008 to stave off their filing bankruptcy due to the collapse of the housing market. Their purpose is to add liquidity to the mortgage markets by buying pools of mortgages issued by financial institutions and then repackaging and reissuing them as collateral for other investments. Outstanding shares of these companies continue to trade on the Nasdaq. See **GNMA (Ginnie Mae)**.

Fed funds rate: the rate that banks charge other banks for overnight loans. The banks may be either federally chartered or state chartered. Although this rate is not set by the Federal Reserve Board, it sets a target for this rate that it wants other banks to maintain so that bank lending practices will be in line with Fed economic mandates.

Federal Open Market Committee (FOMC): the Federal Reserve committee that meets about once every six weeks to evaluate or alter Federal Bank policies. It is composed of five of the twelve Federal Reserve regional bank presidents and seven members of the Board of Governors. Usually it sets or adjusts the Fed funds target rate and Discount rate. It may also raise or lower money supply by requiring banks to buy government bonds from the Fed, reducing money supply, or requiring banks to sell government bonds back to them, increasing money supply. That activity is referred to as Open Market Operations.

Federal Reserve Board (FRB or the Fed): the governing body of Federal Reserve System, an organization created December 23, 1913, with the passage of the Federal Reserve Act. It regulates the U.S. banking industry and sets domestic (and sometimes foreign) economic policy. Fed spokesmen will often refer to its dual mandate of controlling inflation and regulating unemployment.

Fiat currency: money in circulation that is not backed by a physical asset. It is simply a token of exchange that people as a whole accept as a legitimate form of money with which to facilitate financial transactions. The word *fiat* literally means "let it be done", implying a command with the authority and power to accomplish its purpose. All money in circulation in the U.S. has been fiat currency since 1971 when the country went off the gold standard. Virtually all the paper money in the world is fiat currency. The quantity of money in circulation is a tool for creating and controlling inflation and recession cycles.

Fiduciary: someone who makes financial decisions on behalf of another. Pension fund managers, for example, act as fiduciaries when they make investment decisions for employees' interests in retirement plans. Stockbrokers may also have fiduciary responsibilities to their clients.

Financial Industry Regulatory Authority (FINRA): a private corporation owned by member financial service companies that acts as a self-governing overseer for setting standards of ethics and knowledge for the industry. It was formed as a successor to the National Association of Securities Dealers with the merger of the NASD and the regulatory arm of the NYSE. Even though the NASD is no more, the Nasdaq Exchange still bears the acronym for the organization that created it.

Fiscal policy: the actions Congress takes to influence economic growth or contraction through legislative action affecting tax revenues and spending. This is usually coordinated with the monetary policy actions of the Federal Reserve Board. See **Monetary policy**.

Fiscal year: the twelve month period beginning with the first month of the formation of a new company. Many companies later alter their fiscal years to correspond to the calendar year, beginning on January 1 and ending on December 31. This has created the phenomena of "earnings seasons" as many companies file their quarterly financial reports following the end of the months of March, June, September, and December.

Fixed-return investments: a term for securities that are obligated to pay a specified amount of money to investors. Fixed-return investments would include bonds, preferred stock, government sponsored enterprises (Ginnie Maes, etc.), certificate of deposits (CDs), or other similar investments. See **Variable-return investments**.

Front-end load fund: a class of mutual fund shares, class A, where the investor is charged a fee when the shares are purchased. This fee is expressed as a percentage of the net asset value (NAV) of the fund. (See **back-end load fund** and **no load fund**.)

Forbes 400: a list compiled by *Forbes* magazine of the 400 richest people in the America. That periodical also publishes other lists of wealthy people, including the world's billionaires.

Fortune 500: a list compiled by *Fortune* magazine of the 500 largest companies in America.

Future value: a prediction of the amount of money an investor will have after a given period of time. Assuming the investment pays a fixed rate of return over that period, it is computed by the formula $F = P(1 + i)^n$. See **Present value**.

Futures contracts: highly leveraged (typically 80 – 95 percent) commodity investments allowing the purchaser (long position) of the contract to profit from a rise in the price of the underlying asset and the seller (short position) to profit from a decline. Contracts are available on several exchanges in various groups such as precious metals, industrial metals, energy, financial rates and indexes, foreign currency, and food, which is separated into softs, grains, and livestock. The quantity of the underlying commodity, margin requirements, and length of time for each contract is set by the exchange. Speculators are attracted to the futures market because of high returns possible from the use of high leverage, but with that leverage also comes high risk. Unlike options contracts, there is no limit to the downside risk with futures. Speculators may be required to deposit additional margin if the price of the underlying commodity moves contrary to the speculator's contract.

GNMA (Ginnie Mae): an acronym for Government National Mortgage Association, a government agency whose function is to buy Federal Housing Authority (FHA) or Veterans Administration (VA) approved home mortgages from lending institutions and reissue them as government guaranteed pools. Investors in Ginnie Maes will receive monthly payments of interest and principal from the underlying pools of mortgages until all principal is paid down. Unlike Fannie Mae and Freddie Mac, Ginnie Mae pools are backed by the "full faith and credit of the U.S. government", like U.S. Treasury debt. See **Fannie Mae** and **Freddie Mac**.

General obligation bond (G.O.): a municipal debt issue backed by the full taxing authority of the issuer, usually state government. Such bonds were formerly considered more secure than comparable revenue bonds, backed by cash flow from specific municipal projects. However, with the declining financial integrity of many states, the triple-A rating on many state G.O. bonds has been downgraded lower than some comparable revenue bonds. See **Revenue bond**.

Good-till-canceled order (GTC): instructions to a broker to buy or to sell a security that will remain in effect until it is canceled, also called an open order. GTC orders are usually entered as limit orders, setting a minimum price at which it could be executed. Brokers may have a policy of notifying clients who have open orders on their books that are well away from the current market and have been in force for a long period of time, but investors are responsible for cancelling open orders they enter. Some brokers only allow GTC orders for a specified period of time.

Goodwill: on a company's balance sheet it is an intangible asset representing the difference between what a company paid for that asset in a merger or acquisition and what the current market value of that asset is. Often companies pay more than the market value of a physical plant because they expect to increase their earnings from the company's ongoing business.

Greed-Hope-Fear Cycle: an illustration of the psychological effect of market price movements on investors, showing that a person's emotions will typically cause him or her to buy near the top of a market cycle and sell near the bottom. It may also be referred to as the Small Investor Syndrome.

Greenmail: a strategy of buying a large block of voting shares and using that power to intimidate the Board of Directors by threatening a proxy battle to replace members of the board or influence company policies. The hostile suitor will usually then negotiate to sell back the shares to the company at an inflated price. It is called greenmail because it is similar to blackmail, but it is not illegal. Those who engage in this type of activity are often referred to as activist investors.

Gross domestic product (GDP): the total output of goods and services produced within the geographical boundaries of a country. It is computed by measuring the amount of spending and investing by all entities in that country. In the U.S. the GDP Deflator adjusts the actual amount of spending to a constant dollar value by taking out the effects of rising prices due to inflation, thus more accurately expressing the real growth (or shrinkage) of the economy.

Hedging: investing strategies usually designed to mitigate the risks associated with some investments. Stock investors may use options to hedge their positions. Bankers may use futures or interest rate options to hedge the risk on their loans. Manufacturers who buy large quantities of raw materials may hedge their costs by buying commodities futures contracts. Hedge funds are investment companies that also use options and futures, but they are misleadingly named because they generally use those contracts to increase their returns by assuming a greater degree of risk.

IPO (Initial Public Offering): a company that begins trading on an exchange for the first time. An investment banker will usually form a syndicate group with other brokers and will determine the price at which to bring a company's stock public and the number of shares that will be issued. This is referred to as the primary market.

IRA (Individual Retirement Account): a plan offering tax advantages that will help employees to supplement other savings—such as social security, 401(k) plans, or pension funds—set aside to produce income when they stop working or work fewer hours due to age. The two main types of IRAs are Traditional and Roth. Traditional IRAs allow for a tax-deductible contribution but earnings are taxable when withdrawn. Roth IRA contributions are not tax deductible, but regular distributions are usually not subject to income tax. Contributions to these types of IRAs must be from earned income only. Only a Spousal IRA allows a working spouse to contribute to an IRA for a non-working spouse. IRAs are important to individual investors because social security is forecast to be insolvent before the younger members of the workforce today will reach retirement age.

Income (or Earnings) Statement: a financial report showing a company's revenues (or sales) and expenses over a period of time, quarterly and annually. It is organized from top to bottom in the order of priority that the company meets its financial obligations.

Indenture: the formal agreement on the face of a bond certificate. It states the legal rights and obligations of the bond issuer and the investor.

Inflation: the measure of the loss of purchasing power of money due to increasing money supply. Often inflation is associated with rising prices, and to a layman the loss of purchasing power and rising prices sound the same. But to an economist, inflation is a result of the abundance or scarcity of money. They reference the Weimar Republic in Germany following World War I and the Zimbabwe one hundred trillion dollar bill in the 2010s as examples of how uncontrolled money supply causes hyperinflation.

Initial margin requirement: the percentage of equity required to be deposited by securities investors who borrow some of the cost of an investment from their broker. It is referred to as Regulation T and has been at 50 percent for many decades; however, some brokers may set the requirement higher. Setting the initial margin requirement is the only rule-making authority the Federal Reserve Board exercises in conjunction with FINRA, the Financial Industry Regulatory Authority. The initial margin requirement for futures contracts is set by the exchange and varies from contract to contract.

Insider: anyone who has access to nonpublic information about a company's business. According to SEC regulations, it is illegal to profit from investments made on the basis of insider information. In recent years, the regulatory arm of the SEC has stepped up its prosecution of cases involving insider trading.

Institutional investor: individuals or organizations who invest in large quantities (blocs) of securities, including investment companies, pension funds, corporate and government account managers, etc. Often institutional investors trade blocs of securities between themselves off the exchange in the fourth market.

Interest rate risk: type of risk associated with the price of fixed-return securities during periods of interest rate volatility. There is an inverse relationship between the direction of interest rates and the price of the fixed-return security, by approximately the same percentage amount. For example, if interest rates on bonds moves from 5% up to 5.5%, that would be a 10% upward move. The price of a bond would move down approximately 10 %, from 100 to 90.91 (100 ÷ 1.1 = 90.91). Note a 10% rise from 90.91 to 100 would be 10%. The rate of change of a rising rate is not the same as the rate of a declining one. The percentage change from 50 to 100 is a 10%, but the change from 100 to 50 is 50%.

Investment: the use of money to make more money.

Investment banker: the title of the broker responsible for bringing initial public offerings (IPOs) to the market. Investment bankers may also be referred to as underwriters, and the group of underwriters as the syndicate. Usually investment bankers are divisions of brokerage firms or financial institutions.

Investment grade bonds: debt instruments rated BBB (Baa) or higher by the major bond rating agencies. See **Junk bonds**.

Junk bonds: term used to describe all bonds rated below BBB by Standard & Poor's or Fitch, or Baa by Moody's, popularly referred to by the euphemism high yield bonds. Most junk bond mutual funds or CEFs that identify themselves as "High Yield" are primarily invested in junk bonds. See **Investment grade bonds**.

Large-cap company: See **Market Capitalization**.

Leading Economic Indicators (LEI): a statistical measure of ten segments of the economy designed to forecast the level of economic activity six months to one year out. It is a proprietary statistic compiled by Thomson Reuters Jefferies, which also releases indexes of lagging and coincident indicators, primarily used to verify the accuracy of the leading indicators.

Leverage: the use of a smaller amount of capital than the cost of an underlying investment to control the total amount. The use of leverage increases risk. Investors could receive a higher return on their capital than the percentage move of the underlying security, but they could also lose more than their original investment if it moves against them. In the securities industry leverage is used with margin accounts, options, commodity futures contracts, etc.

Libor rate: acronym for London Interbank Offered Rate, the percentage of interest charged on short term loans set by the British Bankers' Association. It determines the rate on loans to banks ranging from overnight to one year, somewhat similar to the Discount Rate set by the FRB in the U.S. It is extremely important because so many rates around the world are based on it, probably hundreds of trillions of dollars. In the U.S. many adjustable rate mortgages are based on Libor.

Limit order: instructions given to a broker to buy or sell a security at a set price, or better. A limit order to buy will usually be at or below the current market price. A limit order to sell will be at or above the current market. See **Good-till-canceled orders**.

Liquidity: the ease with which an investment may be turned into cash with little or no loss in market value. Money market funds are considered the most liquid security investments.

Long-term capital gain (or loss): the difference between the purchase price and the sale price of an investment held over one year. Favorable tax treatment on long-term capital gains has been used sometimes to encourage investing.

Long-Term Equity Anticipation Securities (LEAPS): put and call options that expire in the month of January two or three years out from the current year. LEAPS are similar to other options, except for the expiration date. There are two series of LEAPS available for each of the two years following the longest expiration date of the regular options.

M2: the most watched measure of money supply recorded by the Federal Reserve Board. Usually the Fed has considered the growth of M2 measure of money supply to be the best indicator of inflation, but recent disinflation during periods of rapid growth in M2 have revealed the Fed's limited ability to influence economic activity through fiscal policy alone. See **Money supply**.

Macroeconomic risk: See **Risk**.

Market Capitalization (Market Cap): the size of a company as determined by the number of shares outstanding times the current market price of the stock. This term should not be confused with the capitalization of a company, which is the sum of a company's debt and equity. Standard & Poor's categorizes companies as Micro Cap, Small Cap, Mid Cap, Large Cap and Mega Cap. Although the size of these categories changes dramatically over time, and financial commentators often have their own definitions; here is an approximate guideline: Micro Cap – under $1 billion; Small Cap – over $1 billion; Mid Cap – over $3 billion; Large Cap – over $15 billion; Mega Cap – over $50 billion.

Margin: for the securities industry, the percentage of equity that must be deposited for an investment with the remaining funds being borrowed. If a margin account with $10,000 of securities is said to be at 40 percent, then the debit balance is $6000 and the equity is $4000. Interest is paid to lender on the outstanding debit balance at a rate set by the lender based on the broker loan rate.

Margin maintenance requirement: the minimum percentage equity margin account must maintain. Most brokers set this at 30 percent, but it may be higher for some investors or for some positions. The NYSE and Nasdaq Exchanges set the maintenance requirement at 25 percent, so brokers set it higher in order to avoid noncompliance with the exchange rules.

Market order: instructions to a broker to execute a buy or sell transaction at the best available price at the time the order hits the exchange. For a sell order that would be at the highest bid price; for a buy order at the lowest ask price.

Mark to market: the process of journaling (transferring) money between an equity margin account (usually type 2) and a short account (usually type 4) in order to maintain a credit balance equal to the full market value of the short position. A short seller must maintain equity in the margin account equal to at least 30 percent of the value of the short account.

Micro cap company: See **Market capitalization**.

Microeconomic risk: See **Risk**.

Mid-cap company: See **Market capitalization**.

Monetary policy: the actions the Federal Reserve Board takes to influence economic growth or contraction, usually by controlling money supply. This is usually coordinated with the fiscal policy actions of Congress. See **Fiscal policy**.

Money market fund: an open-end mutual fund that invests exclusively in short term debt securities. Since these debt securities will be redeemed at par value in a short time, their market value usually does not change. Thus, the share price remains stable, usually at $1 per share. The most frequently used investment in money market funds is commercial paper, typically averaging around 30 days to maturity. They may also invest in T-bills. Because the portfolio of debt securities in money market funds is likely to change daily, the interest rate they pay will change correspondingly.

Money supply: a four tier system of reporting the total amount of cash and liquid investments in circulation, reported weekly by the Federal Reserve Board. M1 is the amount of currency and coins in circulation plus demand deposit (checking) accounts, savings accounts, and traveler's checks. M2 is the total of M1 plus money market funds and certificates of deposit (CDs). M3 is the total of M2 plus institutional money funds and jumbo CDs. The fourth tier is L, long-term liquid assets, and is the total of M3 plus nonbank U.S. Savings Bonds, short-term U.S. Treasury securities, commercial paper, and bankers' acceptances.

Municipal bonds: fixed-return securities issued by state of local governments or government agencies, usually referred to as munis. The interest paid on munis is except from federal income tax for all taxpayers and from state income tax for most residents of the state in which the bond is issued—double tax free. Muni bonds issued by U.S. government territories, such as Puerto Rico, are federal and state tax-exempt for residents of all states.

Mutual funds: professionally managed portfolios of investments in which each share of the fund represents ownership of many different securities or investments. Most retirement accounts, such as 401(k)s and pension plans offer a selection of mutual funds to their participants. Mutual funds are referred to as open-ended because there is an unlimited number of share that can be issued.

Nasdaq Exchange: the second largest electronic communications network (ECN) that makes a market for publicly traded securities, after the NYSE/Euronext. It was formerly referred to as the over-the-counter (OTC) market.

Net Asset Value (NAV): the calculation of the per share value of the total of the investments in an investment company fund, such as a mutual fund, CEF, ETF, or ETN. For most mutual funds and ETFs, the NAV is usually determined once a day after the close of the markets. Open-end mutual funds are usually bought or sold at the closing NAV the day the order is entered.

Net profit margin: a financial ratio from the Income Statement calculated as net income (earnings) divided by net sales (revenues). It is the percentage of total sales, the company keeps after paying all expenses and taxes.

No load fund: a class of mutual fund shares that does not charge a sales commission or a contingent deferred sales charges CDSC, usually identified as class C shares. Investors should realize that even though no-load funds do not have sales charges, the investment company will still charge a fee to cover administrative and operating expenses. (See **front-end load fund** and **back-end load fund**.)

Open-end fund: an ordinary mutual fund whose capitalization is not fixed. It can issue more shares as investors add money to the fund and reduce the number of shares when investors sell.

Options: a derivative security characterized as a contract to buy or sell a set quantity of an underlying security, usually 100 shares, at a set price, the strike price, within a given period of time. See **Call option** and **Put Option**.

Par value (of bonds): the principal or face amount of a debt security. The amount the bond investor will receive at maturity.

Par value (of stock): The per share value that is assigned for the purpose of balance sheet accounting. If the par value is $1, and a company has 50 million shares outstanding, the Balance Sheet will carry the equity value of the common stock at $50 million. Most of the equity on a balance sheet will be the result of retained earnings. The par value of stock has no relationship to its market value.

Penny stock: the traditional definition is any company whose share price was under $3, because at that price the stock is not eligible for purchase on margin. However, the term is more frequently used now as any stock trading under $1. Most penny stocks do not trade on a major exchange and consequently have larger bid-ask spreads than other companies. They also have limited independent research coverage and the price may be more easily manipulated because they often have only one, or a few, market makers.

Poison pill: a corporate strategy to discourage hostile takeover attempts. If a hostile suitor or activist investor acquires a certain percentage of a company's stock, a poison pill usually allows the company to issue more shares to investors the company deems friendly, such as current management, making it impossible for the suitor to amass a voting majority. It is called a poison pill because of the dilution of outstanding shares, affecting all shareholders. The price of the stock will drop in approximately the same percentage as the dilution.

Portfolio: all the securities owned by an investor. Most investment advisors recommend keeping your portfolio diversified in securities that are not correlated, which do not rise and fall during in unison with economic cycles. For example, defensive companies such as utilities and pharmaceuticals usually perform better than basic industry companies during periods of economic recession.

Preferred stock: an equity security that pays a dividend at a fixed rate similar to interest on a debt security. The dividend is senior to common stock dividends but junior to bond interest. Most preferred stock dividends are cumulative. If the company omits preferred stock dividend payments, the skipped dividends must be paid before a common stock dividend can be. Also, some preferred shares are convertible into common stock.

Precious metals: to the financial markets, one of the mined elements that has a high economic value—gold, silver, platinum, and palladium. The market for precious metals generally runs counter to economic cycles. During times of economic or political chaos, the market for precious metals, especially gold, is likely to be the best performing asset. Copper, aluminum, titanium, and nickel are usually classified as industrial metals.

Pre-market (or pre-open) trading: the two and a half hours, 7:00 – 9:30 a.m. ET, that electronic communications networks execute securities trades before the large exchanges open. Market hours for the NYSE and Nasdaq are 9:30 a.m. to 4:00 p.m. ET. See **After-hours (or after-market) trading**.

Present value: the inverse of the Future Value formula, $P = F/(1+i)^n$. This formula calculates how much money must be invested at the present time to receive a predetermined value in the future at a fixed rate of interest. See **Future value**.

Price earnings ratio (PE): a financial ratio computed by dividing the current market price of a stock by the most recent annual earnings per share. It is also referred to as the earnings multiple because it is the number that when multiplied by the EPS will equal the price of the stock. The future PE ratio is the price of the stock divided by next year's estimated EPS.

Primary market: the process of bringing an initial public offering (IPO) to a secondary exchange or ECN where it can be traded. The primary market involves the operations of an investment banker, usually a department of a securities firm. See **Secondary market**.

Producer price index (PPI): the Labor Department's measure of inflation of wholesale (producer's) prices. It is reported monthly, a day or two before the Consumer Price Index. It is considered to be a leading indicator of consumer inflation.

Program trading: the use of computers to generate buy and sell orders for large blocks of securities. Program orders are frequently entered in risk arbitrage trading involving major indexes and options or futures contracts on the indexes. There are restrictions on program trading when the market goes through periods of high volatility.

Prospectus: a document issued for all companies in the primary market, representing full disclosure of the company's business. No other information may be disseminated regarding an IPO except the prospectus, and all potential investors must receive a prospectus.

Proxy: someone who votes on behalf of another. Companies send out annual proxy solicitation letters to their shareholders to vote on matters that may come up at the next shareholder's meeting. Those proxy votes will be recorded at the meeting.

Put option: a type of derivative security that give the purchaser (holder) the right to sell a set number of shares (100) at a set price within a predetermined period of time. See **Call option**.

Quadruple Witching Days: the third Friday in the months of March, June, September, and December. Four derivative contracts related to equities and indexes expire on the same day: stock options, index options, stock futures, and commodity futures. You may still hear this term called *triple* witching days, referring back to the time before stock futures were traded. There can be high volatility in markets around these days as institutional traders and program traders rebalance their positions before the derivative contracts expire.

Quantitative Easing (QE): the process of the Federal Reserve Board increasing the money supply in the banking system on a larger scale than would normally be accomplished in open market operations. Often QE is accomplished by issuing more Treasury bonds as direct result of increasing fiat currency. QE is meant to create inflation by stimulating spending or investing. However, since government bonds represent public debt, QE policies will increase the burden on taxpayers in the future when that debt comes due. Thus, QE could ultimately have the opposite effect of that intended.

Random walk hypothesis: the belief that the direction of market movements are completely unpredictable and that there is no discernable cause-and-effect relationship between economic developments and security prices. It is often used by short term option speculators.

Real estate investment trust (REIT): the type of investment company that holds a portfolio of real estate properties or mortgages. Like all investment companies, it is not taxed at the corporate level and must pass through at least 90 percent of its net income to its shareholders.

Record date: the date on which an investor must own a stock to be eligible to receive the next dividend payment. The settlement date for a trade must be on or before the record date for a new owner to be the legal shareholder of record for the next dividend. There are two business days between the ex-dividend date and the record date because there are three business days between the trade date and settlement date. A trade entered on the ex-dividend date will settle the day after the record date.

Red herring: the preliminary prospectus that must be issued to all prospective investors before a company goes public (IPO). It is so named because of the SEC's red-lettered disclaimer on the cover.

Return on assets (ROA): the calculation of net income divided by total assets from a company's financial statements.

Return on equity (ROE): the calculation of net income divided by total shareholders' equity (net worth). This is a very important financial ratio, revealing the percentage return the company made on its equity. It is often compared to the riskless rate of return as a means of how efficiently the company invested shareholders equity.

Revenue bond: a municipal debt issue where the interest payments and the repayment of principal are secured by the cash flow generated from the project the bond is funding. Some revenue bonds would include waste disposal, toll roads or bridges, water revenue, hospitals, sports or entertainment arenas, etc. See **G.O. bond**.

Risk: the unpredictability of a future outcome. For investments it is often separated into microeconomic and macroeconomic risk. *Macro*, meaning large, refers to factors that affect most securities. Some of these factors are inflation, interest rate movements, government policies, and economic cycles. *Micro*, meaning small, refers to factors that only affect a specific company or product. Some micro risk factors are business competition, the use of debt to finance operations, and industry business cycles.

Risk on/Risk off trading strategies: when traders invest in more speculative investments, they are described as risk on; and when they become more defensive, they are risk off. Speculative investments follow more volatile trading patterns; defensive ones would include income equities, bonds, gold, and other investments that traditionally do well in a bear market.

Riskless rate of return: interest rate available on U.S. Treasury securities. Because of credit risk, all other bond issuers pay a higher interest rate on equivalent bonds than the riskless rate. So, when the Treasury raises interest rates, other bond issuers—corporations, municipalities, foreign entities, and so on—must raise their rates commensurate with the assumed risk associated with them.

Round lot: one hundred shares of stock. This has traditionally been the most frequently used multiple for securities trading. Fewer than 100 shares is called an odd lot.

S&P 500 Index: a value-weighted market indicator of 500 large cap companies selected by Standard & Poor's. The index changes as the total market capitalization of the companies in the index changes. Market capitalization is the result of multiplying the market price of a company by the number of shares outstanding, the measure of the value of the company. An index, as opposed to an average, uses an arbitrary base as a beginning so that changes in the index will represent percentage changes from that base. The S&P 500 is almost universally used by mutual fund managers and institutional investors as a statistical representation of the overall market. Speculators can invest in options or futures on this index and on other S&P Indexes. Also, it is used for the computation of beta. See **Dow Jones Industrial Average (DJI or Dow)** and **Beta**.

Secondary market: the term used to describe all stock exchanges and ECNs. The primary market is the process of bringing a new company to the secondary market. See **Primary market**.

Secular trend: used in the securities industry to imply a long-term market expectation. Speculators and traders would more likely be interested in short-term trends, and investors, secular ones.

Securities and Exchange Commission (SEC): the U.S. government agency that is the chief regulatory body for the securities industry. It was created under the Securities Exchange Act of 1934.

Securities Investors Protection Corporation (SIPC): a federally mandated corporation owned by member financial industry firms that provides insurance protection for investors' accounts in the event of the failure of the broker. It does not provide insurance coverage for investment losses; there is no insurance for market risk. Current coverage is limited to $500,000 in investments and $250,000 in cash. The SIPC is to financial services industry as the FDIC is to the banking industry.

SEP-IRA: acronym for simplified employee pension-individual retirement account, a tax-advantaged account for self-employed individuals. Contribution limits change, but at the time of this writing, participants could contribute up to $54,000 on $270,000 of earned income, or 25 percent of after-tax earned income from their business. All funds are tax deferred until withdrawn at retirement. There is generally a 10 percent penalty if withdrawn before the year in which the participant turns age 59½.

Short sale: the act of selling shares of a security that are borrowed from the broker. The strategy is used to profit from a price decline. Short sellers hope to buy back the borrowed shares at a lower price than they sold them. If the price of the short security rises above the short sale price, the short seller will be losing money. A short position must be closed at some point to repay the borrowed shares, and since short sellers do not own the shares, the short will be profitable if it is covered when the market is lower. See **Mark to market**.

Small-cap company: See **Market capitalization**.

Speculation: investment strategy involving a higher degree of risk than investing. Speculators usually expect a higher rate of return or quicker results than more conservative investors.

Stochastic: a technical market indicator based on the moving average of the position of the closing price as a percentage of the range for the day (or other period). The range is treated from the low to the high as a scale going from 0 to 100. If the closing price is at the low, the stochastic number would be 0, and if it is at the high, the stochastic would be 100. If the close is exactly half way between the low and the high, the stochastic would be 50. The stochastic indicators use complex formulas for comparing moving averages of these high/low calculations.

Stock rights: contracts giving shareholders the opportunity to purchase additional shares. Stock rights are distributed to shareholders a month or so prior to the company issuing new shares on the primary (IPO) market, diluting existing shareholders' percentage ownership. The rights will allow shareholders to increase the number of shares they own. Thus, they can maintain their same percentage ownership after the offering. The exercise price of the rights will usually be at a price below the current market price by the approximate percentage of dilution.

Stock split: a method by which companies can issue more shares of stock to current shareholders. A split will cause the price of the stock to be reduced by the same percentage as the increase in number of shares. There is no material benefit to shareholders of a stock split. If a stock splits 2-for-1, the number of shares owned will double, but the price of each share will be halved. Stock splits are usually the result of management's decision to keep the price at a lower level to make round lots more affordable.

The market: in daily use this term generally refers to the Dow Jones Industrial Average of 30 blue chip companies. It is a simple arithmetic average of the prices of the stocks with the divisor being adjusted for changes to the makeup of the companies in the indicator. Dow Jones also publishes a Transportation Average of 20 stocks, a Utility Average of 10, and a Composite Average of the 60 companies in those three averages. It also publishes many other global and composite indicators.

Tick: term used to describe the smallest unit of incremental change in securities prices, usually one cent, $0.01, but it can be higher for high priced securities. If a stock is on an up-tick, the last trade was at a higher price than the previous one, and a down-tick would be the opposite.

Trade date-settlement date: the three business day period between when a securities trade is executed (trade date) and the day when the money is due to change hands from the buyer to the seller (settlement date). A business day is a day that banks are normally open for business, so that excludes weekends and holidays. Another important factor for investors has to do with dividend payments. The settlement date for a trade must be on or before the record date for the dividend payment. See **Record date** and **Ex-dividend date**.

Transfer agent: the institution, usually a commercial bank, responsible for registering security certificates and recording changes in ownership.

Treasury bills: the shortest term fixed-return securities issued by the U.S. Treasury Dept. T-bills are usually sold at a discount to face value and do not pay current interest. The return is factored into the appreciated value of the bill at maturity. There are scheduled auctions for T-bills that mature in 4, 13, 26, and 52 weeks. Also, there are cash management bills that mature in a few days and are not auctioned on a regular cycle.

Treasury notes and bonds: fixed-return securities issued by the U.S. Treasury Dept. that make semiannual interest payment like most other bonds. T-notes are sold with original maturities of 2, 3, 5, 7, and 10 years and in $100 minimum denominations. T-bonds have the same features as T-notes, but they are only sold in 30 year original maturities.

Variable-return investments: a common designation for equity securities as opposed to debt securities, such as bonds and preferred stock. It is a term meant to remind the investor that

GLOSSARY ◊ 341

there is more inherent risk, unpredictability of future outcome, with equities than with bonds. See **Fixed-return securities**.

Warrant: a contract that, like a call option, gives the owner the right to buy shares of an underlying security at a set price and usually expires after a period of time, usually several years. Warrants trade on stock exchanges, like equities, whereas call options trade on option exchanges. There are not many companies that issue warrants, because investors realize they represent future dilution of their percentage ownership.

Wash sale: in current use, the term used to describe the repurchase of a security, or its equivalent, 30 days or less after the date of sale, if that sale had resulted in a tax-deductible capital loss. The IRS may not allow taxpayers to deduct capital losses if the trade is a wash sale. Taxpayers must wait over 30 days to repurchase a security they sell for a capital loss if they want to claim that as a tax deduction.

Yield-to-maturity: the calculation of the total return of a fixed-return investment, including the interest rate and the change in value of the principal invested, either positively or negatively, from the time of purchase to the due date. It may also be referred to as the bond's basis.

Zero coupon bond: a fixed return investment that does not pay current interest because it is purchased at a discount to par value and the interest is represented by the appreciating value of the bond until maturity. U.S. Treasury bills and Series EE Savings Bonds are example of the structure of zero coupon bonds, but the term itself is usually applied to non-interest paying corporate or muni bonds. The IRS identifies any non-interest paying debt security as an OID, original issue discount and requires investors to report the annual appreciated value of the bonds as if interest had been paid. That is referred to as taxable phantom income.

Recommended Reading

Gilder, George (Foreword by Steve Forbes). *Wealth and Poverty*, 2nd Ed. Washington, D.C.: Regnery Publishing, 2012.

Graham, Benjamin and David L. Dodd (Foreword by Warren Buffett). *Security Analysis*, 6th Ed. New York: McGraw-Hill Trade, 2008.

Graham, Benjamin and Jason Zweig (Warren Buffett, Collaborator). *The Intelligent Investor: The Definitive Book on Value Investing*. New York: Collins Business, 2003.

Hayek, Friedrich A. *The Road to Serfdom*. Chicago: University of Chicago Press, 2007.

Friedman, Milton. *Capitalism and Freedom*. University of Chicago Press, 2002.

Lynch, Peter, and John Rothchild. *One Up on Wall Street: How to Use What You Already Know to Make Money in the Market*. New York: Fireside, 2000.

Malkiel, Burton G. and Charles D. Ellis. *The Elements of Investing*. New York: Wiley, 2009.

Sowell, Thomas. *Basic Economics: A Common Sense Guide to the Economy*. New York: Basic Books, 2014.

Index

Accredited investor, 295
Accrued interest, 121-2
Advance/Decline Line (ADL), 192
American Depositary Receipt (ADR), 25
Annuitant, 290-291
Annuity, 289-291
Arbitrage, 221, 241
Arbitrageur, 221, 241
Ask price, 27, 69-74, 120-1, 229
Austrian School, 12, 300

Back-end load, 204, 206
Balance sheet, 125-28, 152, 299
    Book value, 133-6
    Capital asset, 126
    Current assets, 126, 135
    Current liabilities, 125, 134-5
    Current ratio, 133, 135
    Fixed assets, 126
    Formula, 125
    Intangible assets, 126, 134
    Retained earnings, 130
Balanced investing, 146, 152, 198, 209, 213
Bank of International Settlements (BIS), 299
Bankruptcy, 47, 91-3, 103-4, 117, 135, 164-6, 236, 266
Bear (bearish) market, 35, 176-8, 182, 185, 191-5, 223, 237
Beta, 54-5
Bid price, 27, 69-74, 120-1, 179, 206, 229, 233
Bitcoin, 221
Black Monday, 34, 241, 258
Blue chip, 18, 20
Blue sky laws, 256
Bonds, 91-123
    Basis point (bp), 120
    Basis price, 109
    Bearer, 107-8
    Buying of, 91, 109-5
    Classification of issuers, 94-6
    Collateralized, 92-3, 99
    Collateralized Mortgage Obligation (CMO), 99
    Convertible, 102, 127
    Corporate, 77, 91, 93, 96, 101-2, 114
    Current yield, 111-3, 122
    Credit risk, 113, 209
    Debenture, 93
    Definition of, 91-2
    Discount, 108-10, 119-20
    Fixed return, 92
    General obligation (GO), 97
    High yield, 116-7, 209-10, 217
    Indenture, 94, 102, 117

Investment grade, 77, 114-6, 209
Junk, 95, 116, 209-10, 218
Mortgage backed, 92, 218, 298-9
Municipal (muni), 95-6
Par value, 97, 102, 106, 110-1, 118-20
Premium, 108-10, 118-9
Ratings, 113-7
Revenue, 97
Risks of, 111-8
Subordinated debenture, 93-4
Yield curve, 112-3
Yield-to-maturity (YTM), 108-11, 119
Zero coupon, 97, 106
BRICS, 308, 311
Brokers,
    Discount, 58-9
    Full-service, 58-9
    Online, 58-60
    Selection of, 62, 67-8, 144
Brokerage accounts,
    Commissions and fees, 58-61
    Community Property, 62-3
    Joint Tenants with Rights of Survivorship (Jt Ten), 62
    Opening of, 57-62
    Services, 58, 73-4, 132, 207-9
    Title designation, 62-3
    Tenants in Common, 62
    Types of, 76-7
    Wrap fee, 58, 65, 268
Broker loan rate, 78, 85, 150, 253
Bubble market, 165, 255-6
Bull (bullish) market, 176, 182, 185-6, 191-5
Bulletin Board stocks, 26
Buttonwood Agreement, 4

Call options:
    Definition, 190, 210
    ETFs and ETNs, 224, 234
    Leverage from, 224. 234
    Technical indicator, 191
CalPERS and CalSTRS, 50
Capital gain, 77, 108-11, 120, 218, 224. 257, 276, 279
Capital intensive business, 136
Capital loss, 77, 257, 276
Cash account, 76, 81-2
Cash flow statement, 124, 129-31
    Quality of earnings, 130, 140
C-Corporation, 44
Certified Financial Planner (CFP), 31, 33
Charts (charting), 176
    Bar charts, 174-5, 183
    Bollinger bands, 180-3
    Candlestick charts, 174

344 ◇ INDEX

Channel, 174-8, 189
Double bottom, 176-7
Double top, 176-8
Gap, 72, 178-9
Head and shoulders, 178-80
Inverted head and shoulders, 176-8
Line charts, 174
Patterns, 144, 171, 174, 176-8, 189. 199
China, 60-1, 218, 308-10
Churning, 66, 267-8
Closing tick, 16
Commercial paper, 113, 209
Commodity futures contracts, 153, 162-3, 235, 240, 244-9
Communism, 60-1, 261-3
Compound interest, 105-7
Consumer price index (CPI), 98, 158-62
Consumption tax, 274-5
Contrarian investing, 40, 173, 185, 192, 194
Cooking the books, 264
Cost-of-living adjustment (COLA), 159
Crash of 1929, 34, 254, 256-58, 260
Creation units (ETF), 222
Creative accounting, 263-4
Cryptocurrency, 222
Cumulative preferred, 107, 127

Day trading, 73, 171, 268
Derivative securities, 99-100, 190, 247, 254
Designated market maker (DMM), 70
Dilution, 247-9
Discount rate, 149-51
Disposable income, 148, 151
Dividend,
    Cumulative preferred, 107, 129
    Dates of, 86-88, 242
    Definition, 86
    Ex-dividend date, 86-89
    Payable date, 86
    Payout ratio, 50, 87-8, 135
    Preferred, 104, 127, 129
    Record date, 51, 86-8
    Reinvestment Program (DRIP), 88-9
    Yield, 27, 85
Dollar cost averaging, 196-98, 205
Dow Jones divisor, 18- 20
Dow Jones Industrial Average (DJIA), 17-21, 23-4, 133, 220-1, 258

Earnings per share (EPS), 27, 129, 138, 249
Earnings season, 46
Economic cycles, 55, 118, 145-7, 153
Economic Stimulus bill, 167
Economy,
    Definition, 5-8, 10-15
    Description of, 10-14
    Events that affect, 297-9
    Theory, 12
EDGAR, 125
Electronic Communications Network (ECN), 3, 14, 17, 27, 71
Enron, 103, 265-6, 285-6

Fed funds rate, 149-53
Federal Deposit Insurance Corp., (FDIC), 251-4
Federal Home Loan Mortgage Corp., Freddie Mac (FHLMC), 93-4, 99-100, 165, 190, 254-6
Federal National Mortgage Assoc., Fannie Mae (FNMA), 93, 99-100, 165, 190, 254-6
Federal Open Market Committee (FOMC), 153
Federal Reserve Board (FRB), 77, 149-54, 160-3, 167, 170, 252-4, 259, 297-302
Fiduciary, 28, 116
Final prospectus, 49
Financial Industry Regulatory Authority (FINRA), 14, 65-7, 77, 79, 208, 227, 264, 267-70
Financial plan/planning, 31-3, 245
Fiscal year, 46, 124-6, 131, 135, 138
529 Plan (Education Savings), 287-9
Fixed amount investing, 196, 198
Fixed return investments, 92, 103-5, 113
Flat tax, 273-5
Forms 10K and 10Q, 125, 259
401(k), 403(b), & 457 Plans, 28, 212, 278-91
Fourth market, 48
Free market capitalism, 7-8, 13, 15, 17, 60-1, 261-3, 302-6
Full employment, 148, 152
Fundamental analysis, 144-63
    Debt-to-asset ratio, 133-4
    Future PE, 139-40
    Gross profit margin, 133
    Horizontal analysis, 140-1
    Net profit margin, 138-9
    Operating profit margin, 133-6
    Price earnings ratio (PE), 28, 131, 138-9, 211
    Return-on-assets ratio (ROA), 140
    Return-on-equity ratio (ROE), 139-40
    Vertical analysis, 141
Future value, 105, 110

Gambling, 2, 5, 29, 53-4, 57, 73, 83, 173, 240, 249
General partner (GP), 292
Glass-Steagall Act, 209, 254
Global markets, 24, 255, 307
Good-till-canceled order (GTC), 73, 87
Goodwill, 126
Government National Mortgage Assoc., Ginnie Mae (GNMA), 99-100
Greed-Hope-Fear cycle, 34-6, 40-1, 173, 177, 192, 195, 211
Gross Domestic Product (GDP), 148, 157-8, 163, 163
Growth stock, 52, 88, 135, 140

Hayek, F A, 12, 306
Hedging, 224-6, 230-6, 245-6

Hyperinflation, 169

Income statement, 128-9
    EBITDA, 131, 136
    Gross profit, 128-9
    Net income, 129
    Operating income, 131
Income tax, 31, 43, 47, 95-6, 101, 104, 126, 200, 219, 257, 271-9
Index of Leading Economic Indicators (LEI), 160-1
Individual retirement account (IRA), 276-81
    Custodian, 276-7
    Required minimum distribution (RMD), 280
    Rollover, 281, 284, 287
    Roth, 277-82, 284, 287
    SIMPLE, 282
    Simplified Employee Pension (SEP-IRA), 278, 281-2
    Spousal, 277, 280
    Traditional, 277-8, 284
Industrial life cycle, 154-6
Inflation, 11, 28-30, 55, 147-54, 156-62, 169, 264, 298
Initial margin requirement, 77-8, 257-9
Initial public offering (IPO), 14, 47-9, 134, 203, 247-9, 259
    Syndicate group, 49
    Underwriting, 47, 49, 243
Insider trading, 259-60, 263
Intercontinental Exchange (ICE), 4
Interest rate spread, 253
Investment company,
    Closed-end fund (CEF), 216-225
    Definition, 200
    Exchange traded fund (ETF), 102, 116, 199, 201, 220-4, 233-41, 277
    Exchange traded note (ETN), 220, 233-4, 241
    Hybrid fund, 201
    Open-end fund, 201-2, 216-20
Investment Company Act of 1940, 203-4, 260
Investors' rights, 251-5

Keynesian theory, 12, 300, 306

Labor intensive business, 136
Laffer curve, 275
Laissez-faire, 12, 166
Last trade, 16, 27, 72, 229, 244
Level 1, 2, and 3 quotes, 73-4
Leverage,
    Commodities, 266
    Debt, 189, 209-19
    Funds, 213, 119
    Margin, 76, 82-3
    Options, 223-4, 234
    Rights and warrants, 249
Liability,
    Bond, 91
    Insurance, 47

Investment, 43, 47
    Shareholder, 50
    Tax, 96, 273-6, 293
Limit order, 69, 72-6, 87
Limited liability corporation (LLC), 43
Limited liability partnership (LLP), 43
Limited partnerships, 219, 224-5, 271, 282, 297-300
Long-term liabilities, 126, 134
Margin account, 76-85, 125, 234, 238. 252
Margin agreement, 79, 83, 227, 238
Margin call, 79-81, 246
Market cap, 21-4, 26, 48, 212, 265
Market efficiency, 116-7, 172
Market multiple, 138
Market order, 36, 69-75
Market timing, 34, 40, 75, 172-3, 196, 217
Mark to the market, 84
Master limited partnership (MLP), 218, 294-5
Minimum maintenance requirement, 78-9, 252
Money flow index (MFI), 180, 185
Money supply, 151-3, 160, 168, 298-302, 324, 328
Mortgage derivatives, 320
Mutual funds, 200-25
    Blended fund, 212
    Commission breakpoints, 204-6
    Definition of, 21, 201
    Family, 206-9, 215, 277, 291
    Fees, 201-9, 223
    Front-end load fund, 204-8
    Growth fund, 209, 211-2, 217
    Letter of intent (LOI), 196, 205
    Load, 203-08
    Management style, 211
    Money market fund, 105, 113, 151, 209, 214, 217, 253
    Net asset value (NAV), 201-2, 206, 217, 220-2
    No-load fund, 211, 214
    Regulation of, 262
    Rights of Accumulation, 205
    Selection of, 213-5
    Value fund, 211

Nasdaq Exchange, 13, 23-6, 48, 71-2, 190, 193, 221, 240, 315
Nasdaq market makers, 71-2
Nasdaq 100 Index (QQQ), 24, 190, 221-3
New York Stock Exchange/Euronext (NYSE), 3-4, 14, 17, 24-6, 48-9, 52, 72-4, 103, 197, 227-8, 260, 303, 317
NYSE Index, 24

Odd lot trading theory, 193-3
Open market operations, 153
Options,
    Chain, 229
    Closing transaction, 232-3
    Covered call, 230-7
    Definition, 226

Effect of stock split, 234
ETFs and ETNs, 240-4
Expiration date, 227-32, 235-6, 239-42
Holder, 234, 237-8, 240-2, 245, 248
In the money, 239-30
Long-term Equity Anticipation
   Securities (LEAPS), 329
Opening transaction, 232, 242
Open interest, 229, 232-3
Option Industry Council (OIC), 226
Out of the money, 230, 239
Premium, 227-39, 243-4, 246
Put, 226-30, 236-40,
Series, 227-9, 232-3
Spread, 233, 239, 246
Straddle, 239-40
Strike price, 227-39
Writing calls, 230-6
Writing puts, 236-8
Options Industry Council (OIC), 226
Order book, 69, 73, 179

Partnership, 14, 42-3, 47, 50, 219
Preferred stock, 48, 93, 103-4, 111, 127-8
Present value, 105
Price-weighted average, 18, 22, 186
Primary market, 14, 47, 49, 98, 122, 203, 248
Prime rate, 150
Pink sheets, 26
Principal, broker acting as, 48
Private company (enterprise), 44-5, 49, 303, 310
Private placement, 295, 315
Private sector, 7, 12, 168
Producer price index (PPI), 160
Program trading, 201, 240-1, 316
Prospectus, 49, 203-8, 210-8, 259
Proxy, 2, 51-2, 259
Prudent man rule, 269
Public Utility Holding Company Act of 1935, 260

Quadruple witching days, 241, 250
Quantitative easing (QE), 168-9, 298
Quote spread, 54, 70-1, 120-1

Random walk hypothesis, 172
Real estate investment trust (REIT), 216-8
Real GDP, 157-8
Recession, 5, 30, 35, 55, 147-54, 161, 166, 272
Red herring, 49
Regulation T (Reg T), 77-8, 80
Risk,
   Arbitrage, 221, 241
   Bonds, 110-18
   Definition of, 53
   Exchange traded fund, 223
   Leverage, 76, 82-3, 134, 153, 189
   Macroeconomic, 56, 120
   Measurement of, 58
   Microeconomic, 55, 118

Mutual fund, 209-10, 213
Options, 234, 237
Stock market, 53-4
Tolerance, 116, 212, 237
Round lot, 27, 70, 195, 228
Royalty trust, 218-9
Rule of 72, 106
Russell Small Cap 2000 Index, 24, 221

S&P Global Index, 24
S-corporation, 43
Sarbanes-Oxley Act, 266, 286
Secondary market, 14, 47, 98, 120-2, 259
Securities, 14
Securities and Exchange Commission (SEC), 49, 65, 77, 203, 222, 259-60, 264
Securities Act of 1933, 258-9
Securities Exchange Act of 1934, 259, 266
Securities industry, 1, 49, 58, 60, 67, 77-8, 166, 256, 258, 260,263. 270
Securities Investors Protection Corp. (SIPC), 251-3
Settlement date, 68-9, 76, 86, 122
Shareholder rights 50-2
Shareholders' Equity Statement, 124, 131-2
Shares of beneficial interest (SBI), 201, 219, 294
Short interest ratio, 194-5
Short selling, 86-8, 198-9
Simple interest, 106, 109
Small investor syndrome, 34, 40, 51, 173, 195-6, 218
Sole proprietorship, 42-3, 47
Spot contract (futures), 245
Stock,
   Certificate, 44-5
   Growth, 56, 94
   Preferred, 111, 118, 184
   Quotes, 26-30, 74, 76, 78-9, 127, 145
   Split, 18-20, 233-4
   Trading, 36-9, 73-4, 85-6
   Transfer,
   Value, 225
   Variable return investments, 92, 291
   Voting rights, 52-3, 129
Stock certificate,
   Street name, 45, 63-4, 88, 107
   Transfer agent, 45, 91
   Transfer of, 3, 13, 15, 45-6, 63-4
Stock exchanges, 3-4, 13-4, 17, 51, 103, 259
Stock market,
   Crashes, 34-5, 40, 254-8, 260
   Definition, 13, 17
   Free market capitalist system, 13, 60, 261, 303
   Participation in, 28
   Risk capital, 29
   Timing techniques, 34-40
Stock purchase rights, 247
Stock split, 18-20, 227-8
Stop order, 69, 74-6, 85-7, 223
Stop-limit order, 69, 75-6

INDEX ◊ 347

Supplement liquidity providers (SLPs), 70
Supply and demand, 32, 70-1, 101, 116, 171, 175. 195, 201
Supply and demand curve, 15-6

Term Asset-Backed Loan Facility (TALF), 167
Troubled Asset Relief Program (TARP), 12, 166-7
Technical analysis,
    Breadth of market, 192-3
    Exponential moving average (EMA), 180, 188
    High-Low Index, 193-4
    Moving average, 180-3, 186-8, 194
    Moving average convergence/ divergence (MACD), 186-8
    Rate of change (ROC), 184-5
    Relative Strength Index (RSI), 185-6
    Put/call ratio, 194-6
    Simple moving average (SMA), 180-24, 186
    Stochastic, 180, 186-9
    Timing techniques, 196-8
    Volume graph, 188
Tender offers, 259
Third market, 48, 101, 294

Tick, 16-7
Ticker symbol, 16, 25, 27, 190
Thomson Reuters/CRB Index, 161
Total capitalization, 126, 133, 201, 210, 221
Trade date, 68-9, 86, 122
Treasury Inflation-Protected Securities (TIPs), 980
Trust Indenture Act of 1939, 260
Typical price, 186
Unauthorized trading, 267
U.S. National debt, 94, 163-5, 313

Value Line Composite Index, 24
Value-weighted index, 21-2, 186
Variable annuity, 291
VIX, volatility index, 222-3, 243-5

Warrants, 247-9
Wash sale (trades), 256-7
Wash sale (taxes), 257
Wells Notice, 264-5
Wilshire 5000 Equity Index, 24
www.usdebtclock.org, 163, 301

Zimbabwe, 169

Printed in the USA
CPSIA information can be obtained
at www.ICGtesting.com
LVHW021309200824
788467LV00004B/34